Jazz Musicians of
the Early Years, to 1945

ALSO BY DAVID DICAIRE
AND FROM MCFARLAND

*More Blues Singers: Biographies of 50 Artists
from the Later 20th Century* (2002)

*Blues Singers: Biographies of 50 Legendary
Artists of the Early 20th Century* (1999)

Jazz Musicians of the Early Years, to 1945

David Dicaire

McFarland & Company, Inc., Publishers
Jefferson, North Carolina, and London

LIBRARY OF CONGRESS CATALOGUING-IN-PUBLICATION DATA

Dicaire, David, 1963–
    Jazz musicians of the early years, to 1945 / David Dicaire.
      p.   cm.
    Includes bibliographical references, discographies, and index.

    ISBN 0-7864-1583-5 (softcover : 50# alkaline paper)

    1. Jazz musicians—United States—Biography.   2. Jazz singers
—United States—Biography.   I. Title.
ML394.D52   2003
781.65'092'2—dc21   2003009258

British Library cataloguing data are available

Cover photograph ©2002 Digital Vision

Manufactured in the United States of America

McFarland & Company, Inc., Publishers
  Box 611, Jefferson, North Carolina 28640
  www.mcfarlandpub.com

To Jim and Rose
Thanks for the support!

Contents

Introduction

The mere mention of the word "jazz" conjures up a different set of images for each generation. To many the picture of Louis Armstrong's round friendly face, cheeks puffed out as he blows his trumpet under a full moon overlooking the shimmering waters of the Mississippi River, is the very essence of jazz. To others it is the excitement generated by the sounds, sights, and lights of Bourbon Street in New Orleans. To an older generation it is the swinging, big band styles of Benny Goodman, Duke Ellington, Count Basie, and Glenn Miller sending the enlisted men off to battle. To others it is a dimly lit, smoky nightclub in Greenwich Village where the innovative, frenetic sounds of bebop fill the air. To many newer fans it is an open-air concert, a celebration of music, art and culture.

Undoubtedly, the history of jazz is deep and wide. It is commonly believed that the music is a blend of European classical harmonies and West African rhythms. Although the two styles were at different ends of the musical spectrum, their elements combined over a three-hundred-year period to create something new and exciting. But the roots of jazz grew from other musical styles as well.

One of those styles, a very important one, was the blues. The primitive rhythms of the blues came with the captives from Africa brought to the new world to work as slaves on the Southern plantations, and the music branched out in different directions. By the late nineteenth century, the blues had been dissected and reorganized into separate styles. The tonality of the blues had a direct, profound, and lasting influence on jazz. Where blues turned in one direction, however, jazz turned in another.

Another essential element of early jazz was ragtime. Although scholars debate just how much ragtime contributed to the development of jazz, it is certain that ragtime supplied, at the very least, a crucial sense of syncopated rhythms. Ragtime's rhythms incorporated the same timekeeping elements found in the New Orleans marching bands. Although one ingredient missing from ragtime was improvisation, many ragtime composers and pianists, such as Scott Joplin, James P. Johnson, Fats Waller, and Eubie Blake, were essential in shaping jazz in the early part of the twentieth century.

While the Mississippi Delta is the cradle of the blues, New Orleans is the cradle of jazz. There are many reasons why New Orleans, Louisiana, became the jazz center and remains one of the music's most vibrant spots today. History, demographics, geography, an economic boom and cultural blending were all factors in making the Crescent City unique. It was only fitting that a new music emerged from this environment.

The history of New Orleans is quite interesting. For its first forty-six years it was a French possession, and certain customs established in that period continue to this day. In 1764, the city was ceded to Spain and for the next thirty-six years lived under Spanish rule. But the French influence was still dominant, and New Orleans resembled the French West Indies, with the dominant music based on the rhythms found in Haiti and Martinique. In 1800, Napoleon reclaimed New Orleans as French territory, and in 1803, he sold the land to the United States.

With the largest black population in the United States, the African American influence on the culture—including its music—was enormous. Immigrants from Haiti, Cuba, Martinique, Santo Domingo, and Trinidad added their own influence as they brought their customs, their religions, and their musical motifs.

The western migration of millions to tame the rugged frontier opened by the Louisiana Purchase created an economic boom. The new settlers needed supplies, and the cheapest way to deliver goods to the people was by riverboat from New Orleans. The city's strategic position on the Mississippi made it one of the most important trading ports in the world, and the commercial activity created many opportunities for other industries to flourish, including music.

The economic boom sparked a population explosion as British Protestants arrived in New Orleans to join the Creoles (those of Spanish, French and African ancestry), runaway slaves from the French West Indies, and blacks from the plantations surrounding the city. Each group brought its own music, and the blending of the various elements—European classical music, white folk songs, African rhythms, and the blues—created something special.

The combination of these musical sources with the second-line rhythms developed by the New Orleans marching bands, as well as the spirituals, work songs, and ragtime, gelled to create the popular music of the day. Long before it was christened "jazz," this new sound played a vital role in the daily lives of the citizens of New Orleans in the nineteenth century. Brass bands played at parades, funerals, parties, and dances.

The citizens of New Orleans contributed two other elements that influenced the development of jazz. The first was Voodoo ceremonies, and the other was public performances in Congo Square. The religion of Voodoo arrived with those who emigrated from Haiti, and New Orleans became the Voodoo capital of America. There are few historical accounts of Voodoo ceremonies, mainly because of the rigid privacy code that was attached to them. But the dances at the Congo Square were lively public performances often depicted by writers and artists whose works now serve as invaluable sources on the development of jazz. The dances at Congo Square also helped to usher in the popularity of the marching band and the use of European instruments.

Once all of these various influences were consolidated, the music began to gain some attention. Buddy Bolden, a New Orleans resident, was the first musician to organize a band that played jazz. The spark he struck ignited a fire that would spread quickly throughout the continental United States and eventually the entire world. Ironically, while it is a fact that the blues preceded jazz, jazz musicians were the first to record. Though historically credited with beginning the first genuine jazz band, Bolden was not the first to put the music on vinyl for the buying public. That distinction belongs to the Original Dixieland Jazz Band, a white group from New Orleans, who were the quintessential jazz outfit at the time. Although the records of the ODJB sound dated because of the inferior equipment they were recorded on, the fact that they were the first band to record jazz music ensured their place in history.

The success of the Original Dixieland Jazz Band created opportunities for other groups to record this hot new music. Although in its earliest recorded form jazz bears little resemblance to the freer styles of today, the music created excitement that would last throughout the twentieth century and beyond. The early pioneers like Bolden, Buck Johnson, Joe "King" Oliver, Kid Ory, Freddie Keppard, Jelly Roll Morton and Pops Foster, to name a few, played in the famous Storyville red light district of New Orleans. When the Storyville section was closed, jazz musicians took their music to the large metropolises of Chicago and New York and, later, Los Angeles.

In the 1920s, prosperity reigned as America enjoyed an unprecedented upturn of economic fortunes. The hot, sassy sound of jazz was the soundtrack of the Roaring Twenties and dominated the decade musically, despite some stiff competition from the blues. Interestingly, the noted jazz musicians of the day played on many of the recordings of the classic female blues singers—including the greatest of them all, Bessie Smith. Lonnie Johnson, a fine blues guitarist, was closely associated with the great names in jazz of the era and recorded with Eddie Lang, a noted jazz guitarist.

Major evolutions in the music occurred during this period. In its infancy jazz was the music of ensemble as a group participated in collective improvisation. The aim of the early jazz bands was to provide dance music in the dozens of saloons and bordellos of the Storyville district. When the new form moved to the big cities it was still intended as dance music, but a fuller, more diverse style was needed to please the citified crowds. Inspired by the need to create a more exciting sound and the urge to stretch creatively, soloists began to steal the spotlight. The best of the early soloists—like Louis Armstrong—learned to improvise within the context of the group sound. Others took their cue from Armstrong, and from this point on, each band featured its prize soloist(s) on a horn, on strings, on piano.

Many of the musicians who helped make Chicago the prime jazz scene in the early 1920s arrived from New Orleans, including Armstrong, Sidney Bechet, Jelly Roll Morton, Joe "King" Oliver, Johnny Dodds, Baby Dodds and Zutty Singleton. In Chicago, the Austin High Gang, a group of white high school musicians, in an effort to replicate the sound of their heroes, frequented the clubs where Armstrong *et al.* played. While many musicians remained loyal to the New Orleans traditional style of jazz, others developed a more sophisticated brand of music complete with rhythmic variations, adventurous chords, and complex arrangements. It was the latter style that evolved into the big band sound. Despite the timeless music created during this period and the good times enjoyed during the Roaring Twenties, the fun came abruptly to an end with the stock market crash of 1929.

In the early part of the 1930s, the popularity of jazz was at its lowest ebb. The bottom had fallen out of the recording industry when the United States economy tumbled into depression. There were fewer jobs for musicians. However, by the middle of the decade, the sounds of the twenties had matured into something hot and new. The era of big band swing was born. Suddenly the music was not a bitter reminder of the past, but the prominent sound of the day and the bright hope for the future.

The big bands of Fletcher Henderson, Benny Goodman, Duke Ellington, Glenn Miller, Count Basie and others filled the demand for hot dance music. The introduction of radio into millions of homes and the resurgence of the recording industry made jazz once again the musical heartbeat of the nation. The bands grew in size and were divided into strict seating arrangements. The brass section included trumpets and trombones; the woodwinds included the clarinet and various saxophones; the rhythm section included drums, bass, piano, guitar and other string instruments.

Although New Orleans and Chicago remained important jazz centers, it was New York that became the jazz capital of the nation in the late 1920s and 1930s. Territory bands from the Midwest and Southwest also emerged during this period, playing unrefined blues-drenched music that swung hard, which was in direct contrast to the more polished and more commercial efforts of their city cousins. Undoubtedly, one of the hottest jazz centers was Kansas City, which produced many of the top jazz musicians of the period including Coleman Hawkins, Ben Webster and Lester Young.

The era of the big band, whose sound came to prominence around 1935, lasted until the end of the Second World War. Millions of enlisted men and their girls shared one last dance to the swinging big band sound before they crossed the Atlantic or ventured to the Pacific to fight for their country. Despite the popularity of the big bands, however, jazz was reinventing itself. The musical heroes of the World War II era were eventually replaced by a new generation of jazz artists.

This book is dedicated to the men and women of the first fifty years of jazz—1895–1945—and is divided into five distinct parts. Part One, "The New Orleans Tradition," features those who gained fame in the Crescent City. Part Two, "The Jazz Age," features those who helped spread the music from New Orleans to the urban centers of Chicago and New York. Many of the alumni from New Orleans traveled to the big city to seek national recognition. The third part is entitled "The Big Band and Swing Era: The Bandleaders" and features those who rose to prominence as the head of a big band. The fourth part, "The Big Band and Swing Era: The Musicians," highlights players who made swing such a hit and laid the foundation for the buildup of bop that was on the horizon. The fifth part, "Other Major Figures," features seven special individuals who made enormous contributions to the first half century of jazz.

The first fifty years of jazz were filled with many of the greatest musical names of the twentieth century. Scott Joplin, Louis Armstrong, Fats Waller, Duke Ellington, Count Basie, Benny Goodman, Billie Holiday, and Ella Fitzgerald continued to exert their influence on all musicians of the latter part of the century and the new millennium. The evolution of jazz from the local music of New Orleans flavor to an international force is the story of the individuals who made it happen.

PART ONE

The New Orleans Tradition

Since New Orleans is the cradle of jazz and for much of its early history jazz was confined to the Storyville district, it is easy to see why nearly all the early jazz artists were from the Crescent City or the state of Louisiana. Although not every musician of the era could be called a pure jazz artist, many of them were essential pioneers in the translation of the early elements of popular music into what eventually became known as jazz.

The first jazz bands were essentially collective ensembles rather than groups with a featured soloist. Since most of the musicians of the day could not read music, their playing was improvised, establishing improvisation as a key element throughout the history of the genre. The beat of those early groups was based on the simple one-two rhythms of the marching bands that supplied music to parades, dances and funeral processions. The cornet was the dominant instrument of the era, as well; other brass instruments such as the trombone were also prominent.

The piano also played a significant role in shaping the sound of early jazz. The guitar, bass, banjo and drums were relegated to a strict role as rhythmic tools. The saxophone was considered a novelty instrument.

The first jazz band formed by Buddy Bolden played simple dance music that was appreciated by the hard-working African-Americans of the time. A typical aggregation in Bolden's day consisted of two or three lead horns weaving improvised melodies in and around the beat, laid down by string instruments like the guitar or the banjo and by the tuba or bass as well as by the drums.

During the 1910s, the important outfits included John Robicheaux's Orchestra, the Onward Brass Band (that featured King Oliver), the Excelsior band with Lorenzo and Louis Tio, the Original Creole Band (with Freddie Keppard on trumpet), the George Lewis–led bands, Bunk Johnson's groups, and the Original Dixieland Jazz Band.

The hot sound of "jass"—as it was known from the late nineteenth century to the early twentieth century—includes some of the most colourful characters in the annals of American and international music. Many musicians of this era were never given the chance to record. Bunk Johnson, Albert Nicholas, Fate Mariable, James Reese Europe, William Marion Cook, George Bacquet, Wooden Joe Nicholas and Kid Punch Miller are a few of the dozens of New Orleans artists who are not prominently featured in this book but played an important role in shaping the sound of jazz. Those featured in this section were some of the pioneers integral to the popularization of the New Orleans jazz tradition.

Buddy Bolden was the first player to put together a jazz band. He was a pioneer on the cornet and blazed the path for others to follow, including Freddie Keppard, Joe "King" Oliver, Louis Armstrong and Bix Beiderbecke.

Nick LaRocca was one of the first important white players who led the Original Dixieland Jazz Band into the history books with its groundbreaking recording. He tarnished his image later on by claiming he had invented jazz.

Joe "King" Oliver gained fame before the advent of the jazz age, and was an important musician for over twenty years. He followed in the cornet tradition established by Buddy Bolden.

Kid Ory was the first great trombone player who epitomized the tailgate style.

Freddie Keppard was one of the true giants of the early jazz age, taking off where King Oliver stopped. His cornet recordings are of historical significance.

Pops Foster was a pioneer of the bass. He laid down a simple rhythm compared to the complexity of sounds achieved by today's players.

Jelly Roll Morton was the most important piano player of the New Orleans tradition and later found fame in Chicago. He worked with many of the greatest names in jazz history.

Johnny Dodds, a New Orleans native, established himself in Chicago. He was the best clarinet player of his generation and paved the way for future licorice men.

Sidney Bechet was a giant of jazz who changed the course of the music forever. He was a talented musician who excelled on two instruments. Like a host of other New Orleans jazz players Bechet would enjoy his greatest success in the big cities of Chicago and New York as well as overseas.

Zutty Singleton, along with his counterpart Baby Dodds, was a pioneer on the drum kit.

Baby Dodds, the little brother of Johnny Dodds, was the greatest drummer of the first twenty years of jazz and set the standard for many of the stickmen who would follow in his footsteps.

BUDDY BOLDEN (1877–1931)

The Cornet Pioneer

The very seeds of jazz that were planted in New Orleans were nurtured for over a hundred years by the first group of musicians that came along who possessed a special affection for the music. Although its exact beginnings are a serious point of debate among scholars, pundits, and fans, many agree that the man known as the "Cornet Pioneer" organized the first true jazz band. His name was Buddy Bolden.

Charles "Buddy" Bolden was born on September 6, 1877, in New Orleans, Louisiana. As with the obscure bluesman Blind Blake, the details of Bolden's life are sketchy. He acquired a taste for the roots of jazz by participating in the marching bands that were so prominent in the Crescent City at the time, the dances at Congo Square, the secret meetings where voodoo was practiced, and the shouting congregation at the church he attended. The sounds, textures, rhythms and colors of the music that surrounded him enthralled the young Bolden and steered him towards a career in entertainment.

When he was a young boy Bolden suffered a tragedy that would shape the rest of his life. His father and sister died of yellow fever, and the subsequent depression that enveloped his mother allowed him to run unsupervised up and down the rough streets of New Orleans. It was on these mean streets that he learned how to survive and play the cornet. He also acquired a marketable skill—cutting hair—that put food on the table.

In 1890, at the age of thirteen, he left school and was ready to earn his living as a genuine jazz player. He paid his dues by cutting hair during the day and playing dance pieces at night, biding his time until he would lead his own band and fulfill his musical visions. New Orleans was a hotbed of music and Bolden was just one more cornet player trying to earn a living. The stiff competition ensured that he kept his instrument sharp and ready.

In 1895, after completing apprenticeships with a variety of groups that played some form of early jazz, Bolden formed his own band, borrowing elements from ragtime, blues, popular music, marches, minstrel songs, polkas, and quadrilles. Then he shaped those elements into an advanced style. It is believed that while he was leading the first jazz band into the pages of history, Bolden was also running a barbershop and might have been an editor of a scandal sheet, underlining the fact that musicians made very little money in the genre's formative years.

However, by 1900, Bolden was hailed as the "King of the Cornet" and was the most popular musician talked about in barbershops, on street corners, in parlors and every other place in New Orleans where jazz fans gathered. The instruments in his dance band consisted of the cornet, clarinet, trombone, violin, guitar, string bass, and drums. Some of the musicians who were part of Bolden's outfits (it was believed that he simultaneously led six bands bearing his name) at one time or another included Louis Keppard, Bunk Johnson, Big Eye Louis Deslisle, George Biquet, Albert Glenny, and Wallace Collins.

Buddy Bolden reigned supreme for seven years. His cornet was the most recognized instrument of the earliest days of jazz, which boasted an appreciative but regional audience in New Orleans. Jazz had not yet branched into the bigger metropolises of Chicago, New York and Los Angeles. Although he would never achieve national or international status, Bolden established his legend in his hometown from 1900 to 1907.

He was a boisterous man who enjoyed a stiff drink and a pretty lady on his arm. He cultivated the image of the New Orleans jazz musician with his high life of good times and good music that would reverberate throughout the decades. He earned a reputation as a *bon vivant* and played the loudest, clearest cornet in the country. Eyewitness accounts dutifully stated how Bolden's horn could be heard in every quarter in New Orleans and across the entire Louisiana landscape.

In 1907, Bolden suffered a mental breakdown during a parade and was committed to the local hospital. He would remain in a mental institution for the remainder of his life. Some believe that his condition was inherited from his mother while others attributed his deterioration to a case of syphilis. While he was institutionalized many changes occurred in jazz and the music world left him behind. On November 4, 1931, in Jackson, Louisiana, twenty-four years after he played his last concert, he died a seemingly forgotten man.

Buddy Bolden was a pioneer of jazz and arguably its first important performer. Ironically, the man who is believed by many to be the starting point of jazz made no legitimate records of the music he created. Unfortunately, a rumored cylinder roll of his work has never been found. It remained for those who played with him to relate to the world his musical expertise and his exploits.

Bunk Johnson would claim in later interviews that Bolden was the best cornet player in the world. Louis Armstrong candidly stated how he often snuck into the backs of jazz clubs where Bolden's group was playing and absorbed the entire show. For Satchmo, there was no one that compared to Bolden. Many of Bolden's bandmates boasted that when Buddy blew his horn everyone throughout the city came running to listen to him play. Whether this is true or just another part of the Bolden legend is pure speculation. Without any proper evidence of his playing, any assessment is open to discussion.

Although none of his recordings exist, the influence Bolden had on jazz can be measured in other ways. He gave several jazz musicians their first break, including Bunk Johnson who would go onto forge a respectable career. Freddie Keppard was another who benefited from being in Bolden's band and would succeed the latter as the next great New Orleans cornet player. Bolden's touch on the cornet also shaped the sounds of Joe "King" Oliver and Red Nichols. He was also a prime inspiration to Louis Armstrong.

All of the early traditional New Orleans jazzmen owed a great debt to Buddy. Despite the dearth of recordings, his music was the prime building block of the early jazz sound that was extended by the next generation. The stunning style he created could be heard in the work of every cornet player that followed him, including Keppard, Oliver, Nichols, and Armstrong.

Bolden made the cornet the prime musical instrument in the earliest days of jazz. Although the saxophone, piano, drums, bass, guitar, clarinet, and trombone would eventually equal and surpass the cornet in popularity, the birth of jazz is associated with the cornet. Bolden made the cornet to jazz what Charlie Patton made the acoustic guitar to the blues.

Although only one of his many original compositions survives— "Buddy Bolden's Blues"—it is believed that Bolden played a blues-drenched cornet. He jammed on such standards of the day as "Maple Leaf Rag," "Don't Go Away Nobody," "Careless Love," and "219 Took My Baby Away." Perhaps his style can best be described as a combination of ragtime and the earliest form of jazz. But without a doubt, his music was hot and sassy and created great excitement.

There were other dimensions to Bolden's music. Not only was his sound blues oriented, but he also possessed the ability to instantly improvise—the two key ingredients of jazz. Bolden played simple lines behind the one-two march rhythms that he had grown up listening to. Although his style was not the most sophisticated ever created, it contained the essential elements of jazz, if the reports of witnesses are deemed credible.

In many ways, Bolden's music was like the city of New Orleans itself. It was a joyous, spirited sound that flowed freely with a rhythm to tap to and a melodic hook that allowed the average citizen of the Crescent City to hum along. There was an undeniable *joie de vivre* attached to the famed city along the Mississippi River and Bolden was intelligent enough to propel the good times along with his piercing cornet sound.

While Charley Patton is credited with laying down the blueprint of a bluesman's life, Buddy Bolden is the pioneer who settled the boundaries of a jazzman's behavior. Bolden lived hard and died young. His offstage behavior was a lifestyle copied by hundreds of jazz musicians over the years, including Bix Beiderbecke, Lester Young, Billie Holiday, Charlie Parker, Miles Davis, and countless others. There was a burning desire in his restless spirit that he was able to instill in his playing. He burned the candle at both ends and passed on the thirst for creating fire to every generation of jazz artists.

There has been much research into the sketchy details of Bolden's life in an attempt to right historical facts. One of the most important books in jazz history, *In Search of Buddy Bolden*, written by Donald Marquis sheds much needed light on the great cornetist's life. A cleverly crafted book, it not only proved that Bolden was the first important jazz artist, but also brought to life an era that has been neglected because of a lack of well-kept historical documents.

The legend of Buddy Bolden has endured the test of time. Every "revival" of the New Orleans sound only endears him to a new generation of fans who rediscover the important influence of the man who put together the first jazz band. Some of the latter day musicians that have carried on the New Orleans tradition influenced by Bolden and bands of his era include Bob Crosby's Bobcats, Lu Watters (Yerba Buena Jazz Band), Bob Scobey, Bob Wilbur, Yank Lawson and Bob Haggart (World's Greatest Jazz Band), The Dukes of Dixieland, Turk Murphy, Climax Jazz Band, Black Eagle Jazz Band, Original Salty Dogs, Jim Cullum and James Dapogny's Chicago Jazz Band.

In the past one hundred plus years of jazz history there have been great innovators, heroes and superstars who have injected the genre with taste, class and heart. Although many musicians may have surpassed Bolden in popularity since he played his last note, the "Cornet Pioneer" remains one of the most fascinating characters in the annals of that brassy New Orleans sound.

NICK LAROCCA (1889–1961)

The History Maker

Although music resembling jazz had existed in various forms prior to the start of the twentieth century, the genre began to forge its true identity around 1910. But in order for the new style to truly catch on in the public's mind, widespread popularity had to be established. The obvious answer was the technology of recording. The Original Dixieland Jazz Band, a group of white musicians steeped in the tradition of the African-American sounds of New Orleans, earned the distinction of being the first band to make the initial out-and-out jazz recordings. The leader of the band was known as "The History Maker." His name was Nick LaRocca.

Nick LaRocca was born on April 11, 1889, in New Orleans, Louisiana. A self-taught musician, he soaked up the music that was all around him and at a very young age was leading his own band. He played all over the city with violinist Henry Young. They both gained invaluable performing experience that would serve them well later on in their careers. When not on stage with his proper group, LaRocca was playing cornet with a variety of outfits including those of Dominic Barrocca, Bill Gallity, and the Brunnies Brothers.

By the time he was in his early twenties, LaRocca's musical career began to take more shape and direction. He was a regular in Papa Jack Laine's Reliance band; that exposed him to some of the biggest crowds in the Crescent City. The apprenticeship in Laine's band looked slick on a hungry young musician's resume. LaRocca was making a name for himself on the New Orleans musical scene, a major accomplishment considering the stiff competition. It was shortly after leaving Laine's group that LaRocca joined Johnny Stein's band.

Stein, a drummer, was a traveling jazzman and exposed LaRocca to the wild city of Chicago. It was here that LaRocca gained a better understanding of the future direction of jazz. Although his stint in Stein's group was short, it enabled him to forge the confidence to form his own ensemble. He called his group Original Dixieland Jazz Band. The personnel consisted of trombonist Eddie Edwards, clarinetist Alcide Nunez, pianist Henry Ragas, drummer Johnny Stein and LaRocca on cornet. All the members were from New Orleans.

There would be personnel changes along the way before the band earned its way into the history books. After a falling out with LaRocca, Nunez was replaced by Larry Shields on the clarinet while Tony Spargo replaced Stein on the drums. In 1919, J. Russell Robinson replaced Henry Ragas after the latter's death that same year.

The ODJB carved a distinct niche for itself in the Windy City, earning the title of one of the top jazz bands in the later half of the 1910s. They made their debut at a popular Chicago restaurant. Because the crowd was accustomed to ragtime, the sassy sound that the group blasted out shocked many in the audience at first. But eventually they conquered the large mid-west city and then took New York by storm, turning the Reisenweber restaurant, an important venue of that period, into a rollicking jazz hothouse. It was these types of concert appearances that enabled the group to take a giant step to make records.

In 1917, a year before the end of World War I, the quintet was the first group to take the rabid, energetic sounds of New Orleans jazz and put them on vinyl. The first two songs they recorded (for Columbia), "Darktown Strutters Ball" and "Indiana," were never released. After they switched over to the Victor label, however, stardom was not far away. They cut the seminal classic "Livery Stable Blues" and "Dixie Jazz Band One Step." Once "Livery Stable Blues" was available to the public, life was never the same for the band. The song, complete with the horns imitating animal sounds, catapulted the ODJB to the forefront of the musical scene. Arguably they were not the greatest jazz outfit on the circuit, but they were one of the most popular.

Over the next few years the band would record and add several songs to its musical canon including "Tiger Rag," "At the Jazz Band Ball," "Fidgety Feet," "Sensation," "Clarinet Marmalade," "Margie," "Jazz Me Blues" and "Royal Garden Blues." They enlarged their fan base when they traveled to Europe in 1919–1920, creating the same excitement they had in the Big Apple a couple of years before.

By the early 1920s, the musical landscape was changing considerably, and not favorably for LaRocca and his groundbreaking band. Larry Shields, the best soloist in the band, left in 1921. The emphasis in jazz was shifting from the ensemble sound that the ODJB specialized in to that of the soloist. The music companies had begun to record the true giants of jazz who were far superior to the ODJB. In 1925, LaRocca suffered a nervous breakdown and broke up the band.

Although LaRocca retired, others in the band continued to make music. Spargo took over as leader, augmented the band's personnel, and enjoyed a long residency in New York. He left the group in 1927 and joined Lacey Young's Orchestra soon after. By the early 1930s he was heading his own outfit, hustling to book gigs during the tough economic times. He would return to work with LaRocca and take over the band once again when LaRocca bowed out. Spargo played into the 1940s and retired in the early 1960s.

After the breakup of the ODJB, Edwards formed his own group and played many residencies in New York during the late 1920s. Like LaRocca, Edwards left the music world and worked at various jobs as a vendor and a sports coach. He returned to join LaRocca upon the re-formation of the ODJB and stayed on with Spargo and Shields until the early 1940s. He remained in New York until his death in 1963.

Larry Shields left the ODJB in 1921. He joined Paul Whiteman's band for a period of time, then moved to the West Coast where he led his own groups that appeared at various venues around the Los Angeles area. He tried his hand at acting in the late 1920s, but once the Great Depression set in he worked outside the music business. He took part in the re-formed version of ODJB in 1936 and stayed on until 1940 then retired permanently.

From 1925 to 1936, LaRocca was out of the music business and earned a living as a manager for a contracting firm. In 1936, almost a decade after their breakup, the group reunited to make more recordings on the strength of a revival of the New Orleans tradition. Although Spargo had been the only member to continue his career after the breakup of the ODJB, he, LaRocca, Shields, Edwards, and Robinson gathered together and redid six songs. Later on that year LaRocca formed a large orchestra that cut a handful of tracks. Two years later the comeback was shelved and he never returned to the music scene.

Although he would emerge from retirement in 1959 to partake in a recording session that featured his voice but none of his actual playing, his career as one of the pioneers of jazz music was over. Nick LaRocca died February 22, 1961, in New Orleans, Louisiana.

Nick LaRocca was a seminal figure in jazz history. He was involved in the first recordings that greatly expanded the appeal of the genre. He was never a great soloist in the tradition of Louis Armstrong or King Oliver, but he did have a nice touch on the cornet. Unfortunately, he damaged his reputation years after his career was over with boasts of playing a much larger role than he did. His comments lost him much respect in the jazz world.

LaRocca, more of an ensemble player than a distinct soloist, could groove in the pocket with the rest of the band, but was unable to stand-out and distance himself apart from the other members of his unit. He was never a great influence on future cornet players as a solo artist, but the recordings he made in the 1910s with the ODJB were like a home study kit for future jazz musicians. Even today the re-mastered songs available on CD remain a part of every jazz enthusiast's audio library.

Undoubtedly, LaRocca's claim to fame was as the founder and leader of the ODJB. Their contributions to jazz were essential in popularizing the genre and delivering the whole attitude to a wider audience. Arguably the band was one of the main sparks that ignited the jazz age of the 1920s. Many of the groups of the era looked to them for inspiration. LaRocca's outfit was also responsible for spreading the appeal of the early New Orleans flavor in Europe.

Although the history books have been somewhat ambivalent towards LaRocca and his exact contributions to the music, due mainly to his later exuberant claims, he deserves a permanent place in history. He is a member of the Jazz Hall of Fame. He provided the world with an interesting collection of music and his story has a special place in the annals of the genre's formative period. Without a doubt he was one of the genuine history makers of the initial period of jazz.

Discography

Sensation! ASV/Living Era 5023-2.
The Original Dixieland Jazz Band, Riverside 156.
Original Dixieland Jazz Band, 1917–1923, Jazz Archives 158492.
75th Anniversary, Bluebird 61098-2.
The Complete Original Dixieland Jazz Band, RCA 6608.
Original Dixieland Jazz Band, 1921–1936, EPM Musique JA 157282.
Nick LaRocca's Dixieland Band, Sweetland 230.
Original Dixieland Jass Band Ragtime to Jazz 1, CBC 1035.
Original Dixieland Jazz Band, The First Recordings 1917–1921, CBC 1009.
Original Dixieland Jazz Band, 80 Years of Jazz, 1917–1997, LRHR 1103.
Original Dixieland Jazz Band Sensation 1917–1920, ASL 5023.
Dixieland Jazz Band 1917–1936, Jazz 66608.
Original Dixieland Jazz Band Vol. 1 1921–1936, EPM 157282.
Original Dixieland Jazz Band Vol. 2 1917–1923 EPM 158492.

JOE "KING" OLIVER (1885–1938)

Dippermouth Blues

The New Orleans jazz tradition is one of great pride and distinction. The practitioners of the very first style laid down the foundation for all that was to follow in the next decades. In the Crescent City at the turn of the twentieth century there were many "legends" but perhaps none as great as the Cornet Kings. In this line of succession the first was Buddy Bolden, the second was Freddie Keppard and the third was the man responsible for the Dippermouth Blues. His name was King Oliver.

Joe "King" Oliver was born on May 11, 1885, in New Orleans, Louisiana. Yet another of the early jazz giants who was raised in the Crescent City, he was surrounded by the new music and was bitten by the bug at an early age. Although he started out playing the trombone, he would switch to cornet—the instrument with which he would make his mark.

Oliver cut his musical teeth with the Walter Kinchin's Band and later with the Melrose band, two early apprenticeships that would serve him well later on during his career. Although he lost his sight in one eye during his teen years, Oliver would not be denied. He spent much of the 1910s playing in a variety of groups, including Kid Ory's legendary outfit. Despite the fact that he became well known while playing with Ory, Oliver was only biding his time before he would be able to lead his own aggregation.

After the closure of Storyville in New Orleans, the main jazz center for at least a decade, King traveled to Chicago to join the burgeoning scene there. After a stint in Lawrence Duhe's band, Oliver took it over and finally realized his goal of leading his own jazz group. They played at local clubs like the Deluxe Dave, Peking Cabaret, and Dreamland— every one an important jazz palace in the Windy City in the 1920s. He climbed to the top of the Chicago jazz scene very quickly and cemented his position with the addition of a rising star named Louis Armstrong.

Oliver took the band to the West Coast for a year and they developed a loyal following in Los Angeles, San Francisco, and other California centers. But a year later, he took the group back to Chicago where, not long after, it broke up. In between bands, he recorded with the legendary Jelly Roll Morton. A few months later, he formed the Dixie Syncopators and they played many residences in Chicago, later toured throughout the Midwest in Milwaukee, Detroit, St. Louis, and then went on to New York in 1927. He was as responsible as any other musician for spreading jazz throughout the country. Unfortunately, after his Midwest tour his career began to decline.

On the surface it appeared that Oliver was business as usual. He continued to make records but not with the same consistency as he had in the mid-1920s. Some of the best material of his career was captured during this downward period. He played on the recordings of Clarence Williams and sounded in top form. He formed small bands for specific concerts and studio dates. His name was still well recognized within jazz circles.

But the combination of the Great Depression, the general slack state of the recording industry as a result of the economic fallout, and the phasing out of the cornet as a prime instrument in jazz all spelled the end for Oliver. Like the Jazz Age itself, he faded into the pages of history.

In the last years of his life, he worked around the South as a fruit stand operator and a janitor in a poolroom. On April 8, 1938, in Savannah, Georgia, Joe "King" Oliver, one of the early giants of jazz, died. He was 52 years old.

King Oliver was a jazz musician of great importance for many different reasons. He was one of the main architects of the New Orleans Tradition as well as the Golden Age of Jazz. He helped spread the appeal of the new sound throughout the country and around the world. Although his recorded material might seem outdated to today's fans, one must never forget that for some twenty years he was one of the prime cornet players of his era.

Like the music of many of his fellow musicians from the Crescent City, Oliver's cornet sound reflected his birthplace. His tone was boisterous, rollicking, and joyful. There was a richness and earthy depth to the notes he played with such brilliant precision. Because of his piercing and powerful style it was no wonder that he was called "King."

He was the leader of two key groups (the Creole Jazz Band and the Dixie Syncopators) both of which had a profound effect on a number of other bands. Oliver's outfits blazed a clear path for future groups to follow and provided guidance to those of the same era. He was able to achieve such lofty heights because of the personnel in the lineup.

Oliver was an excellent recruiter and had a remarkable eye for talent. His groups boasted several future "legends" including Louis Armstrong, Baby Dodds, Johnny Dodds, Jimmie Noone, and Kid Ory. Other important names that played with him include Bud Scott, Johnny St. Cyr, Arville Harris, Barney Bigard, Jimmy Archey, Luis Russell, Paul Barbarin, Buster Bailey, Stump Evans, Cyrus St. Clair, Omer Simeon, Darnell Howard, Leroy Harris, Lil Hardin, Albert Nicholas, Honore Dutrey, and Lottie Taylor. Featuring these quality musicians enabled him to reign supreme during his prime.

He was a superb bandleader and always allowed the members of his band to take their turns and shine in the spotlight. It was during his stint in Oliver's band that Louis Armstrong became a household name. Oliver was an important influence on Louis Armstrong. Satchmo, the one individual most strongly associated with the days of the golden age of the genre in the minds of many fans, made his recording debut with King Oliver. The close working relationship between the two is an integral part of that period in jazz history.

Oliver was also an important pioneer in transforming jazz from ensemble music to music featuring the brilliant work of soloists. The change from group sound to featured solo performer paved the way for later modern legends like Charlie "Yardbird" Parker, Dizzy Gillespie, and John Coltrane.

Oliver influenced an entire realm of musicians. A few of the jazz names that followed in his path include Henry "Red" Allen, Muggsy Spanier, Tommy Ladnier, and Wilbur De Paris. He also had a profound effect on such swing era bandleaders as Fletcher Henderson, Duke Ellington, Count Basie, Artie Shaw, Benny Goodman, Glenn Miller, Jimmy and Tommy Dorsey, Jimmie Lunceford, and so many more. They all owed a debt to Oliver. He was able to make the most of the talent that he had available. He was a master politician who was able to smoothly operate his band by making each member feel like he was making major contributions to the music.

Oliver made several records and gave the world some unforgettable classics including "Dippermouth Blues," "Chimes Blues," "Riverside Blues," "King Porter Stomp," "Tom Cat Blues," "Someday Sweetheart," "Dead Man Blues," "Jackass Blues," "Every Tab," "Showboat Shuffle," "West End Blues," "Blue Blood Blues," and "Jet Black Blues." Numerous future jazz artists, as well as blues singers and rock and rollers, shamelessly pillaged his musical catalog. There was an accessibility to his music that instantly hooked the listener. The simplicity and quality of his work made it naturally inviting for others to copy.

During the New Orleans revivals in the 1940s and 1970s, many turned to Oliver's songbook as a guiding source proving that his classics had survived the test of time. An excellent cornet player who may have been the very best, he never disappointed his audience. He is a member of the Jazz Hall of Fame. There is no doubt that the man who gave the world his "Dippermouth Blues" holds a special place in jazz history.

Discography:

King Oliver's Jazz Band, Auvidis 157462.
King Oliver: Louis Armstrong, Milestone M47017.
King Oliver Creole Jazz Band, Olympic 7133.
Sugar Foot Stomp, GRP 34.
King Oliver, RCA 42411.
King Oliver, Brunswick BLP-58020.
Great Original Performances 1923–1930, Louisiana Red Hot Records 607.
Handful of Riffs, ASV/Living Era 5061.
The Quintessence/1923–1928, EPM Musique JA157462.

King Oliver in New York, RCA LPV-529.
Complete Vocalion & Brunswick Recordings, Affinity 1025.
King Oliver, Vol. 1 (1923-1929), BBC RPCD/ZCRP 787.
Okeh Sessions, EMI 260579.
King Oliver, Vol. 1, Classic Jazz Audio 19.
King Oliver & His Orchestra, Epic BA-17003.
King Oliver Creole Jazz Band, 1923–1924, Retrieval 79007.
King Oliver Farewell Blues, Vol. 1, FRG 34.
King Oliver Farewell Blues, Vol. 2, FRG 35.
Dippermouth Blues, ASL 5218.
King Oliver, The Compositions of Jelly Roll Morton, CBC 1027.
Father of the New Orleans Trumpeters 1926–1930, EPM 159242.
King Oliver & His Jazz Band (with Louis Armstrong), EPM 157462.
King Oliver & His Creole Jazz Band, 1926–1928, Classic 618.
King Oliver and His Creole Jazz Band, 1928–1930, Classic 607.
King Oliver & His Creole Jazz Band, 1930–1931, Classic 594.

KID ORY (1886–1973)

Tailgate Trombone

Each instrument in jazz has its pioneer. Buddy Bolden was the early champion of the cornet and set the pace that Freddie Keppard, Joe "King" Oliver, Nick LaRocca, and Louis Armstrong, among others, would follow. Pops Foster was the deacon of the bass and established the parameters of its role in the early New Orleans bands. Zutty Singleton and Baby Dodds were the prime stick men. Johnny Dodds was the first important clarinet player. Jelly Roll Morton, Scott Joplin, and Eubie Blake were the masters of the piano. The man who brought the trombone to prominence did so with his tailgate technique. His name was Kid Ory.

Kid Ory was born Edward Ory, in La Place, Louisiana, on December 25, 1886. As a native of the Bayou State, Ory soaked up the rich musical environment and by the age of ten had begun his musical career. A multi-instrumentalist, he started on the banjo then developed his skills on the clarinet, drums, string bass, and alto saxophone before choosing the valve trombone as his prime jazz voice.

Once he was proficient enough, Ory led a band that performed all over La Place and the surrounding area. While he earned a decent living in his native town, New Orleans was the true musical pulse of the state, and in 1912 Ory moved to the Crescent City. He had a sharp eye for talent and during his period as a bandleader he recruited such greats as Mutt Carey, King Oliver, Sidney Bechet, Johnny Dodds, Jimmie Noone and a young, unknown trumpeter named Louis Armstrong.

In the next few years he established his legend in New Orleans music circles. Already somewhat of a star, Ory introduced his individual style to a larger audience. It was during this productive phase of his long, illustrious career that he became known as the best trombonist in all of jazz.

Despite his success, in 1919 Ory left his native state for the Golden Coast for health reasons. He found a home in California and made history by leading the first small African-American band to record. The songs "Ory's Creole Trombone" and "Society Blues" were cut not under his name but under the moniker Spike's Seven Pods of Pepper Orchestra. Although he made a definite impact on the jazz scene in California, he was convinced that Chicago offered better opportunities for him.

In 1925, when he arrived in the Windy City, Chicago was being hailed as the hottest jazz center. He made valuable contributions to the Chicago scene while recording many sides with his old colleagues from New Orleans, including King Oliver and Jelly Roll Morton. But he utilized his trailing trombone technique to perfection on his good friend Louis Armstrong's Hot Five and Hot Seven sessions. The songs he cut with Satchmo's studio groups became classics. He also toured New York and other major cities with King Oliver during this period. Later, in 1927, he joined Dave Payton's band.

Ory also made his presence felt in a number of other outfits including Boyd Allen's Band, Clarence Black's group and the Chicago Vagabonds. After five years in Chicago, which saw Ory add immensely to his already strong reputation, he returned to Los Angeles to participate in the groups of Mutt Carey, Leon Rene, Emerson Scott, Freddie Washington, and Charlie Echol. Although he was without a doubt one of the true forces in jazz in the 1920s, by the end of the decade Ory was out of the music business.

Another victim of the decimation of the recording industry during the Great Depression, Ory left the world he had known for some thirty years in order to help his brother run a chicken farm. Thankfully, all of the musical gifts that he had delivered in his illustrious career had been preserved on vinyl. But the sheer excitement of Ory on stage was absent until 1939, when he returned to pick up the lost threads of his once successful musical life.

He immediately joined Barney Bigard who was thrilled to have the living legend in his band. At this point in his comeback, Ory played both trombone and bass. After a brief stint in Bigard's band, Ory assumed the leadership of his own group. His combo of musicians played on the Orson Welles radio show and quickly built a strong following. The new band included old pal Mutt Carey on trumpet and Omer Simeon and Darnell Howard on clarinet. The band cooked.

Ory could not have picked a better time to begin the second phase of his career as the New Orleans revival was in full swing. It was also around this time that he made his acting debut in the film *New Orleans*. He later made an appearance on *The Benny Goodman Story*. Although he didn't win an Oscar for any of his acting performances, he helped spread his name to a different type of audience.

The years between 1945 and 1960 were truly golden years for Ory. He worked steadily in the Los Angeles area as well as other West Coast cities, and toured throughout the country and abroad with his Kid Ory Creole Jump Band that included at various times Teddy Buckner, Marty Marsala, Alvin Alcorn, and Red Allen. Although Ory worked with a fabulous list of jazz giants during his distinguished career, Alcorn was the perfect compliment to his style and skill.

After 1960, Ory slowed down considerably. While he still recorded and toured occasionally, his salad days were over. In 1966, he retired to Hawaii but made sporadic appearances including one at the New Orleans Jazz Festival in 1971. On January 23, 1973, in Honolulu, Hawaii, the jazz world lost one of its most prominent pioneers. Kid Ory was 87 years old.

Kid Ory was more than a jazz pioneer. His contributions to the music were plentiful and varied. As a musician, particularly on the trombone, he set the standard for all future players, and his multi-instrumental abilities only added to his assorted credits. He was a unique individual whose bands generated some of the most exciting moments in jazz history.

Despite the many hats Ory wore in jazz, he will always be associated with creating the definite parameters for the trailing trombone. He had an essentially dynamic style that required impeccable timing, and he used his horn to play rhythm bass lines behind the clarinet and the trumpet creating a rich dimension to the blaring first lines of the prime horns. In the first thirty years of the twentieth century the trombone was linked to one name—Kid Ory.

It was Ory's boldness in experimenting with traditional jazz rules that enabled later revolutionists like Dizzy Gillespie and Charlie Parker to reinvent the music. Like all good pioneers, he paved the way for future generations in order to maintain the vibrancy of the genre. Although later trombonists would differ in technique from his tailgate form, he provided

a base from which to begin. His style was firmly rooted in the boisterous, joyful sound of early New Orleans jazz.

Ory was also a survivor. When he quit the music business in the
early 1930s, many jazz pundits believed that he was washed up and that
his playing days were done. But he proved all of his detractors wrong and
arguably enjoyed as much success in the second phase of his career as he
did in the first. Many of the most important artists of the early days of
jazz never recovered from the collapse of the music industry during the
Great Depression.

Ory was also a prime architect of the New Orleans Tradition as well
as of the Jazz Age. During both eras, he shared the stage along with fellow musicians Henry "Red" Allen, Bobby Hackett, Hot Lips Page, King
Oliver, Roy Eldridge, Jack Teagarden, Louis Armstrong, and Sydney
Bechet. Although the "Titan of the Trombone" did not single–handedly
put New Orleans on the world musical map with his outstanding talent
and leadership qualities, his contributions were essential in shaping the
Crescent City's international reputation as the center of jazz. As a glo-
betrotter, he simply restated his love for the music to audiences around
the world.

Ory delivered a vast trove of songs, including "Muskrat Ramble," that
were standards in the 1920s and helped define the era. "Muskrat Rum-
ble" remains one of the great old classics still performed by a variety of
jazz musicians of the new school.

His signature trombone can be heard on many other classics he
recorded on his own and as part of groups headed by Louis Armstrong,
Jelly Roll Morton, King Olivier, and Johnny Dodds. A very short list
includes "Skit-De-De-Dat," "Gut Bucket Blues," "Doctor Jazz," "Black
Bottom Stomp," "Grandpa's Spells," and "Tailgate!"

One of Ory's greatest skills as a musician was his versatility. He was
a capable leader as well as an in–demand session player. He excelled on a
wide assortment of instruments, although he will be forever linked to the
trombone.

Time has not forgotten Kid Ory. His name re–occurs in many dis-
cussions of the early days of jazz and of jazz music in general. He is also
enshrined in the Jazz Hall of Fame. Although his sound seems dated in
terms of the current trends, his music remains an important chapter in
the annals of the genre. Undoubtedly, the man with the trailing trombone will always hold a special place in jazz history.

Discography

Kid Ory's Creole Jazz Band, Folklyric 9008.

Kid Ory, Columbia CL-835.
Kid Ory at the Green Room, Vol. 1, American Music AMCD-42.
Kid Ory at the Green Room, Vol. 2, American Music AMCD-43.
At Crystal Pier 1947 [live], American Music 90.
Edward Kid Ory and His Creole Band, GNP 519.
King of the Tailgate Trombone, American Music 20.
Kid Ory and His Creole Dixieland Band, Columbia CL-6145.
At the Beverly Cavern, Sounds 1208.
Creole Jazz Band at Club Hangover, Storyville SLP-4070.
Live at Club Hangover, Vol. 1, Dawn Club 12013.
This Kid's the Greatest! Good Time Jazz 12045.
Kid Ory Plays the Blues, Storyville 4064.
Sounds of New Orleans, Vol. 9 [live], Storyville 6016.
Kid Ory's Creole Jazz Band (1954), Good Time Jazz 12004.
Live at Club Hangover, Vol. 3, Dawn Club 12017.
Creole Jazz Band, Good Time Jazz 12008.
Kid Ory's Creole Band/Johnny Wittwer Trio, Jazz Man LP-2.
Kid Ory Favorites! Good Time Jazz 10041-42.
Favorites! Fantasy 60009.
Kid Ory in Europe, Verve 8259.
Song of the Wanderer, Verve 1014.
The Kid from New Orleans: Ory That Is, Verve 1016.
Dixieland Marching Songs, Verve 1026.
Kid Ory Sings French Traditional Songs, Verve 1030.
Plays W.C. Handy, Verve 1017.
At the Jazz Band Ball 1959, Rhapsody RHA 6034.
Dance with Kid Ory or Just Listen, Verve 1022.
The Original Jazz, Verve 1023.
The Storyville Nights, Verve 8456.
Kid Ory Live, Vault 9006.
Ory's Creole Trombone, ASV/Living Era 5148.
In Denmark [Live], Storyville 6038.
Kid Ory's Creole Jazz Band (1944–45), Good Time Jazz 12022.
His Greatest Recording 1922–1944, Best of Jazz/Swing Era 4023.
Kid Ory, 1922–1945, CLC 1069.
Kid Creole and his Jazz Band, 1922–1947, Document 1002.
Kid Creole and his Creole Jazz Band, EPM 157162.
Kid Ory and His Creole Jazz Band, 1944-46, EPM 158872.

FREDDIE KEPPARD (1890–1933)

The Second in Line

The cornet was the prime instrument in the early years of jazz. Buddy Bolden was its first great practitioner and he became a legend. Later King Oliver would take up where Bolden left off. But in between the reign of King Bolden and King Oliver was the second great cornet player of the New Orleans tradition. His name was Freddie Keppard.

Freddie Keppard was born February 27, 1890, in New Orleans, Louisiana. He grew up in a musical family; his brother Louis played the tuba and the piano. Freddie himself began on the mandolin, then switched to the violin. He explored the possibilities of the accordion before settling on the cornet. Once he was proficient enough to perform in front of an audience he organized the Olympia Orchestra. The group played local gigs around the city. He also moonlighted in Frankie Dusen's Eagle Band.

In 1912, Keppard and several bandmates traveled to Los Angeles where he co-founded the Original Creole Orchestra. A successful enterprise, it became the most popular band on the West Coast and extended its appeal in the big cities of Chicago and New York. Although he had a chance to record his material at this time Keppard turned down the offer, a decision that he would later regret. Had he recorded them, his place in history would have been sealed for eternity.

From 1917 on, Keppard split his time between Chicago and Los Angeles establishing his legend. Eventually he settled in the Windy City and secured a permanent residency at the Logan Square Theatre before heading back to the City of the Angels once again to tour the Orpheum circuit. Although he was the unquestionable leader of the newly reformed Original Creoles, he also spent a good part of the 1920s as a hired gun.

Keppard toured with a number of groups including the Tan Town Topics and was a regular fixture at the Entertainers' Café. He also played his cornet in Lt. Tim Brymm's group during a residency in New York. Freddie then began to work with Jimmie Noone while also moonlighting in Mae Brady's Band at the Dreamland club.

From 1923 through 1926, Keppard took part in no less than three different bands: Doc Cooke's, Ollie Powers' and Erskine Tate's outfits. Doc Cook's sixteen-piece band were all prime architects of the Chicago jazz sound and made several recordings that included Keppard's sharp cornet sound. Ollie Powers' Harmony Band was a mainstay at the Dreamland club; Erskine Tate's Vendome Symphony Orchestra (they played at the Vendome Theatre) was a fifteen-piece ensemble. The various situations enabled Keppard to display his great versatility. His ability to excel in any environment ensured that he would always be able to find work.

Between these various engagements he also found time to lead his own group. It was during this time period—1923–1927—that Keppard decided to record his own material. It was a significant achievement since many of the first generation of New Orleans Traditional jazz player never had the opportunity to establish a recorded legacy. These were his peak years and captured him at his best before his decline.

Unfortunately, while he was making great music and playing a pivotal role in the popularization of jazz, Keppard was also developing into an alcoholic. As a result his health began to deteriorate and his gleaming cornet solos began to lose their sharpness and power. By the end of the 1920s, Keppard was out of the music business, a shell of the man who had once been hailed as the greatest cornet player of his day.

Keppard, like many other African-Americans at the time, also suffered from tuberculosis. After a lengthy illness, he died on July 15, 1933, in the Cook County Hospital in Chicago, Illinois. He was 44 years old.

Freddie Keppard was a jazz pioneer. His name can be placed alongside other noteworthy musicians of that early period including Buddy Bolden, Bunk Johnson, Jelly Roll Morton, Louis Armstrong, Sidney Bechet, and King Oliver. His vast contributions to the New Orleans traditional style and as one of the major architects of the Chicago sound only add to his legend. Keppard also helped introduce jazz to the West Coast, in particular to the many nightclubs around the Los Angeles area.

Keppard played a strong horn cutting through the rhythms derived from the funeral and parade marches of the previous century. Although he was one of many in a world of cornet players, he possessed a distinct sound that was instantly recognizable. In an era of ensemble music he stood out with his brilliant ability to improvise.

In order to fully understand Keppard's contributions as a musician he must be put in proper context next to the other two early New Orleans cornet players—Buddy Bolden and King Oliver. Bolden was the first great cornet player who played loudly but never recorded any of his material. Although he was an important influence on Keppard, the student outdistanced the master as he showed a greater range in ability and imagination. Oliver was a bandleader who enjoyed many years of success and was able to add his cornet skills to a band ensemble better than Bolden and Keppard.

But more than just being a great cornet player, Keppard also added his own personal designs to the blueprint of how a jazz musician acted and lived in the genre's formative years. He played hard and partied hard. This practice led to the early demise of many jazz musicians. Perhaps no other style can claim a longer list of early deaths—except for the blues— than jazz. Unfortunately, Keppard's name must be added to list of those who left us before their time.

He was also responsible for changing jazz from the music of an ensemble to music that emphasized the soloist. While examples of his varied talents survived, unfortunately, much of his work went unrecorded. A complete recording of his catalog would greatly elevate his status in the eyes of jazz historians.

Although the Original Dixieland Jazz Band was the first group to be credited with putting the new sound on record, Keppard could have made that claim if he hadn't turned down the opportunity to record in 1915, two years before the ODJB put their material on vinyl. But Keppard, a paranoid individual, was convinced that rivals would steal his ideas if they were able to hear his efforts. These types of decisions hurt his reputation and stunted a quicker blossoming of his career.

Keppard was one of the most well-traveled jazz musicians of all time. He made his mark in four major American cities: New Orleans, Chicago, Los Angeles and New York. In Europe, he became one of the most revered artists and influenced an entire generation with his piercing cornet sound despite having never played there.

In his career he worked with many of the biggest names in jazz. A partial list includes Johnny Dodds, Jimmie Noone, Eddie Vincent, Bill Newton, Johnny St. Cyr, Elwood Graham, Robert Shelly, Fayette Williams, Jasper Taylor, Joe Poston, Jerome Pasquall, George Mitchell, Andrew Hilaire, Jimmy Bertrand, Papa Charlie Jackson, Cookie's Gingersnaps, Clifford King, Arthur Campbell, and Jimmy Bell. Keppard made an undeniable impact on each person that he crossed paths with because of his unique cornet sound and his fast-paced lifestyle.

Despite a brief time in the sun and a major gaffe in not being the first person to record a true jazz record, he was still inducted into the Jazz Hall of Fame. Keppard was an interesting individual whose contributions to the music cannot be overlooked. His dedicated playing, his penchant for introducing the wonders of jazz to the western states, the mythical figure that he cut, and his association with many of the biggest names in the genre of the period ensure that he will always be remembered for his position as second in line.

Discography

Red Onion Jazz Babies/Cook's Dreamland, Fountain FJ-107.
The Complete Freddie Keppard 1923–27, King Jazz 111.
The Legendary Freddie Keppard—New Orleans, Smithsonian/Folkways 15141.
New Orleans Giants, Vol. 1, EPM Musique HS151262.
Legend, Pearl 1052.
1923–1928, EPM Musique 159282.
1923–1926, Challenge 79017.

POPS FOSTER (1892–1969)

The Slap Rhythm Man

In the past one hundred years, the role and importance of the bass, as with the other rhythm instruments, has expanded in jazz. During the New Orleans Tradition, the bass was relegated to simple rhythmic duty and took a backseat to the cornet or trumpet and piano featured in the solo spotlight. In later years, Jimmy Blanton and Charles Mingus proved that the bass could be an effective lead instrument in jazz. The pioneer of jazz bass was one of the best timekeepers and was known as "The Slap Rhythm Man." His name was Pops Foster.

Pops Foster was born George Murphy Foster on a plantation in McCall, Louisiana, on May 18, 1892. He began his musical career on the cello and three years later switched to the string bass. His brother, Willard, studied the banjo and guitar. One of the most important events in George's musical maturation occurred when the family moved to New Orleans when he was ten years old. There he was immediately exposed to the second line rhythms and rich musical environment of the Crescent City.

Foster turned professional in his early teens. The three years he had spent studying the cello enabled him to take immediate command of the bass and he easily found work in the early jazz ensembles. Although his role was timekeeper, he had begun a career as a working musician that would last for the next six decades through many changes in the genre.

He joined Rosseals Orchestra in 1906, left shortly thereafter and played in Jack Carey's group. After a brief stay with the Magnolia Band—one of the many New Orleans working outfits at the time—Foster joined Kid Ory, the king of the tailgate trombone style. Although he would remain with Ory for several years he also found time to play in a variety of other bands including those of Armand Piron and King Oliver.

Along the way, Foster had studied the tuba and although the string bass was his first instrument, he was now a double threat. That only increased his marketability. In 1917, he joined Fate Marable's riverboat summer tours and would work with the famous bandleader for the next four seasons.

Like many other jazz musicians of the era, he traveled the country and played in different locations. In 1921, Foster made his way to St. Louis and found work immediately with Charlie Creath and Dewey Jackson. After his stint in these two groups, Foster played with Ed Allen's Whispering Gold Band before rejoining trombonist Kid Ory on the West Coast.

Foster remained in Los Angeles for the next two years. It was during his tenure with Ory that he made his first recordings. Although he would never lead a recording session throughout his long career, Foster would appear on hundreds of other recordings of many notable jazz artists. When Ory turned leadership of the band over to Mutt Carey so he could return to Chicago (the hot jazz spot in 1925), Foster stayed with Carey for a short time before moving back to St. Louis.

For the next four years—1925 to 1929—Foster found plentiful work in St. Louis, usually in the Charlie Creath and Dewey Jackson bands. By this time, he was recognized as one of the top bass players in jazz circles. His driving slap-bass style propelled the soloists in the band while he kept up a strong rhythm. Although he wasn't adventurous, he was solid and he performed exactly what was expected of him in every group he played in.

In 1929, Foster joined Luis Russell. Russell, born in Panama in 1902, was a noted pianist and arranger who had extensive experience before joining King Oliver's band in Chicago in 1925. Eventually, Russell, after numerous recordings with Oliver, formed a ten-piece unit that played in Harlem. Some of the alumni in his band included trombonist J. C. Higginbottom, an important name of the 1920s and 1930s, drummer Paul Barbarin, trumpeter Bill Coleman, and saxophonist-clarinetist Albert Nicolas.

It was during his stay in Russell's band that Foster was featured on such classics as "Jersey Lightning," "Song of Swanee," "Saratoga Shout," "Feelin' the Spirit," "Panama," "Doctor Blues," and "Louisiana Swing." In these and other songs the definite slap bass of Foster can be heard spurring on Higginbottom, Nicolas, and Russell during their inspiring solo flights. Although he wasn't flashy, Foster was an essential part of Russell's success and definitive sound.

In 1929, Russell's band began to back Louis Armstrong. The opportunity enabled Foster to expand his already impressive credentials. Russell's first-rate band toured and recorded with the trumpet legend and Foster's slap bass can be heard on the V.S.O.P. volumes five and six, as well as on *Complete Works 1935–1940*. The regular work enabled him to keep his career going while other bass players of his era such as Steve Brown, Wellman Braud, and Bill Johnson were not as fortunate.

Due to health problems, Foster was forced to leave the band in 1940. After a brief stay in hospital he was fit once again to resume his career. He spent time with the brilliant pianist Teddy Wilson before joining Happy Caldwell's Happy Pals and remained there for a few months.

At a time when the young bop enthusiasts were reshaping the very sound of jazz, the old guard that included Foster remained dedicated to the New Orleans tradition. While Jimmie Blanton and Charles Mingus were exploring different avenues, Foster carried on with his slap-rhythm style. In the 1940s, the revival of the New Orleans sound enabled him to enjoy a career renaissance.

Foster, who had played a secondary role throughout much of his career, decided to try his hand at being his own boss and formed a duo with guitarist Norman Isadore Langlois. Although the pair proved to be a dynamic pairing, Foster would spend a good chunk of the war years (1942–1945) as a worker for the New York subway system. He moonlighted, playing gigs on the weekends.

Despite the steady pay that his civilian job provided, music was in his blood. He returned to the world of jazz, joining Sidney Bechet's group in 1945. A few months later he found work with Art Hodes' band and remained there for over a year. Foster, who had participated in hundreds of recordings by this time in his career, was also part of the *This is Jazz* radio series, which kept his name vibrant in music circles.

After the Second World War, travel to Europe became feasible once again. Foster joined the Mezz Mezzrow Band and played at the festival in Nice, France, with the famed leader. Upon his return to the United States, he joined Bob Wilber's Band based in Boston. Jimmy Archey assumed leadership in 1950, and Foster toured Europe with him two years later.

In the hard bop/cool jazz days of the 1950s, Pop Foster continued to find work as a session player and remained with Archey's band, which had a regular gig at the Central Plaza in New York. The audience had not lost its taste for the traditional style that Foster remained loyal to and played with such pride. In 1954, he added another dimension to his resume when he appeared in the movie *Jazz Dance*.

In 1954, he returned to his boyhood home of New Orleans where he played briefly in Pops Celestine's outfit. He later joined Sam Price's Bluesicians and remained with them for six months, touring in Europe with the band during the winter months of 1955–56. Upon his return to America, Foster moved to San Francisco and made it his home base for the remainder of his career.

He found work immediately in the Bay area with Earl Hines and stayed with the talented pianist for the next few years playing in many of the local venues. In 1962, he left Hines and freelanced, first appearing with Eddie Smith's Band, then with Elmer Snowden's Trio for much of 1963 and the following year. In 1966, he toured Europe once again as part of the New Orleans All-Stars. Upon his return to the United States he moved to his California home. Although he was stationed in the Golden State, he toured regularly throughout the rest of the United States and Canada.

In 1968, Foster suffered a serious illness, but recovered to resume playing. However, on October 30, 1969, in his San Francisco home, the great slap bassist from another era of jazz died. He was 77 years old.

Pops Foster was a jazz pioneer. He was the first important bassist, and although he never distinguished himself as a great soloist he was a steady rhythm man. His forte was the ability to propel the various horn players in the band to reach higher while he kept an even beat. This dual ability was the starting point of all aspiring bass players who arrived on the jazz scene long after Foster had already established his impeccable credentials.

Although he never led his own recording session he took part in literally hundreds of dates with many of the biggest names in jazz history. A short list includes Louis Armstrong, Henry "Red" Allen, Sidney Bechet, Kid Ory, Jelly Roll Morton, Baby Dodds, James P. Johnson, Earl Hines, Fats Waller, Jack Teagarden, and Coleman Hawkins. He also played on blues discs with Sonny Terry and Brownie McGhee and with Alberta Hunter. There is scarcely a major jazz artist from the first half of the twentieth century who doesn't feature Pops' driving slap bass.

He worked with a number of other jazz artists that he never recorded with including Zutty Singleton, Sidney "Big Sid" Catlett, Eddie Condon, Lee Blair, Bernard Addison, Jack Teagarden, Wellman Braud, Will Johnson, Bingie Madison, Wilbur De Paris, George Washington, Teddy Hill and Baby Dodds. No matter who he worked with Foster could be counted on to provide a rock-steady bass sound slapping the root notes in perfect rhythm.

Although he never gained the solo status that Blanton, Oscar Pettiford, and Charles Mingus all basked in, Foster remains an important member of the bass playing family. He was the first real "star" (although in a background role) of the instrument. It was Foster who established the foundation for future bass virtuosos to improve on. He was also an important influence on John Kirby and Walter Page. His style can also be heard in the early rock and roll records of Bill Haley and the Comets, Elvis Presley, and others.

Foster's career spanned six decades and because of his long, illustrious years in jazz, he was a historian who witnessed first hand the many changes that occurred in the music. He was also able to provide a very personal glimpse into the lives of the many greats with whom he played including Armstrong, Bechet, and Morton. His life in jazz was captured in his autobiography *Pops Foster: An Autobiography of a New Orleans Jazzman* that was posthumously published.

While other bassists such as Blanton, Mingus, Charlie Haden and Ray Brown brought greater recognition to the instrument, Foster remains an important figure. Because of his enormous contributions he was inducted into the Jazz Hall of Fame. Although he is not the first bass player to be named in a discussion of bassists, there is no denying the slap rhythm man's unique place in jazz history.

Discography

The following is a partial list of the many records that Pops Foster appears on.

Henry "Red" Allen Collection, Volume 1, JSP 332.
Henry "Red" Allen Collection, Volume 2, JSP 333.
Henry "Red" Allen Swing Out Pearl 1037.
Henry "Red" Allen Swing Era Best of Jazz 4031.
Jimmy Archey, Dr. Jazz Series, Volume 4, Storyville 6044.
Louis Armstrong, Portrait of the Artist as a Young Man, Sony 57176.
Louis Armstrong, West End Blues, Ind. 2035.
Louis Armstrong, Back O' Town Blues 1939–45, EPM 156732.
Louis Armstrong, Thanks a Million 1935–1940, AVD 574.
Louis Armstrong, Masterpieces, Vol. 1, EPM 158132.
Louis Armstrong Hot Fives & Sevens, Volume 4, JSP 315.
Mildred Bailey Blue Angel Years 1945–1947 Baldwin Street Music 306.
Sidney Bechet Port at Harlem Jazzmen, Blue Note BLP-7022.
Teddy Bunn (1929–1940), RST 1509.
Hoagy Carmichael, Sometimes I Wonder, ASV/Living Era 5345.

Hoagy Carmichael, Old Music Master, Memoir 527.
Eddie Condon & His All-Star band, Live at Town Hall (1944), Jass 634.
Coleman Hawkins, Body & Soul, Pearl 1022.
Art Hodes Dixieland Jubilee, Blue Note PB-706.
Art Hodes Jazz Records Story, Jazzology 82.
James P. Johnson, Hot Piano, PEA 1048.
King Oliver 1923–1930, Louisiana Red Hot Records 607.
Tommy Ladnier, Goose Pimples, Pearl 1074.
Tommy Ladnier, Steppin' on the Blues, ASV/Living Era 5353.
Eddie Lang/Lonnie Johnson, Blue Guitars, Vol. 1–2, BGO 327.
Leadbelly, Where Did You Sleep Last Night? Smithsonian/Folkways 40044.
Mezz Mezzrow, 1928–1936, Classics 713.

JELLY ROLL MORTON (1890–1941)

Red Hot Pepper Jazz

The annals of jazz are full of eccentric and colorful characters who shaped the early sound and set the standards for the type of music that was to follow. Despite their immense contributions, many of these pacesetters have been forgotten by latter day fans and scholars. However, history has been kind to some of them including the man who shook the world with his "red hot pepper jazz." His name was Jelly Roll Morton.

Jelly Roll Morton was born Ferdinand Joseph Lemott on October 20, 1890, in New Orleans, Louisiana. Morton possessed an ancestry that reflected the very roots of jazz itself. A Creole and a Euro-African American, he started on the guitar and the trombone before finally settling on the piano. When he ran his fingers along the keyboards he felt the magic inside him and knew that he could be something special if he could hone his skills. His patience and dedication paid off handsomely because by his early teens he was already performing in New Orleans' famed Storyville district.

By his late teens, Morton had given up playing piano in the bordellos in New Orleans and drifted throughout the South, spending time in Meridian and Biloxi, Mississippi, among other places. It was during these travels that he accumulated the material for the cycle of songs that would make him famous. Although he was first and foremost a musician, during this period in his life Morton earned a living as a pool hustler, vaudeville comic, and, according to some historians, a pimp. He eventually returned to New Orleans and music in the early 1910s, after creating havoc in San Francisco, Detroit, Chicago, St. Louis and Kansas City.

In 1917, Morton moved to Los Angeles and stayed there for five years. During this time he appeared at various clubs throughout the city, ran his own establishment for a brief period, and most importantly, organized his first band. His small group toured the West Coast, going as far as Vancouver, Canada. After disbanding his outfit, he caught the traveling fever once again and sojourned to Alaska before returning to the southwestern part of the United States. After working in Denver, Colorado, Morton then relocated to Los Angeles. Throughout his journeys he had continued to improve on the piano and added dimensions to his playing that he would make good use of later on.

In 1923, Morton arrived in Chicago, which was fast becoming the prime jazz city in the country. He immediately recorded with the Jazz Rhythm Kings and although the songs were somewhat uneven and rough, there was no denying Morton's prowess on the piano. He was regarded as one of the prime players by 1923. His style was heavily influenced by New Orleans jazz, but because of his extensive travels he incorporated elements of many other types of music into his playing.

It was in the Windy City that he cemented his legend. In 1926, after bouncing around in various groups, he formed his own Red Hot Peppers and recorded some of the most definitive music of any era. His group included trombonist Kid Ory and guitarist Johnny St. Cyr. Although the 1920s was one of the golden eras of jazz and there were literally hundreds of bands throughout the land competing for jobs, Morton's Red Hot Peppers was one of the most recognizable. Although much of the credit rests with Morton, the members of his band made enormous contributions.

Johnny St. Cyr was born in New Orleans, Louisiana, on April 17, 1890. He played with a number of jazz giants including Freddie Keppard, Louis Armstrong, Fate Marable and Doc Cook. St. Cyr became an excellent guitarist and was arguably one of the first important six string slingers in jazz along with Lonnie Johnson and Eddie Lang. The trio opened the doors for Charlie Christian who arrived a decade later.

Another important member of Morton's Hot Peppers was Omer Simeon. Omer Simeon was born in New Orleans but moved to Chicago when he was twelve. He made his professional debut at the age of eighteen in his brother's group and also played for Charley Elgar's Creole Jazz Band. He later toured and recorded with King Oliver's Dixie Syncopators before moving on to Morton's group. By the time that he joined Jelly Roll's band he was an accomplished player.

Other essential sidemen in his band included cornetist George Mitchell, trombonist Gerald Reeves, clarinetists Barney Bigard, Darnell Howard, and Johnny Dodds, bassist John Lindsey, C-melody saxophonist Stomp Evans, and drummer Andrew Hilaire. While Morton wasn't recording with his own group, he cut some interesting albums with Baby and Johnny Dodds.

Although Chicago remained an important jazz center, New York eventually eclipsed it in the late 1920s and as a result Morton moved to the Big Apple. He continued to record mostly for the Victor label with sidemen like trumpeters Ward Pinkett, Red Allen and Bubber Miley, trombonists Geechie Fields, Charles Irvis, and J. C. Higginbottom, as well as the faithful Simeon. Others who appeared with Morton during this time included clarinetists Albert Nicholas, Barney Bigard, banjoist Lee Blair, guitarist Barnard Addison, tuba player Bill Benfore, bass pioneer Pops Foster, and drummers Zutty Singleton, Tommy Benford, and Paul Barbarin. One aspect that separated Morton from other jazz musicians was his use of different instruments like the banjo and tuba in his band.

Morton's fortunes in New York turned sour in the early 1930s. He had lost touch with the pulse of jazz and his music was considered old-fashioned. The recording industry, decimated by the Great Depression, didn't have time to record Morton. His lack of popularity was guaranteed not to sell records—something none of the struggling labels could afford. His abrasive personality blocked any chances of being used as a sideman, a lucrative source of employment for many musicians during the tough days of the early 1930s. Because of his inability to record Morton's once illustrious career suffered a sharp decline.

He drifted around the East Coast for some time before eventually ending up playing in rat-infested, run-down places where he was unrecognized as one of the major contributors of jazz. He managed to survive the Dirty Thirties eking out a meager existence until a savior by the name of Alan Lomax arrived on the scene to record Morton for the Library of Congress series that became Jelly Roll's last flash in the sun. Unfortunately, the Library of Congress recordings were not released for a decade.

Morton was inspired by the success of the Library of Congress recordings and believed he could make a strong comeback in order to regain his past glory. He returned to New York determined to retake his place among jazz's elite; however, he enjoyed only limited success. The jazz world seemed to have passed him by.

He moved to the West Coast in the early 1940s in an attempt to once again rekindle his career, but he died on July 10, 1941, in Los Angeles, California. He was 50 years old.

Jelly Roll Morton was an important jazz pioneer. He was an exceptional piano player who became an idol to the many who followed him. He was also a sound composer of many jazz classics. He was part of the distinguished group of musicians who served as a link between the birth of New Orleans Traditional jazz and the spreading of the genre to the urban centers (particularly Chicago). The recordings he made as leader of the Red Hot Pepper band are genuine classics and essential additions to any fan's collection.

Morton was a terrific piano player who was able to extend the boundaries of the traditional New Orleans parade and barroom sound. Later, in the 1920s, he was one of the great improvisers. He swung as hard as anyone else, preceding the Big Band era by at least a decade. He combined elements of ragtime, blues, opera, New Orleans brass band, Spanish and folksong into his style. But there was more to Morton's musical skills. Like all other great musicians there was an individuality to his playing that transcended all styles and categories. His particular touch is instantly recognizable.

One of Morton's most important influences was Scott Joplin; however, Jelly Roll was able to develop beyond the stringent boundaries of ragtime. His songs contained more than one theme and often contained two or more fully developed melodies. He understood the subtleties of harmony and was able to weave a rich, complex sound over the rhythm section. He never received adequate credit for his knowledge of musical textures.

He was able to work both hands independently, forging an amazing style all of his own. His left hand created breathtaking runs while his right hand kept a solid beat with the bass player and drummer. He was able to juxtapose what his two hands could do adding layers of sound. He was instrumental in transforming ragtime into classic jazz.

Although he was an eccentric character, a rascal, a liar, and someone who was hard to get along with, he was also a formidable bandleader who worked with many of the legends of the early days of jazz. The list includes: Kid Ory, Omer Simeon, Barney Bigard, Albert Nicholas, Bud Scott, Baby Dodds, Stump Evans, George Mitchell, Zutty Singleton, Quinn Wilson, Gerald Reeves, Lee Blair, Tommy Benford, Johnny St. Cyr, Ward Pinkett, Darnell Howard, Geechie Fields, Andrew Hilaire, and Wellman Braud.

Despite a reputation that dogged him throughout the years as someone who took much credit for things he hadn't done, Morton was still a special influence on a number of later jazz musicians. A partial list includes Little Brother Montgomery, Bob Brookmeyer, Dave Burrell, Art Hodes, Dick Hyman, Rahsaan Roland Kirk, Turk Murphy, Lonnie Liston Smith,

Mike Westbrook, Don Ewell, and Ikey Robinson. But he also had an effect on those of his generation including Earl Hines, Fats Waller, Louis Armstrong, Sidney Bechet, Johnny Dodds, Kid Ory, and Omar Simeon.

He was a talented composer and arranger and is responsible for giving the world a number of classics. A partial list includes "King Porter Stomp," "Grandpa's Spells," "Wolverine Blues," "The Pearls," "Mr. Jelly Roll," "Shreveport Stomp," "Milenburg Joys," "Black Bottom Stomp," "The Chant," "Original Jelly Roll Blues," "Doctor Jazz," "Wild Man Blues," "Winin' Boy Blues," "I Thought I Heard Buddy Bolden Say," "Don't You Leave Me Here," and "Sweet Substitute." Many of his compositions became standards and staples in the repertoires of other jazz players. Although he was accused of stealing songs from others and then copyrighting them under his own name, Morton's recorded catalog is a deep well from which all jazz students are able to draw.

Jelly Roll Morton was an original and did as much to perpetuate the legend of jazz musicians as anyone else. Some of his testimony was true, other parts were greatly exaggerated. But there was a burning fever inside him that would never allow him to rest. He was a determined man, had odd habits, was loyal to those who needed him and was above all charismatic. Like so many other musicians of his day including Louis Armstrong, Bix Beiderbecke, King Oliver, and Buddy Bolden, Morton cut a personal as well as a musical swath through the history of jazz.

Jelly Roll Morton remains a distant name from the past to many new fans, but a deeper investigation reveals that he was a man of immense talent. He is one of the foundations of the early days of jazz and his memory lives through the large body of work he left to the world as well as those who have recorded his songs. Despite the controversy that has tarnished his image long after his death, Morton will always be remembered for his red hot pepper jazz.

Discography

Jelly Roll Morton, Riverside RLP-1018.
Ferd "Jelly Roll" Morton, Retrieve 79002.
Rarities Vol. 2, Rhapsody 6030.
Jelly Roll Morton, Everest 267.
Kansas City Bop: The Library of Congress, Rounder 1091.
Animule Dance, The Library of Congress, Vol. 2, Rounder 1092.
The Pearls, The Library of Congress, Vol. 3, Rounder 1093.
Winin Boy Blues, The Library of Congress, Vol. 4, Rounder 1094.
The New Orleans Rhythm Kings, Riverside RLP-12-102.
Birth of the Hot, RCA 66641.

New Orleans Memories, Commodore DL-30000.
Jelly Roll Morton, Milestone 47018.
Jelly Roll Morton, Dr. Jazz 1926–1927, Arpo 3.
Jelly Roll Morton, Vol. 1 1923–1924, Masters of Jazz 19.
Jelly Roll Morton, Vol. 2 1924–1926, Masters of Jazz 20.
Jelly Roll Morton, Vol. 3 1926, Masters of Jazz 33.
Jelly Roll Morton, Vol. 4 1927–1928, Masters of Jazz 58.
Jelly Roll Morton, Vol. 5 1928–1929, Masters of Jazz 72.
Jelly Roll Morton, Vol. 6 1929, Masters of Jazz 80.
Jelly Roll Morton, Vol. 7 1929–1930, Masters of Jazz 108.
Jelly Roll Morton, Vol. 8 1930–1934, Masters of Jazz 139.
Jelly Roll Morton, 1930–1939, CLC 654.
Jelly Roll Morton, 1939–1940, CLC 668.
Jelly Roll Morton, The Original Mr. Jelly Lord, AVD 696.
Jelly Roll Morton, Last Sessions—The Complete General Recordings, 1939–1940, CMD 403.
Jelly Roll Morton, Jelly Roll Morton Plays Jelly Roll Morton, Legends 467.
Jelly Roll Morton, Blues & Stomps from Rare Piano Rolls, Biograph 111.
Jelly Roll Morton, 1926-1930 JSP 903.
Jelly Roll Morton, Sweet & Hot, PEA 1003.
Jelly Roll Morton, Jelly Roll Stomp 1920's TRD 1075.
Jelly Roll Morton, Centennial: His Complete Victor Recordings 1926–1936 (5 CDs), BLBD 2361.
Jelly Roll Morton, The Pearls, 1926–1939, BLED 6588.
Jelly Roll Morton, Absolutely the Best, FUE 6191.
Jelly Roll Morton, Greatest Hits, Victor 68500.
Jelly Roll Morton, Mr. Jelly Lord, Rhino, 70384.
Jelly Roll Morton, Piano Rolls, NON 79363.
Jelly Roll Morton, Smoke House Blues, 1923–1930, CRG 12003.
From Chicago to New York, Vol. 2, EPM 151192.

JOHNNY DODDS (1892–1940)

Weary Way Blues

The legends of jazz encompass a variety of characters who made a serious impact on the music they loved so much. While the word "greatest" is often attached to these pioneers, in reality, the term was often misused. However, when the term "greatest" is associated with the licorice man who gave the world his weary way blues, it is justified. His name was Johnny Dodds.

John M. Dodds was born April 12, 1892, in New Orleans, Louisiana. Dodds was from a musical family; his younger brother, nicknamed "Baby," would later make his mark as one of the first important jazz drummers. However, unlike many of the early jazz artists, Johnny had a late start, not picking up the clarinet until he was seventeen. Although he was mostly self-taught he did receive some lessons from Lorenzo Tio and Charlie McCurdy.

Once he had become proficient enough to perform in front of a live audience, Dodds began a long apprentice in Kid Ory's band. He stayed there from 1912 through 1919 with a few stints in Fate Marable's riverboat jazz groups during the summer months. When the Navy forced the closing of the Storyville district he moved to Chicago to be part of King Oliver's Jazz Creole Band. It was from this point on that he established his reputation as the best clarinetist of the Jazz Age.

He recorded with King Oliver and his distinguished touch can be heard on such classics as "Canal Street Blues" and "Mandy Lee Blues." He also added his clever and clear clarinet sound to sessions with Jelly Roll Morton and Louis Armstrong. However, some of his most important recordings done at this time were with his own band, the Black Bottom Stompers, that included Natty Dominique. Because of their long association together it is necessary to briefly shift the spotlight to Dominique.

Anatie "Natty" Dominique was born in New Orleans, Louisiana, in 1896 and began to play the trumpet at an early age, soaking up the music that surrounded him. He became proficient enough to play in front of an audience by his early teens and was one of the many underage New Orleans jazz artists to perform in the red-light Storyville section. In the 1920s he backed blues singer Sippie Wallace and also recorded with Jelly Roll Morton before he settled with Dodds. Although he never attained the supreme status of Louis Armstrong or King Oliver, Natty was still regarded as one of the premier trumpet players from New Orleans. Dominique was able to blend his sound with Dodds' perfectly. The duo fit together musically like a well-penned two-part harmony song. They joined forces permanently in 1928 and spent many years performing in the same group.

From 1924 to 1930, Dodds worked regularly at Kelly's Stables in Chicago. As the house band he ensured the owner a top-notch act. This was the most productive period of his career and he became a big star on the Chicago jazz scene of the 1920s. He was starring with some of the biggest names in jazz as well as backing up blues singers Ida Cox and Lovie Austin. His outside work with the classic female blues singers underlines the great respect that so many other artists had for him.

However, at the beginning of the depression, like so many of his fellow musician brothers, Dodds saw his career plummet. The recording industry was in limbo and he was forced to find additional work running a cab company. Although times were tough he would not be deterred and continued to lead a band (that included Dominique) throughout the 1930s, appearing in many Chicago clubs including the Three Deuces, New Plantation, Calahan's, Lamb's Café, The 29, and others. He was able to continue to earn a slim living making music while many others were out of the business.

By the end of the 1930s, Dodds had returned to music full-time and he made some important recordings in late 1938 and 1940. He led his own group, the Chicago Boys, which consisted of pianist Lil Armstrong, guitarist Teddy Bunn, trumpeter Charlie Shavers and drummer/vocalist William Spencer. The group did not include Johnny's long time partner, Natty Dominique. The aforementioned band recorded in New York during Dodd's one and only trip to the Big Apple.

Unfortunately, for Dodds, his comeback was a little premature as the New Orleans revival that would occur in the 1940s went on without him. On August 8, 1940, Johnny Dodds, the greatest clarinetist of his generation died of a cerebral hemorrhage after suffering a heart attack. He was 48 years old.

Johnny Dodds is an important figure in jazz history. He was the premier clarinetist of his era and one of the best that ever lived. He was a prime architect in the creation of the Jazz Age. He played with many of the greatest names and was the leader of his own special unit.

Dodds was a superb blues player, a man who understood the genre so deeply that he was able to take it in a different direction and create his own brand of hot jazz. His music contained a creative excitement that inspired the listener and those around him. He was technically sound and played with such enthusiasm that he inspired all those who shared the stage or a recording date. In many ways he was the complete musician full of creative ideas and with the talent to turn them into a marketable commodity.

He was a fantastic soloist and was able to go head to head with the great Louis Armstrong and gave no quarter. He dueled with Jelly Roll Morton for instrumental supremacy during their recordings together and never backed down from the challenge. Dodds was an asset to every group he recorded with, giving the overall sound a sizzling dynamic dimension of pure emotion.

His solos were interesting for many reasons. Although he explored different avenues, his playing was not so outrageous as to offend. There was a familiarity to his sound but at the same time a hint of something more dangerous. He invited the listener into his private world with carefully chosen notes that complimented one another. His solos also had a dream-like quality that allowed everyone to forget the drudgery of his or her everyday existence. He played harmonies that were instantly recognizable that made people hum a tune without realizing that they were singing. Eighty years later his music continues to provide a brand of familiarity as well as that inviting edge.

Dodds had great technical ability in the upper and lower ranges. His expert control and masterful touch enabled him to explore areas that other clarinetists were unable to reach because they lacked his unbounded skills. There was smoothness to his playing, but there was also a spark of pure imagination, inventiveness, and a unique touch. His individual voice assures him a special place among all licorice men.

His resume is very impressive. He was instrumental in assuring that a number of groups were able to claim a slice of the historical jazz pie. The list includes: Louis Armstrong's Hot Five and Hot Seven session groups, Jelly Roll Morton's Red Hot Peppers, and King Oliver's Jazz Creole Band. These were the three top jazz bands of the 1920s, and Dodds played a major role in the popularity of each one. Without him, the entire musical catalog of the 1920s would sound much different and less spectacular.

Johnny Dodds, along with Sidney Bechet, Baby Dodds, Albert Nicholas, Barney Bigard, George Lewis, Bix Beiderbecke, Louis Armstrong, Jimmie Noone, King Oliver, and Jelly Roll Morton, remains a vital name from the early days of jazz. Along with his contemporaries he created a mood that dominated the country for only a few scant years, but one that is still talked about today.

As with other jazz musicians, one way to measure the influence and impact Dodds had on the history of jazz is to examine those who followed him. A partial list includes Pee Wee Russell, John Surman, Johnny Mince, Frank Teschemacher, Clifford Hayes, Tommy Dorsey, Glenn Miller, and Omer Simeon. Undoubtedly, he had profound reach and influenced numerous musicians who came after his reign.

Another way to measure a musician's impact is from the catalog of songs that he gave to the world. Dodds provided jazz fans with "Melancholy Blues (Harlem on Saturday Night)," "Wild Man Blues," "Blue Clarinet Stomp," "Hear Me Talkin'," "Pencil Papa," "Indigo Stomp," "Mr. Jelly Lord," "Wolverine Blues," and "Carpet Alley Breakdown," to name just a few. There are also the many songs from the sessions that he took part in. It is difficult to find a jazz classic of the 1920s without Dodds' imprint all over it.

While the sound of modern jazz has traveled a long way since the days when Johnny Dodds was delighting audiences with his brilliant playing, there remains a trace of his influence in today's musicians. Jazz artists of Dodds' stature hold a special place in history since they were the founding pioneers of the genre. For his efforts he was inducted into the Jazz Hall of Fame. With his "Weary Way Blues" he has never been forgotten.

Discography

Johnny Dodds, Vol. 1, Riverside RLP-1015.
Johnny Dodds, Vol. 2, Riverside RLP-1002.
Johnny Dodds (1923), Best of Jazz 4014.
Chicago Mess Around, Milestone M-2011.
Johnny Dodds and Kid Ory, Columbia 16004.
Blue Clarinet Stomp, Bluebird 2293-2.
Sweet Side Chicago Jazz, MCA MCAD-42326.
In the Alley, Riverside RLP-12135.
1923–1940, Best of Jazz 4014.
Wild Man Blues: 24 Clarinet Classics, ASV/Living Era 5252.
Great Original Performances 1923–1929, Louisiana Red Hot 622.
Myth of New Orleans, Giants of Jazz 53077.
The Complete Johnny Dodds, RCA 741110/111.
King of New Orleans Clarinet (1926-1938), Brunswick BL-58016.
Sixteen Rare Recordings, RCA PV-558.
Johnny Dodds & Tiny Parkham, Paramount 261201.
Dixieland Jug Blowers, Victor 261211.
Johnny Dodds & Tiny Parkham, Paramount 270401.
Johnny Dodds Trio, Vocalion 270421.
Dodds Black Bottom Stompers, Vocalion 270422.
Dodds Black Bottom Stompers, Vocalion 271008.
Johnny Dodds Trio, Victor 280705.
Johnny Dodds' Washboard Band, Victor 280796.
Johnny Dodds' Orchestra, Victor 290116.
Johnny Dodds' Orchestra, Victor 290130.
Johnny Dodds' Orchestra, Victor 290207.
Johnny Dodds Trio, Victor 290207.
Johnny Dodds' Orchestra, Victor 290207.
Johnny Dodds' Chicago Boys, Decca 380121.
Johnny Dodds' Orchestra, Decca 400605.

SIDNEY BECHET (1897–1959)

Coal Cart Blues

In the beginning, jazz was ensemble music and the skillful improvisation of the soloist was not highly developed. But, gradually, the music evolved and the focus on a very talented individual to provide a contrast to the harmony and rhythm that the group played was encouraged. One of the first great soloists to emerge out of the band concept and advance the progress of jazz was the man responsible for the "Coal Cart Blues." His name was Sidney Bechet.

Sidney Joseph Bechet was born on May 14, 1897, in New Orleans, Louisiana. Although destined to become the most famous musician in his family, he was not the only one of the family's seven children to pursue a musical career. His brother Leonard was a professional trombonist before he left to pursue a career in dentistry, and another brother, Joseph, played guitar.

Bechet's musical roots go deep. He was a Creole, a descendent of early French and Spanish settlers. His grandfather was an ex-slave who sang and danced in Congo Square. He also played the drums, and his intricate sense of rhythm seemed inborn. Bechet's father was a shoemaker, but played music for pleasure. He was also an excellent dancer having inherited a strong sense of rhythm from his father. This musical pedigree enabled Bechet to join his brother Leonard's band, The Silver Bells, at a very young age when he stunned listeners with his proficiency on the clarinet.

In his teens, Bechet sat in with some of the most important jazz musicians, including cornet king Freddie Keppard. He also marched with Manuel Perez, and absorbed the rhythm structures of the famous second line of the New Orleans parade bands. Bechet further honed his skills when he teamed up with New Orleans legend cornetist Buddy Petit.

There were others who helped Bechet's progress during his formative years, including Lorenzo Tio, Big Eye Louis Nelson and George Baquet. Bechet became such a proficient student that he himself became a teacher to Jimmie Noone, although Sidney was two years younger than his pupil. This dedication to teaching others what he knew was the key to the continuation of jazz.

Sidney served a long apprenticeship in his native New Orleans before striking out on his own. He played in the Silver Bells Band with his brother Leonard for a brief period and with Buddie Petit's Young Olympians and John Robichaux's Orchestra. Bechet also played with a group called the Eagles from 1911–1912 and even spent time in one of Bunk Johnson's groups.

Although New Orleans presented fantastic opportunities for a talented trumpeter like Bechet, he could not be confined to the Crescent City and left in his late teens. He joined a traveling show and added the names of King Oliver, Louis Wode, and Clarence Williams to his already impressive resume. Although he did return to his birthplace on occasion, in 1917 he left for good and traveled throughout the south and the mid-west, sitting in on various bands. He eventually arrived in Chicago in 1918.

It was in the Windy City that Bechet would make his greatest impact. He joined Will Marion Cook's band and traveled to Europe near the end of World War I. He developed a fan base in Europe, particularly in France, which would grow over the next few decades. It was also across the Atlantic that Bechet spotted a soprano saxophone in a store and before long had mastered the rudiments of the instrument; it became one of his main musical voices in jazz. He was now a double threat musician.

Upon his return to the United States in 1921, he moonlighted as an actor, appearing in the revue *Negre* with Josephine Baker as well as the play *How Come?* In 1923, after playing jazz for some fifteen years, Bechet was finally able to make his first recordings with the Clarence Williams Band. In the next couple of years he expanded his recorded catalog by backing up many of the classic female blues singers including Bessie Smith, Ma Rainey, Ida Cox, and Mildred Bailey. During this period he was able to play alongside and against the legendary Louis Armstrong. Their competitive, interactive, fiery solos are some of the purest moments of jazz magic ever created.

He also toured Russia with Benny Payton's band and when he returned to New York he joined Duke Ellington's group. Ellington, who was just beginning his long, brilliant career, greatly benefited from someone with Bechet's experience and skill. Throughout his career Bechet was an asset to every band he played in no matter how brief his stay. He always provided a wealth of musical knowledge and history.

Europe held an irresistible charm over Bechet so he returned there in 1926, and stayed for four years. He had residencies in Germany, Paris, and England. In 1930, in Paris, he was involved in a shooting incident that earned him a stint in jail. He was later deported back to America. The ugly scandal was like a foreshadowing of future events because from this point on his career suffered a downward turn.

With the record industry practically wiped out because of the stock market crash, Bechet and many other musicians found themselves out of work. He opened and operated a tailoring business with fellow musician Tommy Ladnier. Although there were some hot jam sessions in the store that attracted many of the top players of the day, Bechet's musical career was at a standstill for much of the 1930s.

It wasn't until near the end of the decade that Bechet began to make a serious comeback when he scored a hit with the song "Summertime." He was eventually signed to the Bluebird label, famous for its stable of blues singers like Sonny Boy Williamson I, Tampa Red, and Big Bill Broonzy. Bechet enjoyed a career renaissance and added a large number of stone classics to his already impressive musical canon. By this time he was based in New York and played at many of the era's most notable clubs, including the Log Cabin, Fonda Mimo Club, Nick's, Ryan's and other now-defunct jazz spots. He also played summer residencies in Philadelphia, New Jersey, Springfield, Illinois, Boston, and New Orleans with his old friend Louis Armstrong.

After World War II, Bechet's career was in limbo once again. He opened up what he hoped would be a successful music school and had one prize pupil—Bob Miller. It seemed that Bechet, one of the greatest clarinet and soprano sax players of the past three decades, would be forgotten. But his fortunes took an upward swing in 1949 when he received an invitation to play at the Salle Pleyel Jazz Festival in Paris. He made the most of the opportunity by stunning the crowd with his still remarkable abilities and although he made periodic visits to the United States, he remained a permanent resident of the City of Lights. Bechet became one of the most endeared entertainers in France and played major concerts all over the country.

On May 14, 1959, Sidney Bechet succumbed to cancer in Paris. He was 62 years old.

Sidney Bechet is one of the most important pioneers in the history of jazz. From 1920 until his death, he was one of the finest clarinet and soprano saxophonists in the business. He was a major architect of the Jazz Age and though he played all over the world, he never truly abandoned his New Orleans roots.

It is rare in jazz for a performer to excel at two instruments, but Bechet was proficient on the clarinet, as well as on the soprano saxophone. His vibrant tone, complete with superior vibrato technique, was combined with his uncanny ability to swing and improvise—two of the foundations of jazz. His solo work was aggressive, with long improvised lines and an incredible dexterity played at a high speed. His warmth and spirit shined through his crisp playing. Like his fellow New Orleans jazz musicians, there was a boisterous, rollicking side to his sound as well as a sophistication that few ever achieved.

He was a gifted storyteller, with a strong charisma that was an important part of his music. The dimensions of his personality gave his style an edge that wasn't found in other jazz players. Interestingly, though his playing was unique in jazz history, by the time he started to record Bechet had already reached his full maturity. He never progressed beyond that point but always guaranteed a strong musical presence in any concert he performed in or recording session he participated in.

His relationship with Louis Armstrong was of particular interest. Armstrong and Bechet were two of the giants of 1920s jazz and together they propelled the popularity of the genre to dizzying heights. Although Armstrong is noted as being the stronger soloist, Bechet was the first soloist to record in jazz history, beating out his friend and rival by a few months.

Bechet's vast talents were always in demand. Ellman Braud, Pops Foster, Louis Armstrong, Baby Dodds, Manzie Johnson, Sidney "Big Sid" Catlett, Zutty Singleton, Clarence Williams, Mezz Mezzrow, Charlie Irvis, J.C. Higginbotham, Jimmy Archey, Earl Hines, Lawrence Lucie, Claude Jones, Cliff Jackson, Bernard Addison, Teddy Bunn, and Jelly Roll Morton all recorded and played live with Bechet.

He also had a strong influence on a diverse group of musicians that includes Albert Ayler, Kenny Davern, Johnny Hodges, Rahsaan Roland Kirk, Courtney Pine, Tab Smith, Cecil Taylor, Bob Wilber, Captain John Handy, Klaus Doldinger, Jimmie Noone, Duke Ellington, and Duke Heitger. His playing has reverberated throughout the decades.

Bechet was one of the greatest ambassadors of jazz and enhanced the music's reputation throughout the world. While many of his contemporaries became stars in America, only a handful had the same impact on the international scene. Bechet brought his distinctive brand of jazz to Russia, Germany, France, Great Britain, Argentina, Chile, Belgium and a dozen other countries around the globe.

To study the life of Sidney Bechet is to study the life of jazz itself. He was one of the prime forces responsible for turning early New Orleans jazz into America's classical music. Undoubtedly, the great soloist with the full, clear beautiful tones on his "Coal Cart Blues" will forever occupy his own jazz throne.

Discography

Unique Sidney, CBS 63693.
Jazz From California, Jazz Archives JA-44.

Superb Sidney, CBS 62636.
Summertime, Musical Memories 30382.
Double Dixie, Drive Archives 71051.
Bunk & Bechet in Boston [live], Jazz Crusade 3040.
Jazz Nocturne, Vol. 1–12, Fat Cat's Jazz 001/012.
Sidney Bechet Sessions, Storyville 4028.
In the Groove, Jazz Society 670506.
The Fabulous Sidney Bechet, Blue Note BLP 1207.
The Fabulous Sidney Bechet and His Hot Six, Blue Note BLP 7020.
Sidney Bechet, Centenary Celebration—1997: Great Original Perfor-
    mances 1924–1943, Louisiana Red Hot Records 632.
The Chronological Sidney Bechet, 1923–1936, Classics 583.
The Best of Sidney Bechet, EMD/Blue Note B2 28897.
Sidney Bechet, In New York, 1937–1940, JSP 338.
Sidney Bechet, Great Original Performances 1924-1943 LRHR 632.
Sidney Bechet, Shake 'Em UP, AVD 694.
Sidney Bechet, Young Sidney Bechet, 1923–1925, CBC 1028.
Sidney Bechet, Really the Blues, ASL 5107.
Sidney Bechet, In New York, 1950–1951, STC 6039.
Sidney Bechet, The Legendary Sidney Bechet, 1932–1941, BLED 6590.
Sidney Bechet, Sidney Bechet at Storyville, Great Jazz Masters, 9014.
Sidney Bechet, Up a Lazy River, 1940s, GTJ 12064.
Sidney Bechet, Runnin' Wild, Blue Note 21259.

ZUTTY SINGLETON (1898–1975)

A Monday Date

One of the essential elements that separated jazz from the blues and popular music at the turn of the century was rhythm. The first jazz brass bands duplicated the rhythm produced by the second line timekeepers found in New Orleans parades and funeral processions. Later on, a new sophisticated language would emerge from the world of jazz, but in the beginning there were two important drummers who dominated during the traditional years. There was Baby Dodds and the man who was always keen on playing at a Monday date. His name was Zutty Singleton.

Arthur James "Zutty" Singleton was born in Bunkie, Louisiana, on May 14, 1898. He came from a musical family; his uncle was Willie "Bontin" Bontemps who played the bass, guitar and banjo. Although there was a variety of instruments to choose from, Singleton opted for the drums because of his admiration for the second line rhythms he heard in the marching bands during trips to the big city.

He practiced hard and honed his skills until he was proficient enough to play professionally. His first gig was with pianist/composer Steve Lewis at the Rosebud Theatre. He would also spend some time in the John Robichaux Orchestra until the advent of the First World War when Singleton served in the U.S. Navy. After the war, he worked as a chauffeur briefly before returning to the music business.

In the next three years he would freelance with Tom's Roadhouse Band, Papa Celestin, and "Big Eye" Louis Nelson. Although he added an important dimension with his percussionist skills to every band he worked with, Singleton was keen on leading his own group. His style was evolving into more self-expressionism, and he desired to explore this special side of his talent. He eventually formed his own outfit for a short time with a residency at the Orchard Cabaret before joining Luis Russell in 1921.

Like dozens of other New Orleans musicians, Singleton played in Fate Marable's riverboat band. He cruised up and down the Mississippi River for two seasons before returning to New Orleans. In the Crescent City he rejoined his old friend John Robichaux and his orchestra for a brief time before heading off to St. Louis. The Arch City was a hot spot of jazz in the early 1920s and he had no trouble finding work. He eventually settled with Charlie Creath. Singleton also took time off from his hectic musical career to marry Creath's sister.

Despite the positive direction his career had taken, he grew restless in St. Louis and returned to New Orleans where he joined trombonist Charlie Lawson's band. However, as it was to so many other New Orleans musicians of the era, the Windy City was calling, and Singleton headed down there to be reunited with other expatriates including Johnny Dodds, Sidney Bechet, Louis Armstrong, Jimmie Noone, and his drumming peer Baby Dodds. In Chicago, there was no shortage of work. He played in Vernon Roulette's Band as well as with Doc Cooke, Dave Peyton, Jimmie Noone and Louis Armstrong.

After his stint with Armstrong (in a band that included pianist Earl Hines), he rejoined Dave Peyton's band. He would also play in Jimmie Noone's group before joining Carroll Dickerson's band, which featured his old friend Louis Armstrong. Singleton would be a part of many recordings that Armstrong would make during the period between 1927 and 1929, recordings that became classics. He also participated in a recording as a trio with pianist Jelly Roll Morton and clarinetist Barney Bigard. Like the Armstrong sessions, the songs he cut with Morton and Bigard enhanced his popularity. At the tail end of 1929, Singleton joined the migration of big name jazz artists headed to New York.

In New York, he was part of Dickerson's group before joining Allie Ross for a brief stay. Later that year he would lead his own band during a residency at the Lafayette Theatre. Although the stock market crash of 1929 would have a serious impact on his career, he continued to find work in a succession of bands led by Vernon Andrade, Fats Waller, Bubber Miley and Otto Hardwick. He would later play with Tommy Ladnier and Pike Davis where he backed Bill "Mr. Bojangles" Robinson.

In 1933, Singleton toured with Norman and Irene Selby and got stranded in Chicago, one of his old stomping grounds. He remained in the Windy City and enjoyed a period of relative steadiness. Throughout most of 1934 and 1935, he divided his time between playing in Dickerson's band and heading his own group at such famous places as the Three Deuces and the Flagship. After his residency at the Three Deuces was over he disbanded his outfit to join Roy Eldridge in the fall of 1936. Upon leaving Eldridge's group the following year he returned to the Big Apple where he worked with Mezz Mezzrow's Disciples of Swing. Upon leaving Mezzrow, he joined forces with Sidney Bechet, an old running buddy from his younger days in New Orleans.

For most of 1939 and 1940, Singleton led his own group at such now defunct places as Nick's, Village Vanguard and Kelly's before enjoying a period of stability playing Ryan's. It was the era of swing, and Singleton, who had arrived on the scene playing in strict New Orleans time, had been able to adjust to the more challenging big band stomp. It was this flexibility that allowed him to continue to work while many musicians remained unemployed.

In 1943, Singleton moved to the West Coast and led his own quartet during a long residency at Bill Berg's. No stranger to jamming after hours, he managed to play with Paul Howard's Band and electric guitar blues legend T-Bone Walker. Their time together was brief because he was busy once again with his band in 1944 and was a prominent fixture on Orson Welles' radio show.

After a short period of time with guitarist Teddy Bunn's group, he joined the Slim Gaillard Trio for much of the spring of 1945. But Singleton was a restless spirit and was soon leading another of his bands throughout much of the remaining decade of the 1940s. However, he also found time to play in groups led by Wingy Manone, Eddie Condon, Joe Marsala, Nappy Lamare and Art Hodes. After playing in Buddy Hackett's band for a brief spell, he joined Bernie Billings.

In November of 1951 Singleton made his first trip to Europe where he wowed audiences with his mature style that included some of the best drum solos of the era. He remained there until 1953 and worked with Mezz Mezzrow and Hot Lips Page. Singleton would eventually become a member of the Mezz Mezzrow band. A year later he toured with the Bill Coleman All-Stars.

Upon his return to the United States, Singleton settled in New York and worked steadily at the area clubs including the Metropole, Central Plaza, and Stuyvesant Casino for the remainder of the decade. He later joined Wilbur De Paris for a few months in 1954 but then struck out on his own again. No matter the current flavor of jazz, he was always able to find steady work in the clubs and made a good living there.

In 1963 he joined Tony Parenti's band. But Singleton continued to front his own bands when not working with Parenti and enjoyed long residencies at many of New York's hottest clubs, including Ryan's, in the middle of the decade. He broke his stay at Ryan's to play the New Orleans Jazz Festival in 1969 before returning to New York once again.

In 1970, the career of one of the most illustrious jazz musicians in the history of the genre was cruelly ended when Singleton suffered a stroke. He never played again. On July 14, 1975, Zutty Singleton died in New York City. He was 77 years old.

Zutty Singleton, along with Baby Dodds, was the most important drummer to emerge from the New Orleans scene in the 1910s. He was instrumental in ensuring that the drums gained the attention they deserved. Singleton was the first drummer to make the solo an important weapon in his arsenal. His use of brushes added color and tonality to his steady playing.

There was flexibility to his drumming. Although, like Dodds, Singleton copied the rhythm lines he heard in the marching bands while a youngster in New Orleans, he eventually learned how to swing. During the Big Band era his drumming remained vibrant because of his ability to match the styles of Jo Jones, Gene Krupa, and Buddy Rich. Although not as technically sound as the trio aforementioned, he was still an exciting drummer.

With the advent of bebop, when many of the New Orleans clan faced extinction and were singled out as dinosaurs by the young, hip bop contingent, Singleton found himself behind the drum kit and backed Dizzy and Bird. Although he never reached the superior level of Kenny Clarke and Max Roach or the great Art Blakey, Singleton could hold his own in bop circles. It was his ability to be a musical chameleon that ensured he always had work.

Singleton was also a journeyman who played behind a coterie of jazz individuals including Claude Jones, Bernard Addison, Jack Teagarden, Cozy Cole, Lawrence Lucie, Earl Hines, Coleman Hawkins, Joe Sullivan, Luis Russell, Fred Robinson, Lionel Hampton, and Bud Scott. Although he recorded with everyone mentioned above and many others, he did cut a few sessions as leader for a variety of labels throughout his long career. However, he will best be remembered as part of Armstrong's Hot Fives and Hot Sevens sessions.

Singleton had a large influence on a number of drummers who followed him including his counterpart Baby Dodds. In an era that contained several good drummers including Dodds, Paul Barbarin, Cozy Cole, and Dave Tough, Singleton was better than each of them. His drum solos were more expressive, more adventurous. He also cleared the path for the important swing drummers Jo Jones, Chick Webb, Gene Krupa, Buddy Rich and Louie Bellson. All of the bop and post-bop rhythm makers such as Clarke, Blakey, Roach, Chico Hamilton, Philly Joe Jones, Elvin Jones, and Ronald Shannon Jackson owe a debt to Singleton. Zutty's influence can also be heard in the styles of the fusion players Billy Cobham, Alphonse Mouzon, Tony Williams, and Jack DeJohnette. To listen to some of the young drummers today, including Jeff "Tain" Watts, is to be transported back to the heyday of Singleton's career.

Zutty Singleton played a large role in jazz history. He appeared in three movies—*Stormy Weather*, *New Orleans*, and *Turned-Up Toes*. He was instrumental in the emergence of the drums as a vital part of a jazz band. He added dimensions in the recording studio and as a live performer that were copied by countless others. But most of all, Zutty Singleton was always ready to jam on a Monday date.

Discography

Battle of Jazz, Vol. 2, Brunswick B 58038.
Zutty and the Clarinet Kings, Fat Cat FCJ 100.
Henry "Red" Allen, Vol. 1, JSP 332.
Henry "Red" Allen Collection, Vol. 2, JSP 333.
Henry Allen Swing Out, Pearl 1037.
Henry "Red" Allen Swing Era, Best of Jazz 4031.
Louis Armstrong Portrait of the Artist as a Young Man, Sony 57176.
Complete Hot Fives & Sevens 1925–1928, Sony 635527.
Louis Armstrong Back O' Town Blues 1939–1945, EPM 156732.
Thanks a Million 1935–1940, AVD 574.
Louis Armstrong Masterpieces Vol. 1, EPM 158132.
West End Blues, Ind. 2635.
Coleman Hawkins Been Stalkin,' Pablo BACD 2310 933-2.

Lionel Hampton Classics 1937–1939, EPM 157372.
Planet Jazz, BMG 74321511502.
Sidney Bechet, Vol. 1, 1923, Masters of Jazz 5.
Sidney Bechet, Vol. 2 1929–1930, Masters of Jazz 14.
Sidney Bechet, Vol. 3, 1931–1937, Masters of Jazz 27.
Sidney Bechet, Vol. 4, 1937–1938, Masters of Jazz 43.
Sidney Bechet, Vol. 5, 1938–1939, Masters of Jazz 60.
Sidney Bechet, Vol. 6, 1939, Masters of Jazz 76.
Sidney Bechet, Vol. 7, 1940, Masters of Jazz 97.
Sidney Bechet, Vol. 8, 1940, Masters of Jazz 100.
Sidney Bechet, Vol. 10 1941, Masters of Jazz 127.
Sidney Bechet, Vol. 11, 1941–1942, Masters of Jazz 140.
Little Jazz, Inner City 7002.
James P. Johnson Hot Piano, PEA 1048.
Tommy Ladnier Goose Pimples, Pearl 1074.
Tommy Ladnier Steppin' in the Blues, ASV/Living Era 5353.

BABY DODDS (1898–1959)

The Great Anchor

Throughout the history of jazz most of the adulation has been accorded to the horn players such as Louis Armstrong, Sidney Bechet, Bix Beiderbecke, Lester Young, Dizzy Gillespie, Charlie Parker, John Coltrane, and Miles Davis. However, the men who were part of the rhythm sections made enormous contributions to the genre including the timekeeper known as "The Great Anchor." His name was Baby Dodds.

Warren Dodds was born in New Orleans, Louisiana, on December 24, 1898. The youngest of six children, he was surrounded by music from the very start, particularly through the endeavors of his older brother Johnny. Not to be outdone, the youngest of the Dodds brothers tried to emulate his sibling. While Johnny elected to play a horn, Warren drifted to the rhythm instruments.

Warren received his first drum lessons from Dave Perkins, a fine New Orleans stickman. Later Dodds was also given instruction by Walter Brundy and Louis Cottrell, Sr., two other important New Orleans drummers. He learned the popular parade and funeral march rhythms that dominated in the beginning of jazz. But he knew that the instrument was capable of more intricate patterns and would have to bid his time until he could prove his theory.

By his early teens he was leading a double life. During the day he worked in a sack-making factory and at night he jammed with local bands and worked parade gigs with the legendary Bunk Johnson. Eventually he was able to break out of the heavy factory work after he appeared in his first gig with Willie Hightower's American Stars.

The young Dodds learned much from his brief stint with the trumpeter Hightower, but gained more practical experience in his next musical adventure with Fate Mariable. Dodds stayed with the Mariable band that played on a riverboat for three seasons. Already, at this point, he was experimenting with different rhythms trying to break out of the age-old metered structures of the New Orleans style.

Although his previous stints in several groups had been learning experiences, it was his time in King Oliver's Jazz Creole that brought him the most satisfaction as well as recognition. He joined Oliver's unit in San Francisco and then moved on to Chicago. It was an extra thrill to play in Oliver's top New Orleans band because Dodds' older brother Johnny was also a member. Baby was now on par with his boyhood idol.

A year later Baby left King Oliver and joined his brother and Freddie Keppard to work a residency at Kelley's Stables in Chicago. Baby enjoyed his greatest success between the years 1924 and 1930. He played in many of the noted Chicago jazz groups of the time including those led by Lil Armstrong, Willie Hightower, Ralph Brown, Charlie Elgar, and Hugh Swift. While his regular work was impressive it was his freelancing on numerous recording sessions that truly brought him fame.

His work with Armstrong's Hot Seven and Jelly Roll Morton's Hot Peppers elevated his status from well-known percussionist to the most important jazz drummer of the era. While other players continued to play the tired old New Orleans rhythms, Dodds had explored different paths. He was able to fuel some of the best solos that Armstrong, his brother Johnny and Jelly Roll Morton could muster with more complex rhythmic structures.

Dodds slowed down in the 1930s. With the advent of the Great Depression, work was sometimes hard to find even for a respected musician like Warren. He played many gigs with his brother Johnny in a small band capacity and helped his other brother Bill run a taxi service. In 1936, he landed a somewhat steady job as house drummer at the Three Deuces club in Chicago and stayed there for three years before moving on.

During most of the war years, 1940–1944, Dodds remained in

Chicago where he found plentiful work at the 9750 Club, and also spent time in Jimmie Noone's band. He took over his brother's band when the latter was forced to leave because of trouble with his teeth. In 1944, Baby helped Bunk Johnson make a comeback. He traveled to New York with Johnson where he impressed a new audience with his unique skills as a drummer.

After the war, Dodds continued his storied career, spending time with Art Hodes and being featured on the *This Is Jazz* series on the radio. By this time radio had been broadcasting jazz jams for about twenty years, helping spread the popularity of the music throughout the country. The legend of Baby Dodds was enhanced by these radio sessions as people who had never heard him play could enjoy the experience through the magic of the airwaves.

In 1948, he helped spread the appeal of jazz beyond the borders of his home country when he joined Mezz Mezzrow to play at the Nice Festival in France. They briefly toured other European clubs before returning home. It was a satisfying venture for Dodds, who had a deep influence on the drummers in Europe who were trying to emulate American jazzmen.

Upon his return to the United States, he stayed in New York and worked with Art Hodes again before pushing on to Chicago where he found work with Miff Mole at the Beehive Club. It was upon a return visit to the Big Apple in the spring of 1949 that Dodds suffered his first stroke. He recovered nicely, but suffered a second stroke the following spring. But Dodds recuperated enough to allow him to play in Natty Dominique's band from 1951 to 1952.

Late in 1952, a third stroke forced Dodds to give up his regular job (he was playing at Ryan's in New York), and he relocated to Chicago to convalesce. Two years later, he made an appearance in the Big Apple playing with the Don Frye Trio. He returned to the Windy City shortly after suffering from partial paralysis.

A stubborn individual born to make music, Dodds did not retire completely until 1957. Two years later, on February 14, 1959, Warren "Baby" Dodds, who had revolutionized the art of drumming and would influence many generations, died in Chicago, Illinois, of natural causes. He was 61 years old.

Baby Dodds was an innovator of extreme importance. By the time of his death he had left a legacy that had enriched jazz drumming forever. He had changed the art of percussion and made the timekeeper the focus of the band. All drummers who followed in his footsteps—no matter their style—owed a great debt to Baby Dodds.

He developed a system of drumming that enabled him to use the entire kit to maximum effect. He was a multi-timekeeper. His method included the ability to keep different times on different parts of the drum. With the pedal he pounded out a solid rock steady beat that fed the bassist and pianist. On the snare drum he played a faster beat that spurred on the soloists, usually the horn players. This innovation—the increased use of the snare drum—was a trick many future drummers including the bop and hard bop men Kenny Clark, Max Roach, Elvin Jones and Art Blakey, included in their arsenal.

Dodds utilized a unique set up of drums that became the standard unit. His setup included a large bass drum (that resembled those from his marching days) that was brought to life with his fancy foot skills on the big head pedal. There was the precious snare drum that enabled him to sound like a ferocious, finely-tuned machine racing down the highway at top speed. The choke cymbal was another of his available weapons that allowed him to unleash a stinging round of bullet-like attacks. There was also a rack of wood and other percussion accessories that allowed him to extend his rhythmic dimensions as well as embellish the music that his bandmates created.

Although he was an excellent solo drummer, Dodds was an even more impressive team player. He tuned his drums to the other instruments and created a syncopated element of harmony and melody. He was a master of the give and go, supporting his bandmates during their ferocious solos while taking his own cue from time to time. His multi abilities enabled the entire group to stretch a song out and take it in directions that other less talented drummers were not able to in a band atmosphere.

It was his adventurous streak that made him a favorite jazz player in the 1920s and 1930s. He could swing with the best of them and paved the way for Gene Krupa, Jo Jones, Chick Webb, Buddy Rich and Louis Bellson, the best of the swing drummers. Later, Kenny Clarke, Max Roach, Art Blakey and Elvin Jones would not only incorporate many of the Baby Dodds innovations into their own style but cite Dodds as their most important inspiration.

Although he recorded very little on his own, Dodds was an integral part of Armstrong's Hot Seven, which produced some of the most legendary jazz music in history. Also, his playing with Jelly Roll Morton's Red Hot Peppers only added to his status as perhaps the best of the jazz drummers to emerge from the New Orleans scene. There are hundreds of jazz classics recorded during the golden age that feature Dodds on drums. Some of these songs include "West End Blues," with Louis Armstrong, "Blame it On the Blues," and "Old Stack O'Lee Blues," with Sidney Bechet and Albert Nicholas. He can also be heard with his brother on such recordings as "Weary Way Blues," "Come Back Sweet Papa," "Gut Bucket Blues," "Willie the Weeper," "Wild Man Blues," "Melancholy Blues," and "Gully Low Blues."

In many ways, Dodds is the granddaddy of drummers much the same way that Pops Foster is the granddaddy of the bass players. Those who tried to emulate him have never forgotten Dodds' contributions to jazz. His press rolls, his unflappable rock steady beat and his overall ability are still held in awe by today's young jazz drummers.

He was the first timekeeper to record solos and in many ways opened the doors for the rock drummers who would come along forty years later and bash their way into history. Certainly, one can hear the influence of Baby Dodds in the styles of such legendary rock stick men as John Bonham, Ginger Baker, Carl Palmer, Keith Moon, Charlie Watts, and the entire rock drumming fraternity. Dodds was also an inspiration to the blues drummers of the 1950s who played on the famous Chess sessions. That group includes Fred Below, Francis Clay, Elgin Evans and Leroy Foster.

Warren "Baby" Dodds was the first legitimate drummer to achieve recognition in jazz. He strived for more freedom behind the drum kit and found it because of his exuberant and adventurous style. His personality shone through his playing. Despite the fact that much of the music that made him famous was recorded some eighty years ago, the solid reputation of "The Great Anchor" has not suffered the ravages of time.

Discography

Baby Dodds Trio, GHB 50.
Baby Dodds Drum Method: Band, American Music 1.
Baby Dodds Drum Method: Trio, American Music 2.
Baby Dodds Drum Method: Solo, American Music 3.
Classics, Blue Note 6509.
Footnotes to Jazz, Vol. 1, Smithsonian/Folkways 2290.
Baby Dodds, Smithsonian/Folkways FP 30.
New Orleans Drums, EPM Musique 159632.

PART TWO

The Jazz Age

While jazz was born in New Orleans, it soon spread to other parts of the country. In 1917, when the Storyville section was closed, there began a migration of jazz players to the metropolises of Chicago, New York and Los Angeles. Many of the early performers who began their careers in New Orleans found fame and fortune in the Windy City and the Big Apple.

The change in venues dictated a change in style. At its start, jazz had been the music of ensembles. Now, in order to appease the cosmopolitan crowds, the appeal of the star soloist was encouraged. The horns battled for position and rode atop driving bluesy rhythms. Jazz was truly the music of the age of prosperity and good times. All of the previous elements—ragtime, blues, West African rhythms, West Indies rhythms, spirituals, and work songs—were crystallized and synthesized to create the golden age of jazz.

It was during this era that Louis Armstrong, Sidney Bechet, Jimmie Noone, Jelly Roll Morton and others emerged as stars. In addition, Johnny Dodds, Baby Dodds, James P. Johnson, Fletcher Henderson, Bix Beiderbecke, Jimmie Noone, and Fats Waller expanded the appeal of jazz that swept across North America and Europe.

The following is a partial list of the musicians, bandleaders, and vocalists who made the jazz age what it was in the 1920s. Outstanding trumpeters and cornetists of the era include Henry "Red" Allen, Doc Cheatham, Sidney De Paris, Tommy Ladnier, Kid Punch Miller, Red Nichols, Mugsy Spanier, Rex Stewart, Bunny Berigan, Buck Clayton, Clarence Williams, Harry "Sweets" Edison, Cootie Williams, Hot Lips Page, and Jimmy McPartland. Notable pianists include Jimmy Blythe, Lil Armstrong, Horace Henderson, Don Lambert, Lucky Roberts, William "The Lion" Smith, and Mary Lou Williams. The best of the trombonists include George Brunis, Will Bradley, and Albert Wynn. Although there were hundreds of groups, some of the more important ones include The California Ramblers, McKinney's Cotton Pickers, Mills

Blue Rhythm Band, New Orleans Rhythm Kings, New Orleans Owls, North Carolina Ramblers, The Original Memphis Five, Red Onion Jazz Band, and the State Street Ramblers. Albert Burbank, Bud Freeman, Frank Jackson, George Lewis, Pee Wee Russell, Frankie Teschemacher all made their mark on the clarinet. Lewis also played a fine alto sax, while Freeman starred on the tenor sax. Frank Jackson was another important tenor saxophonist. Noted bandleaders include Cab Calloway, Paul Whiteman, and Luis Russell. On guitar, Eddie Condon, Johnny St. Cyr, and Lonnie Johnson were special talents; Condon and St. Cyr also doubled on banjo. Sonny Greer, Dave Tough, and Big Sid Catlett were the best timekeepers. Multi-instrumentalists of note include Junie C. Cobb, Frankie Trumbauer, and Andy Kirk. Julia Lee and Annette Henshaw were two of the many exciting vocalists who made their mark during the decade. Interestingly, many of the finest jazz singers were also excellent blues singers such as Sippie Wallace, Ida Cox, Alberta Hunter, Mamie Smith and, the greatest of them all, Bessie Smith.

The following figures are featured in this book.

James P. Johnson was an influential New York piano player and composer who created a bridge between ragtime and jazz.

Jimmie Noone was one of the most important clarinetists of the era and, like many New Orleans graduates, found fame in Chicago.

Ethel Waters was a pacesetter who sang blues-tinged jazz numbers and also had a prominent movie career. She paved the way for the big three of Billie Holiday, Ella Fitzgerald and Sarah Vaughan.

Fletcher Henderson was a prime bandleader and arranger who moved between the early New Orleans style and the sophisticated swing of the 1930s.

Louis Armstrong was a fountainhead of jazz. He was and remains the best known of all jazz artists as a featured trumpet player and singer.

Eddie Lang was an inventive guitar player who developed the blueprint for all other jazz guitarists to follow. He often also teamed with violinist Joe Venuti.

Bix Beiderbecke was one of the leading figures of the Roaring Twenties as one of the main inspirations of the Chicago-style jazz sound. He has often been referred to as Louis Armstrong's white alter ego.

Earl Hines was an excellent piano player and a longtime bandleader. He was a fixture of jazz for decades.

Fats Waller was a noted piano player, composer, and one of the era's truly lively characters.

Jack Teagarden succeeded Kid Ory as the best trombone player in jazz. He paved the way for the bop trombone of J. J. Johnson.

JAMES P. JOHNSON (1894–1955)

The Stride King

The piano has played a pivotal role throughout the entire history of jazz. From the earliest days of ragtime to boogie-woogie, from big band to bebop and beyond, the instrument shaped and defined the very sound of each style. Many of the greatest musicians in the annals of jazz were piano players, including the man known as "The Stride King." His name was James P. Johnson.

James P. Johnson was born February 1, 1894, in New Brunswick, New Jersey. He was one of only a handful of jazz musicians born outside New Orleans to become a star in the 1920s. From the moment he discovered the piano he became a fervent disciple because it contained all of the mysteries of the world, and the desire to unlock its many secrets proved irresistible. Once he had access to one he played constantly in a feverish attempt to master the instrument that so fascinated him.

As a youngster he was open to a variety of musical ideas, including the blues, classical music, and the ragtime riffs of Scott Joplin. In addition, square dances, church hymns, stomps, marches, popular tunes, folk songs, and barrelhouse ballads formed the bedrock of his practical education. Because of his unlimited abilities, his visionary scope, and his powerful presence, he was earmarked for success.

The proving ground for musicians was New York City. It was a hotly competitive arena and also the hub of the music publishing industry. Johnson arrived in the Big Apple in 1912, at the age of eighteen, to seek his fame and fortune. It is important to note that at the time of his arrival, New York piano players like Lucky Roberts, Richard McLean, and Bob Hawkins had already established a style that revolved around an urban ragtime bass and was supplemented by blues melodies and country dance rhythms; it was the earliest form of stride.

Once in the big city, Johnson, forever a student of new sounds, absorbed the symphonic concert music, cabaret show tunes and grand opera, adding all three to the eclectic mix of his musical bag. He also was enchanted with the New Orleans pianist Jelly Roll Morton who had a regular gig in Harlem. For four years Johnson went to "school" as he watched and listened attentively to his heroes like Morton perform at the house rent parties and other locales. Johnson was taking down notes in his head and storing them for future use. He was also continuously honing his piano technique and adding musical phrases to his ever-increasing vocabulary.

Finally Johnson had polished his skills to the point that he was proficient enough to play in front of an audience, and he made his professional debut at Coney Island. He also toured Southern vaudeville circuits before settling down to work in the New York club venues. His repertoire consisted of popular songs, showpieces, hits from the current musicals, rags (most notably those written by Scott Joplin), as well as some of his own compositions. All of his devotion and dedication to honing his craft began to pay off handsomely.

One of his first regular gigs was at the Jungles Casino. Johnson learned very quickly that in order to be popular and not booed off the stage he had to play music that people could dance to. Any music played that people couldn't dance to was quickly thrown aside. Many of the patrons at the Jungles Casino were from the south and demanded the type of swinging music that reminded them of home. It was in this kind of environment that Johnson would create from his myriad of influences the "Charleston," a ragtime arrangement of a set dance.

By 1918, Johnson was an important piano player on the New York circuit. He played café jobs, made piano rolls, was a prolific songwriter, did some Broadway stage work, and performed on vaudeville tours for the Theatre Owner's Booking Agency (or TOBA, as it was more popularly known). For someone of Johnson's skill and his ability to adapt to new tastes, there was never a shortage of work. It was also around this time that he began to tutor the young pianist Henry "Fats" Waller.

By 1920, Johnson was a favorite of the rabid crowds and acknowledged as the stride king among his contemporaries. He had managed to combine the raw power of the blues with tinges of classical and ragtime. He had paid his dues for seven long years and was now ready to reap the rewards of his hard work.

During the 1920s, there was no greater stride pianist on the Harlem rent party circuit—with the possible exception of Willie "The Lion" Smith—than Johnson. Every night he dazzled audiences with his unmatched skills and his ability to swing. He was a talented improviser borrowing ideas from a variety of sources including Broadway shows and other pianists like Eubie Blake, as well as from classical sources, to create something fresh and new. He also knew how to make an audience dance. He teamed up with Fats Waller (his dedicated pupil) and William "The Lion" Smith.

William "The Lion" Smith was born William Henry Joseph Bonaparte Bertholoff Smith on November 25, 1897, in Goshen, New York. His mother was a fine organist and piano player and taught her son the rudiments of the instrument beginning when he was six. By his teens he was earning a living as a piano player, but the war disrupted his career. He returned from overseas with the nickname "The Lion," which would last for the rest of his life. After his discharge, he quickly became a star on the Harlem rent party circuit and appeared on Mamie Smith's groundbreaking hit "Crazy Blues." Most of his career was spent as a freelancer. With his trademark cigar and derby hat, he cut an imposing figure in jazz circles. He was an accomplished player who developed a light touch that influenced a number of jazz figures including Duke Ellington. He recorded with his group the Cubs in 1935, and later cut some piano solos for the Commodore label. His memoir, *Music on My Mind*, provides an important link to the rich musical decades of the 1920s and 1930s. He was—along with James P. Johnson and Fats Waller—one of the big three in New York piano circles in the 1920s. He died in 1955.

Although he was recognized as a prime force in the new music that had been coined jazz, Johnson's career would explode in many different directions in the 1920s. He was an ambitious composer and wrote the scores to several Broadway shows including *The Charleston* and *Old Fashioned Love* and for the revue *Running Wild*. He also wrote *Yamekraw*, a longer, more complex work that made its debut at Carnegie Hall, certainly a major achievement for a jazz musician at that time. He also wrote the score for *Plantation Days*, which he performed in Europe in 1923. The exposure to an overseas audience helped him expand his fan base.

Despite a hectic schedule of tours, writing, and sessions, he found time to work in two revues—*Black Sensations* and *Smart Set*. In the 1920s, the revue was a staple of the black entertainment industry since there were very few other forms available to black performers, and Johnson was one of the major contributors. In the 1920s, white authorities often suppressed any form of African-American expression because they felt it encouraged the populace to gain confidence and courage.

Johnson also backed some of the best blues singers of the era including Bessie Smith and Ethel Waters. He can be heard on Smith's recordings of "Backwater Blues," "Blues Spirit Blues," "Wasted Life Blues," and "Worn Out Papa Blues." His link to the classic female singers only emphasizes the vast territory he covered as a musician. In many ways Johnson was the perfect accompanist for the female blues singers because of his stride style. He was able to play blues with several layers. While his left hand provided a steady rhythm, his right hand played melodies and breathtaking runs of pure blues notes. He provided the classic female singers with an entire dimension of sound that linked the blues and jazz together, enabling them to attain a greater audience.

He continued recording his own works and also played on the records of Perry Bradford and Clarence Williams. On a few occasions, he also shared the spotlight with his old friend Fats Waller. By the end of the 1920s, Johnson had established himself as a noteworthy pianist, composer, arranger, guest accompanist, and bandleader. The 1930s, however, would be much different.

Like so many other musicians Johnson saw his career disintegrate during the Depression years. He was semi-active in music and composed some very ambitious pieces, including "Harlem Symphony," "Symphony in Brown" and a blues opera. Unfortunately, Johnson was way ahead of his time and some of his most aspiring works have been lost over the years. Once he had been in perfect harmony with the tastes of black culture but by the middle of the decade had fallen out of favor.

Johnson returned full-time to the jazz world in the latter part of the 1930s. In 1939, he sat in with Eddie Condon and once again dazzled all with his remarkable skills, proving that he had not lost any of his technical powers. Although he had suffered a major blow to his once flourishing career due to circumstances that were beyond his control, he was determined to regain his lost appeal. The 1940s proved to be more fruitful.

Unfortunately, he began to suffer a series of minor strokes in the 1940s. He remained active, however, and added some memorable performances and new recordings to his legendary status. Ironically, he was playing with many of the piano players who were inspired by the recordings he made in the 1920s. Many of the bebop pianists like Bud Powell and Thelonious Monk looked up to Johnson.

In 1951, a major stroke ended Johnson's brilliant career. Four years later, on November 17, 1955, in New York City, James P. Johnson, the great stride player who made enormous contributions to jazz, died. He was 61 years old.

James P. Johnson was a jazz hero. For the better part of two decades he astounded all with his uncanny touch on the eighty-eight keys. His range was wide and deep. His legacy can still be heard in the playing of other major jazz piano players such as Oscar Peterson. But there is more to the Johnson legacy than his great ability on the piano.

He developed a magical musical style by combining the best elements of blues, ragtime, and classical. He took the power of the blues, the novelty of ragtime, and the structure of classical to create his stride piano classics. Rarely has one person been able to blend three distinct musical forms into something so magnificent. By being able to combine all these parts, he paved the way for fusion-jazz, rhythm and blues, soul, rock and roll, and many other types of post-war music that incorporated elements from many genres.

He was the all-important link between ragtime and early jazz piano. He studied the works of Scott Joplin and began where the great ragtime master left off. He was able to advance beyond the boundaries that Joplin set because of advances in technology and the simple fact that he, Johnson, was a better musician. But the influence that Joplin had on Johnson cannot be denied. Every musician needs a starting point, a mentor, and an idol. The ragtime master was that and more to the stride king.

Like Joplin's, Johnson's playing had a large influence on an incredible number of jazz pianists spanning many eras. A partial list includes Count Basie, Ran Blake, Art Hodes, Lonnie Liston Smith, Ralph Sutton, Art Tatum, Fats Waller, Don Ewell, Dick Wellstood, Duke Ellington, Fletcher Henderson, Walter Roland, and Willie "The Lion" Smith. Johnson's compositional skills also made a strong impact on the group of aforementioned pianists.

Johnson was blessed with a tremendous amount of talent and parlayed his abilities into writing and arranging a number of songs that still remain vital to the standard jazz repertoire of the modern artist. A partial list of the treasures he gave the world includes "If I Could Be With You (One Hour Tonight)," "The Charleston," "Runnin' Wild," "Old Fashioned Love," "A Porter's Love Song to a Chambermaid," "Eccentricity," "Arkansas Blues," "Ole Miss Blues," "Harlem Choc'late," "Babies on Parade," and "Carolina Shout."

James P. Johnson belongs to a select group of jazz musicians, one with its own style that lives on in the music, old photographs, and old films. Many of his songs have been re-mastered and have reached a new generation of jazz fans. In his era, he was a star of stellar magnitude. Although the history of jazz can lay claim to a long impressive list of great pianists, there was only one stride king.

Discography

Carolina Shout, Biograph BCD 105.
Yamekraw and Other Selections, Smithsonian/Folkways 2842.
James P. Johnson, Columbia CL 1780.
Watch Me Go, IAJRC 52.
Snow Morning Blues, GRP GRD604.
Rent Party Piano, Blue Note 7011.
Smithsonian/Folkways 2850.
Jazz Band Ball, Blue Note 7012.
Ain'tcha Got Music, Pumpkin 117.
The Daddy of the Piano, Decca DL-5190.
Stomps, Rags and Blues, Blue Note BLP-7011.

Rent Party, Riverside PLP-1011.
Rare Piano Solos, Blue Note BLP-1009.
Rare Piano Roll Solos, Vol. 2, Biograph 125.
Parlor Piano Solos from Rare Piano Rolls, Biograph 150.
Father of the Stride Piano, Columbia 1780.
Running Wild, Tradition 1048.
King of Stride Piano, 1918–1944, Giants of Jazz Piano 52201.
James P. Johnson, 1921–1928, CLC 658.
James P. Johnson, 1928–1938, CLC 671.
James P. Johnson, 1938–1942, CLC 711.
James P. Johnson, 1943–1944, CLC 824.
James P. Johnson, 1944, CLC 835.
James P. Johnson, 1944 Vol. 2, CLC 856.
James P. Johnson, 1944–1945, CLC 1027.
James P. Johnson, 1945–1947, CLC 1059.
James P. Johnson, Hot Piano, PEA 1048.
James P. Johnson, Carolina Shout, 1921–1949, ASL 5355.
James P. Johnson, The Original James P. Johnson, 1942-1945, SFW 40812.
Harlem Stride Piano, Harlem Stride Piano, 1921–1929, EPM 158952.
James P. Johnson, Vol. 2, Riverside 1917.

JIMMIE NOONE (1895–1944)

Apex Blues

The jazz age produced a plethora of stars who dominated the scene in the 1920s and then were soon forgotten. Although many of these musical figures continued to tour throughout the rest of their careers, many never enjoyed the same peak of popularity that they had during the golden age of jazz. One such artist reached the height of his musical career during the decade with his Apex blues. His name was Jimmie Noone.

Jimmie Noone was born on April 23, 1895, in Cut-Off, Louisiana, on a family farm ten miles from the lights, sounds and excitement of New Orleans. Noone showed an early interest in music and took up the guitar as a young boy. Later on, as a teenager, he switched over to clarinet and received lessons from Lorenzo Tio, Jr., and Sidney Bechet. Bechet would turn out to be one of Noone's contemporaries.

A studious fellow, Noone quickly became proficient enough on the clarinet to join Freddie Keppard before his twentieth birthday. His stint in Keppard's group enabled him to gain valuable performing experience and prepared him for future endeavors including a seat in Buddy Petit and the Young Olympian Band. Noone eventually formed his own group, but was unable to keep it together.

Like so many other New Orleans jazz musicians, Noone followed the path to Chicago where he rejoined Keppard's Creole Band. A year later he was a member of King Oliver's band and retained a permanent residency in the group for two years. But his true big break came when he joined Doc Cooke's Dreamland Orchestra.

Doc Cooke was born in Louisville, Kentucky, in 1891. He studied music from an early age and by eighteen was working as a composer-arranger in Detroit. Eventually, Cooke moved to Chicago where he formed his first band. He also moonlighted as musical director for Riverview Park. From 1922 through 1928, he led his sixteen-member band at Harmon's Dreamland. He moved to New York in 1930 and became staff arranger for Radio City Music Hall. He obtained the name "Doc" because he gained a doctorate of music at the Chicago College. He retired in the 1940s. During his long residency at Harmon's Dreamland many important musicians of the 1920s played in his orchestra including Jimmie Noone.

Noone recorded with Doc Cook's Dreamland Orchestra and during his six-year tenure with the band established himself as one of the prime clarinetists of the era. Although the experience was a positive one, Noone had greater ambitions. He wanted to lead his own group once again and was given the chance at the Apex Club.

While the history of jazz is filled with the glory names of the people who created the music and their names still retain a powerful quality, many of the clubs that these greats starred in have been demolished and turned into parking lots. The Apex Club, in Chicago, was a fine establishment that hosted hundreds of jazz concerts, creating magical moments that live forever in the memories of those fortunate to attend the events. Although it has since been torn down, the Apex was one of the top clubs in the country.

At the Apex Club, Noone, along with Earl Hines and altoist Joe Poston, managed to harness all of their creative powers and attained legendary status. It was during this time that Noone recorded many sides for Vocalion, one of the early record companies. He also wrote many of the songs that made him famous, including "Four or Five Times" and his signature piece "Sweet Lorraine." He established credentials as a solid bandleader, musician and songwriter.

Noone's popularity reached its climax in the 1920s, but he was quickly swept from the spotlight like so many other musicians when the stock market crashed on Black Tuesday in 1929. He remained in Chicago throughout the 1930s and continued as one of the true great clarinet voices of jazz, but his fame receded. His level of talent had not dropped but the times had changed. Even guest appearances by the impressive young singer Joe Williams in his band did little to restore the popularity of Noone's outfit.

In 1940, craving a change, Noone left Chicago, which had been his home base for twenty years, and led his own group throughout the country. His quartet toured Omaha, Nebraska, and played a long stint in San Antonio, Texas, at the Tropics. In 1943, he headed further west with his group, playing at the Streets of Paris club in Los Angeles before breaking up the band to join Kid Ory.

During his time in Kid Ory's band, Noone recorded and played on radio dates. He also appeared with the East Side Kids in the 1944 Monogram film *The Block Busters*. Just when it seemed as if he was on the threshold of recapturing past glories, on April 19, 1944, he suffered a fatal heart attack. He was just a few days shy of his forty-ninth birthday.

Jimmie Noone was a genuine star of the 1920s. His rise, reign and decline reflect the story of the Jazz Age itself. He was able to combine all of his talent and charisma in order to dominate the musical scene for at least a brief period of time. He was a key figure in the transition from the old New Orleans style to the swing of the 1930s. Ironically, he was somewhat lost in the shuffle during the big band and swing era. However, he remained one of the finest clarinet voices throughout his career.

The Noone style has often been imitated but never duplicated. Often accorded the same accolades as Sidney Bechet and Johnny Dodds, the other two outstanding clarinetists of the 1920s, Noone had a smoother tone than either of his contemporaries. He possessed a liquid, fluid technique that was interspersed with speedy solos. There was an overall polished playing to his sound, a definite professional edge. Noone made playing the clarinet look easy even during the most difficult passages and solos.

Interestingly, his style was one of constant evolution. Noone, who had played in New Orleans, arrived in Chicago sounding much like all the other clarinet players from the Crescent City. But during the 1920s he broke out of the strict confinement to become a different player who pointed the way to the swing era.

Although he has often been categorized as a one-decade star, Noone had his hand in the events that unfolded during the next twenty years. His music was a precursor to the subtle arrangements utilized by Duke

Ellington. Noone was also one of the most profound influences on Benny Goodman, the "King of Swing." Both Ellington and Goodman would reach immense popularity in the 1930s.

Noone also had a major influence on Irving Fazola, Jimmy Dorsey, Omer Simeon and Darnell Howard. His fluid playing also had an indirect impact on Sidney Bechet and Johnny Dodds. Jazz musicians have always been conscious of the music that is being produced around them and have been able to incorporate ideas from their contemporaries into their own program. Another jazz artist that Noone had a direct influence on was his son Jimmie Noone, Jr., who emerged in the 1980s to play clarinet and tenor with the Cheathams, a group that enjoyed moderate success.

Noone also gave the world a string of memorable classics. They include "Sweet Lorraine," "I Know That You Know," "Four or Five Times," "Apex Blues," "My Monday Date," "Blues My Naughty Sweetie Gives To Me," "Anything You Want," "Chicago Movie," "Delta Bound," "Crying for the Carolines," "Deep Trouble," "I'd Do Anything for You," "Liza," "After You're Gone," "I've Got a Mystery," "Let's Sow a Wild Oat," "Some Rainy Day," "She's Funny Like That," and "Sweet Sue-Just You." He also supplied songs for motion pictures including "Am I Blue?" and "Birmingham Bertha," which were featured in the movie *On with the Show*. Each song was stamped with the Noone touch on the clarinet. His smooth sound is instantly recognizable. There is no other sound quite like Noone's in all of jazz.

Throughout his career as bandleader at the Apex and other clubs, his band featured many of the top performers of the era. Vocalist May Alix started with Noone in 1921 and stayed for a couple of years. Other singers included Junie Cobb who also played banjo and guitar; Cobb stayed less than a year. Joe Poston supplied Noone's band with vocals as well as alto sax and clarinet. He joined the group in 1928 and stayed until 1930. Helen Savage also was a featured vocalist with Noone.

Other Noone alumni include tuba player Lawson Buford, pianists Zinky Cohn (who stayed from 1929 to 1931), Alex Hill who remained less than a year after replacing Earl Hines, banjo/guitarist Wilbur Gorham, cornetist George Mitchell, tuba player Bill Newton, Bud Scott who played both the banjo and guitar, vocalist Elmo Tanner, drummer Johnny Wells who replaced Ollie Powers when the latter died in 1928 after a two-year stint with Noone's band, as well as trombonist Fayette Williams.

But there is more to the Jimmie Noone story than his impressive contributions to jazz as a very good clarinetist, bandleader, and songwriter. He epitomized the hard-living, fast-playing cool cat image of the jazz singer of the 1920s. He was a suave, neatly attired man who lived to play music and enjoyed all of the fringe benefits that came with being a big star. He relished the fame that playing the clarinet brought him since he loved the women, money and adulation as much as creating music.

Noone and Bix Beiderbecke, Louis Armstrong, Johnny Dodds, Baby Dodds, Sidney Bechet, James P. Johnson and Fats Waller were the prime driving forces behind jazz of the Roaring Twenties. Noone crystalized the era in his personal style. However, while some of the big names of the 1920s were able to continue their careers, he was confined to that period and never fully recovered once the era was over.

Although other artists of the 1920s surpassed Noone in popularity and had more stellar careers, it is very hard to forget Jimmie Noone because of the serious impact he had on the music and the whole scene. While his time in the sun was limited, he became a legend with his Apex blues, and the world was a better place for it.

Discography

Apex of New Orleans Jazz, 1923–1944, ASV/Living Era 5235.
Jazz Heritage: At the Apex Club, MCA 1313.
Jimmie Noone and his Orchestra, IAJRC 10.
Apex Blues, Decca 633.
Oh! Sister Ain't That Hot! MCA 1367.
Volume Three, 1929, Swaggie 845.
The Apex Club Orchestra, Brunswick BL-58006.
At the Apex Club, Decca DL-9235.
New Orleans, RCA 35627.
His Best Recordings: 1923–1940, Best of Jazz 4034.
Complete Recordings, Vol. 1, Affinity 1027.
Volume Two, 1928–1929, Swaggie 842.
The Jimmie Noone Collection, Vol. 1 (1928), Collector's Classic 6.
Volume Four 1929–1930, Swaggie 844.
1930–1934, Classics 641.
1934–1940, Classics 651.
New Orleans 1928–1929, Milan 731101.
1923–1928, Classics 604.
1928–1929, Classics 611.
1929–1930, Classics 632.

ETHEL WATERS (1896–1977)

Jazzin' Babies Blues

The legion of great female singers spans the entire history of the genre. Often, these women were multi-talented vocalists capable of blending various elements of pop, blues, and spirituals into their repertoires. Many of the best singers started out in the blues field and later adopted a jazzier sound. One of these exceptional performers delivered her "jazzin' babies blues" to the delight of fans around the world. Her name was Ethel Waters.

Ethel Waters was born Ethel Howard on October 31, 1896, in Chester, Pennsylvania. Like so many of her blues and jazz contemporaries, Waters' first musical experience was through the church and gospel music. She sang in the choir and developed a love for singing that would remain with her throughout her life. Because of her interest in different styles she was destined to move beyond gospel.

Waters grew up poor and didn't have much schooling. By her teens she was working as a domestic, one of the few employment opportunities that a young African-American girl could obtain in those days. Music and singing enabled her to get through the drudgery of her hard labor. Some reports indicate that she may have been married as early as thirteen. Whether this is true or not there is little doubt that Waters—like millions of other African-American children growing up in the country before the advent of World War I—had a rough struggle.

But Waters had tremendous courage as she continued to scrape and claw her way to the top. She caught her first big break when she won a talent contest as a teenager and soon was singing all over the Philadelphia area. She managed to find work on the stage at the Lincoln Theatre in Baltimore where her showstopper was the John C. Handy classic "St. Louis Blues." She also performed in other places in Baltimore, spreading her name in two cities on the East Coast.

She then toured the South, billed as "Sweet Mama Stringbean" (because of her height and slim figure), and starred in carnivals, tent and vaudeville shows. She expanded her horizons by playing in *Hello, 1919!* at the Lafayette Theatre in Harlem. Her first recordings were "The New York Glide" and "At the New Jump Steady Ball" on Cardinal Records in 1919. Then in 1921 she cut two songs for Black Swan Records: "Down Home Blues" and "Oh, Daddy," which became a best seller.

Her first professional tour was with the Black Swan Troubadours, one of the popular touring companies at the time. She was backed by Fletcher Henderson's band and developed a reputation as an exciting and versatile performer. After this, Waters continued to play the vaudeville circuit and worked in several theatrical revues. When she turned down an offer to go to Paris with Revue Negre, she gave the unknown Josephine Baker, Waters' replacement, her big break in the entertainment business.

Waters began to distinguish herself with the recordings she made in 1921; they set her apart from the other female blues and jazz singers of the era. She had the powerful edge of Bessie Smith in her voice, but she was also very jazz-oriented and her music had a strong swing feel to it. Also, her delivery was clear and easily accessible.

Although she was considered a blues singer at the beginning of her career, Waters eventually incorporated more jazz material in her repertoire by the middle of the 1920s. But Waters was not content to sing just blues and jazz songs; she had greater ambitions. She starred in theatre productions and established a movie career. Her multiple accomplishments enabled her to enjoy a diversified career that rivaled that of any other female singers of the era and often surpassed the stature of many.

She appeared on Broadway for the first time in 1927 in *Africana*, and traveled to Europe in 1930. Irving Berlin wrote four songs for her for his Broadway show *As Thousands Cheer*. This show toured the south where Waters received star billing with the white players.

While many of the female classic blues and jazz singers of the 1920s saw their careers disintegrate in the 1930s, Waters made the smooth transition to pop star. She continued to appear in films and in theatre productions throughout the decade. She also sang with her husband Eddie Mallory, a trumpeter, who led his own band that toured the country.

Eddie Mallory was born in Chicago in 1905 and learned how to play the trumpet as well as the sax. His interest in music stretched beyond his playing ability to include arranging and composing. In 1927, he joined the Alabamians and remained with them for four years. He worked in a variety of bands until he hooked up with Waters in the middle of the 1930s. From 1935 until 1939, Mallory was the director of the band that backed Waters. The marriage, however, was brief and the two split up after only a few years together. By the middle of the 1940s he was out of the music business.

In 1938, Waters gave a recital at Carnegie Hall and then began to appear in dramatic roles, including *Mamba's Daughers* a year later. She also continued to do recordings on a variety of labels. From this point on Waters would devote more time to her acting career than to her singing career.

However, as the 1940s unfolded, Waters did not completely aban-
don her love for the stage or the concert hall. She continued her career as
a singer and an actress, adding many solid credentials to her already
impressive resume. In 1943, she appeared in *Cabin in the Sky* in which she
introduced three classic songs: "Cabin in the Sky," "Taking a Chance,"
and "Happiness Is Just a Thing Called Joe."

Waters, who always craved a new challenge, starred in nonmusical movie
roles in the 1940s and the 1950s, while still retaining her title as one of the
best singers of blues, jazz, and pop on the circuit. Her dual career as singer
and actress kept her busy and enabled her to achieve a wider audience. She
was a veteran performer who always left the crowd screaming for more.

The 1960s saw Waters come full circle as she returned to singing in
the church, the original point of her entertaining career. She worked with
the evangelist Billy Graham and won over an entire new section of fans.
Although she did perform the occasional concert, Waters' days of multiple concert dates were over.

On September 1, 1977, Ethel Waters, the multi-talented singer,
actress, died in Chatsworth, California. She was eighty years old.

Ethel Waters was a jazz queen throughout her career. But she was
more than that. She had the ability to explore and conquer many different
media, placing her in a very special category among artists of the twentieth century. Her contributions to jazz alone would have been enough to
earn her entry into the Jazz Hall of Fame.

Throughout her career she worked with a large number of the most
important jazz musicians including Duke Ellington, Benny Goodman,
Bing Crosby, Fletcher Henderson, Benny Carter, Tommy Dorsey, Manny
Klein, Jimmy Dorsey, Pearl Wright, Stan King, Cootie Williams, Joe
Venuti, Dick McDonough, Joe "Fox" Smith, Freddy Jenkins, Milt Hin-
ton, Rube Bloom, Lou Kosloff, and Eddie Mallory.

She gave the world a treasure trove of classics including "New York
Glide," "At the New Jump Steady Ball," "Am I Blue?," "Memories of You,"
"Heatwave," "Takin' a Chance on Love," "You Brought a New Kind of
Love to Me," "Don't Blame Me," "I Just Can't Take It Baby," "I Can't
Give You Anything But Love," "Stormy Weather," "Porgy," "You Can't
Stop Me from Loving You," "Heat Wave," "Jeepers Creepers," "West End
Blues," "Georgia on My Mind," "Black and Blue," and "A Hundred Years
from Today," to name a few. Her songbook is an oral history of Ameri-
can music from the 1920s through the 1970s.

Although many of her recordings became well known, she also
guested on a number of sessions including "Cotton Club" with John Berry,
and "Melody Lingers On" with Irving Berlin. She also added her distinct
vocals to recordings by Hoagy Carmichael, Benny Carter, the Dorsey

Brothers Orchestra, Duke Ellington, Ella Fitzgerald, James P. Johnson, and Cole Porter.

Waters fits into many categories. She is ranked with the best of the early classic female blues singers who include Bessie Smith, Ida Cox, Alberta Hunter, Sippie Wallace, Mamie Smith, and Ma Rainey. She is also put in the same category of jazz singers as Mildred Bailey, Maxine Sullivan, Billie Holiday, Josephine Baker, and Ernestine Anderson. She had a large influence on Pearl Bailey, Lena Horne, Helen Humes, and Ella Fitzgerald. Her influence can be heard in the diverse styles of Dinah Washington, as well as in newcomer Diana Krall and everyone in between including Koko Taylor, Aretha Franklin, Sarah Vaughan, Big Mama Willie Mae Thornton, Tina Turner, and Etta James.

Her ability to handle several mediums opened the door for many of the divas of the past forty years. Madonna, Whitney Houston, Mariah Carey, Diana Ross, and a host of others all owe a great debt to Ethel Waters. She stood boldly in the face of racism and was determined that her career would not suffer in spite of it. Her lessons are carried on today.

A list of some of the movies she appeared in include: *On with the Show, Rufus Jones for President, Gift of Gab, Bubbling Over, Cairo, Tales of Manhattan, Cabin in the Sky, Stage Door Canteen, New Orleans, Let's Sing a Song from the Movies, Pinky, Beulah, The Member of the Wedding, Caribbean Gold, The Heart Is a Rebel,* and *The Sound and the Fury.* She also appeared on television on *Route 66* and *The Borden Show.* She also showed up in archival footage in *That's Entertainment, That's Dancing!, That's Black Entertainment,* and *Jazz,* a mini-series.

Waters also conquered the publishing world. During her long career she wrote two autobiographies: *His Eye Is on the Sparrow* and *To Me It's Wonderful.* Both are an invaluable source of information for anyone interested in further exploring the life, the triumphs, and tragedies of a truly remarkable jazz lady.

Ethel Waters provided the world with many memorable songs and moments on the big screen and on stage. Her talent was undeniable and she was a fixture on the entertainment scene for seven decades. Her career serves as a lesson that obstacles can be overcome if one has the perseverance, confidence, and dedication to achieve her goals. She will be remembered as a brave lady who changed the world with her "Jazzin' Babies Blues."

Discography

Cabin in the Sky, Milan 356062.
Ethel Waters, Remington RP-4105.
No Ethel Waters on Mercury, Mercury MG 20051.

Performing in Person Highlights from Her Illustrious Career, Monmouth
    Evergreen 6112.
Ethel Waters Sings, Continental 16008.
Favorite Songs, Mercury MG-290051.
Timeless Historical Presents Ethel Waters, Timeless 5326.
Jazzin' Babies Blues, Vol. 2 (1921–1927), Biograph 12026.
1921–1923, Classics 796.
Oh Daddy, Vol. 1 (1921–1924), Biograph BP-12022.
An Introduction to Ethel Waters: Her Best Recordings 1921–1940, Best
    of Jazz 4013.
1923–1925, Classics 672.
Ethel Waters (1924–1928), Wolf 1009.
Ethel Waters' Greatest Years, Columbia Kg-31571.
1925–1926, Classics 672.
Ethel Waters on Stage and Screen (1925–1940), Columbia CCL 2792.
1926–1929, Classics 688.
1929–1931, Classics 721.
1931–1934, Classics 755.
Foremothers, Vol. 6, Rosetta 1314.
Who Said Blackbirds Are Blue, Sandy Hook 2030.
1938–1939, Jazz Archives 157472.
American Legend, Delta 12747.
1935–1940, Classics 755.
Ethel Waters 1929–1939, Timeless 7.
1931–1940, Giants of Jazz 53294.
Am I Blue? ASV/Living Era 5290.
Takin' a Chance on Love: The Complete Bluebird Recordings, Definitive
    11114.
Ethel Waters Singing Her Best, Jay 3010.

FLETCHER HENDERSON (1897–1952)

Smack's Blues

In the annals of jazz there have been many talented individuals who
not only excelled on one or more instruments but also made a serious

impact as arrangers. Their compositions became classics that have inspired future generations of musicians. One of these immensely gifted artists was an important piano player, a respected bandleader, and a brilliant arranger who gave the world his Smack's Jazz. His name was Fletcher Henderson.

Fletcher "Smack" Henderson was born Fletcher Hamilton Henderson, Jr., on December 18, 1897, in Cuthbert, Georgia. He grew up surrounded by music as both his parents were good piano players and encouraged their children to practice until they had complete command of the instrument. Fletcher began studying the piano at the tender age of six and continued for several years, earning many awards in numerous competitions.

Despite his early success young Fletcher wasn't keen on a music career. The ability to create harmony and melody was a pastime, a hobby that was one part of his life. He had greater ambitions. It is ironic that one of the most important cogs in the history of jazz was not fervent about a pursuing the life of an itinerant musician. It was a decision that he would soon reverse, but by his teens music was not Henderson's first love.

Unlike many black children of the era, Henderson did not grow up in poverty. His father was a school principal in Macon which enabled young Fletcher to pursue a college diploma, a rarity among young African-Americans in the 1910s. He gained a degree in chemistry and mathematics from Atlanta University and moved to New York City to find work. But his dream of becoming a chemist was dashed because of the racism that existed at the time.

Instead, he found work as a song demonstrator with the Pace-Handy Music Company. When the founder of the company launched his own label (Black Swan), Henderson assumed an important role in the new organization. It was apparent that Henderson's talent as a songwriter and arranger were already being recognized. The job on the new label enabled him to further polish his already strong composition skills.

Many jazz historians insist that Henderson was a fine pianist, but lacked the talent to gain the same respect accorded greater players such as Art Tatum or Oscar Peterson. However, in 1922, he was asked to put a group together to back Ethel Waters on tour. Henderson recruited clarinetist Garvin Bushell and the Aiken brothers, trumpeter Gus and trombonist Buddy. The group appeared in the largest venues throughout the winter months of 1922–23, and upon their return to New York disbanded. However, Fletcher played a further role in the career of Ethel Waters by supervising the recordings of her "Oh Daddy!" and "Jazzin' Babies Blues" sessions.

In 1923, Henderson's schedule was a very hectic one. Aside from backing Waters in the studio, he accompanied the great blues singer Bessie Smith on her Columbia recording dates, recorded some piano solos of his own for Black Swan, and performed with a band for a couple of different labels. Many of the musicians whom he used in the recording studio would later form the nucleus of the first big band he assembled the following year. The cast of musicians included trumpeter Howard Scott, bassist Rafael Escudero, arranger-composer-saxophonist-clarinetist Don Redman, trombonists Teddy Nixon and Charlie Green, drummer Kaiser Marshall and the incomparable saxophonist Coleman Hawkins. Later that year the great Louis Armstrong joined the band elevating the talent level considerably and making Henderson's outfit the top band in the land.

The group's first engagement was a six-month residency at the Club Alabam in New York in 1924. Their early sound was based on New Orleans jazz. The group itself followed King Oliver's model. There was an instrumental lineup backed by a steady four-beats-to-the-bar rhythm section. Henderson also borrowed the call-and-response phrasing that was prominent in other jazz bands including those of Paul Whiteman and Art Hickman.

For the next three years the Fletcher Henderson band remained unchallenged despite the departure of Armstrong (who had taught the quick learning Redman how to really swing) in 1925. With Redman contributing excellent arrangements (he was without a doubt the best arranger in the business at the time), and the tender, sweet sounds of Coleman Hawkins on tenor saxophone, it was easy to understand why Henderson's outfit was the darling of the jazz world. It would remain on top playing residencies at the Alabam and the Roseland until being eclipsed by Duke Ellington and his Orchestra.

Henderson and the musicians in his band formed endless recording combinations. The cornetist Joe Smith, clarinetist Buster Bailey, Redman, Henderson, Charlie Green, and a mature sounding Coleman Hawkins backed many of the blues singers of the period including Ma Rainey, Bessie Smith, Ida Cox, Ethel Waters, Alberta Hunter, Clara Smith, Trixie Smith, and Maggie Jones. Henderson's Hot Six were the elite of the jazz world in the mid–1920s.

Despite the success and the additions of trumpeter Russell Smith, Joe's brother, and Fats Waller, the pressures began to mount. Henderson was not the greatest bandleader and his mistakes started to cost him dearly. Although Waller contributed excellent original compositions that Redman shaped into major hits for the band, Waller was not hired on a permanent basis. A much stronger leader than Henderson, Waller would have solidified the group for a longer period. Also the recordings of the band decreased and those that were made tended to be sloppy and lacking precision.

The departure of Don Redman in 1927 was a critical blow, but Henderson managed to keep his band together and it continued to be a first-rate group. But the cracks were evident. It was impossible to replace someone of Redman's superior caliber and Henderson's outfit began to fizzle. The major reason was the lack of recordings made. After the departure of Redman in 1927, until 1931, Henderson's band recorded perhaps a couple of dozen songs, most of the arrangements scavenged from other sources.

The band carried on despite numerous personnel changes. The talented Joe Smith left to join Redman in McKinney's Cotton Pickers. But Henderson was able to recruit Benny Carter who came very close to filling Redman's shoes as arranger in the band. Jimmy Harrison, Claude Jones, Walter Johnson, Clarence Holiday, and John Kirby gave Henderson's group a new identity and in 1931 they began to record more prolifically. That marked the maturation of Henderson the arranger. It was a slow, painstaking process, but eventually Henderson began to compose scores for his band that heavily copied what Redman and others were doing. Often the arrangements came from within the band, as Henderson's sidemen were always eager to contribute their own musical ideas.

Although there was never a shortage of ability in the Henderson big band because of the leader's sharp eye for new talent, more bad business decisions led to the demise of his group in 1934. One of the most important factors was the lack of directional skill that Henderson possessed. The break up of the band was spurred on by the departure of Coleman Hawkins after a ten-year tenure in the band. He seemed irreplaceable.

In 1935, Henderson had no band and his frustrations were very real. By this time he had polished his arrangement skills until they were first rate. But instead of being able to write for his own group, he provided the bulk of compositions for Benny Goodman who was on the verge of unparalleled popularity and earned the title of "King of Swing" on the back of Henderson's excellent arrangements. The meteoric rise of Goodman's band from obscure musical outfit to the hottest show in the country would not have been possible without Fletcher's essential contributions.

In 1936, he reformed his big band. The second incarnation of the Fletcher Henderson Band dripped with outstanding talent—clarinetist Buster Bailey, trumpeters John Kirby, Dick Vance, Roy Eldridge, and Joe Thomas, saxophonists Jerome Pasquall and Chu Berry, and Walter Johnson on drums. The band scored an immediate hit with "Christopher Columbus" and was quickly booked in top clubs like the Grand Terrace in Chicago. But the project fizzled by 1939, as they were unable to score another big hit.

He rejoined Goodman as arranger and piano player despite his limited range on the instrument. Henderson, a stubborn individual, refused to wallow in his own failure and rejuvenated his big band once again in 1941 with the blessing of Goodman. Henderson was able to put together another formidable lineup that included drummer Art Blakey, tenor saxophonist Dexter Gordon and trombonist Vic Dickerson. Although they showed much promise the band didn't have any staying power. As a consolation prize Gordon became an important player in the bop revolution and Blakey went on to form the Jazz Messengers, one of the best modern groups, for over forty years.

Meanwhile, Henderson returned to Goodman's band as arranger. The following year he was reunited with Ethel Waters and toured with her. After that adventure Henderson put his arranging talents to good use writing a revue with J. C. Johnson called *Jazz Train*. They premiered the show in the Big Apple to enthusiastic reviews.

But Henderson was a bandleader born to direct a variety of talented musicians and create music for the masses. In 1945, he enjoyed a return to glory, albeit briefly, with a fifteen month residency in Chicago. He would later front a sextet that included Lucky Thompson and Jimmy Crawford. They played at the Café Society among other venues. The engagement lasted until 1950 when Henderson suffered the first of a series of strokes. A benefit was held later on to help defray medical costs and the performers included the Benny Goodman trio, Buck Clayton, Johnny Smith and many others. It was clear that Henderson still commanded a great amount of respect throughout the jazz community.

Henderson returned to his birthplace of Cuthbert, Georgia, before heading off to the Big Apple one last time. On December 29, 1952, in New York City, in a Harlem hospital, Fletcher "Smack" Hamilton Henderson, Jr., died. He was fifty-four years old.

Fletcher Henderson was an integral figure in the jazz milieu of the 1920s and 1930s, yet never received the credit he deserved. He played many roles: brilliant arranger, composer, studio session man, and bandleader of the first trend-setting jazz big band. The imprint he left on the genre remains significant even today.

Henderson was a terrific arranger and composer. His keen intelligence and imagination helped catapult Benny Goodman to the designated throne of "King of Swing," a title that Henderson richly deserved but was never accorded. Henderson also supplied songs to groups headed by Teddy Hill, Will Bradley, Isham Jones, Jack Hylton, The Casa Loma Orchestra, the Dorsey Brother and the revered Count Basie.

Henderson brought many innovations to jazz that paved the way for the reign of the big bands. He initiated the winning format that established a rhythm section playing tight compositions but also provided wide-open spaces that enabled the brilliant soloists of the era to shine. It was Fletcher, along with Redman, who established the instrumentation of big bands in the 1930s, which included three trumpets, two trombones, four saxophones and four rhythm pieces.

Henderson had a keen eye for talent and a partial list of the great jazz names that he discovered and whose careers he helped nurture boasts a virtual who's who of jazz. The list includes trumpeters Louis Armstrong, Tommy Ladnier, Cootie Williams, Roy Eldridge, Rex Stewart and Red Allen, trombonists Charlie Green, Bennie Moten, J. C. Higginbotham, as well as the clarinetist Buster Bailey. Perhaps the richest crop of musicians was the saxophonists. They included Ben Webster, Lester Young, Benny Carter, Coleman Hawkins, and Chu Berry. His rhythm section alumni consisted of John Kirby, Israel Crosby, Kaiser Marshall, Walter Johnson, and Big Sid Catlett. Even the great stride piano player Fats Waller spent time in Henderson's outfit.

Henderson's eye for talent did not stop with musicians; he was also able to recruit top-notch arrangers. The great Don Redman, Benny Carter, Edgar Sampson, and Horace Henderson all honed their craft while part of Fletcher's outfits. It was these men who helped transform jazz from its early constricted New Orleans form and give it the widespread popularity as the hottest music on the planet. Henderson was a prime mover in spearheading the change from the traditional style to sophisticated swing.

He was also an ambassador of jazz, spreading the music throughout the world by playing residencies in New York, Chicago, the West Coast and Europe. He was one of the key members who truly believed in the music and elevated the status of jazz from dirty street rhythms to the lofty position as America's classical music.

He gave the world a treasure trove of songs. They include "Sing You Sinners," "Moten Stomp," "Can You Take It?," "Shanghai Shuffle," "Down South Camp Meeting," "Wrappin' It Up," "Hotter Than 'Ell," "Go 'Long Mule," "Copenhagen," "Everybody Loves My Baby," "How Come You Do Me Like You Do?," "Sugarfoot Stomp," "Tell Me Dreamy," "My Rose Marie," "Twelfth Street Blues," "Blue Moments," and "My Gal Sal." The songs served as the starting point for many of the compositions written by other jazz musicians. Many of the arrangers from 1920 to 1940 utilized the same devices that Henderson incorporated in his style.

Like so many other jazz musicians, Fletcher was a valued session man and appeared on an incredible number of records made by Buster Bailey, Benny Goodman, Louis Armstrong, Mildred Bailey, and many of the greatest blues singers of the 1920s. Although no great talent on the piano he was well respected among his contemporaries for the sheer brilliance of his all-around abilities. He was a genuine talent in every area. Fletcher Henderson was a big band innovator, a tremendous composer of brilliant swing material for his group and others, a key session man, and an eagle-eyed talent scout. He was a formidable force in the early days of jazz and is as important as anyone else from the 1920s and 1930s era. His efforts set the table for all of the jazz that would happen during the rest of the century. Despite the lack of recognition he received and shortcomings as a bandleader, there is no denial of the enormous contributions he made with his Smack's Jazz.

Discography

Fletcher Henderson (1923), BYG 5290083.
Henderson Paths, Fountain FJ 112.
Fletcher Henderson's Orchestra, Biograph BLP-12039.
Fletcher Henderson and Louis Armstrong, Timeless 3.
Indispensable, RCA 66676.
The Crown King of Swing, Savoy 254.
Tidal Wave, GRP/Decca 643.
Under the Harlem Moon, ASV/Living Era 5067.
Fletcher Henderson with Slam Stewart and the Jazz Tones, Sutton 286.
Fletcher Henderson's Sextet (1950), Alamac QSR 2444.
Fletcher Henderson, Riverside RLP-1055.
The Big Reunion, Jazztone J1285.
Yeah Man, Hep 1016.
Wild Party, Hep 1009.
Fletcher Henderson's Orchestra, Vol. 1: 1923–24, Historical HLP-13.
Fletcher Henderson's Orchestra, Vol. 2, Historical HLP-14.
Rarest Fletcher, Vol. 1 (1923–1924), MCA 1346.
The Pathe Sessions (1923–1925), Swaggie 803.
Introduction to Fletcher Henderson, 1921–1941, Best of Jazz 4019.
Father of the Big Band, 1925–1937, EPM Musique 159352.
The Harmony & Vocalion Sessions, 1925–1926, CBC 1064.
Live at the Grand Terrace Chicago 1938, STC 2053.
Complete Works Vol. 1 1921–1923, Document 5342.
1924–1927, EPM 157532.
1921–1923, Classics 794.
1923, Classics 697.
1923–1924, Classics 683.
1924, Classics 673.
1924, Vol. 2, Classics 657.

1924, Vol. 3, Classics 647.
1924–1925, Classics 633.
1925–1926, Classics 610.
1926–1927, Classics 597.
1927, Classics 580.
1927–1931, Classics 572.
1931, Classics 555.
1931–1932, Classics 546.
1932–1934, Classics 535.
1934–1937, Classics 527.
1937–1938, Classics 519.
Horace and Fletcher Henderson, 1940–1941, Classics 648.

LOUIS ARMSTRONG (1901–1971)

The Fountainhead

In its infancy, jazz was primarily a New Orleans fascination. But as it began to spread rapidly a leader was needed, someone with the skill and personality to sell the music to the American populace and around the globe. The messiah appeared on the scene ready to conquer the world and assume his role as the fountainhead of jazz. His name was Louis Armstrong.

Louis Daniel Armstrong was born August 4, 1901, in New Orleans, Louisiana. While Armstrong would be known internationally by the time of his death in 1971, no one could have predicted that kind of fame, given his humble beginnings. He was born in the poorest section of New Orleans and sang on the street for whatever spare change he could make. His life was further thrown into chaos when at the age of twelve during a New Year Eve's celebration when Armstrong, adding his own touch to the festivities, shot off a pistol and was caught and put in a home for delinquent youth. Perhaps the incident was a blessing in disguise, because it was while in the place of detention that that he discovered his best friend, the cornet, which would lead him out of the life of abject poverty that he knew during his childhood.

He emerged from the juvenile home armed with his cornet and ready to take on the world. He began his musical career playing all over New Orleans, paying his dues and biding his time. Eventually, he caught his first break when he joined Kid Ory's band on a recommendation by King Oliver. Oliver, who had a sharp eye for talent, was ensuring that the future cornet player was developing properly. After four years in Ory's band, Armstrong was summoned to Chicago to be in Oliver's Creole Jazz Band. It was in King Oliver's band that Armstrong began to make his mark on the world of jazz. The Creole Jazz Band was the top act of the era and played a ripping traditional New Orleans style of jazz, but it also left space for short, inspirational solos. It provided just enough room for Armstrong to flash his developing brilliance because by this time he had asserted himself as the top cornet player of the era. It was also as a member of Oliver's Creole Jazz Band that Armstrong was given his first chance to record.

Although he was quickly becoming the main attraction in Oliver's octet, Armstrong jumped groups and joined Fletcher Henderson's outfit in 1924 at the suggestion of Lil Henderson, who would become Louis' second of four wives. In Henderson's big band in New York, Armstrong directed the course of future jazz with his uncanny sense of rhythm and electrifying solos. He was instrumental in ensuring that New York would become the main center of jazz. Although he had made great strides in shaping the music while a member of Oliver's group, it was in Henderson's band that Satchmo really made an impact. He taught them how to swing, and jazz would never really be the same again. While not teaching Henderson and his bandmates to rock to the rhythm, Armstrong was playing behind the classic songs recorded by female blues singers Bessie Smith and Ma Rainey, which only furthered his appeal.

Even though he had greatly influenced those in Henderson's band and created the groundwork for the big band and swing era that would occur a few years after, Armstrong returned to Chicago where he joined Clarence Williams' Blue Five. It was while a member of the Blue Five that he was able to trade hot, sassy solos with the great Sidney Bechet. It seemed that no matter what project Armstrong participated in he was only adding to his all-star status.

In 1925, at the prime of his career, Armstrong organized his first band called the Hot Five. The group consisted of Johnny Dodds on clarinet, Kid Ory on trombone, Lil Armstrong on piano, Johnny St. Cyr on banjo, and Armstrong on trumpet after he had discarded the cornet for the modern version of the instrument. The band really cooked from the very start and during this period Armstrong managed to add many classics to his growing musical canon.

At the height of the jazz age Armstrong was the most important and most popular jazz figure, a remarkable feat considering that Duke Ellington, Fletcher Henderson, Johnny Dodds, King Oliver, Sidney Bechet, Bix Beiderbecke, Earl Hines, and dozens of other jazz giants were practicing their trade during the era. Armstrong was not only the greatest trumpeter and soloist, but he was also establishing his credentials as one of the most unique and recognizable voices in jazz. More than anyone else, Armstrong shaped the music, the attitude, and the feeling of the jazz era.

His Hot Five sessions were expanded to include Baby Dodds and the new group was christened the Hot Sevens. Louis and his band created some of the most incredible music in the history of civilization. By this point Armstrong's virtuosity was second to none and his influence on future musicians was undeniable.

In 1928, Armstrong progressed beyond his previous work by organizing a group that emphasized the dynamics between trumpeter Armstrong and piano player Earl Hines. This new concept enabled Armstrong to add a fistful of classic songs to his already impressive collection. The interchange between the two competitive fireball musicians set a new standard for others to follow.

Armstrong continued to stretch his creative muscle with each new project he tackled. While his Hot Five and Hot Seven groups were spectacular on record, their live performances were limited to one appearance. Instead, Armstrong was appearing with Erskine Tate's and Carroll Dickerson's groups in Chicago. Louis, who had been born with the gift of the showman, had matured into a first-class entertainer. Every night he gave the audience a taste of the Armstrong magic building upon one successful performance after another.

Satchmo, as he was affectionately called, delivered a plethora of jazz classics that extended the usual realm to include blues and pop songs. His enormous and various gifts allowed him to wear many hats in the decade of the 1930s, more so than the previous decade. While many musicians were out of work during the Great Depression, Armstrong was continuously involved in one project after another. His two stints in Europe in 1932 and 1934, respectively, established his fame across the Atlantic. His name became synonymous with the word jazz.

However, despite his stature, Armstrong was considered old news by the early 1940s as the bebop movement turned the jazz world upside down. Yet he didn't allow this criticism to derail his ambitions. He continued to blow his trumpet with great confidence and expanded his legend by appearing in movies, on stage, on radio, and in recording studios. In 1947, he formed the All-Stars, a sextet that featured quality musicians such as trombonist Jack Teagarden, clarinetist Barney Bigard, and his old friend Earl Hines on piano. The group toured extensively and it was this format that Armstrong practiced for the rest of his career.

Despite the harsh criticism that the All-Stars show was nothing more than a circus act, Armstrong continued to do what he did best: entertain people. He played hard-driving Dixieland and swing standards, joked around with the audience, and remained one of the mainstays in jazz. Although the personnel in his All-Stars would change over the years (Hines, Teagarden, and Bigard all eventually left, replaced by Trummy Young and Edmond Hall, among others), they carried on. Satchmo also teamed up with many of the biggest names in jazz, including Ella Fitzgerald, and enjoyed continued commercial success. In 1967, he had a number one hit with "What a Wonderful World."

By the time of his death Armstrong had reached complete legendary status. He was a household name to many people who had never heard him play and didn't even like jazz. On July 6, 1971, in New York City, Louis Armstrong, the colorful, comedic, larger than life figure, died. It was an international day of mourning. His death was not only a blow and a loss to the world of jazz, but to the entire musical community.

Louis Armstrong was a fountainhead of jazz. His stature continued to grow long after his passing. One of the truly great musical personalities of the twentieth century, he possessed a rare combination of instrumental and comedic talent, charisma, and compositional and vocal ability. His magic transcended musical, racial, and cultural barriers. His contributions to jazz and to the international world of music were many.

Louis Armstrong was the king of the trumpeters. While many fine fellow trumpet players were stars before him, and there have been many great trumpeters who followed him, none matched his unique, individual talent. His sharp, piercing solos set the standards that all modern jazz is built on. No matter the style, or the era, there is a little bit of Satchmo's playing in every jazz trumpeter.

Although he was not the first soloist to record, Armstrong developed the parameters for soloists that many tried to copy but none could match. His efforts propelled the music from an ensemble format to one featuring star soloists and improvisation, two cornerstones of jazz. In his prime Armstrong's power could not be matched. Of all the early cornet players, Louis stands out as the king of them all.

Armstrong was first and foremost a bluesman. His understanding of blues textures was second to none. But where Blind Lemon Jefferson turned right with his blues efforts, Armstrong turned left. He expressed the blues in his own inimitable style. Many of his songs were blues sharpened to a fine point with his potent, stinging trumpet solos. While many of the early blues singers used the guitar as their main musical voice, Armstrong used the horn.

He was also instrumental in laying down the foundation for the big band and swing sound that would explode in the 1930s. No one could ever deny that Armstrong was incapable of swinging. His knowledge of rhythmic structures and his inborn ability to hear the beat in his head was pure musical genius. He taught a generation of jazzmen to swing. He released the music from the confining staccato rhythms that had characterized the genre since its birth.

But his musical prowess did not end with his accomplished musicianship. He was also one of the great vocal talents in jazz and his sound is instantly recognizable. His gravelly, friendly tone pulled at heartstrings. He was one of the first scat singers blurting out rapid-fire nonsense syllables in an attempt keep up to the fast-paced music. In one hundred years of jazz his singing ability has been matched by only a handful of performers including Billie Holiday, Ella Fitzgerald, Sarah Vaughan, Frank Sinatra, and Bing Crosby, all of whom were greatly influenced by Armstrong.

The combination of his singing and musical talent allowed Armstrong to give the world a treasure chest full of classic songs. They include "Cornet Chop Suey," "You're Next," "Mabel's Dream," "Canal Street Blues," "Riverside Blues," "Snake Rag," "Tars," "Buddy's Rabbit," "Chattanooga Stomp (West End Blues)," "How Come You Do Me the Way You Do?," "Shanghai Shuffle," "Alabamy Bound," "Copenhagen," "Heebie Jeebies," "Jazz Lips," "Skid-Da-De-Dat," "Gut Bucket Blues," "Twelfth Street Rag," "Struttin, with Some Barbecue," "I'm a Ding Dong Daddy," "Stardust," "Wrap Your Troubles in Dreams," "Hello Dolly," "What a Wonderful World," "Swing That Music," "Mack the Knife," "Blueberry Hill," and countless others.

Armstrong was one of the first jazz musicians to use television to increase his popularity. He conquered Hollywood and appeared in a number of movies including *Rhapsody in Black and Blue*, *Copenhagen Kalundborg*, *Pennies from Heaven*, *Artists and Models*, *Cabin in the Sky*, *Atlantic City*, *Pillow to Post*, *New Orleans*, *A Song Is Born*, *The Strip*, *The Glenn Miller Story*, *High Society*, *Satchmo the Great!*, *Jazz on a Summer's Day*, *The Five Pennies*, *Paris Blues*, *A Man Called Adam*, and *Hello Dolly*.

He was an international star and dubbed "America's Goodwill Ambassador." He toured the entire planet, bringing his unique music to different generations during his career, and in doing so, influenced hundreds of future musicians who would eventually make their mark in jazz. Just a partial list includes Lester Bowie, Clifford Brown, Art Farmer, Lionel Hampton, Terumasa Hino, Harry James, Cecil Taylor, Jack Walrath, Kenny Baker, Phil Wilson, Howard McGhee, Coleman Hawkins, Wild Bill Davison, Doc Cheatham, and Tommy Dorsey.

Louis Armstrong remains entrenched in the hearts and minds of generations of people all over the world. The enormous gift of music that poured from the very depths of his soul is beyond remarkable. Undoubtedly he was the fountainhead of jazz and there will never be another musician like him.

Discography

Louis Armstrong, Vol. 1, 1923, Masters of Jazz 1.
Louis Armstrong, Vol. 2, 1923–1924, Masters of Jazz 2.
Louis Armstrong, Vol. 3, 1924, Masters of Jazz 21.
Louis Armstrong, Vol. 4, 1924–1925, Masters of Jazz 26.
Louis Armstrong, Vol. 5, 1925, Masters of Jazz 38.
Louis Armstrong, Vol. 6, 1925, Masters of Jazz 55.
Louis Armstrong, Vol. 7, 1925, Masters of Jazz 94.
Louis Armstrong, Vol. 8, 1925–1926, Masters of Jazz 162.
Louis Armstrong, Hot Fives and Sevens, JSP 100.
Louis Armstrong, Hot Fives and Sevens, Vol. 1, JSP 312.
Louis Armstrong, Hot Fives and Sevens, Vol. 2, JSP 313.
Louis Armstrong, Hot Fives and Sevens, Vol. 3, 1928–1929, JSP 314.
Louis Armstrong, Hot Fives and Sevens, Vol. 4, 1929–1930, JSP 315.
Thanks a Million 1935–1940, AVD 574.
Great Original Performances: 1923–1931, LRHR 618.
Louis' Love Songs 1929–1947, LRHR 640.
Satchmo at Symphony Hall, GRD 661.
Blues For Yesterday 1940s, AVD 670.
Volume 9 1944–1949, AMD 1909.
1944–1946, Classic 928.
1946–1947, Classic 992.
October 6, 1944, Can 1019.
Musical Autobiography: Vol. 1, 1956–1957, STC 2003.
Musical Autobiography: Vol. 2, 1947–1957, STC 2004.
20 Golden Pieces, BDL, 2007.
West End Blues, 1926–1933, Ind 2035.
Louis Sings, Armstrong Plays 1935–1942 JASM 2547.
The Big Band Recordings, 1930–1932, JSP 3401.
V-Disc Recordings, CCM 4510.
Mahogany Hall Stomp, ASL 5049.
25 Greatest Hot Fives & Sevens, ASL 5171.
Pops: The 1940's Small Band Sides, BLED 6738.
Best of the Decca Years, Vol. 1-The Singer, MCA 31346.
The Katanga Concert, 1960 Mi 35908.
The Hot Fives, Vol. 1, Sony 44049.

The Hot Fives & Hot Sevens, Vol. 2, Sony 44253.
The Hot Fives & Hot Sevens, Vol. 3, Sony 44422.
Louis Armstrong & Earl Hines, Vol. 4 1927–1928, Sony 45142.
Louis In New York Vol. 5 1929, Sony 46148.
St. Louis Blues V.6 1929–1930, Sony 46996.
West End Blues—The Very Best of the Hot Fives & Sevens, MCI 50134.
Satchmo the Great 1955–1956, Sony 53580.
Portrait of the Artist as a Young Man, 1923–1934, Sony 57176.
The Complete Hot Fives & Sevens 1925–1928, Sony 63527.
100th Birthday Celebration 1932–1947, RCA 63694.
Plays W.C. Handy 1954, Sony 64925.
Satch Plays Fats, Sony 64927.
Louis Armstrong at Town Hall 1947, Jazz 66541.
The Complete Victor Recordings 1932–1956, Victor 68682.
Swing That Music!, EPM 157312.
Masterpieces Vol. 1, EPM 158132.
West End Blues 1926–1933, EPM 158722.
Back O'Town Blues, 1939–1945, EPM 158732.
The Glorious Big Band Years 1937–1941, EPM 159752.
The Ultimate Collection, 1920s–1960s, Verve 543699.
Satchmo Serenades 1949–1953, Verve 543792.
Louis Armstrong & His Hot Five, 1925–1926, Classic 600.
Louis Armstrong & His Hot Five 1926–1927, Classic 585.
Louis Armstrong & His Orchestra 1928–1929, Classic 570.
Louis Armstrong & His Orchestra 1929–1930, Classic 557.
Louis Armstrong & His Orchestra 1930–1931, Classic 547.
Louis Armstrong & His Orchestra 1931–1932, Classic 536.
Louis Armstrong & His Orchestra 1934–1936, Classic 509.
Louis Armstrong & His Orchestra 1936–1937, Classic 512.
Louis Armstrong & His Orchestra 1937–1938, Classic 515.
Louis Armstrong & His Orchestra 1938–1939, Classic 523.
Louis Armstrong & His Orchestra 1939–1940, Classic 615.
Louis Armstrong & His Orchestra 1940–1942, Classic 685.
Louis Armstrong and His All Stars 1947, Classic 1072.
Louis Armstrong's All Stars, Basin Street Blues—In Concert 1956–1957,
     GJM 9007.
Louis Armstrong/Dukes of Dixieland 1959, LSRJ 1052.

EDDIE LANG (1902–1933)

Hot Strings

In the early jazz outfits the brass horns dominated the sound and the rhythm makers were regulated to a lesser role. However, in the 1920s, when jazz took on a more modern shape, other instruments assumed a larger role in the music. One result was that the guitar became more prominent. The first guitarist to make a serious impact had no predecessor and therefore was forced to write the book on jazz guitar. He did just that with his hot strings. His name was Eddie Lang.

Eddie Lang was born Salvatore Massaro on October 25, 1902, in Philadelphia, Pennsylvania, into a musical family of sorts. His father was a maker of banjos and guitars. However, Lang's first instrument of choice was the violin, which he began to study at the age of seven. It was in grammar school that Lang met his best friend, Joe Venuti, a violin player. The friendship would last for the rest of their lives.

Joe Venuti was born in Italy, in 1899, but moved to Philadelphia when a youngster. Lang and Venuti practiced long hours together on their violins trading licks and unlocking the mysteries of music. Since the violin was relatively unheard of in jazz, the two listened to classical music. Lang studied under a couple of professors who armed him with the basis of a formal education in harmony, chords, and melody.

Since the two had grown up together they were keen on working as a unit and caught their first big break when they landed a gig with Bert Estlow's quintet in Atlantic City. The two city boys enjoyed the adventure and were eager for more musical experiences. It was around this time that Lang abandoned his violin in favor of the four-string, then the six-string guitar and the banjo. Finally he concentrated solely on the guitar. Although the guitar was not a prime force in jazz circles Lang was determined to make it one.

Lang's next gig was with Charlie Kerr's orchestra where he played guitar behind Venuti's violin. The dynamic and intricate interplay of the pair, who had been practicing together for years, was a sensation. There was plenty of work for them and they were favorites in Atlantic City where they often performed. In the winter of 1923, Lang joined Billy Lustig's Scranton Sirens. Six months later he joined The Mound City Blue Blowers, an experimental band from St. Louis. The quartet included Red

McKenzie on comb, Dick Slevin on kazoo and Jack Bland on banjo. The group had scored a hit with "Arkansas Blues." The Mound City Blue Blowers played many places in New York and later traveled to England. In Great Britain, Lang treated audiences to his unique developing jazz guitar style.

Lang recorded with the Blue Blowers in 1924, adding another dimension to their limited sound. It was on cuts like "Deep Second Street Blues," "Play Me Slow," "Tiger Rag," and "Getting Together" that his highly personalized sound shined through so clearly. He was beginning to gain some attention. He would remain with the Blue Blowers throughout most of 1925 including on dates in Atlantic City that also included his boyhood pal Joe Venuti.

But Lang matured beyond what the Blue Blowers could do and left them in the fall of 1925. Because of his distinct guitar sound that was revolutionary for the times, recording offers were plentiful. He earned a nice living doing radio and studio work where his partners included Red Nichols, Miff Mole and Jimmy Dorsey. On many of these cuts his guitar was featured as a solo instrument. Although he was a master of laying down chunky chords, he also had developed a large amount of single note runs that no one else was playing at the time.

In 1926, Lang and Venuti played on their first album together called *Stringin' the Blues*. Lang was also playing sessions with Earl Carroll's Vanities, Roger Wolfe Kahn's group, and Jean Goldkette's band. He was much in demand and was never short of work. But one of the most important sessions that Lang played on was in 1926–27 with Red Nichols and the Five Pennies. The group consisted of Nichols on clarinet, Vic Berston on drums, Jimmy Dorsey on alto saxophone, Arthur Schutt on piano, and Miff Mole on trombone.

More recording dates came his way in 1927 as he teamed with the legendary Bix Beiderbecke. Bix and Lang were for a short time in the Adrian Rollini band. Lang, along with Venuti, played in Paul Whiteman's orchestra briefly. But the talented jazz guitarist could make much more money as a hired gun than working within a group context. He continued recording duets with Venuti at the time as well as cutting records with bluesman Lonnie Johnson. In the 1920s, Johnson and Lang were the two big name guitarists. But while Johnson was more blues Lang was more jazz.

Lang continued his hectic pace in 1928. He appeared live with the Venuti-Lang quartet, and recorded with the top jazzmen of the era including Jack Teagarden, Louis Armstrong, and pianist Joe Sullivan. He was also recording under the pseudonym Blind Willie Dunn and backed such blues singers as Bessie Smith, Victoria Spivey and Texas Alexander. The years 1927–1929 were Lang's halcyon days when he earned enormous amounts of money (for the times) and created the definite jazz guitar sound.

In 1929, Land and Venuti returned to the Paul Whiteman Orchestra and remained there for a year. It was during his stay with Whiteman that Lang played behind some of the era's greatest singers including Mildred Bailey and a young crooner named Bing Crosby. Lang and Crosby became fast friends and soon the former was backing the singer on a steady basis. Lang also appeared in the movie *The Big Broadcast.*

Lang was also involved in other projects, including recording sessions with the Boswell Sisters, a group whose singing style set the precedent for all vocal trios, quartets, and quintets that performed with the big bands. He also performed with the Venuti-Lang All-Star Orchestra, whose members included Jack Teagarden and Benny Goodman.

By 1933, he was in his prime. During the past seven years he had established a reputation as one of the greatest jazz musicians with his influential guitar work that was far ahead of anyone else in jazz, with the possible exception of Lonnie Johnson. Despite the hard days of the Depression, Lang's partnership with Bing Crosby and Venuti enabled him to continue working.

When Lang developed a sore throat it was thought to be a routine malady. But, being somewhat suspicious of doctors and hospitals, he refused treatment for his ailment. Eventually he did consult a doctor who insisted that he needed a tonsillectomy. Eddie Lang, virtuoso guitarist extraordinaire, died on the operating table on March 26, 1933, in New York City.

Eddie Lang was a jazz pioneer. He proved that the guitar could be used effectively as a band instrument as well as a mighty solo weapon. He also demonstrated how the guitar could be used to accompany singers as well as—and in some instances even better than—the piano. His sense of intricate chord arrangements and his excellent solos inspired generations of guitar players in jazz as well as other styles of music.

In many ways, Lang along with Lonnie Johnson, was one of the first guitar heroes long before the term was ever coined. The Lang style—the elegantly picked single note runs, precise and inventive chord patterns, and distinctive rhythmic style—has been copied a thousand times over. Although influenced by classical music, Lang invented his own rich tapestry of sound that echoed throughout the decades.

In an era that featured many good guitarists, including Lonnie Johnson, Blind Lemon Jefferson, and Teddy Bunn, Lang stood out because of his keen ear and superior powers of invention. Lang was also more technically advanced than his contemporaries, capable of playing a greater number of complex chord combinations and more brilliant solo runs. He often sounded like a room full of guitarists.

His influence on future guitarists as well as on the role of the guitar in jazz is phenomenal. Three immediate disciples of Lang were Karl Cress (whom Lang recorded with), Dick McDonough, and George Van Eps. All three used the Lang guitar style on which to build their own careers. Van Eps would later play with Benny Goodman. Al Casey and the Texan Oscar Moore also appreciated Lang's genius. During the swing era, Freddie Green, who starred with the Count Basie Band, incorporated many of Lang's ideas into his own style. Other swing guitarists such as Eddie Condon, Tiny Grimes, Les Paul and Chuck Wayne owe a debt to Lang.

The greatest of the swing era guitarists, Charlie Christian, the brilliant virtuoso, shares many musical characteristics with Lang. Both died young, but before they did left a body of work that inspired generations. Christian started from Lang's blueprint of jazz guitar and extended the parameters to include longer solos mixed with complex and rhythmic variations. In turn, Christian had a large influence on the bop guitarists Barney Kessel, Herb Ellis, and Kenny Burrell. The Christian influence on these players can be traced to Lang's guitar vocabulary.

Later virtuosos like Wes Montgomery, George Benson, Tad Farlow, Gabor Szabo, and fusioneers Larry Coryell, Al Dimeola, John McLaughlin, Pat Metheny, and John Scofield were jazz guitarists who studied Lang closely and expanded on his original musical statements. Any of the new generation of jazz guitarists—including Mark Whitfield—have proved the powerful influence of Lang by incorporating many of his phrases into their own.

Although Lang never had the chance to plug in (sadly, he didn't live long enough for that to happen), he was an inspiration to many who did including blues guitarists T-Bone Walker, B. B. King, and later on, rockers like Chuck Berry, Bo Diddley, Keith Richards, Jeff Beck and the entire rock brethren. Undoubtedly, Lang is the guitar fountainhead of jazz and his unique elements of style were carried over into the blues and rock universe.

Lang recorded many jewels and left behind a superb catalog of classic songs. A partial list includes: "That's No Bargain," "Singin' the Blues," "For No Reason at All in C," "Sleepy Time Gal," "Lonesome Gal in Town," "No More Worryin'," "Black and Blue Bottom," "Washboard Blues," "Get a Load of This," "Cornfed," "Riverboat Shuffle," "I'd Climb the Highest Mountain," "Eddie's Twister," "Perfect," "Rainbow Dreams," "I'll Never be the Same," "Church Street Sobbin' Blues," "There'll Be Some Changes Made," "Bugle Call Rag," and "Walkin' the Dog." Many of these songs were recorded with his boyhood pal Joe Venuti as well as with Jack Teagarden, Louis Armstrong, Red Nichols, Lonnie Johnson, and a host of others.

It has been almost seventy years since Eddie Lang's untimely death and the role and sound of the jazz guitar has greatly changed since then. But no matter if it is acid jazz, free jazz, jazz-fusion, avant-garde, hard bop, cool jazz, blues or rock, the guitar elements that Lang created remain prevalent. The man responsible for his hot strings left an indelible impact on the entire musical world.

Discography

Stringin' the Blues, Columbia C-2124.
Jazz Guitar, Yazoo 1059.
Handful of Riffs, ASV/Living Era 5061.
Quintessential, Timeless 1043.
Pioneers of Jazz Guitar 1927–1938, Challenge 79015.
Blue Guitars, Vol. 1–2, BGO 327.
Joe Venuti/Eddie Lang (1926–1933), ABC 836200.
Violin Jazz (1927–1934), Yazoo 1062.
The Golden Day of Jazz: Eddie Lang–Joe Venuti Stringing the Blues, Koch 7888.
Joe Venuti/Eddie Lang, Vol. 1 & 2, 1920s and 1930s Sides, JSP 3402.

BIX BEIDERBECKE (1903–1931)

Singin' the Blues

The early days of jazz are replete with the exploits of the genre's pioneers. It is the storied material that created legends of many of the initial performers. One cornetist who did much to color the history of jazz was more interested in singin' the blues then creating a legacy. His name was Bix Beiderbecke.

Bix Beiderbecke, the first important jazz musician not from New Orleans, was born Leon Beiderbecke on March 10, 1903, in Davenport, Iowa. His mother was a pianist and his father was a merchant in Iowa. From the onset, it was apparent that Bix was a special musical talent with an incredible ear. As a young boy he would recreate note for note the songs that he heard his mother play. Because music came to him so easily, he never developed proper work habits, and that would haunt him later in his professional life. He was also a difficult student to teach musically since he memorized the lessons instead of learning to read them.

In high school, Bix was transfixed by the sound of the Original Dixieland Jazz Band and their early recordings. He also acquired a cornet, the instrument he would make his mark with in jazz. Although many cornetists would switch to the trumpet in the twenties, Beiderbecke never did.

Despite his love of music his parents were not impressed with his choice of career paths and he was dispatched to Lake Forest Military Academy in order to save his sagging high school career. Luckily for Beiderbecke and unfortunately for his parents, the academy was situated close to Chicago, then one of the prime centers for the emerging jazz sound. Like later rebel Miles Davis, Bix spent more time tracking the jazz sounds around the various nightclubs than attending to his scholarly studies. The result was his expulsion from the academy.

While still at the academy Beiderbecke formed a group with Cy Welge, dubiously named the Cy-Bix band. They played gigs around the area and at school functions. Bix garnered a solid reputation as a fine player. Although he learned a lot from the trumpet players of the day including Nick LaRocca (from the Original Dixieland Jazz Band) and others like Leon Rapollo of the New Orleans Rhythm Kings, it was obvious that Bix had his own distinctive sound.

After his expulsion from Lake Forest, Bix paid his dues as a musician traveling to New York and then working on a touring boat job with leader Bill Grimm. The itinerant life of the jazz musician was something Bix could not get enough of and he eventually found himself in a group called the Wolverines that included George Johnson on tenor sax, Jimmy Hartwell on clarinet, Dick Voynow on piano, Bob Gillette on banjo, Min Leibrook on tuba, and Vic Morre on drums. It was with the Wolverines that Bix made his initial recordings for the Gennett label in Richmond, Indiana, in 1924.

One of these songs from this session, "Jazz Me Blues," began to draw attention and opened up concert dates for the band. Bix was singled out as the most talented member of the outfit. However, despite an increased working schedule and two more recording dates, all was not well with the Wolverines. It was obvious that Bix had grown beyond the abilities of the other members of the band. After an engagement in New York, Bix left the group.

After a brief stint back in Iowa, where he naturally incurred the anger and disappointment of his parents, Bix left the farmland of Iowa for the big city and bright lights of Chicago. In 1925, he spent a brief time in

Jean Goldkette's band but was released because of his poor ability to read music. It wasn't until the fall of 1925 that Bix found a steady gig with Frankie Trumbauer.

Trumbauer was born on May 30, 1901, in Carbondale, Illinois. He caught his first break when he was spotted playing in Chicago Benson's Band by Beiderbecke and joined Jean Goldkette's orchestra. Trum paid his dues and developed into the supreme white saxophonist of the 1920s. Eventually he led his own outfit but not before spending some time in Paul Whiteman's band. Together, they cut some of the definitive classics of the decade. Eventually Trum fell out of favor in the late 1950s, but he played an integral part in the story of Bix Beiderbecke.

After a year in St. Louis Bix and Trum returned to Chicago and joined Goldkette's band. It was by this time—1926—that jazz had truly shed its early New Orleans skin and had adopted a more explosive sound. The soloist was the focus of the band and three men helped pave the way for this innovation—Louis Armstrong, Sidney Bechet, and Bix Beiderbecke.

Beiderbecke had grown as a musician and had reached his creative zenith. The heights he scaled owed a debt to Bill Challis who scored the arrangements for Goldkette. Challis took an immediate shine to Bix and understood his unbridled genius and wrote sections that allowed the hot cornet player to flex his full creative muscles. Goldkette's string band included a wealth of talented artists like guitarist Eddie Lang, Trumbauer, violinist Joe Venuti, and reedman Don Murray. Before leaving the band, Bix made several memorable recordings often in a small group setting with Trumbauer and Lang; the arrangements were most often supplied by Challis.

In the fall of 1927, Goldkette could no longer keep his outfit together. Bix joined Adrian Rollini in New York for a brief period but that venture also proved to be unfeasible. Beiderbecke rejoined Paul Whiteman's orchestra, which was at the time one of the most prestigious in the business. Bix loved the attention he received as the prime soloist and recorded many unforgettable tracks. He was at the height of his fame and on top of the jazz world.

Before taking up with Whiteman, Beiderbecke recorded six sides for Okeh. The session group included Bill Rank on trombone, Don Murray on clarinet, Chauncy Morehouse on drums, Frank Signorelli on piano and Rollini on bass saxophone. The songs they cut included "At the Jazz Band Ball," "Royal Garden Blues," a reprise of "Jazz Me Blues," "Goose Pimples," "Sorry," and "Since My Best Gal Turned Me Down." These selections demonstrated Bix at his very best.

Although he would spend two years with Whiteman, Bix never made the same impact as he had before. His playing leveled off and he began his descent. Beiderbecke, a chronic alcoholic, suffered a breakdown in the late fall of 1928. He moved to Iowa for a few months in order to work himself back into playing shape. Upon his return in February of 1929, the frantic pace of recording, radio shows, and concerts once again took their toll on his worn out body. It was a difficult time for Bix but he proved that he still had the old magic on the recording of "China Boy." However his hectic lifestyle had finally caught up with him.

Bix attempted many comebacks. After leaving the Whiteman band in October of 1929, he returned to Iowa for the winter. In the spring of 1930, Bix arrived in New York in decent physical condition, but just as the economic woes of the nation had literally destroyed the music business. There was little work for him, although he did record a few solo sides; however, much of the magic of his playing was gone.

Bix spent the winter of 1930–31 in Iowa and returned to New York the following spring to revive his sagging career. But nothing he tried worked and he was a shell of his former self. He talked of forming his own group and touring Europe, but his body was worn out and his soul was old. The great Bix Beiderbecke died from pneumonia on August 6, 1931, in New York. He was just twenty-eight.

Bix Beiderbecke is a jazz legend. He epitomized the image of the carefree musician of the Roaring Twenties. He was like a comet in the sky, his career brief, but powerful; one moment he was the hottest cornetist in jazz, the next moment he was gone. Factoids about his life were commonplace and already wildly exaggerated long before his death. But beyond his hard drinking, womanizing, and fast ways, he was a very talented musician who left a permanent stamp on jazz.

Bix Beiderbecke impacted jazz in four major ways. Arguably, he was the first modernist in jazz because of his attitude towards the music and his method of playing. It was Bix who opened the portal for all innovators who would follow in the later years. Red Nichols, Miff Mole, Eddie Lang, Vic Berton, Fud Livingstone, Adrian Rollini, Frank Trumbauer, and Pee Wee Russell, who were inspired mostly by Beiderbecke's improvisations, influenced many of the modernists. Teddy Wilson had great admiration for Red Nichols, and in turn, Wilson made a serious impact on modern jazz pianists. Trumbauer and Russell had a special effect on Lester Young, who in turn was the idol of Charlie Parker. Beiderbecke's influence had a spin off effect on numerous musicians in every decade after his death.

Beiderbecke's extensive use of the ballad style of playing cornet had a direct impact on Pee Wee Russell, Bobby Hackett (an important influence on Dizzy Gillespie), Bud Freeman, Bunny Berigan, Lester

Young, Gerry Mulligan, Paul Desmond and Miles Davis. Of course, Miles Davis is the most important trumpet player of the modern school of jazz, which includes cool, fusion and electric jazz.

Beiderbecke's revitalization of the Dixieland art has continued to fuel modern jazz. Eddie Condon, Joe Sullivan, Frank Teschemaker, Bud Freeman, Rod Cless, Dave Tough, Jess Stacy, George Wettling, Jimmy McPartland, and Pee Wee Russell were some who picked up where Bix left off. The evolved style of Dixieland-swing that Bix played with such brilliance can still be heard in the music of modern artists eighty years after the fact.

The fourth great influence that Bix cast over jazz was his individualistic style, which became an audio-bible for all interested students. Bill Davison, Jimmy McPartland, Andy Secrest, Doc Evans, Brad Gowans, Joe Rushton, Rex Stewart, Yank Lawson and Bud Freeman are just some of the jazz names that went through a Bix period before finding their own distinct voices.

If it had not been for Louis Armstrong, Beiderbecke would have been easily declared the greatest cornet player of the rip roaring twenties. He had a direct approach to the instrument and his concentration on the middle range was in direct opposition to others who worked on the high squeaks and low rumbles. His hot solos contained poetic overtones; he crafted brilliant improvisations that were supremely logical in development and, most of all, lyrical. No one had heard that kind of sound produced from the cornet before and his unique style enthralled both black and white musicians.

His beautifully sculptured solos made him one of the leading lights of the Chicago Jazz School. In fact, along with King Oliver, Louis Armstrong, Jimmy Noone, Red Nichols, Johnny Dodds, Baby Dodds, Pops Foster, Jelly Roll Morton, and Sidney Bechet, Beiderbecke helped shift the emphasis of the jazz scene from New Orleans to Chicago in the 1920s.

But Beiderbecke was more than just the most brilliant white cornetist of the era blowing hot solos. His innovative musical arrangements were more intricate than those that existed at the time and were soon adopted by some of the composers of the era including Fletcher Henderson. In turn, Henderson had a huge influence on jazz for twenty years and wrote for Benny Goodman, "the king of swing." Beiderbecke had an indirect hand in the creation of the swing style that focused on complex group arrangements. Unfortunately he didn't live long enough to see it or to reap the rewards of his genius.

Although he made his greatest mark as a cornetist, Beiderbecke also created clever compositions for piano. His vision would later resurface in the works of Hoagy Carmichael and Marian McPartland. But more importantly, the threads of his melodic impressionistic pieces would be adopted later on by members of the cool style of jazz including Miles Davis. Even guitarist Eddie Condon was touched by the unique piano sound displayed by Beiderbecke.

Bix gave the world a great number of songs that will forever keep his name inscribed in the pages of jazz history. A partial list includes: "Wringin' & Twistin'," "For No Reason at All in C," "Singin' the Blues," "In a Mist," "I'm Coming, Virginia," "Jazz Me Blues," "Since My Best Gal Turned Me Down," "You Took Advantage of Me," "Changes," "There Ain't No Sweet Man Worth the Salt of My Tears," "Love Nest," and "Dardanella."

The Bix legend has been told and retold in books and in movies. *The Stardust Road, We Called It Music, Frontiers of Jazz, A Bio-Discography of Bix Beiderbecke, Kings of Jazz: Bix Beiderbecke, Trumpet on the Wing, Really the Blues, Jazzmen, The Jazz Makers,* and *Bugles for Beiderbecke* are just some of the books that made the man larger than life.

After his death tributes poured forth and many bands were formed for the sole purpose of playing his music and carrying on the spirit of Bix. Despite his personal troubles, without a doubt, Bix Beiderbecke, the white Midwest boy, left an indelible mark on the world of jazz while singin' the blues.

Discography

And the Chicago Cornets, Milestone MCD-47019-2.
Bix Beiderbecke, Milestone M 47019-2.
Singin' the Blues, Drive Archives 41068.
The Indispensable, RCA 66540.
Bix Beiderbecke, Vol. 2, Riverside RLP-1050.
Bix Beiderbecke and the Wolverines, Timeless 013.
Bix Beiderbecke, Vol. 1: Singin' the Blues, Columbia 45450.
Bix Beiderbecke, Vol. 2: At the Jazz Band Ball, Columbia 46175.
Bix Lives! RCA 6845.
Giants of Jazz, Time-Life STL J04.
Bixology, 1924–30, Joker 71/14.
The Complete Bix Beiderbecke, Everest 317.
Early Bix, Riverside RLP-1023.
The Bix Beiderbecke Story, Vol. 2: Bix and Trum, Columbia CL 845.
The Bix Beiderbecke Story, Vol. 1: Bix and his Gang, Columbia CL 507.
The Bix Beiderbecke Legend, RCA 2323.
The Legendary Bix Beiderbecke, Riverside 8810.
The Bix Beiderbecke Story, Vol. 3, Columbia CL 509.

Great Original Performances: 1924–1930, Louisiana Red Hot 620.
Bix Beiderbecke, Vol. 1, 1924–1926, Masters of Jazz 6.
Bix Beiderbecke, Vol. 2, 1927, Masters of Jazz 7.
Bix Beiderbecke, Vol. 3, 1927, Masters of Jazz 15.
Bix Beiderbecke, Vol. 4, 1927–1928, Masters of Jazz 16.
Bix Beiderbecke, Vol. 5, 1928, Masters of Jazz 28.
Bix Beiderbecke, Vol. 6, 1924–1926, Masters of Jazz 50.
Bix Beiderbecke, Vol. 7, 1928–1929, Masters of Jazz 65.
Bix Beiderbecke, Vol. 8, 1929–1939, Masters of Jazz 92.
Tiger Rag, MAGC 11.
Great Original Performances 1924–1930, LRHR 620.
1927–1930, Classic 788.
1924–1925, CBC 1013.
At the Jazz Band Ball 1924–1928, ASL 5080.
The Genius of Bix Beiderbecke, Pearl 9765.
At the Jazz Band Ball Vol. 2, 1927–1928, Sony 46175.
The Indispensable Bix Beiderbecke 1925–1930, JAZZ 66540.
Felix the Cat, EPM 157952.

EARL HINES (1903–1983)

Fatha's Sound

There are in every era a handful of musicians who draw attention to themselves because of their overpowering charisma as much as for their incredible musical ability. The pages of jazz history overflow with such irrepressible characters. However, during the Jazz Age, one piano player exceeded the popularity that was normally showered on the great ones by giving the world his Fatha's blues. His name was Earl Hines.

Earl Kenneth Hines was born on December 28, 1903, in Dusquesne, Pennsylvania. He grew up in a musical family; his mother was an organist, his father was a cornet player in local brass bands, and his sister, a pianist, led her own bands around the Pittsburgh area in the 1930s. One of his uncles was a multi-instrumentalist. Earl began on the cornet but switched to the piano at age nine after his mother had traded in her parlor organ for a piano. Hines was a keen student and made quick progress racing through songbooks with relative ease. His musical education also included a favorite aunt who took him to revues at the local theatre. At a young age, Hines had developed a taste for Czerny, Chopin and Debussy.

He majored in music in school and also played gigs around his hometown in a band he formed with a couple of friends. Eventually Hines quit school to pursue the life of a jazz man and caught his first big break when an area musician, Lois Deppe, discovered the young talent and hired him to be his accompanying pianist for a series of concerts scheduled at the Liederhouse in Pittsburgh. This experience, combined with an admiration for pianists Johnny Waters and Jim Fellman, was the last element in Hines' musical development.

Hines made a few recordings with Deppe in the early 1920s, appeared on radio and toured with him. Hines also played in Arthur Rideout's Orchestra—a job he secured through the recommendation of his former boss. A short time later Hines was leading the Pittsburgh Serenaders, a group Deppe had initially formed. It was while a member of violinist Vernie Robinson's quartet, which played in a club in Pittsburgh called the Elite #1, that Hines got another break. The owner of the club was excited with the band and decided that they would be perfect in Chicago at the Elite #2. So Robinson took his quartet to Chicago, a city with a burgeoning reputation as the hottest jazz center in the world in 1924.

Hines thrived in Chicago. Upon his arrival in the Windy City, the big name among piano players was Jelly Roll Morton. Other talented pianists at the time included Glover Compton and Teddy Weatherford. Hines was particularly taken with Weatherford and studied the performer until he had learned all of his tricks. Fatha, whose roots of piano playing were firmly in the East Coast tradition, was able to combine the lessons he took from Weatherford (a better use of his left hand) with his firm touch and technical superiority to quickly ascend the piano throne.

In 1925, Hines played at the Entertainer's Café with Carroll Dickerson's big band, a highly talented outfit that included trumpeter Natty Dominique, trombonist Honore Dutrey, and saxophonist Cecil Irwin. They were a tight group that toured throughout the States all the way to California before returning to the Windy City. Dickerson, a savvy bandleader, realized that Hines was quickly becoming the best piano player in the city.

It was only a matter of time before the most talented piano player in Chicago hooked up with the greatest trumpet player—Louis Armstrong. He received his chance when he started playing in Erskine Tate's group, which featured Armstrong. After leaving both Dickerson's and Tate's group, Hines joined the famous New Orleans trumpeter and his Stompers; Earl was elected as musical director. Hines also found time to work in the movie theatres where his powerful and elaborate piano skills were much in demand.

It was during this period that Hines led his first sessions. Although his initial recordings with Johnny Dodds as leader did not feature Fatha's best playing, a later engagement demonstrated a more comfortable performance where Earl cut "Chicago Breakdown." The song became a staple among all piano players.

In the fall of 1927, Hines, Armstrong and drummer Zutty Singleton opened a club together. Unfortunately neither was much of an entrepreneur and the venue was not a financial success. Although the three were keen on playing together and possessed a solid fan base, the competition in Chicago was so cutthroat that their business venture lasted less than a year.

Hines returned to New York for a brief spell, then made his way back to Chicago. When he arrived in the Windy City Armstrong and Singleton had joined Dickerson's band and there was no room for Hines. He found work with Jimmie Noone at the Apex Club and gave the clarinetist's band a dimension it hadn't previously possessed. Although Noone was from the old guard of New Orleans jazzmen, he readily accepted the new ideas that Hines introduced, which found their way into the recordings that the quintet made in 1928. Alto saxophonist Joe Poston, banjo player Bud Scott, drummer Johnny Wells, Hines and Noone were able to make exciting recordings by combining the best elements of New Orleans jazz and first rate musicianship into a highly entertaining style.

During his second stint in Chicago, Hines was the king of the piano players and was a serious influence on a new generation of young pianists that included Joe Sullivan, Jess Stacy, and Casino Simpson. The aspiring piano players hung around the Apex in order to watch their hero Hines in action. He provided them with a priceless musical education.

It was his reunion with Armstrong and Singleton, and the additions of trombonist Fred Robinson, clarinetist Jimmy Strong, and guitarist Mancy Cara that revealed Hines' mature sound. Many of the songs recorded during this session (on the Okeh label), such as "Fireworks," "Skip the Gutter," "Tiger Rag," "Sugar Foot Strut," "Squeeze Me," "Monday Date," and "West End Blues," were pure classics. The interplay between Armstrong and Hines was genuine jazz magic.

In the fall of 1928, Hines left the Noone band but there was no shortage of work. He recorded some fourteen sides with Armstrong and twelve piano solos, and debuted his own big band. Hines secured a residence at the Grand Terrace in Chicago and over the next decade became a permanent fixture at the club to the point that his group was called the Grand Terrace Band. Also by this time Hines' solo material (recorded in New York before his tenure at the Grand Terrace) proved his undeniable genius.

The Grand Terrace Band included trumpeters George Mitchell and Shirley Clay, trombonist William Franklin, saxophonist Cecil Irwin, tenor saxophonist Lester Boone, and Hines. The group developed a large following and recorded several sides for Victor. Everyone contributed arrangements and Hines' piano playing changed while in the group. He was given more freedom and was not forced to be the center of attention because of the talented sidemen in the band. Despite the economic crunch of the fall of 1929, Hines managed to keep his band together and expanded it to include twelve members by the early 1930s. Omar Simeon, Darrell Howard, Trummy Young, John Ewing, Ed Burke, Walter Fuller, Edward Sims, George Dixon, Jimmy Mundy, Budd Johnson, and Robert Crowder all spent time in Hines' band. Later, the addition of Alvin Burroughs on drums enabled Hines' outfit to swing hard and powerful like it had never done before.

The Earl Hines band's tenure at the Grand Terrace Ballroom became a jazz institution. Many jazz musicians made it a point to check out Earl's band when they swung through Chicago. Also, the group performed live on radio shows that were broadcasted throughout the country, which only increased its popularity. Sometimes the band featured singers like Ethel Waters and Bill "Mr. Bojangles" Robinson. In an era when many musicians were out of work, Hines and his group continued to record and perform.

In 1934, Hines began recording for Decca. He cut a number of songs including "Sweet Georgia Brown," "That's a Plenty," "Angry," "Maple Leaf Rag," "Copenhagen," and "Wolverine Blues." Although they proved to be successful, the songs were not a testament to the true talent of Hines and his band. But in the dark days when the music business was trying to get back on its feet, any musician was happy to make recordings even if it wasn't exactly what he wanted to do.

In 1936, the band's long stay at the Grand Terrace ended. Ever since they had started to broadcast over the radio the group's popularity had forced them to do more traveling. The dates were there and Hines, a weak businessman, felt that the work was necessary in order to survive. Eventually Fletcher Henderson's group replaced Hines' big band at the Grand Terrace. The defection of arranger Jimmy Mundy to the Benny Goodman band was a crucial blow to Fatha's fortunes.

The decline of the Earl Hines band can be traced to his errors as a manager. Also, Hines, still a powerful pianist, was being eclipsed by Teddy Wilson, the new reigning hero of the keyboard in 1937 and 1938. The fact that Wilson played with Benny Goodman, the hottest band in the land, certainly didn't hurt his reputation. Hines realized that he would have to rebuild his outfit in order to compete.

In 1940, Hines secured a contract with Bluebird and with the help of Budd Johnson began to retool his music to fit a different style. One of the new recruits was singer Billy Eckstine. One of the essential keys that separated Hines from others was his versatility and ability to adapt to new sounds while never losing his base. That year, while boogie-woogie was extremely popular, Hines took the best elements of this style and incorporated them in his playing, which resulted in a new sound for the band.

By 1941, Hines was recording new ideas, hinting at the musical explosion that would pit the old guard against the new cats in the near future. Much credit goes to Johnson who recruited some of the young players that had new ideas for the band. Between 1941 and 1943 Hines added Charlie Parker on tenor (not alto) saxophone, Dizzy Gillespie, Jerry Valentine, Freddie Webster, Shorts McConnell, Bennie Harris, Bernie Green, and the great singer Sarah Vaughan. Unfortunately, due to the ban on recording because of the union strike, the dynamics of this group were never fully realized on vinyl. Sadly, an entire chapter in jazz history was never recorded.

By 1944, Hines had decided to head in a different direction by creating a large orchestra lineup that included a string section. The experiment was short-lived as Hines reduced the band to seventeen members that included reedman Scoops Carry, trumpeter Willie Cook and tenor saxophonist Wardell Gray. Later he would add Cozy Cole and Charlie Shavers to the group that recorded a few sides for the Keynote label. This period also marked Hines recording with big names in jazz such as Coleman Hawkins, Jo Jones, and on one session for Apollo with Johnny Hodges, Oscar Pettiford, and Sidney Catlett.

Although he had featured some of the leading voices that would take the jazz world by storm, Hines was never able to fully enter the realm of bop. The harmonic, long melodic lines, rapid-fire articulation and rhythmic adventures of the bop world clashed with Hines' middle of the road approach. The result was a bland period in his career that proved commercially unsuccessful.

In 1947, Hines' last attempt at a big band failed and he retreated to the comfort of Louis Armstrong's All-Stars. He remained with Armstrong for four years and appeared on the following recordings: *Louis Armstrong, Vol. 2 & 3*, and *Satchmo at Symphony Hall, Vol. 1 & 2*. Although they had provided many musical memories in the 1920s, Armstrong and Hines were unable to rekindle the same kind of energy and fire of those bygone days.

Hines put together a new sextet in late 1951, but once again his lack of business sense doomed the group. They did enjoy a residency at Chicago's Terrace Club, his old stomping grounds, for a brief period, but a lack of recording dates hurt the band despite a talented lineup that included trumpeter Jonah Jones, Benny Green, bassist Tommy Potter, drummer Art Blakey, and reedman Aaron Sachs. In 1955, Hines spent a few months on the West Coast at San Francisco's Hangover Club. While bop and hard bop now dominated jazz, Hines was still pounding out swing and big band music to interested crowds, though the audiences were shrinking yearly. By the late 1950s he had fallen out of favor with much of the jazz crowd.

In 1957, Hines teamed with Jack Teagarden and together they toured Europe and were received enthusiastically. It was a triumphant Hines who returned to America having caught his second wind. He was once again ready to rock everyone with his inimitable Fatha's blues.

In the 1960s, musical tastes favored Hines and he took full advantage of it. While he had recorded at a steady pace, he had never been one of the most prolific artists in jazz history. However, this all changed when he began to be featured as a solo artist, which was always the best venue for him. Although he worked well in a group situation, Fatha was pure magic when it was just him at the piano. He also operated a dinner club in Oakland during the decade and traveled to the East Coast for concert dates.

He continued to reap the rewards of his newfound acceptance, appearing in a series of performances mostly on the West Coast where he had moved in 1960. Although he returned occasionally to New York for a series of engagements at places like the Little Theatre and Birdland in 1964, by this time he was considered a West Coast jazz artist. He also played dates all over the United States, in Europe and all over the world.

In 1965, he completed a successful tour of Europe. More impressively, in 1966 he ventured to Russia with his sextet—a feat that was rare considering the Communist ban on everything American. He returned to Europe in 1967 and in 1968 was featured at London's Jazz Expo. While across the Atlantic he swept through the continent, entertaining his faithful legions of fans. His most triumphant concert was his solo appearance at the 1974 Montreux Jazz Festival that brought the house down.

Hines, who had begun his recording career in 1928, recorded his last work in 1978—a span of fifty years. Sadly, five years later, the great Earl Hines, who had written his own chapter in jazz history, died in Oakland, California, on April 22, 1983. He was 79 years old.

Earl Hines was the first modern jazz pianist. A powerful musician with an uncanny sense of rhythm and melody, his ability never diminished significantly throughout his career. His talent was wide and deep and because of its immensity was in some ways never appreciated. There were so many sides to the Hines piano style that a complete array of his skills was never fully presented.

The Hines style was derived from the stride pianists of the early 1920s—James P. Johnson, Fats Waller, and Willie "The Lion" Smith. But he evolved from that style and took jazz piano into the modern era with his dexterity and technical improvisations. With his left hand, Hines broke up the very rhythms and unusual accents that were the basic foundation of stride. His magical left hand experimented with the rhythm of a song but he never lost the beat. It is simply the technique of a genius. His right hand produced quick and powerful runs up and down the keyboard that left everyone stunned. Although it appeared as if the hands worked independently from each other, they were in constant unison, producing one coherent sound with many rich layers.

Hines thought of the piano as a little trumpet and imitated the sound of a horn with his gifted hands. His right hand was able to capture the vibrato of a trumpet, and even imitate the single-note attack of piercing notes sounding something like a Louis Armstrong solo. Because of his unique approach to playing the piano, Hines created a myriad of ideas that were simply dazzling.

Hines influenced a variety of jazz artists including Claude Bolling, Milt Buckner, Erroll Garner, Stan Kenton, Eiji Kitamura, Dave McKenna, Jay McShann, Bud Powell, Hazel Scott, George Shearing, Art Tatum, Ross Tompkins, Lennie Tristano, Teddy Wilson, Mary Lou Williams, and Nat King Cole.

Hines gave the world a wealth of classics including "Rosetta," "My Monday Date," "You Can Depend on Me," "A Monday Date," "Blues in Thirds," "57 Varieties," "West End Blues," "Fireworks," "Basin Street Blues," and the timeless trumpet-piano duet with Louis Armstrong, "Weather Bird." Aside from his own compositions, Hines was also a master at putting his own stamp on the works of others. He performed cover versions of material penned by Duke Ellington, Fats Waller, George Gershwin, Harold Arlen, Andy Razaf, Spencer Williams, Gus Kahn, Louis Armstrong, W.C. Handy, Jimmy Mundy, Irving Mills, Charles Carpenter, Vincent Youmans, Ted Koehler, Henri Woode, Johnny Green, Roger Graham, Eddie DeLange, and Ned Washington, among others. Hines became as famous for playing his own songs as well as those written by others.

It is easy to say that Earl Hines touched everyone in jazz during his long reign. He was an original, an irrepressible musician who played the piano with a passion and a skill that remained constant throughout his long, distinguished career. The jazz world and the music world will never see anyone like the man who gave us his "Fatha's Blues."

Discography

Earl Hines, BYG 529090.
57 Varieties, CBS 63364.
Earl Hines, Raretone RTR 24003.
Harlem Lament, Portrait 44119.
The Earl Hines Collection-Piano Solos 1928–1940, STC 11.
Fatha's Blues 1964, Trd 1028.
Piano Man! 1939–1942, ASL 5131.
Original Historic Recordings-Vol. 14, EPM 158332.
Earl Hines & The Dixieland All-Stars at Club Hangover 1955, STC 6036.
Earl Hines & His Orchestra 1928–1932, Classic 545.
Earl Hines & His Orchestra 1932–1934, Classic 514.
Earl Hines & His Orchestra 1934–1937, Classic 528.
Earl Hines & His Orchestra 1937–1939, Classic 538.
Earl Hines & His Orchestra, 1939–1940, Classic 567.
Earl Hines & His Orchestra 1941, Classic 621.
Earl Hines & His Orchestra 1942–1945, Classic 876.
Earl Hines & His Orchestra, 1945–1947, Classic 1041.
Earl Hines & His Orchestra 1947–1949, Classic 1120.
Earl Hines Trio, Dial 303.
Earl Hines All-Stars, Dial 306.
Swingin' and Singin', Craftsmen 8041.
Up to Date, Bluebird 6462.
Fatha Plays Hits He Missed, M & K Real Time 105.

FATS WALLER (1904–1943)

Honeysuckle Rose

Many of the individuals in jazz history gained a tremendous amount of popularity for their charisma as well as for their remarkable skills. Their ability to blend musical aptitude with personal appeal propelled them to legendary status and enabled them to expand the appeal of jazz beyond its humble beginnings. Such is the story of the man who delivered his "Honeysuckle Rose" jazz to the world. His name was Fats Waller.

Thomas Wright Waller was born on May 21, 1904, in New York City. Like many blues and jazz singers, Waller's first introduction to music was through the church. His father was a minister and Waller played piano and organ at Sunday Baptist services. His mother was skilled at both the piano and the organ. Waller himself began to take piano lessons at the age of six.

One of Waller's first instructors was Edgar Sampson, who led the school orchestra that Fats played in. Sampson would later work with some of the biggest names in jazz including Duke Ellington, Fletcher Henderson, Chick Webb, Benny Goodman, Artie Shaw, Teddy Hill, Teddy Wilson and the Ella Fitzgerald Band. Waller also received instruction from Carl Bohm and Leopold Godowsky.

At age fourteen, Waller quit school and performed odd jobs waiting for a break in order to fulfill his musical ambitions. In his free time he haunted the Lincoln Theatre, sometimes sitting in for the organist, where he gained valuable experience about how to do movie work. When a spot opened up, Waller, then fifteen, became the official organist for the Lincoln Theatre. It was around this time that he began to receive favorable notices from many of the important piano players in New York City including James P. Johnson.

But Waller had greater musical ambitions than to remain at the Lincoln Theatre his whole life. In order to pump some life into his stagnant career, the ingenious young pianist sought out the most famous player in New York City during the era, James P. Johnson, who took Fats under his wing. The prime lesson of the stride technique of using both hands to create different layers of sound was one Waller incorporated into his basic style.

After the death of his mother and a marriage that ended quickly (the alimony payments would haunt him for years), Waller went on the road with a vaudeville show in early 1921 and used the best weapon in his arsenal—comedy—to survive the rigors of traveling. He was very prolific at this time, creating an immense body of work that would not only make him famous but also enable him to keep up with his support payments.

Waller's diversity ensured him a solid income in an era replete with skilled piano players. Although a master of the piano, he never lost his affection for the organ. He returned to the Lincoln Theatre as often as his hectic schedule allowed him to and when that venue was closed to him (it was sold), he found a job at the Lafayette Theatre also playing the organ. At this point his work schedule included rent-parties, theatres and movie houses, as well as backing up blues singers Sara Martin and Alberta Hunter on the sessions that produced the latter's songs "Sugar" and "Beale Street Blues."

Fats made his first personal recordings in 1922. The songs "Muscle Shoals Blues" and "Birmingham Blues" didn't earn him instant stardom, but they were a good debut. He blended the basics of stride with classical, blues, and popular song to create something excitingly fresh. He cut the songs as a solo performer.

A year later, in 1923, Waller made his first radio broadcast from the Fox Terminal Theatre in Newark, New Jersey. He was also creating piano rolls on which he abandoned some of the ragtime influence of Johnson to forge his own unique sound. Because of his increasing fame he was able to strike up friendships with Clarence Williams, Fletcher Henderson and Don Redman.

It was also about this time that Waller met Andy Razaf, who would have a huge influence on his career. Andy Razaf was born in 1895, in Washington, D. C. He was a gifted writer who worked with many of the biggest names in jazz including Don Redman, Paul Denniker, James P. Johnson, Eubie Blake and William Weldon. Although Razaf cut songs as a solo artist, his best work came in collaboration with Waller. Together they were a winning combination and Razaf contributed lyrics to some of Fats' biggest hits including "Honeysuckle Rose" and "Ain't Misbehavin'."

By 1924, Waller was part of the circle of top New York pianists that included Eubie Blake, James P. Johnson, and William "The Lion" Smith. Like his contemporaries, Fats was busy composing, publishing, recording, touring, and writing for musical shows. It was one of the most celebrated periods of creation and he was very much part of the history-making process.

In 1925, at the age of 21, Waller was already a veteran of the jazz scene and one of its most highly regarded performers. However, Waller, not one to rest on his laurels, continued his education that consisted primarily of European music, which meant the classical composers. His favorites were Bach, Liszt, and Chopin. Many of the ideas of these geniuses could be found scattered through the countless songs that he composed at the time.

In 1926, Waller, who was good friends with Fletcher Henderson, contributed some compositions for the latter and sat in on a couple of sessions that included Fats' first pipe organ recording on the song "The Chant." He energized the recordings of Henderson and his band with unbridled enthusiasm.

The pipe-organ recordings he made with Henderson served as a precursor to the records he made with Victor later on that year. Some of the songs from this session include a version of "St. Louis Blues," "Lenox Avenue Blues," "Soothin' Syrup Stomp," "Stompin' the Bug," "Hog Maw Stomp," and "Rusty Pail."

The wealth of music he created was like a new jazz language that would influence countless musicians in the following decades.

In 1927, Waller moved to Chicago, arriving at the tail end of the Windy City's reign as the supreme jazz spot. Although his time there was brief, he made a lasting impression on the likes of Johnny Dodds, Baby Dodds, Louis Armstrong and Jelly Roll Morton (one of his great rivals), among others, with his zany personality, polished skills and *bon vivant* humor.

He returned to New York where he teamed up with his hero and mentor James P. Johnson. Together they worked in the *Keep Shufflin'* review for a few months. Later that year (1928) they performed at a special concert for W. C. Handy at Carnegie Hall honoring the great songwriter for his vast contributions to early American music. Handy not only had a hand in the creation of the blues, but also, to a lesser extent, jazz.

Waller had another good year in 1929. He was churning out songs at a super-human pace, but often sold them for less money than what he should have received. He worked on another revue, *Load of Coal*, which was a financial and critical success. He played a memorable concert at Carnegie Hall that only enhanced his popularity. He continued to record many hits that formed his impressive song catalog including "Honeysuckle Rose," "Zonky," and "My Fate Is in Your Hands," all written in collaboration with Razaf. Not even the economic disaster of Black Tuesday could slow him down.

Waller continued to record under his own name in the 1930s, but also found time to team up with Jack Teagarden, Fletcher Henderson, Ted Lewis and McKinney's Cotton Pickers. These sessions demonstrated that Waller was not only a solid solo performer, but was also an accomplished band pianist. He also held his own against such legends as Louis Armstrong. The two distinct personalities working together proved to be an interesting experiment.

In 1931, Waller recorded his first vocals on the songs "Dallas Blues," "Garden City Blues," and "I'm Crazy about My Baby." Although he didn't possess a truly magnificent voice, he was able to inject his jovial personality and showmanship into his singing and made the recordings memorable. His vocal talent was another dimension of his musical talent.

Because of the Depression work was hard to find for many musicians. Radio was one of the few outlets that allowed them to make a few dollars. It seemed that Waller was tailor made for radio because although he was more of a visual performer, he was able to transmit his fervor over the airwaves in a neat package of boisterous singing and uplifting playing. It was exactly what the sad times called for in the early part of the 1930s.

A 1932 trip overseas to Paris with songwriter Spencer Williams seemed to re-energize Waller's career. Although his stay in Europe was brief, when he returned he played with more enthusiasm. In 1934, Waller signed a new recording contract with Victor Records. He would cut hundreds of sides for the company, but few of them were piano solos. Instead, he recorded with his group the Rhythms, which consisted of bass player Charlie Turner (who directed the group), Al Casey on guitar, Herman Autry on trumpet, Gene Sedric on tenor saxophone and clarinet, and Slick Jones on drums. Waller also traveled with Don Donaldson's orchestra at the time.

Waller made his film debut in 1935 in the movie *Stormy Weather*. Three years later he returned to Europe and played dates in Great Britain. Because of the popularity of his records, he was able to develop a large and loyal following across the Atlantic. The tour only added to his burgeoning reputation.

During the late 1930s, Waller, a jazz chameleon, divided his time between recording and performing with his Rhythms, appearing as a solo performer, and participating in different groups including a stint with Les Hite. In 1939, he paid another visit to Europe, but left just before the outbreak of war.

His next trip was a solo one as he performed around Britain, in Glasgow and in Denmark, and then returned to London to appear on the BBC. Waller did as much as anyone else in jazz at the time to promote the music on an international level. On a domestic level, he performed with his band at the Yacht Club, Famous Door, and the Apollo Theatre in New York and at the Hotel Sherman in Chicago, as well as all over the Midwest. But, despite his status as one of the biggest names in jazz, his star began to fade.

In 1943, the musician's ban on recording halted a very prolific side of Waller's career. He produced a musical, *Early to Bed*, and although it wasn't his best work it received solid reviews. He also broke up his band.

That same year, on a train returning to New York from Los Angeles, he contracted pneumonia, and on December 15, in Kansas City, Missouri, Thomas "Fats" Waller, the comedic piano man with the flair for writing hits, died. He was thirty-nine years old.

Fats Waller is one of the most colorful personalities in jazz history. But he was more than a showman able to please a crowd with his theatrics. He was a good pianist and organist, and an exceptional songwriter. He was also an adequate singer. He took part in hundreds of sessions as a solo performer and as a player in group ensembles.

Although classified with the stride piano school—mainly due to his association with James P. Johnson—Waller used stride as a launch pad for his own style. He had the uncanny ability to make the left hand do something completely different from the right hand yet made it sound as if the were working in tandem and not on an individual basis.

He was also a great improviser. He would play the familiar melody of a song once, introducing it to the listener, and then head in a completely different direction. With his right hand he would take the original notes of the song and invent something new with it all the while adding substance and embellishments. With his left hand he kicked out thick chords that reminded one of Johnson and other stride pianists, as well as the school of ragtime players. He also added bass notes that created a bottom for the lighter flourishes he weaved with his right hand.

Waller was not only a noted pianist; he was also a pioneer on the organ. He had begun to experiment with the possibilities of the instrument when he played at his father's Baptist church in Harlem. Fats recorded many of his spirituals on the organ including "Sometimes I Feel Like a Motherless Child," a reflection on his mother passing away when he was a teenager. He also recorded one of the first songs on a Hammond organ in Great Britain in the early 1940s shortly before his death. An exceptional organist, he could have easily made a good living playing solely that instrument.

A Fats Waller concert—whether solo or accompanied on stage by a band—was a package of pure delight. The audience was presented with a verbal, as well as a visual act, from a man who knew how to work a crowd. He was a natural entertainer and combined his fine musicianship with his irrepressible humor. He touched the crowds in many ways with laughter, sadness, excitement, and suspense—the entire spectrum of human emotion.

Despite his numerous contributions he will be best remembered for his songwriting abilities, usually in conjunction with Andy Razaf. From 1930 through 1943, Fats made over five hundred recordings. A few of the classics they gave the world include "Honeysuckle Rose," "Ain't Misbehavin'," "Keepin' Out of Mischief Now," "Black and Blue," "Blue Turning Gray Over You," "Sugar," "Southin' Syrup Stomp," "Messin' Around with the Blues," "Loveless Love," "Squeeze Me," "Jitterbug Waltz," "Laughin' Cryin' Blues," "18th Street Strut," "T'ain't Nobody's Biz-ness If I Do," "I've Got a Feeling I'm Falling," and "I'm Crazy About My Baby."

He not only recorded with a number of jazz greats—Louis Armstrong, Fletcher Henderson, Jack Teagarden, James P. Johnson, Benny Carter, Coleman Hawkins, Eddie Condon, Henry "Red" Allen, and Pee Wee Russell—but made an everlasting impact on the careers of dozens of others.

He tutored Count Basie, and had a hand in the development of the great blues pianist Roosevelt Sykes as well as Speckled Red, Art Tatum (considered the greatest jazz pianist of all time), Eddie Boyd, Mary Lou Williams (the first lady of jazz piano) and the classic Dave Brubeck. He also had a direct influence on Oscar Peterson, Nat Cole, Erroll Garner, George Shearing, Johnny Guarnieri, Ralph Sutton, Bobby Henderson, Dick Wellstood, Martha Davis, Don Ewell, John Bunch, Al Casey, Rahsaan Roland Kirk, Lonnie Liston Smith, Hilton Ruiz, Ross Tompkins, and countless others.

Waller was one of the first entertainers—black or white—to understand the power of the visual medium. He was probably the first jazz singer to make an appearance on television while on a tour of Great Britain long before the tube became a standard in every living room in America. He appeared in numerous films including *Hooray for Love*, *King of Burlesque*, *Stormy Weather*, and several film shorts including *Ain't Misbehavin'*.

Fats Waller, a member of the Jazz Hall of Fame, sparked the history of jazz with his versatility, ability and personality. Although his personal life reached crisis points (he often fought with his ex-wives over alimony payments), the entertainer in him would never let the audience down. With his rascal-like smile, his huge, popped-out eyes, and the musical talent to back his showmanship, Thomas Fats Waller, Mr. Charisma, made enormous contributions with his "Honeysuckle Rose" jazz.

Discography

L'art Vocal, Vol. 4: 1934–1939, LAV 4.
Classic Jazz from Rare Piano Rolls, Biograph 104.
Lay Down Papa, Biograph 114.
The Very Best of Fats Waller, CCM 141.
I'm 100 Percent for You, EPR 824.
Fats Waller, 1922–1936, Classic 664.
Fats Waller, 1926–1927, Classic 674.
Fats Waller, 1927–1929, Classic 689.
Fats Waller, 1929, Classic 702.
Fats Waller, 1929–1934, Classic 720.
Fats Waller, 1934–1935, Classic 732.
Fats Waller, 1935, Classic 746.
Fats Waller, 1935, Vol. 2, Classic 760.
Fats Waller, 1935–1936, Classic 776.
Fats Waller, 1936, Classic 797.
Fats Waller, 1936–1937, Classic 816.
Fats Waller, 1937, Classic 838.

Fats Waller, 1937, Vol. 2, Classic 857.
Fats Waller, 1937–1938, Classic 875.
Fats Waller, 1938, Classic 913.
Fats Waller, 1938–1939, Classic 943.
Fats Waller, 1939, Classic 973.
Fats Waller, 1939–1940, Classic 1002.
Fats Waller, 1940–1941, Classic 1030.
Fats Waller, 1941, Classic 1068.
Fats Waller, 1942–1943, Classic 1097.
20 Golden Pieces, BDL 2004.
Yatch Club Swing & Other Radio Rarities, JASM 2549.
More Radio Rarities, JASM 2555.
Fats at the Organ, 1923–1927, ASL 5007.
You Rascal You, 1929–1934, ASL 5040.
Ain't Misbehavin', ASL 5174.
The Joint Is Jumpin', 1929–1943, BLED 6288.
Fats Waller, V-Disc Recordings, CCM 6672.
Fine Arabian Stuff, 1939, HIN 7053.
Original Recordings, Pearl 9742.
The Very Best of Fats Waller, RCA 63731.
Breaking the Ice—The Early Years Vol. 1, 1934–1935, BLED 66618.
I'm Gonna Sit Right Down—The Early Years, Vol. 2, 1935–1936, BLED
    66640.
Fractious Fingering—The Early Years Vol. 3, 1936, BLED 66747.
Fats Waller & His Rhythm Makers—The Middle Years Vol. 1, 1936–1938,
    BLED 66083.
The Last Years 1940–1943, BLED 9883.
Fats & His Buddies, 1927–1929, BLED 61005.
Greatest Hits: 1929–1943, Victor 68495.
A Handful of Keys—Live Radio Transcriptions from 1938, RCA 99603.
Take It Easy, CRG 120016.
Masterpieces Vol. 3, EPM 158152.
Piano Masterworks: Vol. 2, 1929–1943, EPM 158992.
Young Fats at the Organ, Vol. 3, 1926–1929, EPM 159262.
Fats Waller and his Rhythmakers, Yacht Club Swing 1938, EPM 157192.
A Career Perspective, 1922–1943, Music Memoirs 515.

JACK TEAGARDEN (1905–1964)

Prince of the Trombone

In every era of jazz each instrument can claim its own proper champion. Louis Armstrong was heralded as the greatest trumpet player of the 1920s. Art Tatum was acknowledged as the earl of the eighty-eights during the 1930s and 1940s. Charley Parker was deemed the "Dark Baron" of the alto saxophone in the 1940s and 1950s. Art Blakey became the "Duke of the Drum Kit" from the 1950s and thereafter. This list must also include the "Prince of the Trombone" during the 1920s and 1930s. His name was Jack Teagarden.

Jack Teagarden was born Weldon Leo Teagarden on August 29, 1905, in Vernon, Texas. Teagarden was from a musical family: his father was an impressive amateur cornet and baritone horn player; his mother was a piano teacher steeped in classical music but who could also play ragtime. Even his siblings were musical; his brother Charlie was a trumpeter, sister Norma played the violin as well as piano, and brother Clois was a drummer.

Jack's musical education began at five when he studied the piano with his mother who taught him scales, keys and some harmony. But he left the keyboard behind when he acquired a baritone horn. At the age of seven his father presented him with a trombone. By ten, he was playing trombone, and he debuted in public at thirteen playing in the high school band. That same year the family moved to Nebraska where Teagarden played in theatres accompanied by his mother on piano.

Teagarden absorbed the myriad musical ideas around him. In Vernon he first heard a mixture of gospel and blues from the revival not far from his home that sent a shiver up and down his spine. Along the railroad tracks he listened and hummed along with the poor, blind folks who sang the sinful, spiritual blues. In Nebraska, he became acquainted with the intricate rhythms of the Native Americans.

A year later the family moved once again, this time to Oklahoma City. Like so many other jazz legends, Teagarden left home in his early teens to seek his fame and fortune. He moved to Texas where he worked in his uncle's theatre. When he wasn't running the projectors, he was jamming with the numerous local dance bands. His proficiency on the trombone reached a high level.

Eventually Teagarden became part of a quartet that included Cotton Bailey on drums, Fred Hamilton on piano, a banjoist, and Tea on trombone; the little group cooked. The band found work in the Horn Palace in San Antonio. During their one-year residency the group added piano player Terry Shand and C-melody saxophonist Porter Trest. With the increased number of musicians they could play more intricate arrangements.

When the band broke up, Teagarden, a savvy professional all of sixteen years old, landed his first true professional job in Peck Kelley's Bad Boys in the early 1920s. He remained in the group for two years but never made any recordings during this period. The highlight of his tenure in the band was a chance meeting with a powerful cornetist from New Orleans named Louis Armstrong.

Teagarden left at loose ends after pianist Peck disbanded his outfit and found work outside of the music world in the booming oil fields. Jack returned to nearby Vernon, Texas, and did every job that an oil field hand had to perform including delivering nitroglycerine from one area to another. Although there was money to be made in the oil fields, as many would become tycoons, music was in his blood and he yearned to return to the life of a jazz artist.

He failed in his audition to join Doc Ross's Jazz Bandits and went back to working in the oilfields. When his uncle's claim went bust, Jack joined the Southern Trumpeters and paid his dues traveling in less than ideal conditions and for very little money. But his extraordinary talent was beginning to gain him a reputation as the South's Greatest Sensational Trombone Wonder. But the band was unable to stay together and Teagarden was once again left looking for employment. He rejoined Peck Kelly's reformed outfit and toured with the group for a brief spell before frustration set in and Teagarden headed out to Kansas City in search of better musical opportunities.

In Kansas City he quickly joined Willard Robinson's band but didn't stay long. He found a spot with Doc Ross, but then left to become part of the Herb Berger Orchestra. But he was denied a working card by the local musician's union so he traveled to Louisiana and hooked up with the Johnny Youngberg group called the Peacocks. A short time later the restlessness set in once again and Teagarden returned to Doc Ross' Jazz Bandits. Jack remained with the Jazz Bandits for a long spell and began to write songs for the group. By this time the group had graduated to better working conditions and played many of the big venues in the Southwest and California.

In the fall of 1926, Teagarden became a member of the New Orleans Rhythm Masters but the band broke up soon after. He was supposed to rejoin Doc Ross' Jazz Bandits but the job vanished right before his eyes. He eventually found work with Johnny Johnson and recorded on a couple of sessions. However, up to this point, Teagarden's jazz career had been one of frustration and lost opportunities. After barely surviving on one pick up gig after another that never fully showcased his style, he joined Ben Pollack's group in Chicago. The band also contained a young clarinetist by the name of Benny Goodman, as well as Jimmy McPartland and Bud Freeman.

It was the big break Teagarden was waiting for as he stayed with Pollack for five long years. During this period—1928–1933—he grew as a musician, arranger and songwriter. Pollack not only encouraged his sidemen to contribute ideas, he also allowed them to record outside of the group. Jack played on dozens of sessions with Pollack as well as the Dorsey Brothers, Sam Lanin, Irving Mills, the Mound City Blue Blowers, Eddie Condon's Hot Shots, Red Nichols, Jimmy McHugh's Bostonians, Fats Waller and the great Louis Armstrong. On one of the sessions with Condon, Teagarden sang "Makin' Friends." In 1929 alone, he participated in over one hundred sides.

His flourishing career also included radio programs and series, dance dates, a movie, and revues. There was hardly enough time to indulge in all of the opportunities that came his way but Teagarden made the most of the good times while they lasted. In 1933, Pollack could no longer hold the band together. The various members, including Teagarden, drifted away.

After stints with his younger brother Charlie and old friend Wingy Manone, Teagarden joined the Mal Hallett Orchestra for a brief spell. Later that same year, he joined Paul Whiteman's Band and remained with the group for five years. Although it was not the most popular jazz group on the scene, it did afford him a chance to record on a regular basis. But, more importantly, membership in the band provided financial security in uncertain times for the famous trombone player.

In 1939, he left Whiteman's group. Teagarden, after playing in innumerable groups for his entire career, finally decided to front his own big band. His timing was disastrous. America would soon go to war and it was nearly impossible to keep a group together because nearly every able-bodied musician was enlisted in the armed forces.

Nevertheless, he determinedly plodded on for the next eight years with his group despite the fact that he was not born to be a leader and businessman. On a more positive side, Teagarden had the opportunity to record with such luminaries as Ben Webster, Rex Stewart, Barney Bigard, and drummer Dave Tough.

In 1947, he joined Louis Armstrong. Teagarden had suffered health problems while burdened with running his own business. But he regained his coolness and spirit once he joined Armstrong's all-stars. The group included Barney Bigard on clarinet, Dick Carey on piano, Big Sid Catlett on drums, Jack Lesberg on bass and Satchmo on trumpet. Jack and Louis shared the vocal chores.

In his four year tenure with the group, Teagarden appeared on Armstrong's recordings: *Satchmo at Symphony Hall, Louis Armstrong Vol. 1 & 2, Satchmo's Greatest, Vol. 4 & 5,* and *Town Hall Concert: The Unissued Part.* The two giants of jazz even sang a duet together called "Rockin' Chairs." Of all the musicians whom Armstrong collaborated with—and there were many—arguably his best partner was Teagarden. Since Armstrong's name was still magic in jazz circles, their collaboration meant first class traveling conditions, appearance in venues that otherwise would have been closed to them, and tours of Europe.

In 1951, he left Armstrong's All-Stars and formed a small combo of his own that included his brother George and Ray Bauduc, who had played with Teagarden in Pollack's band. They toured throughout the world and made several recordings. With the era of the big band forgotten, small combos were the order of the day and he excelled in this format. In 1953, his sister Norma took over piano duties in the band. Augmented to a sextet, they continued to perform and record for the next three years although personnel changes were frequent.

In 1956, he disbanded his group to tour with Ben Pollack. Once his work with Pollack had finished he reformed a small combo that included Earl Hines. The Hines-Teagarden unit toured Europe in 1957 to enthusiastic reviews. A couple of years later with monetary aid from the State Department, he toured Asia with his own small band minus Hines. At this period in jazz history, Asia was still virgin territory for western musicians. Teagarden was breaking new ground for future generations. From 1959 until 1964, Teagarden continued to play and record but without the same success he had earlier in his career.

On January 15, 1964, in New Orleans, Louisiana, one of the greatest voices of the trombone was silenced forever with bronchial pneumonia. Teagarden was 58 years old.

Jack Teagarden was one of the genuine giants of early jazz. He is one of the best trombonists in history and ranks with Kid Ory and J. J. Johnson as one of the top three all-time greats. Teagarden was also a strong singer; his warm tone and impressive vocals are his legacy. He was an excellent studio musician and added something to the mix in every recording session he took part in. He was also a credible bandleader who knew how to squeeze the best from the members of his small combos.

Teagarden was a superb technician whose major asset as a trombone player was his uncanny knowledge of the limitations of the instrument. He possessed a liquid fluidity in his playing that veered the trombone from the early tailgate sound that was practiced so well by Kid Ory. Although they had diverse styles and approached the instrument from a totally different point of view, Tea had a major impact on the development of Johnson and set the table for the latter's musical exploits.

During Teagarden's era, there were many fine trombone players including Vic Dickerson, Tommy Dorsey, Benny Morton, Dickie Wells, and Trummy Young. There were also the trombone players who starred with Duke Ellington's band including Lawrence Brown, Quentin Jackson, Tricky Sam Nanton, and Juan Tizol. Despite this talented group Teagarden stands head and shoulders above them. He could do more with the instrument with his sure touch and concise abilities. He was a huge influence on Bob Brookmeyer, Urbie Green, Roswell Rudd, George Masso, Porky Cohen, and J. C. Higginbotham, to name a few.

Teagarden gave the world many memorable songs as a leader, as a session man, and in unison with other jazz artists. A short list includes "She's a Great, Great Girl," "Knockin' a Jug," "Announcer's Blues," "Ain't Misbehavin'," "St. James Infirmary," "Lover," "Stars Fell on Alabama," "Basin Street Blues," and "A Hundred Years from Today." The entire catalog would fill a book.

Jack Teagarden remains a vital figure in the early part of jazz and is in the Hall of Fame. Although J. J. Johnson overshadowed him in the modern era, during the 1930s and 1940s Teagarden was the very best trombonist the genre had to offer. Because of his many contributions to the music there is no doubt that he deserves the title "Prince of the Trombone."

Discography

Bridgeport, Connecticut, Can 1000.
Big T., Pearl 1001.
Jack Teagarden, V-Disc Recordings, CCM 4509.
I Gotta Right to Sing the Blues, 1929–1934, ASL 5059.
Jazz Greats: 1954, Rhino 75784.
Vol. 1, 1928–1931, EPM 157022.
Jack Teagarden & His Orchestra, 1930–1934, Classic 698.
Jack Teagarden & His Orchestra, 1934–1939, Classic 729.
Jack Teagarden & His Orchestra, 1939–1940, Classic 758.
Jack Teagarden & His Orchestra, 1940–1941, Classic 839.
Jack Teagarden & His Orchestra, 1941–1942, Classic 874.
Jack Teagarden & His Orchestra, 1944–1947, Classic 1032.

Jack Teagarden & His Orchestra, Meet Me Where They Play the Blues, 1954, GTJ 12063.
Personal Choice, Modern Jazz Classics 1205.
A Hundred Years from Today, Memphis Archives 7010.
Jack Teagarden and His All-Stars, Jazzology 199.
Big T, Pearl 1001.
Club Hangover Broadcast with Jackie Coon, Arbors 19150.
I Gotta Right to Sing the Blues, Living Era 5059.
Introduction to Jack Teagarden 1928–1943, Best of Jazz 4025.
It's Time for Tea, Jazz Classics 5012.
Jack Teagarden, Members Edition 30222.
Jazz Great, Avenue Jazz 75784.
Live at Frank Dailey's Meadowbrook, Vernon 13199.
Live at the Royal Room, Hollywood, 1951, Vernon 83199.
Live at the Trianon Ballroom, Vernon 22799.
Masters of Jazz Vol. 10, Storyville 4110.
That Man of the Blues, Vernon 32899.
Think Well of Me, Verve 557 101.
Jack Teagarden—V-Disc Recordings, V-Disc 4509.
Vol. 1 1928/1931, Jazz Archives 157022.
Jazz Gallery, MAKIN 21141752.
Planet Jazz, RCA 21612362.

PART THREE

The Big Band and Swing
Era: The Bandleaders

The major impact jazz had made on American culture by the end of the 1920s enabled the music to survive the Great Depression. The recording industry, which had brought jazz to every living room in the country and many other parts of the world, was decimated by the stock market crash. In order to maintain the momentum live jazz was broadcast over the airwaves.

By the middle of the 1930s, the recording industry had made a strong comeback and propelled jazz to previously unattainable heights. Jazz now boasted a four-prong attack in its arsenal. There were the live radio broadcasts, records for home enjoyment, a vibrant juke box industry, and concert tours that covered the entire country and many parts of the world.

Before the explosion of the swinging big bands there were many that laid down the groundwork. In New York City, at the turn of the century, the James Reese Europe–led 50-piece Hell Fighter's Band swung with a mighty force and was years ahead of its time. Europe and his large ensemble played tight compositions that created the feel that many of the big bands would capture two decades later. William Marion Cook was the proud conductor of the 50-piece New York Syncopated Orchestra and experimented with genuine African rhythms. Later in the 1920s Paul Whiteman, erroneously heralded as the "King of Jazz," became quite popular though he played more pop than serious jazz.

In Chicago Ben Pollack featured future big band leaders like clarinetist Benny Goodman, trumpeter Harry James, trombonist Glenn Miller, as well as sax man Bud Freeman and trumpeter Jimmy McPartland.

In Detroit, Jean Goldkette formed a popular dance orchestra that featured important jazz musicians of the 1920s including future big band leaders Tommy and Jimmy Dorsey as well as cornetist Bix Beiderbecke

119

and violinist Joe Venuti. From the ranks of Goldkette's band emerged a new group called the Casa Loma Orchestra led by saxophonist and clarinetist Glen Gray. They were one of the first popular white swing bands. Of course, one of the most important groups was Fletcher Henderson's, a prime pioneer of the big band and swing sound. Later important bands included Cab Calloway's group, Benny Carter's (he was a brilliant multi-instrumentalist, composer and arranger), Andy Kirk's Clouds of Joy, and McKinney's Cotton Pickers. They carried jazz into the 1930s.

During the early part of the decade jazz was music of sympathy reflecting the tough economic times. But by 1935 there was a renewed hope as the younger generation wanted to have fun and forget the economic woes of the country. They demanded dance music and the timing was ripe for the emergence of the big bands.

There were many types of ensembles that captured the imagination of the country. The outfits of the Midwest and Southwest were louder, featuring hot horn sections, intensive sax solos, and swinging rhythm packs composed of guitar, drums, piano, and bass. Bennie Moten's group (that later evolved into the Count Basie Big Band), Walter Page's Blue Devils, and Jess Stone's Blues Serenaders were some of the important territory bands. The smoother groups featured a more commercial sound, as well as the appeal of dance, and the hot soloists format of the earlier New Orleans Jazz tradition. The sweet bands played melodic tunes that weren't even considered serious jazz by many players. Guy Lombardo and His Royal Canadians, Hal Kemp, Isham Jones and Wayne King are just a few examples of groups with a saccharine sound.

Duke Ellington's Orchestra, Jimmie Lunceford's group, and others appealed to a crowd that wanted to really swing and as a result jazz developed into a more sophisticated music that included complex arrangements utilizing the immense talents of musicians to maximum effect. The tightly written arrangements created specific spaces for the star soloists to shine. In earlier days, jazz bands had relied more on improvisation that limited the breaks for solo performances.

It was the power of the big band and swing sound that would take the country through the end of the Second World War. In 1939, while most of the planet was in the shadow of war, the big bands were at their height of power, popularity and creativity. Many of the bandleaders of the era (1935 to 1945) were former players who attempted to lead their own outfits. A list of the most important musicians not featured in this book includes Charlie Barnet, Les Brown and His Band of Renown, Bob Crosby (Bing's brother), Xavier Cugat (who combined Latin rhythms with swing), Billy Eckstine (who would include many of the early bebop artists), Woody Herman, Harry James, Stan Kenton, Les Hite, and Red Norvo. The contributions made by the aforementioned bands as well as dozens of others were vital to the power that the music had on succeeding generations and they should never be forgotten.

Duke Ellington is perhaps the greatest figure in jazz history. His immense donations, his towering presence, his unqualified genius, made him one of the most important personages in not only 20th century jazz, but also across the entire spectrum of music.

Walter Page was one of the leading bandleaders of the territory bands along with Bennie Moten. It was Page's Blue Devils that blazed the path followed by Moten and later on Count Basie.

Jimmie Lunceford was a prime bandleader of the swing era. Although his band never boasted many exciting soloists, he made up for it in daring showmanship and style. Lunceford entertained audiences musically, as well as visually, with his relaxing swing.

Glenn Miller was a frustrated musician and bandleader until he finally managed to consolidate his immense talents. Once he had found out how to swing properly he led one of the most famous dance bands in the country.

Jimmy Dorsey was a fine bandleader who attained incredible popularity with his younger brother and as the leader of his own outfit. A noted musician, Dorsey was an important figure in the transformation from Chicago jazz to the big band sound.

Count Basie was one of the greatest bandleaders whose effervescent spirit and crisp piano playing made him a legend. Many important players made their debut in his band and during one period the Basie Band had the most formidable lineup in all of jazz.

Tommy Dorsey, the younger brother of Jimmy Dorsey, was successful as part of the Dorsey Brothers Orchestra and as leader of the Tommy Dorsey Orchestra. It was Tommy Dorsey who gave a young Italian singer by the name of Frank Sinatra his first break.

Benny Goodman was the King of Swing and his stature in the world of jazz was defined and permanent. He was also an excellent clarinetist. Perhaps more than anyone else his name is associated with the Swing Era.

Chick Webb was the best of the swing drummers and that alone would make him a valuable member of the jazz community. However, he was also an excellent bandleader who gave Ella Fitzgerald her big break. His ability to overcome physical deformity is a triumph of the human spirit.

Artie Shaw was a grand bandleader who put together many winning combinations only to break them up. Among the best-known bandleaders, Shaw's name was synonymous with jazz of the 1940s.

DUKE ELLINGTON (1899–1974)

Beyond Category

There have been many important contributors who helped shape the sound of jazz and insured the genre's immense and everlasting popularity. Within the realm of jazz these artists are acknowledged giants. However, one seminal figure, because of the multiplicity and significance of his vast achievement not only in jazz, but in twentieth-century music, remains beyond category. His name is Duke Ellington.

Edward Kennedy Ellington was born April 29, 1899, in Washington, D.C. His parents both played piano and he began his own musical studies at the age of seven. However, the lessons did not go far because young Ellington was much more interested in sports. When not indulging in games with his neighborhood pals, he was dabbling in all the arts. He was a gifted graphic artist who eventually co-founded his own sign painting company.

But he was destined to make his mark on the world of jazz and at the beginning of his teens was turned on by ragtime. The sounds intrigued the adolescent Ellington. They had the allure of a mistress he was yearning for. One of the turning points in his life was during summer vacation when he heard Harvey Brooks pounding the keys with the attack and ferocity of a lion. Ellington was completely sold.

The fire to play and create music raged inside him and he caught a minor break when he was hired to be a soda jerk at the Poodle Dog Café. The place had a piano and when the regular pianist couldn't perform, Ellington was thrust into the role. In an effort to imitate ragtime, he composed the "Poodle Dog Rag," the first of his thousands of compositions. It was during this stint as a piano player at the soda place that he learned the invaluable lesson of how to disguise the same song by playing in different styles.

During this formative period the stride piano school that included James P. Johnson, Fats Waller, and Willie "The Lion" Smith provided Ellington with musical heroes. There were also local "geniuses" in his hometown of Washington who helped his development significantly. One of these men, Oliver "Doc" Perry, taught Ellington how to read music. Slowly, the young Duke was getting his act together.

He began to play dances, clubs and cafes in the Washington area.

He broadened his repertoire and was composing music that contained a surprisingly high level of sophistication for someone in his middle teens. A student of music more than academia, Ellington quit school in his senior year and turned professional. He played in the ensembles of Louis Thomas and Russell Wooding as well as with other Washington bands. While the music did not earn him a sufficient amount of money, his job as a sign painter paid the bills nicely.

When he was nineteen Duke took a huge step towards becoming a serious professional musician when he formed his own group, The Duke's Serenaders. They played the popular songs of the day: mostly rags, blues pieces and danceable instrumentals. The small band included Ellington and close friends Otto Hardwick and Arthur Whetsol. Later on, Duke would call on these two bandmates to join him in New York.

By his early twenties, Duke was earning a good living as the leader of a popular dance-band in the Washington area. However, despite the comfort of family in his hometown, the opportunity to travel to the Big Apple and make his mark there was irresistible. In 1923, he arrived in New York City ready to conquer the music world, but the adventure was not as successful as the young maestro had hoped it would be and he returned to Washington. The next time he visited Harlem, things would be very different.

Later that year, at the urging of his band mates who had made their way to New York, Ellington returned. This time he stayed and together they paid their dues before their luck began to change. They landed a long residency at the Hollywood Club and the promise of work greatly excited the band that now called itself the Washingtonians, since most of them came from the country's capital city.

Once their residency was finished at the Hollywood Club, the Washingtonians were just another of the dozens of bands trying to find work in New York City. The sextet included Ellington, Sonny Greer, Charlie Irvis, Elmer Snowden, Otto Hardwick and Bubber Miley. When Snowden left the group Ellington took over as leader and occupied that role for the next fifty years.

In 1926, the group's name was changed to Duke Ellington and His Washingtonians. Ellington, who would compose thousands of musical pieces, had begun the practice of writing for the individual players in his group. It was a clever idea because it satisfied the ambitious musicians, added more power to the music, and enabled Duke to focus on one particular member and develop the song from his point. The group became something of the house band at the Kentucky Club, and when the place was closed they had no problem finding other outlets.

The genius of Ellington had many facets. Not only was he an artic-

ulate spokesman, gifted piano player, and inspired songwriter, but he had
a way with people. He could strike up a friendship with just about anyone. A smooth talker and ultimate charmer, Ellington met Irving Mills
around 1926 and their subsequent partnership would accelerate the Duke's
rise to the top. It was through Mills' efforts that Ellington was first signed
to a major label. Although he had made initial recordings in 1923, the
Ellington assembly line of making records truly began in 1926.

In 1927, Ellington started to perform at the Cotton Club in Harlem
and remained there for six years. It was during this period that he enhanced
his popularity with regular radio broadcasts. By 1929, the Duke Ellington Orchestra, as it was now known, totaled twelve members. Many of
them would stay with Ellington for years, including Harry Carney and
Johnny Hodges. Loyalty was something that Duke demanded from his
band and he received it in abundance. Ellington's ability to compose for
individual players and his royal treatment of them made playing in his
band inviting.

With the advent of the Great Depression, the music industry suffered
greatly, but Ellington continued to press on. He made a few recordings,
but the majority of his income was derived from live performances. The
Duke Ellington Orchestra became true road warriors playing all over the
United States and Canada. Many of the tours were long residencies instead
of one-night stops since his name was a strong drawing card that enabled
him to spend a week at a sold-out club. In 1932, Ellington added singer
Ivie Anderson, who gave the orchestra an interesting vocal dimension.

In 1933, Ellington toured Europe for the first time; he would return
overseas six years later. While he was a hit across the Atlantic, he made
a greater impact in America—including in the Deep South. Since Ellington was an outspoken figure against all types of racism and prejudices, he
feared traveling down in Old Dixie, but, in fact, he was extremely popular there. At the Majestic Theatre in Dallas the standing room only crowd
created mayhem and excitement that mirrored the frenzy that would be
exhibited years later at rock concerts.

In 1935, swing became the heartbeat of the nation. Ellington, who
saw himself as a creator of sophisticated music on a level with classical
composers, knew that while his band could play hot, fast moving music,
they weren't really considered a pure swing band. Would Duke change
his style or continue on his individual path? As he had done before and
would during his entire career, Ellington found a compromise between
the new style and his own thing; he became the ultimate voice of com-
plicated swing. His music remained beyond category.

In 1939, Ellington severed his business relationship with Irving Mills.
But while he lost the services of one key member he added another to his

kingdom with the addition of a young arranger named Billy Strayhorn from Pittsburgh, who had a classical music background. Ellington, who was one of the greatest composers of the twentieth century, brought Strayhorn into his universe to become his lyricist. The artistic partnership would last for 28 years until Strayhorn's death in 1967. Together they would score thousands of songs and worked so closely as two individuals that they were like one gifted mind.

The 1940s produced many triumphs and tragedies for Ellington. He would add to his substantial catalog of written music but would have trouble getting some of it on albums because materials used in producing records were being saved for the war effort. He remained busy performing concerts all over the country, including Carnegie Hall, the most prestigious musical venue in the country. The ban on recording due to the union's strike created a backlog of Ellington material and forced him to turn to other media like motion pictures and revues in order to channel his music. Ellington had been involved in both media outlets for years, but at this point they became increasingly important to him.

There were many personnel changes including the introduction of Jimmie Blanton, who would revolutionize the approach to bass. Unfortunately, after two groundbreaking years in the Ellington Orchestra, the young protégé would die of tuberculosis. Duke, always a class act, sent numerous bouquets of flowers and even paid for the casket. Cootie Williams left to take a spot in Benny Goodman's band, a serious rival to Ellington's outfit. Ray Nance replaced Williams and added the dimension of his violin playing. Others would leave, including Barney Bigard and Ivie Anderson. But despite the toll of the war, the ban on recording, the departure of key personnel, and the decline of the popularity of the big bands, the Duke Ellington Orchestra continued to prosper when other groups could not find work.

In 1950, when Johnny Hodges, Sonny Greer and Lawrence Brown left Ellington to form a combo, the jazz world was in shock. For the next four years, Ellington would be without the services of these three masters. Of the three, Hodges would be the one that Ellington missed the most and with the return of his masterful alto and soprano saxophone touch in 1955 everything was once again in proper order in the Ellington universe.

The 1950s saw Ellington perform at the first of the outdoor concerts that would later become a staple in his performing schedule. One of these was the Newport Jazz Festival and the ensuing album would be his biggest seller. He continued to make masterful records that sold well, but by this time his audience consisted of an older set. The young jazz fans were listening to hard bop; other teenagers screamed for their rock and roll heroes.

In 1956, Ellington began a series of recordings for Columbia which would revitalize his career. A meeting with Queen Elizabeth was a triumph for the Duke and inspired him to write "The Queen's Suite." It was not issued to the public until after his death. In 1959, he returned to Hollywood and together with Strayhorn wrote the score for *Anatomy of a Murder*.

He continued to write film scores in the 1960s, among them *Paris Blues*. The band personnel continued to change but there was also stability among the ranks as Hodges, Carney, and Brown continued their long tenures with the orchestra. In 1962, Ellington made his debut as a soloist. But he was also recording albums with collaborators whose styles included the free-spirited approach of John Coltrane, the bluesy riffs of Count Basie, and the edgy sound of Coleman Hawkins.

In the 1960s, the core audience for the Duke Ellington Band was quickly shrinking as the world was turned on by Beatlemania and pop music. In order to combat a steady decline in his career, Duke regularly took his show outside of the United States. In 1964, the group traveled to the Middle East, India, and the Near East, after touring Sweden and other European countries. Although it was a gamble performing for people who had rarely seen a jazz concert, much less experienced the challenging music of Duke Ellington and His Orchestra, the tour was so successful that it was filmed by CBS for television. Television was a new medium for Ellington and he made the most of it. He toured every year, adding new countries to his list of conquests including many in Africa in 1966.

On May 31, 1967, Billy Strayhorn died of cancer, and it had a devastating effect on Ellington. For years as collaborators the two had weathered good and bad times. Duke never fully recovered from this personal loss.

But amid tragedy there were triumphs. Ellington became a favorite of the White House and performed many times when Lyndon B. Johnson was president. On the occasion of Duke's seventieth birthday, there was a celebration at the White House with a guest list that included the elite of the jazz world such as Count Basie, Dizzy Gillespie, and Benny Goodman.

Ellington entered the 1970s as one of the grand ambassadors of jazz. With the death of Louis Armstrong in 1971, Duke became the most important spokesman for the genre. He performed in Russia, a great honor since the Communist government usually regarded all Western culture as a corruptive force. Sadly, he lost the services of Johnny Hodges at the beginning of the decade.

Three years later, on May 24, 1974, Duke Ellington, the greatest composer in jazz history, succumbed to a painful bout with cancer. It was an international day of mourning as tributes poured from all over the world in honor of him. He had just celebrated his 75th birthday.

Duke Ellington was a jazz institution for fifty years. He is arguably one of the most important figures in jazz history as well as one of the greatest contributors to twentieth century music. He was a superb bandleader, composer, pianist, ambassador, and cut a swath across the musical landscape that will never be repeated.

Ellington was the composer of thousands of pieces of music including rags, blues, jazz, concert pieces, sacred pieces, suites, stage shows, film scores, and other works that have yet to see the light of day. He made over 200 records, sold untold millions of albums and is responsible for the most enormous body of music in jazz. A partial list of his many songs regarded as masterpieces include "Mood Indigo," "Rockin' in Rhythm," "It Don't Mean a Thing If It Ain't Got That Swing," "Sophisticated Lady," "Drop Me Off at Harlem," "In a Sentimental Mood," "I Let a Song Go Out of My Heart," "Prelude to a Kiss," "Solitude," "Satin Doll," "Boy Meets Horn," "Do Nothing Till You Hear from Me," "I Got It Bad," "I'm Beginning to See the Light," "Just Squeeze Me," "Azure," "Battle of Swing," "Blue Light," "Subtle Lament," and "Serenade to Sweden." A complete list would fill over fifty notebooks.

He wrote longer pieces such as "Black, Brown & Beige," "Such Sweet Thunder," "Liberian Suite/A Tone Parallel to Harlem: The Harlem Suite," "A Drum Is a Woman," "The Far East Suite," "The Latin-American Suite," "New Worlds A-Coming," "Harlem: The Golden Broom and the Green Apple," "The Togo Brava Suite/The English Suite," "Suite Thursday," "Deep South Suite," and "Peer Gynt Suites, Nos. 1 & 2." Many of his compositions reflected his observations on African-American life in Harlem and across the United States.

His many film scores include *Paris Blues, Anatomy of a Murder, Black and Tan, A Bundle of Blues, Murder at the Vanities, Symphony in Black, Cabin in the Sky* and *Reveille with Beverly.* He appeared on television several times and produced film documentaries for National Education Television including *Love Her Madly* and *Concert of Sacred Music.* He appeared in countless specials that examined his life and music including *On the Road with Duke Ellington, The Twentieth Century: Duke Ellington Swings through Japan, Duke Ellington in Amsterdam and Zurich,* and *Goodyear Jazz Concert: Duke Ellington and His Orchestra.*

Ellington was a superb bandleader and throughout the years he was able to boast the most loyal musicians. Although some stayed for brief periods, others stayed for many years.

He was an ambassador of jazz and played in nearly every concert and dance hall in America. He performed concerts in Canada as well as Great Britain, France, The Netherlands, Belgium, Poland, Hungary, Romania, Austria, Denmark, Norway, Sweden, Italy, Germany, Spain, Brazil, Uruguay, Argentina, Chile, Peru, Ecuador, Colombia, Venezuela, Puerto Rico, Panama, Nicaragua, and Mexico. He visited the Far East and Southeast Asia including Japan, Taiwan, the Philippines, Hong Kong, Thailand, Burma, India, Ceylon, Singapore, Malaysia, Indonesia, Australia, and New Zealand. He also played in the Soviet Union. There is barely a corner of the globe he did not perform in.

He received the Presidential Medal of Freedom, several postage stamps were made in his honor, and he was honored with fifteen honorary degrees from universities and colleges. His music is included in study programs all over the United States and the world. In 1988, a large collection of Ellington artifacts was turned over to the Smithsonian Institution for posterity. He received hundreds of trophies, medals, plaques and awards. They could easily fill several rooms. He is, of course, a proud inductee in the Jazz Hall of Fame.

He was a suave, elegant man, whose moniker Duke fit him perfectly. He was from a different universe, a different world; the court of Ellingtonia had its own style and reigned supreme for six decades. He was a known aficionado of billiards, a major flirt, and a workaholic.

The scope of Duke Ellington's achievements is immeasurable. There has never been anyone before him or since who has captured so much of the world, lived a life so full of triumphs and tragedies. Adding up all of his accomplishments—the thousands of recordings, hundreds of albums, too many concerts, his sidemen, the awards bestowed upon him—truly emphasizes the fact that he was beyond category.

Band Members 1927–1974

SAXOPHONES

Tenor Saxophone

Barney Bigard 27–42
Johnny Hodges 28–51, 55–70 (also played soprano sax)
Ben Webster 35, 36, 40–43, 48–49
Jimmy Hamilton 43–68
Al Sears 44–49
Norris Turney 69–73 (also played flute)
Harold Ashby 68–74

Alto Saxophone

Russell Procope 46–74

Baritone Saxophone	*Bass Trombone*
Harry Carney 27–74	Chuck Connors 61–74

BRASS

Trumpet
William "Cat" Anderson 44–47, 50–59, 61–70
Harold Shorty Baker 42–44, 46–51, 57–59, 61–63
Willie Cook 51–58
Mercer Ellington 65–74 (also served as road manager)
Freddie Jenkins 28–34, 37–38
Wallace Jones 38–44
Taft Jordan 43–47
James Miley 23–29
Terry Clark 51–59 (also played flugelhorn)
Artie Whetsol 20–23, 28–38
Charles Williams 29–40, 62–74

Trombone
Juan Tizol 29–44, 51–53, 60 (also was composer and copyist with band)
Laurence Brown 32–51, 60–69
Buster Cooper 62–69
Tyree Glenn 47–50
Quentin Jackson 48–59
Joe Nanton 26–46
Chuck Connors 61–74

Clarinet	*Cornet*
Otto Hardwick 20–28, 32–43	Rex Stewart 34–45
Barney Bigard 27–42	
Jimmy Hamilton 43–68	
Russell Procope 46–74	

RHYTHM

Bass	*Drums*
Hayes Alvis 35–38	Sonny Greer 1920–1951
Joe Benjamin 70–74	Louis Bellson 51–53, 54–55, 65
Jimmie Blanton 39–41	Rufus Jones 66–73
William Braud 27–35	
Wendell Marshall 48–54	
Oscar Pettiford 45–48	
Billy Taylor 34–39	
Sam Woodward 55–68	

Guitar/Banjo	*Piano*
Fred Guy 25–49	Billy Strayhorn 39–67
	(also was composer, orchestrator,
	collaborator and wrote some of
	the lyrics for the band)

SINGERS

Ivie Anderson 31–42
Alice Babs 63–73
Kay Davis 44–50
Al Hibbler 43–51
Herb Jeffries 39–42
Betty Roche 42–44, 51–53
Joya Sherrill 42, 44–45, 56, 63
Ray Nance 40–45, 46–61, 62–63, 65
        (also was cornetist, violinist, and dancer)

Discography

Afro-Eurasian Eclipse, Original Jazz Classics 645.
All-Star Road Band 1, Sony 40012.
All-Star Road Band 2, Sony 39137.
American Legends, Vol. 8, Laserlight 12731.
And Friends: Compact Jazz, PGD/Verve 33291.
At Basin Street East, Music & Arts 908.
At Birdland, Jazz Unlimited 2036.
At Columbia University, BMG/Musicmasters 65122.
At Newport, Sony 40587.
At Tanglewood, BMG/RCA 5692.
At the Cotton Club, RCA/Camden 459.
At the 1960 Monterey Jazz Festival—Part 1, Status 1008.
At the 1960 Monterey Jazz Festival—Part 2, Status 1009.
Back Room Romp, Sony 44094.
Beyond Category: Musical Genius, BMG/RCA 49000.
Birth of a Band, 1924–26, EPM/Hot 'n' Sweet 151042.
Birthday Sessions Volumes 1–5, Laserlight 15965.
Black & Tan Fantasy, EPM/Hot 'n' Sweet 151112.
Black Beauty 1927–28, EPM/Hot 'n' Sweet 151122.
Black, Brown & Beige, Sony 64274.
Blue Note New York City, Canby Records 1010.
Blues in Orbit, Sony 44051.
Carnegie Hall, Vintage Jazz Classics 1024.

Carnegie Hall Concerts, 1943, Prestige 34004.
Carnegie Hall Concerts, 1944, Prestige 24073.
Carnegie Hall Concerts, 1946, Prestige 24074.
Carnegie Hall Concerts, 1947, Prestige 24075.
Carnegie Hall '64, Moon 61.
Classically Duke, Star Line 61074.
Cool Rock, Laserlight 15782.
Cornell University Concert, BMG/Musicmasters 65114.
Cotton Club Stomp, 1929, EPM/Hot 'n' Sweet 151292.
Creole Rhapsody, EPM/Hot 'n' Sweet 152322.
Digital Duke, Uni/GRP 9548.
Drum Is a Woman, Tristar Music Imports 36658.
Duke Ellington, 1927–34, Nimbus 6001.
Duke Ellington, Featuring Paul Gonsalves, Original Jazz Classics 623.
Duke Ellington, WMO 90324.
Duke Plays Ellington, Topaz Jazz 1020.
Duke's Big 4, Pablo 2310703.
Duke's Men: Small Group, Sony 46995.
Early Ellington, Complete Brunswick Recordings Decca 640.
Echoes of the Jungle, EPM/Hot 'n' Sweet 152332.
Ellington Indigos, Sony 8053.
Ellington Suites, Original Jazz Classics 446.
Ellington—56, Le Jazz 27.
Essence of Duke Ellington, Sony 47129.
Essential Recordings, Le Jazz 2.
European Tour, Band Stand 1509.
Far East Suite, BMG/RCA 66551.
Fargo, Vintage Jazz Classics 1019.
Felling of Jazz, Black Lion 760123.
Festival Session, Tristar Music Imports 36659.
From the Blue Note Chicago 195, Musidisc 550292.
Gold Collection, DeJavu 5110.
Great Chicago Concerts, BMG/Musicmasters 65110.
Great Duke Ellington, Hindsight 335.
Great London Concerts, BMG/Musicmasters 65106.
Great Paris Concert, WEA/Atlantic 304.
Happy-Go-Lucky, WEA/Discovery/Trend/Musicraft 70052.
Happy Reunion, Sony 40035.
Harlem, Pablo 2308245.
Harlemania 1928–1929, EPM/Hot 'n' Sweet 151282.
HIFI Ellington, Tristar Music Imports 80881.
His Mother Called Him Bill, BMG/RCA 6287.

Homage à Duke, Tristar Music Imports 36655.
Hot Summer Dance, Sony 48631.
In a Mellotone, BMG/RCA 51364.
In Boston 1939–1940, Jazz Unlimited 2022.
In Europe, 1965, Rte 15032.
In the Uncommon Market, Pablo 2308247.
Indigos, Sony 44444.
Indispensable, BMG/RCA 66679.
Intimacy of the Blues, Original Jazz Classics 624.
Intimate Ellington, Original Jazz Classics 730.
Jazz at the Plaza, Tristar Music Imports 36660.
Jazz Cocktail, ASV/Living Era 5024.
Jazz Collector Edition, Laserlight 15753.
Jazz Group, 1954, Musidisc 550192.
Jazz Party, Sony 40712.
Jubilee Stomp, BMG/RCA 66038.
Jungle Nights in Harlem, BMG/RCA 2499.
Latin American Suite, Original Jazz Classics 469.
Liberian Suite, Tristar Music Imports 80882.
Live at Newport, 1958, Sony 53584.
Live at 1957 Stratford Festival, Music & Arts 616.
Live at the Blue Note, CEMA/Capitol 28637.
Live at the Rainbow Grill, Moon 49.
Live at the Whitney, Uni/GRP 173.
Masterpiece 2, EPM/Jazz Archives 158142.
Meadowbrook in Manhattan, Black Label 8029.
Midnight in Paris, Tristar 36661.
Mood Indigo, 1930, EPM/Hot 'n' Sweet 152252.
The Mouche: 1928, EPM/Hot 'n' Sweet 151272.
Music Is My Mistress, BMG/Musicmasters 5013.
My People, Sony 52759.
Never Before Released Recording, BMG/Musicmasters 5041.
New Mood Indigo, Sony 40359.
New Orleans Suite, WEA/Atlantic 1580.
Okeh Ellington, Sony 46177.
Orchestra Works Ellington, Uni/MCA 42318.
Part 2—In Concert at the Pleyel, Magic 40.
Passion Flower, Moon 74.
Pianist, Original Jazz Classics 717.
Piano Album, CEMA/Capitol 92863.
Piano in Background, Tristar Music Imports 36663.
Private Collection, Stud Music Deluxe 22.

Private Collection Dance Concerts: California 1958, WEA/Atlantic 91042.
Private Collection Dance Dates: California 1958, WEA/Atlantic 91230.
Private Collection New York & Chicago, '65 '66 '71, WEA/Atlantic 91234.
Private Collection Studio Sessions: Chicago '56 WEA/Atlantic 91041.
Private Collection Studio Sessions: 1957, WEA/Atlantic 91232.
Private Collection Studio Sessions: 1957 & 1962, WEA/Atlantic 91231.
Private Collection Studio Sessions: New York 62, WEA/Atlantic, 91043.
Private Collection Studio Sessions: New York 1963, WEA/Atlantic 91044.
Private Collection Studio Sessions: New York, 1968, WEA/Atlantic 91233.
Private Collection Suites: New York 1968 & 1970, WEA/Atlantic 91045.
Recollections of Big Band Era, WEA/Atlantic 90043.
Reminiscing in Tempo, Sony 48654.
Rockin' in Rhythm, Jazz Hour 73504.
SRO, Jazz Classics 7680.
SRO/Things Ain't the Way, Jazz Classics 9066.
Satin Doll, Jazz Club 3502.
Second Sacred Concert, Prestige 24045.
70th Birthday Concert, Cema/Capitol 32746.
Sir Duke, Drive Archive 41019.
Small Group-1940–46, BMG/RCA 66471.
Solos, Duets & Trios, BMG/RCA 2178.
Sophisticated Duke, Quicksilver Records 5002.
Sophisticated Lady, BMG/RCA 61071.
Standards—Live at the Scalle Plaza, JMY 1011.
Stereo Reflections in Ellington, Natasha Imports 4016.
Such Sweet Thunder, Tristar Music Imports 80884.
Take the "A" Train, Four Star 40063.
Things Ain't the Way They Used to Be, Jazz Classic 9061.
This One's for Blanton, Analogue Productions 15.
Three Suites, Sony 46825.
Through the Roof, Drive Archive 42416.
Togo Brava Suite, CEMA/Capitol 30082.
Uncollected, Vol. 1, Hindsight 125.
Uncollected, Vol. 2, Hindsight 126.
Uncollected, Vol. 3, Hindsight 127.
Uncollected, Vol. 4, Hindsight 128.
Uncollected, Vol. 5, Hindsight 129.
Unknown Sessions, Tristar Music Imports 36664.
Up in Duke's Workshop, Original Jazz Classics 633.

Uptown, Sony 40836.
Uptown Downbeat, Avid 546.
Yale Concert, Original Jazz Classics 664.

WALTER PAGE (1900–1957)

The Blue Devil

After the Storyville section of New Orleans was closed down in 1917, musicians emigrated north and most of them settled in Chicago. However, some never made it to the Windy City and created jazz hotbeds in a number of towns along the Mississippi River including Dallas, Oklahoma City, Tulsa, Kansas City, Memphis, St. Louis and Omaha. The regional outfits that sprang up in these and other centers became known as territory bands. Although often looked down upon by their more sophisticated city cousins, the territory bands were forces to be reckoned with. One mid-western bandleader proved it as a blue devil. His name was Walter Page.

Walter Sylvester Page was born February 9, 1900, in Gallatin, Missouri. He developed an interest in music at an early age and studied the tuba and bass drum. Once he had proficiently honed his skills he played in local brass bands. In high school he added the string bass and the baritone saxophone to his musical abilities.

Although the glamour of the music world greatly interested young Page, he played music for fun. He had decided on a teaching career and was actively taking such a course in a Kansas university while moonlighting for saxophonist Dave Louis' band. Eventually Page realized that music was his true calling and decided to pursue wholeheartedly this ambition.

He took a giant step in achieving his goals when he joined Bennie Moten's Orchestra in 1918. Moten's outfit was a territory band that openly challenged the New Orleans groups of Jelly Roll Morton, Joe "King" Oliver, and the Original Dixieland Jazz Band for supremacy. However, while the aforementioned played mostly in New Orleans and then in Chicago, Moten's concert route was the Midwest where he was immensely popular.

Benjamin Moten was born on November 13, 1894, in Kansas City, Missouri. His mother was a pianist who taught her son the basic rudiments of the instrument. Although Moten would play piano during his days as bandleader, he switched to the baritone saxophone before his teens. At the tender age of twelve he joined his first group, Lacy Blackburn's Juvenile Brass Band, and remained in it for a year. Originally influenced by ragtime, Moten developed a more sophisticated sound by blending ragtime with a heavy dose of Kansas City blues, which was prominent at the time, as well as a touch of barrelhouse, boogie-woogie, and classical. He tied the various elements together to create his own unique style.

Page remained in Moten's band from 1918 through 1923. Then he took his string bass and baritone sax talents with him and joined the Billy King Road Show, a band led by trombonist Emir Coleman. When the group disbanded two years later, Page was left without employment. It was at this point that he vowed he would never again be left in a desperate situation so he took over the remnants of Coleman's band and formed the Blue Devils.

The Blue Devils would boast a number of famous musicians, including Page on bass (who by this time had developed his mature sound), on occasion Emir Coleman, trombonist-guitarist-arranger Eddie Durham, pianist Count Basie, and singer Jimmy Rushing.

Although he possessed a wealth of talent in his Blue Devils, he only recorded the group a couple of times; the band was best captured live. His Blue Devils were serious rivals to Bennie Moten's Orchestra and may have passed them in popularity, but beginning in about 1929, Moten was able to lure away many of Page's best musicians, including Count Basie.

In 1931, Page turned over the band to trumpeter James Simpson and returned to his base of Kansas City where he worked with a number of small bands until he joined his former arch rival Moten. Interestingly, the Blue Devils continued to tour under a variety of leaders, including drummer Earnest Williams, altoist Buster Smith, and trumpeter Leroy "Shake" White.

Page remained in Moten's band until 1934. He joined a Basie-led outfit for a brief period of time before becoming part of the Jeter-Pillars group in St. Louis in the fall of 1934. Although he had gained fame as bandleader of the Blue Devils, he would enjoy more acclaim as part of one of the greatest rhythm sections in jazz history when he joined Count Basie's big band in 1936.

The famed rhythm section was composed of four equal individuals. Page, an excellent bass player, was never adventurous and put down a solid walking bass line that propelled all the soloists in the band. He was joined by the revolutionary drumming of Jo Jones, who opted to ride the cymbals and drop bombs on the snare drum instead of the old New Orleans-style of flailing away at the bass drum. The third member of this group, the supreme guitar and banjo player Freddie Green, was never recognized for his soloing ability but gained notoriety as the consummate swing string slinger. Green, with his killer chord combinations, was always in step with Page, Jones and Basie. The foursome was rounded out by the excellent piano virtuosity of Basie.

From 1936 to 1942 there wasn't a better rhythm section in the big band and swing idiom. The four rhythm makers were able to create and weave a patterned beat that provided the perfect launch pad for the horn players in the group, who included Hershal Evans, Buck Clayton, Harry "Sweets" Edison, Benny Morton and the great Lester "The Prez" Young. It was during this period that Page enjoyed major acclaim for his talents on the string bass. He opened the door for virtuosos like Jimmie Blanton to garner more respect for the instrument.

Despite numerous recordings with the Basie band, Page left in 1942 and found work with small combos in Kansas City. Later he toured with Nat Towle's outfit, then worked with Jesse Price's group in Joplin, Missouri. But after drifting for four years, Page returned to the Basie fold in 1946 and stayed for three years.

In 1949, he joined Hot Lips Page's (no relation) group. He remained there for a couple of years before moving on to back up the singer Jimmy Rushing. Although Page had always been based in Kansas City, he moved to New York in 1951 where he found much work as a freelance artist. Occasionally, his freelance schedule was interrupted by stints in the outfits of Jimmy McPartland, Eddie Condon, and Ruby Braff.

In the summer of 1956, Page toured with Wild Bill Davison and later on in the year with Roy Eldridge. Because of his abilities on bass and other instruments, Page was never out of work for long. By this time he was already a legend from his days as leader of the Blue Devils, as well as the time he spent with Basie at the height of the big band craze.

In 1957, Page contracted pneumonia and the complications that followed resulted in his untimely death on December 20 of that same year.

Walter Page was an important member of the jazz scene from the early 1920s until the 1940s. Although he never achieved superstar status, he struck fame twice as a leader of the famed Blue Devils and as the driving pulse in the Count Basie Band.

In the realm of jazz bassists, Page occupies a special place. Although he was never heralded as a magnificent soloist, he was in many ways an underrated bass player. He could drive and swing the band with his grooving bass to beat the devil. Page understood the textures of swing as well as, and better than, most. He was a vital step in the transition of jazz of the 1920s to the Big Band sound.

Page was a logical extension of Pops Foster. He was able to take the simple timekeeping device of Foster's sound into a different realm. He was able to keep time but in complex patterns that far exceeded what Foster could manage. Any jazz fan can trace the line from Page to Foster just by listening and comparing each of their roles in jazz.

In an era that produced several excellent bass players, Page was a touch better than Milt Hinton, Chubby Jackson, and Slam Stewart. Although he didn't enjoy as long a career as Hinton did, nor was he a showman-type bassist like Jackson, Page was more of a team player than either of them. It wasn't until Jimmie Blanton arrived on the scene that Page fell to second spot among bassists. However, without Page setting the table, the exploits of Blanton would never have happened.

All of the bass players who came after Page owe him a particular debt. Ray Brown, Oscar Pettiford, Charles Mingus, Charlie Haden, Niels-Henning Orsted Pedersen, Ron Carter, Stanley Clarke and Jaco Patorius can trace their roots back to Page. They built upon the foundation that he laid down in over two decades as a serious musician.

Page is unique for yet another reason. Along with John Kirby, he was one of the few bass-playing bandleaders. Others played different instruments. However, Kirby never enjoyed the same success as Page did with his Blue Devils.

As a bandleader, Page is responsible, along with Bennie Moten, for giving the territory bands the respect they deserved. Although Page would eventually lose his best players to Moten, he was more than a capable field general giving instructions from his position. His Blue Devils seriously challenged Moten for the latter part of the 1920s and the early 1930s. His inability to keep his musicians is in no way a reflection on his ability as a leader.

Page worked with many of the greatest names in jazz. A partial list includes Earle Warren, Benny Morton, Harry "Sweets" Edison, Dicky Wells, Dan Minor, Jimmy Rushing, Ed Lewis, Buddy Tate, Eddie Durham, Herschel Evans, Vic Dickenson, Benny Goodman, Ben Webster, Buster Bailey, Allan Reuss and a host of others. Of course his most famous partners were the rhythm section of the Basie band and Lester Young.

Walter Page enjoyed two very distinct and successful phases in his career—as leader of the Blue Devils and as part of the rhythm section of the Basie band—which ensured him a very special place in the history of jazz. He excelled in two different eras. Undoubtedly, the "Blue Devil" was an inspiration to all those he touched with his special musical gifts.

Discography

Basie, Count, Vol. 4, 1937, MJAZ 48.
Basie, Count, Vol. 5, 1937–1938, MJAZ 49.
Basie, Count, Vol. 6, 1938, MJAZ 85.
Basie, Count, Vol. 7, 1938, MJAZ 87.
Basie, Count, Vol. 8, 1938–1939, MJAZ 111.
Basie, Count, Vol. 9, 1939, MJAZ 115.
Basie, Count, Vol. 10, 1939 MJAZ 153.
Basie, Count, Vol. 11, 1939, MJAZ 158.
The Best of Early Basie, 1936-1939, GRD 655.

JIMMIE LUNCEFORD (1902–1947)

Harlem Shout

The era of the big band and swing leaders was an exciting one for many different reasons. The music created during this period was some of the most imaginative and danceable ever produced by the human spirit. Each style boasted its own proper champion. There was the hard-driving swing of Benny Goodman, the forceful Dixieland of Bob Crosby, the simple, riff-filled swing of Count Basie, the highly developed swing of Duke Ellington and the very commercial swing of Glenn Miller. Then there was the king of relaxing swing who never failed to delight audiences with his Harlem Shout. His name was Jimmie Lunceford.

Jimmie Lunceford was born James Melvin Lunceford on June 6, 1902, in Fulton, Missouri. Like so many of his jazz brethren, Lunceford came from a musical family. His father was a choirmaster. Later, when the family moved to Denver, Colorado, Lunceford would study under the tutelage of Paul Whiteman's father. Along the way, little Jimmie learned to play a number of instruments including all the saxophones, guitar, and trombone.

But there was another important part to Lunceford's education: he studied musical theory, familiarizing himself with the inner workings of song. This would prove to be incredibly beneficial throughout his career. Lunceford graduated with a Bachelor of Music from Fisk University in 1926—a time when opportunities for higher learning for African-Americans were rare. Also, while he was studying the structure of music, he was indulging in the practical side, playing alto sax with George Morrison's Orchestra. During summer vacation he filled out his resume by appearing with John C. Smith, Wilbur Sweatman, Elmer Snowden and Deacon Johnson.

Although the idea of forming a band and enjoying the life of an itinerant jazz musician was tempting, he opted for a more secure position in teaching. It was at Manassa High School in Memphis that Lunceford began to recruit and assemble his band from the student pool of his classes. These early formations of the Jimmie Lunceford Orchestra played summer sessions all over the Memphis area.

In 1929, Lunceford and a few of his former students—Edwin Wilcox, Willie Smith, and Henry Wells—joined forces and turned professional. The group found work plentiful in the Memphis area where they had built up a strong local following. They played residencies as well as broadcasting over Memphis radio. Eventually the band broke out of the regional territory and played dates in Buffalo and Cleveland. By 1933, the Jimmie Lunceford Orchestra was ready to be unleashed upon the jazz world.

The group played a residency at the famed Lafayette Theatre, then toured the New England area before returning to New York and starring at the fabled Cotton Club. It was there that the Lunceford band began to gain a reputation as one of the best swing outfits in the nation. The group executed the colorful and wildly imaginative arrangements of Sy Oliver to perfection.

Sy Oliver, born in Michigan and the son of two music teachers, played the trumpet at the age of twelve and toured all over the Ohio area with a variety of bands. He was teaching music and arranging on the side when he caught the attention of Lunceford, who invited the arranger genius to join the group. Oliver played a vital part in Lunceford's rise to national prominence by developing a two-beat swing sound that was copied by dozens of bands.

The band played a mixture of material including simple songs with catchy melodies like "Dream of You" and "On the Beach at Bali-Bali." They also played complex songs like "My Blue Heaven." They delighted audiences with novelty songs like "Organ Grinder Stomp." The variety of material was instrumental in elevating the Lunceford Orchestra above others.

But there was more to the group's success than just the brilliant and diverse compositions; there was a sense of theatrics and inner dynamics. The Lunceford band didn't just play music to entertain the audience; they understood showmanship. They possessed a strong visual side. Trumpeters would point their instruments to the ceiling and the band wore

colorful costumes. It was this entertaining element of the band that separated it from other groups on the circuit.

The group recorded a number of sides for Decca, including "Harlem
Shout," "Harlem Express," "For Dancers Only," "Swinging Uptown,"
"Annie Laurie," "Swanee River," "Muddy Water," "Slumming on Park
Avenue," "Stomp It Off," "Avalon," and "Sleepy Time Gal." Many of these
compositions were some of the most recognized songs of their time.
Although Lunceford had been recording for some time it was the records
he made with his band in the middle of the 1930s that are best remem-
bered.

By the middle of the decade, the Jimmie Lunceford Band was one
of the most popular outfits in the country, challenging the Duke Ellington Orchestra for supremacy. A tour of Scandinavia in 1937 exposed the
band to a European audience and increased their large fan base.

Back in the United States, Lunceford was so much in demand that
the band was constantly on the road. They performed a couple of hundred one night concerts, about twenty weeks of theatres, perhaps one long
residence of a month and a couple of weeks of well-deserved vacation.
The band traveled thousands of miles a year.

Trombonist Trummy Young joined the band in 1937 and became the
group's featured soloist along with altoist Willie Smith. The band was
also composed of Sy Oliver, guitarist Eddie Durham, pianist Ed Wilcox,
tenorman Joe Thomas, trumpeter Eddie Tompkins, and singer Dan Gris-
sam. Although they lacked the presence of truly great soloists (Smith and
Young being the only two genuine virtuosos in the ensemble), the Lunceford Band still managed to become one of the best of the swing groups
in the 1930s. The secret of the band's success was not relying on its star
soloists, but more on the ensemble sounds of a bright brass section, float-
ing saxophones, and a high-spirited rhythm section.

There was camaraderie among the musicians in the Lunceford Band.
The fraternal, almost gang-like atmosphere created a buoyant environment in which to create music. They managed to instill this cheerfulness
into their music and passed it on to the audience. The sense of exuberance created an unusual intensity that many bands could never match.

The good times and unprecedented success lasted until 1939, when
Sy Oliver was lured away by Tommy Dorsey. Although pianist Ed Wilcox,
altoist Willie Smith and Lunceford himself contributed solid arrangements, they were unable to fill Oliver's shoes. Also Lunceford underpaid
his sidemen and many left for better paying jobs, including drummer Jimmie Crawford, the heartbeat of the band, Willie Smith, Paul Webster,
Trummy Young and Freddy Webster. Eddie Tompkins was killed while
serving in the army. Although the replacements in the band included

quality musicians like trumpeter Freddy Webster and bassist Truck Parham, the contagious spirit of the early days was gone.

They never regained the heights of the pre-war days, but remained popular. On July 12, 1947, in Seaside, Oregon, Jimmie Lunceford, the exciting and successful bandleader, collapsed and died of a heart attack during an autograph signing session, although rumors throughout the years have circulated that a racist restaurant owner poisoned Lunceford. His death signaled the end of one of the most successful big bands of the era. While Eddie Wilcox and Joe Thomas were eager to carry on, the group disbanded for good soon after Lunceford's death.

Jimmie Lunceford was a man of many talents. Although he was a fine musician, his fame rests on his role as bandleader. For twenty years Lunceford fronted an incredibly exciting and superbly drilled jazz orchestra. The music he helped create serves as a tribute to an era considered by many as the golden age of jazz. As a bandleader he was able to mesh various personalities, a genuine group of individualists, into a cohesive unit.

The Lunceford Band was less emotionally expressive than Ellington's orchestra and didn't swing as hard as Basie's outfit, but they made up for these two weaknesses in other areas. They were a highly precise orchestra that could play a variety of music with equal brilliance, yet in many ways they were an everyman's band. They were a great dance band kicking out songs that filled the night air and made the audience stand up and dance. They were a visual treat with their showmanship, colorful uniforms, and sense of dynamics. They were daring and took chances playing novelty songs and other material that the Ellington Orchestra or Basie Band would never attempt.

Although not recognized as a brilliant musician Lunceford was capable on a variety of instruments. Evidence of his musicianship is scattered throughout the many recordings he made during his lifetime. In 1929, with his first band, the Chickasaw Syncopators, he played trombone. For most of the 1930s he played alto. On the recording of "Liza," he played the flute. During the Second World War, because many of his band members were called up, Lunceford replaced the missing players himself, fitting right in with his chameleon-like multi-instrumental abilities.

Lunceford was an influence on a number of later big bands, including the outfits of Stan Kenton and Glenn Miller. Stan Kenton was a bebop bandleader who included unusual compositions and arrangements in his repertoire in much the same way as Lunceford had a decade earlier. Miller, one of the most famous bandleaders of the big band era, copied the showmanship ideas such as the trumpeters pointing their instruments to the ceiling. Miller also scored a number one hit, "Chattanooga Choo-Choo," which many considered a novelty song rather than pure jazz. Miller, like Lunceford, died under strange circumstances.

Although many of Lunceford's musicians never gained important reputations, they were well-respected in jazz circles. Trummy Young was perhaps the most famous of the Lunceford alumni. A superb trombonist, he worked with Benny Goodman, Roy Eldridge, and Earl Hines, to name a few. Perhaps one of the underlying points of the Lunceford band is that although individually they were not considered superior musicians, together, as a group, under the excellent leadership of their boss, they were something special.

Lunceford was the glue that held everything together. He was a handsome man who directed the group like a schoolteacher with his baton signaling precise orders. He was a thorough teacher who demanded the best effort from his musicians since he was giving his all. His huge smile was as large as his talent and his heart.

Although it has been sixty years since Lunceford was entertaining his millions of fans throughout the country and abroad, the music remains a vital soundtrack of the swing era in jazz. While he might have had some shortcomings there is no denying the bandleader, multi-instrumentalist, and arranger his rightful place in jazz history as the man who never failed to please with his "Harlem Shout."

Jimmie Lunceford Band Circa 1937

SAXOPHONES

1st Sax	2nd Sax	3rd Sax	4th Sax
Willie Smith	Joe Thomas	Ted Buckner	Earl Carruthers

BRASS

1st Trumpet	2nd Trumpet	3rd Trumpet
Eddie Tompkins	Paul Webster	Sy Oliver

1st Trombone	2nd Trombone
James Young	Russell Boles

RHYTHM

Piano	Guitar	Bass	Drums
Edwin Wilcox	Albert Norris	Mose Allen	Jimmy Crawford

SINGERS

Dan Grissom, Sy Oliver, Joe Thomas, James Young, Paul Webster

Discography

Jimmie Lunceford, Masters of Jazz 17.
Stomp It Off, GRP 608.
Rhythm Is Our Business, ASV/Living Era 5091.
Volume 2, Master of Jazz 18.
Harlem Shout, Decca D 79238.
For Dancers Only, Decca DL-5393.
Lunceford Special, Columbia G 104.
Jimmie Lunceford & His Orchestra (1940), Circle 11.
Jubilee, Joyce KP-5005.
Volume 1 (1927–1934), Masters of Jazz 12.
1930–1934, Classics 501.
The Complete Jimmie Lunceford, Columbia 66241.
Jazz Heritage Jimmy's Legacy (1934–1937), MCAC-1320.
Big Bands, Time Life PT-19311 R959-2.
1934–1935, Classics 505.
Jazz Heritage Rhythm Is Our Business, MCAC 1302.
Jimmie Lunceford, Vol. 1 (1934–1939), Black and Blue 59241.
1935–1937, Classics 510.
1936–1943 Live Broadcast, Jazz Hour 3004.
1937–1939, Classics 520.
1939, Classics 532.
1939–1940, Classics 565.
1940–1941, Classics 622.
1941–1945, Classics 862.
The Uncollected Jimmie Lunceford and His Harlem Express (1944), Hindsight HSR-221.

GLENN MILLER (1904–1944)

In the Mood

There were many types of dance bands during the big band and swing era. There was the hard-driving swing of Benny Goodman, the more relaxed, infectious swing of Jimmie Lunceford, the Dixieland of Bob Crosby, the simple, riff-inspired yet personal swing of Count Basie, and the intellectual swing of Duke Ellington. Every ensemble, no matter what type of music they played, contained an element of commercial appeal. Undoubtedly, the most commercial of the swing bands between 1939 and 1942 was led by the man who was always in the mood to create great music. His name was Glenn Miller.

Glenn Alton Miller was born in Clarinda, Iowa, on March 1, 1904. There was musical talent in the family as Glenn's younger brother Herb became a trumpeter and led his own band for many years. Glenn spent much time roaming the country as the family relocated often. In 1909, they settled in North Platts, Nebraska, where Miller began his musical education, taking up the cornet and then the mandolin. After seven years in Nebraska, the family moved once again to Grant City, Missouri. Missouri, more of a musical state then Nebraska, was a good place for the young, impressionable Miller. It was in Grant City that he picked up the trombone. It seemed that he was born to play the trombone because he honed his skills quickly and joined the town band. The family moved again to Fort Morgan, Colorado, where he attended high school. But music was his future path and he left school to join Boyd Senter's band in 1921.

Miller remained in Senter's band for a brief period before he left to attend the University of Colorado. While a student, he continued to play gigs and started to compose as well as arrange. Eventually he joined Max Fischer's Band in Denver and traveled to the Golden State with them. In 1926, Miller joined Ben Pollack's band and returned to the East Coast. Two years later he left Pollack's band to work briefly with Paul Ash then decided to become a freelance arranger. By this time his skills as composer and arranger had progressed tremendously.

As a hired gun, Miller took part in many freelance recordings and arranged for a number of groups. But his main activity during this period was playing with Broadway shows. He participated in *Strike Up the Band*, *Whoopee!*, and *Girl Crazy*, to name a few. Although he joined Bert Lown's Orchestra for a brief time, he returned to writing and arranging. He toured with Smith Ballew in the early 1930s and then caught his first big break when he joined the Dorsey Brother's Orchestra in the spring of 1934. While he was arranging for the Dorsey Brothers outfit, he continued to study his art with Dr. Joseph Schillinger. In 1935, he left the Dorsey Brothers and went to work with Ray Noble. He would go on to arrange for the Glen Gray Casa Loma Band as well as for Ozzie Nelson. But after years of arranging and composing for others, Miller decided to fulfill his dream of directing his own big band.

In the winter of 1937, he began to assemble his group. He searched for the right combination of musicians who would complement each other and who were also capable of playing the type of music he envisioned. He recruited clarinetist Hal McIntyre from Connecticut. He discovered tenor saxist Johnny Harrell in Texas. Trumpeters Charlie Spivak, Sterling Bose, Manny Klein, guitarist Dick McDonough, piano player Howard Smith and drummer George Simon rounded out the band. Miller, of course, played trombone. He was able to secure a recording contract with Decca where the first edition of the Glenn Miller Band cut "Moonlight Bay," "Peg o' My Heart," and "I'm Sittin' on Top of the World."

After their live debut at the Hotel New Yorker, the band landed at the prestigious Blue Room in New Orleans, the heart of jazz music. They also played dates in Dallas and Minneapolis. Although he had paid his dues extensively for a number of years, it wasn't instant success for Miller. The incredible success he would enjoy during his prime was still two years away. Numerous personnel changes, uninterested crowds, serious competition, and the inability to please the audiences were just some of the frustrations that he experienced during his growing pains as the leader of his own outfit.

The band managed to eke out a meager existence working irregular dates although they were not well received by the audiences at the time. Miller continued to try different combinations and experimented with the arrangements. He introduced clarinet-led songs that would eventually become his trademark. He assigned a trumpet part to clarinetist Johnny Mince who had joined the band. He also allowed a fifth voice on saxophone.

Irving Fazola, a highly touted clarinetist, joined the orchestra, elevating the talent level. The band broadcasted over the radio but still didn't catch on. They cut two sides for Brunswick but neither one was a hit. In late 1937 Maurice Purtill arrived to occupy the drummer's spot for one night since he was on loan from Tommy Dorsey.

One year after forming his outfit Miller disbanded the group. Many of the personnel found work elsewhere including singer Kitty Lane, Fazola, trumpeter Les Biegel, and Jerry Jerome. After two months of inactivity, Miller reassembled his band. He had Hal McIntyre, Chummy McGreggor, bassist Rolly Bundoc and trumpeter Bob Price from his old group. He added clarinetist Wilbur Schwartz, drummer Bob Sprangler, and tenor sax Gordon Beneke. Miller also hired Ray Eberle as his singer.

This new edition performed in Boston and had a semi-steady gig at the Paradise restaurant. Despite the available dates personnel in the group continued to change too frequently. The vocalist, Gail Reese, quit, but her replacement, Marion Hutton, was a true find. She sang like a jewel and fit right in with the band. Paul Tanner, a trombone player, arrived on the scene. A subsequent concert in North Carolina proved to be quite discouraging and Miller almost broke up the band. However, when the group landed the coveted summer booking at the Glen Island Casino he ran his orchestra through their paces at the Meadowbrook. He felt that this was his last chance at making it in the music business.

The group's fortunes began to turn. When Moe Purtill joined the group permanently the problems on drums were solved. Miller also stocked his orchestra with an eight-man brass team. The pieces fell into place during that magical summer of 1939. Once the residency was over the orchestra had created an excitement that ricocheted them into the top spot among dance bands. They were quickly booked into some of the best places in the land and started to break attendance records.

The group also started to make records that people wanted to buy and listen to. They cut "Sunrise Serenade," "Moonlight Serenade," "Body and Soul," and "Now I Lay Me Down to Weep" on the Bluebird label. It was also during this time that the band recorded one of its biggest hits, "In the Mood." It was a very commercial number in which the tenor sax exchange between Beneke and Al Klink gave the song an edge. Soon the song became the band's most requested number and they played it up with the trumpeters and trombonists waving their horns high in the sky, that piece of showmanship Miller had stolen from Jimmie Lunceford. This number one hit was interesting for yet another reason. It featured one of Miller's clever arrangement devices. He would repeat the riff over and over again, then make it fade away before blasting it again and repeating the cycle.

The horn section was boosted by the arrival of trumpeter John Best and Ernie Caceres on clarinet and baritone sax. By this time the Miller band was the number one group in the land as they gigged non-stop. They played three radio programs a week, as well as a marathon five hours of music per night and six hours on the weekends, plus daily rehearsals. They also recorded a number of hit songs including "Tuxedo Junction" and "I'll Never Smile Again." Although Miller was arranging much of the band's music, Bill Finegan was adding his own touch. Later, Jerry Gray arrived on the scene fresh from one of Artie Shaw's disbanded groups.

Despite the band's success there continued to be some personnel changes. Herman "Trigger" Alpert joined the group and immediately sparked the orchestra with his popping bass sound. Trumpeters Billy May and Ray Anthony supplied another energy source when they joined in 1940. A few months later, Miller added the Modernaires, a vocal quartet that consisted of Chuck Goldstein, Hal Dickenson, Ralph Brewster and

Bill Conway. The four new singers helped Miller strike gold immediately with the monster seller "Chattanooga Choo Choo," the featured song in the band's first movie appearance in *Sun Valley Serenade*. Later the group would appear in their second movie, *Orchestra Wives*.

The hits continued to pour forth. Bobby Hackett arrived with his inspired cornet and added a beautiful touch to "Rhapsody in Blue." The band continued to record ballads including "Dearly Beloved." Later, in September 1942, the Glenn Miller Orchestra recorded its last track together, "Here We Go Again." Miller's decision to join the armed forces to help in the war effort spelled the end of the band.

His major activity in the army was to form a dance band to entertain the troops. He was able to assemble a quality orchestra with the talented men who had also decided to join the war effort. He recruited drummer Ray McKinley, trumpeter Zeke Zarchy, arranger Jerry Gray, bassist Trigger Alpert and trombonist Jim Priddy. All had been in Miller's orchestra during his civilian days. He added pianist Mel Powell, trumpeters Steve Steck, Bobby Nichols, and Bernie Privin, saxophonists Hank Freeman, Chuck Gentry, Jack Ferrier, and Gabe Gelinas, guitarist Carmen Mastren, as well as saxist-clarinetist Peanuts Hucko.

Miller brought his group to England and began to entertain the soldiers over the radio and at special concerts. Unfortunately, his reign as the king of the wartime outfits was over much too quickly. On December 15, 1944, he left Bedford, England, on his way to Paris to set things up for the band's arrival there a few days later. The plane never made its destination and his body was never recovered. He was thirty-nine years old.

Glenn Miller was an intelligent bandleader, an amazing arranger, a power on the trombone, and one of the most important figures in the annals of the big band era. Almost sixty years after his death his name continues to be popular among jazz fans and the general music population as a whole. His contributions were many.

He was a formidable trombone player. One of a number of bandleaders to actually play an instrument, he had a certain touch. There exists a school of thought that strongly believes that despite his warm, clear style he never received the credit he deserved because of his accomplishments in other areas. Although he might not have been quite in the same league as the big three of Kid Ory, Jack Teagarden and J. J. Johnson, Miller added to the trombone vocabulary with his poignant, happy style.

He was a noted arranger. Long before he found success with his own group he supplied pieces to numerous other bands including the Dorsey Brothers, Glen Gray, Ray Noble and Ben Pollack. He had a facility and incredible imagination for putting various sounds together. His use of

clarinet openings was unheard of before he did it. He knew how to juxtapose strengths against strengths and create a level of swing that was
unique. Miller fully understood the range of every instrument and was
able to extend every one to its outer limit to create his special brand of
commercial music.

Once he figured out exactly what the audience wanted he supplied
it and they could never get enough of it. The danceable brand of music
highlighted by his signature piece "In the Mood" clearly demonstrates
the creative genius of Miller as an arranger. His understanding of swing
textures was second to none. His ability to deliver audiences the fire and
passion of music was a great gift and underlines the aim of every group
no matter the genre.

Glenn Miller romanticized the swing era like no one before him. He
created a body of music that not only captured the imagination of a generation but also defined its very goals. A stubborn, artistic individual, he
looked like a stern schoolmaster. But there was a depth to his thinking
and actions that has never been duplicated. Although there were great
bandleaders during the swing era, Miller might have been the greatest of
them all. In many ways, he possessed the flexibility and imagination of
swing music itself.

After Miller's untimely death the band carried on. A variety of bandleaders took over the orchestra, but without their revered leader it was
never the same. However the wartime group fulfilled the vision it had been
created to do: entertain the troops. For six months in Europe, the Glenn
Miller orchestra filled the airwaves and urged the soldiers to carry on. He
would have been proud of the members of his band.

Decades after his mysterious passing, the Glenn Miller name continued to sell records at an incredible pace. The fact that the music still
remains vibrant even today is a tribute to the man who helped create it.
The song "In the Mood" is an all-time favorite and is played on numerous radio stations that don't broadcast jazz. It is an immediate hit with
every generation that hears it.

Glenn Miller did not have a long stay in the spotlight, since the band
was only together for five years before he left for the service; but it made
a huge enough impact to garner him entry in the Jazz Hall of Fame. In
1953, the film *The Glenn Miller Story* was made. The big band era is but
a faded memory in the pages of musical history, however, hearing the signature piece "In the Mood" conjures up feelings for those bygone days
and the man who created the legacy.

Glenn Miller Orchestra 1941

SAXOPHONES

1st Sax	*2nd Sax*	*3rd Sax*	*4th Sax*
Al Klink	Hal McIntyre	Ernie Caceres	Tex Beneke

CLARINET
Willie Schwartz

BRASS

1st Trumpet	*2nd Trumpet*	*3rd Trumpet*	*4th Trumpet*
Johnny Best	Ray Anthony	Mickey McMickle	Billy May

1st Trombone	*2nd Trombone*	*3rd Trombone*	*4th Trombone*
Glenn Miller	Paul Tanner	Jimmy Priddy	Frankie D'Annolfo

RHYTHM

Piano	*Guitar*	*Bass*	*Drums*
Chummy McGregor	Jack Lathrop	Trigger Alpert	Maurice Purtill

SINGERS

Dorothy Claire, Ray Eberly, The Modernaires: Bill Conway, Hal Dickenson, Ralph Brewster, and Chuck Goldstein

Discography

On the Air (Live), RCA Victor 6101.
Spirit Is Willing, Bluebird 66529.
On the Radio, Magic 63.
Little Brown Jug, Vol. 3, Vintage Jazz Classics 1038.
The Glenn Miller Carnegie Hall Concert, RCA 1506.
The Carnegie Hall Concert (Live), Bluebird 66147.
Live at the Paradise Restaurant, Magic 42.
Glenn Miller Concert, RCA Victor 1193.
For the Very First Time, RCA Victor 6100.
On the Alamo, Drive Archive 40164.
Live at the Café Rouge, Jazz Hour 1037.
Glenn Miller in Hollywood, Mercury 826635.
Glenn Miller Army Air Force Band, RCA Victor 6700.
Secret Broadcasts, RCA 52500.

War Broadcasts, Laserlight 15740.
Glenn Miller and his Army Air Force Orchestra, Soundlight 1104.
The Complete Recordings on Columbia Records, Everest 4005.
Best of the Big Bands: Evolution of the Band, Columbia 48831.
Greatest Hits, RCA Victor 68490.
Big Bands—Glenn Miller: Take Two, Time-Life 4TL-0021/R929-2.
The Complete Glenn Miller, Vol. 1–13, Bluebird/RCA 61015.
The Popular Recordings 1938–1942, Bluebird/RCA 9788.
1938–1942 Broadcast Versions They Never Recorded, Jazz Hour 1004.
The Chesterfields Broadcasts, Vol. 1, RCA 3873.
The Original Recordings of Glenn Miller and his Orchestra, RCA 829.
String of Pearls, RCA 2-1068.

JIMMY DORSEY (1904–1957)

Blue Champagne Swing

Arguably, jazz is one large family. Although there have always been long standing debates over traditional versus modern, acoustic versus electric, chord versus free, there is a bond that runs deep between all the practitioners of the genre. The friendships, the loyalties, the connections made between everyone is an unbreakable chain. Sometimes there is a genuine link between jazz performers, a fraternity, and a bloodline. During the swing and big band era there were two brothers, both bandleaders who enjoyed incredible popularity. One of them was known for his "Blue Champagne Swing." His name was Jimmy Dorsey.

James Francis Dorsey was born on February 29, 1904, in Shenandoah, Pennsylvania. It was from his father, Thomas F. Dorsey, that Jimmy received his musical education. The elder Dorsey was a music teacher and director of the Elmore Band. Jimmy began his musical career on the cornet and switched to trumpet. Later on, he took up the alto sax as well as the clarinet. From the tender age of seven, Dorsey was playing in his father's band. At the age of nine he would appear briefly in the J. Carson McGee King Trumpeters band.

In 1920, Jimmy formed the Dorsey's Novelty Six with his younger brother Tommy. The band eventually evolved into Dorsey's Wild Canaries and played a long residency in Baltimore. They also became one of the first groups to broadcast over the radio. Despite the popularity of the band Jimmy joined Billy Lusting's Scranton Sirens. That spelled the end of the Dorsey's Wild Canaries. He was with Lusting's long enough to make his debut recording. In 1924, Dorsey joined the California Ramblers.

Upon leaving the Ramblers, Dorsey freelanced on radio and appeared on the records of others including Jean Goldkette, Henry Thies, Ray Miller, Vincent Lopez, Paul Whiteman, and Red Nichols. He also joined these bands on regular club dates. Although the desire to form his own outfit was strong, the lucrative freelance market forced him to resist the temptation. Instead he joined Ted Lewis' group in 1930 and toured Europe with the bandleader before returning to United States and doing more freelance work.

He played on the records of Fred Rich, Jacques Renard, Victor Young, Andre Kostelanetz, Rudy Vallee, Lennie Hayton, and the Rubinoff Orchestras. He was also helping his brother run a part-time group called the Dorsey Brothers. In 1934, Jimmy and Tommy turned the Dorsey Brothers Orchestra into a full-time engagement. They made numerous recordings and played many residencies throughout the New York area. The band quickly built up a loyal following and was ready to ascend the top echelon of the big band circuit when an argument led to irreconcilable differences. The standoff cost both of them immensely as Benny Goodman picked up the slack and achieved unprecedented popularity as the leading big band.

After the break up, Jimmy Dorsey continued to lead the band. He eventually changed the name to the Jimmy Dorsey Orchestra and enjoyed much success for the next few years. The band swung hard with eloquent power on a number of pure jazz classics such as "Stompin' At the Savoy," "Major and Minor Stomp," "Mutiny in the Brass Section," and "Waddlin' at the Waldorf." They also played a number of pop hits such as "Amapola," "Tangerine," "My Prayer," "Yours," "Green Eyes," "Besame Mucho" and "Star Eyes" that featured vocal performances by Bob Eberly, Helen O'Connell and Kitty Kallen. Much of the music was tinged with a Latin flavor.

After his brother Tommy walked out of the band Jimmy needed to find a replacement on trombone. The successful candidate was a sixteen-year-old from Detroit named Bobby Byrne who astonished everyone with incredible tone and range at such a young age and fit perfectly into the fold.

Once they finished up their summer residency at the Glen Island Casino, the band landed in Los Angeles where they managed to capture the coveted "Kraft Music Hall" radio series backing Bing Crosby. They stayed there for eighteen months. During this period Kay Weber moved on and Vicki Joyce replaced her. But Joyce didn't last very long and Martha Tilton joined the band but never recorded with Dorsey and eventually joined Benny Goodman. The revolving door of singers in the band continued as Vi Mele arrived to replace Anne Richmond. Ella Mae Morse replaced Mele but was around for a short time. The shuffling stopped when a very pretty blonde singer named Helen O'Connell joined the group. O'Connell became one of the most popular singers of the time and her renditions of "Six Lessons from Madame La Zonga," "The Bad Humor Man," "Little Curly Hair in a High Chair," and "When the Sun Comes Out," only enhanced her sterling reputation. The band and O'Connell never sounded better than when she sang "Embraceable You" and "All of Me."

O'Connell and Eberly were a special team. The song "Green Eyes" was a big hit, as was "Amapola," "Yours," and "Tangerine." The singers in Dorsey's band propelled it to the top. By 1937, when the band returned to New York, Tutti Camarata was the chief arranger and also played lead trumpet. By 1938, the orchestra had settled into a comfortable twin personality group playing Dixieland two-beat and a modern, more swinging four-beat style. Tenor saxophonist Herbie Hymer, first trumpeter Ralph Muzzillo, jazz trumpeter Shorty Sherock, lead trombonist Byrne, and drummer Ray McKinley were outstanding musicians. Dorsey himself was solid on alto sax and clarinet.

Further changes occurred in the band when Don Redman was added to the arranging staff that included Camarata, Hal Mooney and Joe Lipman. When drummer McKinley left in the summer of 1939, the group was shaken up. Dave Tough replaced him but didn't last long. Buddy Schutz replaced Tough and settled in for a long stay.

It was in 1939 that Jimmy and Tommy reunited briefly. The brothers had barely spoken to each other in the past five years ever since Tommy had walked off the stage. Although they were together for one night, the reunion didn't last and they continued on their separate paths. Jimmy Dorsey would enjoy further success with hits such as "I Understand," "I'm Glad There Is You," "I Get Along Without You Very Well," and "Marie Elena." The songs showcased Bob Eberly's vocals.

The band continued to make popular music for the masses into the early 1940s. But in 1943, when Eberly joined the Army, the Dorsey band suffered a decline in popularity. By this time O'Connell had left the band. A number of singers tried to fill the impossibly large shoes of the Eberly-O'Connell team including Kitty Kallen, Buddy Hughes and Bob Carroll, but weren't successful.

By 1943, Dorsey had enjoyed his greatest success. His nine-piece brass section included five trumpets, most notably Nate Kazebier. Tenor saxist Babe Russin and pianist Johnny Guarinieri were strong soloists. Later in 1946, personnel changes brought in guitarist Herb Ellis, pianist Lou Carter and drummer Earl Kiffe.

By 1945, the appeal of the big bands was waning in the face of the onslaught of bop. In 1947, the Dorsey Brothers commenced a period of reconciliation when they appeared in the biographical film *The Fabulous Dorseys*. However, Jimmy would continue to lead his own groups during the late 1940s and early 1950s. It wasn't until 1953, eighteen years after their breakup, that the Dorsey Brothers were reunited. Jimmy joined Tommy and there was happiness in the Dorsey clan once again.

In 1956, when Tommy Dorsey died, Jimmy took over the band but was soon forced to turn over the leadership to Lee Castle because of his own declining health. On June 12, 1957, Jimmy Dorsey died of cancer in New York City. He was fifty-three years old.

Jimmy Dorsey is an important part of the big band and swing era for many different reasons. He was a superb bandleader, a good musician, and an important symbol during that era. Even today, forty-five years after his death, his name remains synonymous with the big band and swing era. Along with his brother he wrote an important chapter in jazz history.

Jimmy Dorsey was one of the most accomplished musicians of the 1920s and throughout the rest of his career. He provided an important voice on the alto sax and recorded one of the earliest solos on that particular instrument. It was Dorsey who blazed a path for all alto saxophonists, including Charlie Parker, to follow.

Dorsey possessed a distinct tone coupled with a rhythmic sensitivity and a technical dexterity that was far superior to anyone else's during his prime. He was capable of providing an immaculate tone that was a cutting edge sound. Also, Jimmy was a noted clarinetist able to capture the imagination of the audience in a live context or in the studio. He could also play a hot trumpet or cornet, adding still another dimension to his musical abilities.

The best evidence of the magic Dorsey was able to create, aside from his own recordings, is on the records of others. On alto he spiced up the recordings of the Paul Whiteman Orchestra, Bix Biederbecke and Frankie Trumbauer. He added his sure clarinet tone to the studio cuts of Jack Teagarden, Benny Goodman, Miff Mole and Red Nichols & His Five Pennies. Dorsey used his trumpet to good effect on sessions with the Venuti-Lang Blue Five as well as on the classic work *Eddie Condon & His All-Stars*.

Jimmy Dorsey was a solid bandleader. He was capable of coaxing the best from the musicians in his band and managed to keep his group on the road and in the studio on a regular basis. As a solo bandleader, or in the company of his brother Tommy, he ranks at the top of the list. The fact that he could match the members of his outfit on a musical level spurred them on.

But despite being in the spotlight as the head of a big band, he was not a natural born leader. He was a relaxed individual who liked to laugh and joke around. Perhaps one of the major reasons for the success of the Jimmy Dorsey Band was derived from the leader's ability to get along with people. In some ways he was too kind and laid back to compete among the more driven bandleaders during the big band boom. However, somehow he found a way not only to compete, but to excel.

The Jimmy Dorsey Orchestra participated in a number of films including *That Girl from Paris, Shall We Dance? The Fleet's In, I Dood It, Lost in a Harem, Lady Be Good,* and *4 Jacks and a Jeep.* Many of these movies were made during World War II as Dorsey contributed the best he knew how to the war effort. Of course, his most famous big screen project was *The Fabulous Dorseys,* which he made with his brother Tommy.

The body of work he left behind is truly remarkable. A partial list of songs that he gave to the world as a solo bandleader, or with his brother, includes many classics. The songs "Coquette," "Let's Do It (Let's Fall in Love)," "What a Diff'rence a Day Makes," "I Believe in Miracles," "Tiny Little Fingerprints," "Night Wind," "Lullaby of Broadway," "Chasing Shadows," "Every Little Movement," "You Are My Lucky Star," "I've Got a Feelin' You're Foolin,'" "You Let Me Down," "Is It True What They Say About Dixie?," "Change Partners," "The Breeze and I," "I Hear a Rhapsody," "High on a Windy Hill," "My Sister and I," "Maria Elena," "Blue Champagne," and "Ballerina" all possessed the Dorsey touch.

If there is one glitch in Jimmy Dorsey's career it is the fight that he had with his younger brother. Not only did the feud cost both of them considerable momentum, it also denied the world of jazz a missing element. Had they stayed together there is a good chance that they would be recognized as the greatest swing band of the era and would have taken away some of Benny Goodman's fame.

However, despite this shortcoming, Dorsey remains an important jazz personality of the 1920s through the 1940s. In an era that contained Glenn Miller, Duke Ellington, Count Basie, Jimmy Lunceford, Benny Goodman, Lionel Hampton, Artie Shaw, Bob Crosby, Bing Crosby, Tommy Dorsey, Frank Sinatra and dozens of other important jazz figures, Jimmy Dorsey carved out his own special place with his "Blue Champagne Swing."

The Jimmy Dorsey Orchestra Late 1930s

SAXPHONES

1st Sax	*2nd Sax*	*3rd Sax*	*4th Sax*
Milt Yaner	Herbie Hamyer	Leonard Whitney	Charles Frazier

BRASS

1st Trumpet	*2nd Trumpet*
Ralph Muzzillo	Shorty Sherock

1st Trombone	*2nd Trombone*	*3rd Trombone*
Bobby Byrne	Sonny Lee	Don Mattison

RHYTHM

Piano	*Guitar*	*Bass*	*Drums*
Freddie Slack	Roc Hilman	Jack Ryan	Ray McKinley

SINGERS

Bob Eberly, Don Mattison, Helen O'Connell and Kitty Kallen

Discography

Pennies from Heaven, ASV/Living 5052.
Contrasts, Decca GRD-626.
At the 400 Restaurant, Hep 41.
I Remember You, Empire 852.
Featuring Maynard Ferguson, Big Band Archives 1216.
Dixie by Dorsey, Columbia C-6095.
Dorseyland Band, Columbia C-6114.
Latin American Favorites, Decca 5091.
Contrasting Music, Volume 1, Coral CR-56004.
Contrasting Music, Volume 2, Coral 56008.
Muscrat Ramble, Swing House SWH 22.
The Fabulous Jimmy Dorsey, Fraternity 1008.
Dorsey, Then and Now: The Fabulous New Jimmy Dorsey Orchestra, Atlantic 81801-2.
The Early Years, Bandstand 7104.
The Best of Jimmy Dorsey, MCAC2-4073.
The Uncollected Jimmy Dorsey & His Orchestra, Vol. 1 (1939–1940), Hindsight HCD-101.

The Uncollected Jimmy Dorsey & His Orchestra, Vol. 2 (1942–1944), Hindsight HSR-153.
The Uncollected Jimmy Dorsey & His Orchestra, Vol. 3 (1949–1951), Hindsight HSR-165.
The Uncollected Jimmy Dorsey & His Orchestra, Vol. 4 (1950), Hindsight HCD-178.
The Uncollected Jimmy Dorsey & His Orchestra, Vol. 5 (1950), Hindsight HSR-203.
Perfidia, Laserlight 15678.
Jimmy Dorsey's Greatest Hits, Project 3 6036.
Plays His Greatest Hits, Rounder 335.
22 Original Recordings, Vanguard 415.
1942–1943 Broadcasts [live], Soundcraft 5002.
So Rare, Collectables 1175.

COUNT BASIE (1904–1984)

The Catalyst

In jazz, the bandleader is the driving force behind the ensemble of musicians as it is his responsibility to coordinate the various personalities and instruments into one cohesive sound. Often, the bandleader is also more than a conductor; he is a part of the band. One of the most important jazz swing generals who made enormous contributions was always a catalyst and sparked the players in his group to achieve greater heights. His name was Count Basie.

Count Basie was born William Basie on August 21, 1904, in Red Bank, New Jersey. His mother was a pianist, but little Bill began his musical career as a drummer. He gigged in a local kid's band and it was only later on that he took up the piano. Although he received regular lessons from neighborhood instructors, Basie idolized Fats Waller. Later on, Basie would receive formal tutorials from Waller, who took young Bill under his wing. Like Earl Hines before him, Basie mastered the stride style of piano but would evolve as a pianist and create his own personal sound.

He found work in his late teens playing at Leroy's in Asbury Park, and also worked with June Clark's band and Elmer Snowden. He also performed in theatres and accompanied a variety of unforgettable acts as well as better ones such as the Sonny Thompson Band. He spent two years with the Gonzelle White show but left in 1927 and accompanied the Whitman sisters for a brief period of time.

Basie's first big break came in 1928 when, stranded in Kansas City, he landed a job with Walter Page's Blues Devils, one of the top Midwest groups of the era. In Page's outfit he flourished and began to carve out a name for himself. Later he joined Bennie Moten's band, but eventually left to form his own aggregation in 1934. He worked as a solo performer then in a trio before once again joining Moten. Upon the latter's death a few short months later, Basie took over as leader. He renamed the group the Barons of Rhythm and began to slowly rise through the ranks of the big bands.

Despite suffering his fair share of rejection and disappointment, by 1936 some of the pieces were in place that would enable him to grab the attention of the jazz world. It was around this time that he acquired the name Count, a handle that was easily recognizable and carried weight. The name stuck with him for the rest of his life.

In 1936, Basie featured Billie Holiday as his vocalist. Holiday and the Basie band worked together wonderfully. Other personnel changes occurred. Freddie Green was brought aboard as well as trumpeters Harry Edison and Ed Lewis, trombonist Benny Morton and Eddie Durham, lead saxophonist Earle Warren and singer Jimmy Rushing. When Holiday left to join Artie Shaw, Helen Humes arrived to take her place. The new version of the band played the Famous Door in New York and that was when things really began to happen.

The band recorded a few sides for Decca including "Sent For You Yesterday," "Jumpin' at the Woodside," "Every Tub," "John's Idea," and the band's early signature piece "One O'clock Jump." By this time all the right personnel had been recruited as Basie assembled a talented band that featured a dynamic rhythm section comprised of himself on piano, drummer Jo Jones, bassist Walter Page, and rhythm guitarist Freddie Green. Exciting trumpeters like Emmett Berry, Al Killian, Joe Newman, Snooky Young, Clark Terry and Thad Jones joined the group. The top saxophonists included Hershal Evans and the incomparable Lester "Prez" Young on tenor. The singer, Jimmy Rushing, who became known as Mr. Five By Five, from his most famous song, took over the lead vocal spot. Later Joe Williams would replace him.

They swung hard in true Kansas City tradition as everything was arranged around the dynamic swinging rhythm section and left plenty of room for talented soloists like Young and Evans to astonish with their virtuosity. The Basie band was a tight unit that also knew how to improvise instantly. It was a formula that captured the imagination of young people across the nation and meant financial rewards for the Count and his cohorts. There was a simplicity and directness in the band's style that was truly irresistible.

The group's rise to stardom also resulted from the broadcasting of their concerts on station WXBY throughout the entire country. From their residency in Reno Club in Kansas City the Basie big band was heard consistently West of the Mississippi. The radio program caused a ricochet effect as the broadcasts drove record sales as well as the group's appearance fee. When they did appear live the band easily reproduced the simple, yet engaging sound that created their popularity and only enhanced their burgeoning reputation.

From 1936 to 1939, they traveled all over the country appearing in such vital venues as Roseland and the Savoy Ballroom. They also played at the Grand Terrain and the Famous Door in Chicago and at the Vendome Hotel in Buffalo. They toured the West Coast delighting their many fans who demanded to see them in concert. Despite the stiff competition from so many other bands on the jazz circuit the Basie band was constantly working.

The group—no matter who occupied the musical chairs—did not slow down during the following decades. As well as performing in many of the major ballrooms and theatres throughout the United States, they were featured in many full length films including *Top Man, Choo-Choo Swing, Reveille with Beverley, Stage Door Canteen, Hit Parade of 1943, Made in Paris, Cinderfella, Sex and the Single Girl, Jamboree, One More Time,* and *Man of the Family.* They provided the swinging rhythms, delivering a visual excitement as well as a musical thrill.

Their reign was short-lived as personnel changes would destroy the momentum they had built up. Freddie Green and Lester Young left in 1940. Jimmie Rushing also moved on. The war draft claimed Thad Jones, Jack Washington and Buck Clayton. Herschel Evans died in 1939. But despite the large turnover and the pressures to replace the departed, Basie managed to hold the show together. A succession of tenor saxophonists followed including Buddy Tate, Don Byas, Illinois Jacquet, Lucky Thompson, Frank Wess, Frank Foster, Eric Dixon, and Eddie (Lockwood) Davis.

In 1943, the Basie band played the famous Blue Room at the Hotel Lincoln becoming the first black group to perform there. But in many respects their best days were over. By the final years of World War II new faces in the band included Joe Newman, Emmett Berry, Al Killian, Eugene "Snooky" Young, J. J. Johnson, Eli Robinson, Illinois Jacquet, Rudy Rutherford, Rodney Richardson and Shadow Wilson.

The Basie orchestra continued into the late 1940s, but in 1950 Count was forced to break up the group. The band suffered its lowest ebb when they ventured into the realm of pop music with the song "Open the Door, Richard!" which topped the charts. But Basie, firmly rooted in the swing style of jazz, returned to the idiom with a small outfit, an eight-piece group that included players Harry Edison, Dickie Wells, Georgie Auld, Gene Ammons, Al McKibbon, Gus Johnson, and Freddie Green. It was this octet that occasionally supported Billie Holliday during the latter part of her career. Basie eventually broke up the group.

In 1952, Basie reformed his big band and enjoyed a renaissance in popularity. The new assemble consisted of Johnny Mandel, Frank Wess, Frank Foster, Eddie Jones and Charlie Fowikes, with Eric Wilkins and Neal Hefti writing exciting arrangements. They toured extensively throughout Europe and Scandinavia in 1956. Seven years later they performed in Japan. Despite the continued success there were numerous personnel changes. Some of the musicians to appear in the Count Basie Band during this period include Charlie Rouse, Serge Challoff, Clark Terry, Buddy De Franco, Jimmy Lewis, and even Buddy Rich. Another fine addition was singer Joe Williams, who gave the Basie Orchestra a different vocal dimension. An original Kansas City Devil, his growling, working-man sound added a much-needed bottom to the hard driving bluesy style that the Basie band executed so well. Despite the advent of rock and roll and the new thing that so many young jazz cats were playing, the simple Basie formula continued to find an audience.

During the 1960s, Basie continued to roll along and enlarged his audience base while retaining his old fans. He played Las Vegas engagements and also performed before Queen Elizabeth II. Although his outfit still swung, he incorporated a greater variety of songs that included movie themes and even Beatles tunes in an attempt to appeal to a younger crowd. He also backed some of the biggest singers in show biz in the studio and live performances including Bill Eckstine, Tony Bennett, the Mills Brothers, Sammy Davis, Jr., Kay Starr, Bing Crosby and Frank Sinatra.

By the 1970s, while many of the youngsters who had danced to the swing music during the Big Band's halcyon days were becoming grandparents, Count Basie and his swinging collection of musicians continued to please crowds. They were a globetrotting band and still sometimes managed to reach the heights of the group's pre-war glory days. In late 1976 Basie was hospitalized with a heart attack. Not one to slow down, he toured Europe a year later.

As the 1980s dawned, Count Basie could proudly look back upon a career that stretched six decades and won the many milestones he had achieved. However, on April 26, 1984, in Hollywood, Florida, the kid from

Red Bank, New Jersey, who had entertained millions, passed away. It was an international day of mourning.

Count Basie was a jazz legend long before his death and remains one long after. He matured during one of the most exciting eras in musical history. While styles over the years came and went, Basie continued to swing and play music that was in his heart. His contributions to jazz are immense.

Although he never gained widespread acclaim for his piano skills, Basie greatly advanced the art of modern piano playing. Originally from the school of stride piano, he learned how to strip the style down to its basic elements providing a simpler, clearer sound. He had a hand in shaping the music from stride to swing. But there was another dimension to Basie's piano sound. The rhythm and blues craze that fueled rock and roll and later rock music can trace a direct line to Basie's style. Every night Basie rocked audiences with his dazzling display of power chords and single run notes. His ability to incorporate a harder-edged sound to his style makes him an important pioneer. Fats Domino, Johnny Johnson, and Jerry Lee Lewis, three of the finest early rock and roll pianists, stole a page from the Basie catalog.

Many of the rock and roll bands would make the essential elements of a hard, swinging rhythm section dominated by piano, drums, bass and rhythm guitar the focal point of their band. This allowed large spaces for the soloist of the band. Groups such as Led Zeppelin, the global heavy metal force, understood Basie's principals of swing and as a result they were very successful.

Basie was also a pioneer of the organ, preferring the electric version of the instrument rather than the pipe. The electric model allowed him more freedom in his playing and meant he didn't have to completely change his style. Although his keyboard skills were exceptional, Basie rarely recorded songs using the electric organ. A rare example can be heard on *Satch and Josh*, the collaboration with the great Oscar Peterson.

Basie was also a solid bandleader. Although he was criticized for poor money management that led to the break up of his very talented outfit in 1950, Basie was always able to field a solid group whether it contained twenty musicians or a lesser number. A short list of Basie Band alumni includes Lester Young, Jo Jones, Sarah Vaughan, Ella Fitzgerald, Freddie Green, Harry "Sweets" Edison, Buck Clayton, Charlie Fowlkes, Walter Page, Jack Washington, Earle Warren, Marshall Royal, Jimmy Rushing, Billie Holiday, Helen Humes, Joe Newman, Ed Lewis, Dicky Wells, Bill Hughes, Frank Foster, Eric Dixon, and Frank Wess.

Three generations of jazz musicians applied the lessons they learned from Basie in their own styles. Johnny Otis, Big Joe Turner, Burning

Spear, Tito Fuente, Bob Brookmeyer, Michel Legrand, Hugh Masekela, Jay McShann, Buddy Johnson, Phil Nimmons, Al Belletto, Mike Longo, Sir Charles Thompson, Robert Lockwood, Jr., Sammy Price, Manny Albam, Maxwell Davis, and Charlie Parker are just a few who were touched by the Basie magic.

Basie was also a prolific recording artist and gave the world "Roseland Shuffle," "One O'clock Jump," "Super Chief," "Blues by Basie," "Basie's Back in Town," "Bleep Bop Blues," "Nails," "Fancy Meeting You," "Little Pony," "Bread," "Bootsie," "Hob Nail Boogie," "Whirly Bird," "Splanky," and "Please Send Me Someone to Love," to name but a few of his classics. While other jazz artists performed numbers from his catalog the driving rhythms and melodies of his songs are scattered throughout the music of dozens of rock, blues and latter–day jazz groups.

Basie was also an ambassador of jazz and traveled all over the world delivering his hot swinging rhythms to the delight of many different cultures which had never seen or heard a real American jazz performer. He was as responsible as any other jazz personality in spreading the appeal of the music to distant areas of the planet.

In many respects Count Basie was a simple man, a reflection to the straight-ahead blues groove and swing that he made famous. He was a warm, exuberant human being who, despite his easygoing outward façade, was one of the most determined and firm bandleaders of all time. His name remains prevalent today. After his death his band continued to tour and record under the leadership of a variety of directors. Despite delivering the same brand of swing to audiences of the world it could never be the same without him. Because more than anything else, William "Count" Basie was a catalyst whose legacy will live on as long as music is played.

The Count Basie Band Circa 1938

SAXOPHONES

1st Sax	*2nd Sax*	*3rd Sax*	*4th Sax*
Earl Warren	Lester Young	Ronald Washington	Hershal Evans

BRASS

1st Trumpet	*2nd Trumpet*	*3rd Trumpet*
Ed Lewis	Buck Clayton	Harry Edison

1st Trombone	*2nd Trombone*
Dan Minor	Benny Morton

RHYTHM

Piano	*Guitar*	*Bass*	*Drums*
Count Basie	Freddie Green	Walter Page	Jo Jones

SINGERS

Helen Humes and Jimmie Rushing

Discography

Bennie Moten's Kansas City Orchestra, Victor LPV-514.
The Count at the Chatterbox, Jazz Archives 16.
The Best of Count Basie, Decca DXSB-7170 2.
Good Morning Blues, MCA 2–4108 2.
Count Basie at the Famous Door, Jazz Archives 41936–41.
The Complete Count Basie, Vols. I to X, CBS 66101(F).
Lester Young Memorial Album, Fontana.
Super Chief, Columbia G-31224.
The Count, Columbia P-14355.
The V Discs, Vols. I and II, Jazz Society AA-505, AA-506.
Count Basie, RCA FXM 3–7053(F).
One O'clock Jump, Columbia JCL-997.
The Complete Count Basie, Vols. XI to XX, CBS 66102(F).
Basie Jazz (Count Basie Sextet), Clef 633.
Dance Session, Clef 626.
Sixteen Men Swinging, Verve 2–2517.
Dance Session #2, Clef 647.
Basie, Clef 666.
Count Basie Swings, Joe Williams Sings, Clef 678.
April in Paris, Verve 8012.
Hall of Fame, Verve 8291.
At Newport, Verve 8243.
Basie Plays Hefti, Roulette 52011.
Every Day I Have the Blues, Roulette 52033.
Breakfast Dance & Barbecue, Roulette 52028.
One More Time, Roulette 52024.
Chairman of the Board, Roulette 52032.
Not Now, I'll Tell You When, Roulette 52064.
Kansas City Suite, Roulette 52026.
Easin' It, Roulette 52106.
The Count Basie Story, Roulette RB-1.
The Legend, Roulette 52086.

Basie at Birdland, Roulette 52065.
First Time (The Count Basie and Duke Ellington Orchestras Together), Columbia CL 1715.
On My Way and Shoutin' Again, Verve V6–8511.
Count Basie & His Kansas City Seven, Impulse AS-15.
Lil Old Groovemaker, Verve V6–8549.
Basie's Beat, Verve V6–8687.
Straight Ahead, Dot 25902.
Standing Ovation, Dot 25938.
Basie Jam (nonet), Pablo 2310–718.
For the First Time (trio), Pablo 2310–712.
Basie Jam, #2, Pablo 2310–786.
Basie Jam, #3, Pablo 2310–840.
A Perfect Match (with Ella Fitzgerald), Pablo D2312110.
On the Road, Pablo D2312112.
The Count Basie Organization, ARPO 2.
Basie, Count, Vol. 1, 1929–1930, MJAZ 3.
Basie, Count, Vol. 2, 1930–1932, MJAZ 4.
Basie, Count, Vol. 3, 1929–1937, MJAZ 13.
Basie, Count, Vol. 4, 1937, MJAZ 48.
Basie, Count, Vol. 5, 1937–1938, MJAZ 49.
Basie, Count, Vol. 6, 1938, MJAZ 85.
Basie, Count, Vol. 7, 1938, MJAZ 87.
Basie, Count, Vol. 8, 1938–1939, MJAZ 111.
Basie, Count, Vol. 9, 1939, MJAZ 115.
Basie, Count, Vol. 10, 1939 MJAZ 153.
Basie, Count, Vol. 11, 1939, MJAZ 158.
The Best of Early Basie, 1936–1939, GRD 655.
20 Golden Pieces, BDL 2020.
Count Basie & His Orchestra-Fresno, CA 1959, JZU 2039.
The Lang-Worth Transcriptions Mid–1940s, SOU 4128.
The Essential Count Basie Vol. 1, 1936–1939, Sony 40608.
The Essential Count Basie Vol. 2, 1939–1940, Sony 40835.
The Essential Count Basie Vol. 3, 1940–41, Sony 44150.
Swingsation, 1937–1939, GRD 59920.
Greatest Hits 1947–1950, Victoria 68493.
Count Basie Featuring Anita O'Day, EPM 157922.
Count Basie Golden Years with Billie Holiday and Jimmy Rushing, Vol. 1, 1937, EPM 158052.
Golden Years Vol. 2, EPM 158062.
Golden Years Vol. 3, EPM 158072.
Golden Years Vol. 4, EPM 158082.

Masterpieces: Vol. 8, EPM 158232.
Blues & Boogie Woogie 1937–1947, EPM 159122.
April In Paris (Verve Master Edition) 1955–1956, PLG 521402.
Count Basie at Newport w/Joe Williams & Lester Young 1957, PLG 833776.
Count Basie & His Orchestra: The Classic Years Late 1930s—Early 1940s, PRE 172.
Count Basie and His Orchestra 1944, HS 224.
Count Basie and His Orchestra 1936–1938, CLC 503.
Count Basie and His Orchestra 1938–1939, CLC 504.
Count Basie and His Orchestra 1939, CLC 513.
Count Basie and His Orchestra 1939, Vol. 2, CLC 533.
Count Basie and His Orchestra 1939–1940, CLC 563.
Count Basie and His Orchestra 1940–1941, CLC 623.
Count Basie and His Orchestra 1941, CLC 652.
Count Basie and His Orchestra 1942, CLC 684.
Count Basie and His Orchestra 1943–1945, CLC 801.
Count Basie and His Orchestra 1945–1946, CLC 934.
Count Basie and His Orchestra 1946–1947, CLC 988.
Count Basie and His Orchestra 1947, CLC 1018.
Count Basie and His Orchestra 1947–1949, CLC 1107.
Count Basie and His Orchestra August 5, 1958, CAN 1011.
Count Basie and His Orchestra Live in 1958 & 1959, SAS 1037.
Count Basie and His Orchestra Cafe Society Uptown 1941, STC 2006.
Count Basie and His Orchestra Fresno, California—April 24, 1959, STC 8293.

TOMMY DORSEY (1905–1956)

Clambake Seven

Throughout the history of jazz it has been just as important to be a competent musician as an entertainer. During the swing and big band era, competition was fierce and every bandleader tried to give his outfit that extra edge. One of the best marketing strategies was the name of the band. Many became household names, including the group known as the

Clambake Seven led by the "Sentimental Gentleman of Swing." His name was Tommy Dorsey.

Tommy Francis Dorsey was born on November 19, 1905, in Shenandoah, Pennsylvania, into a musical family. Not only was his father, Thomas F. Dorsey, a highly respected music teacher, but his older brother Jimmy (by one year) was a gifted musician who would go on to make a name for himself. Tommy's first instrument was the trumpet, taught to him by his father. Although the leading white trumpet player of the day was Bix Beiderbecke, Dorsey followed the path taken by African-American trumpeters such as Louis Armstrong and King Oliver.

However, Tommy would make his biggest impact as a trombonist during his celebrated career. In his early days, he gained invaluable experience appearing often with his brother in the Dorsey's Novelty Six, which eventually became the Wild Canaries. Tommy was also part of Billy Lustig's Scranton Sirens, Jean Goldkette's Orchestra and the Henry Thies Orchestra. In all of these bands Tommy was paying his dues and biding his time until he would lead his own outfit.

In 1925, Dorsey greatly added to his resume with prolific freelance radio appearances and recordings. In 1927, he joined Paul Whiteman's Orchestra and remained there for a year. He moved on to play with Vincent Lopez, Roger Wolfe Kahn, Nat Shilkret, the Rubinoff Orchestra, Rudy Vallee, Victor Young, Walter Rosner, and Red Rich, among others. He was also leading a band in full partnership with his brother Jimmy, the duo playing dates together.

In the early 1930s Tommy continued his lucrative freelance radio work and appeared on recordings of others until 1934. It was then that he formed The Dorsey Brothers with Jimmy. Although they were a successful act and growing more popular at the cusp of the big band and swing era, it all fell apart one spring evening in 1935. Tommy, well known for his short temper in jazz circles, left the bandstand at the Glen Island Casino after a heated argument with his brother. It would be years before they worked together again.

It would have been very easy for Tommy to return to the insulated world of radio and recording studios. But instead, he chose the hard road and became the leader of big band after departing from his brother's fold. He caught a lucky break when his friend Joe Haymes was going nowhere with his group. Dorsey took over the outfit that included an entire sax and trumpet section and a trombonist, pianist, guitarist, bassist and arranger named Paul Weston.

Dorsey immediately changed the style of the band and once they swung to his liking they made some recordings for RCA. The group's initial efforts "On Treasure Island," "Back to My Boots and Saddle," and

"Santa Claus Is Coming to Town" lacked polish, but that would come with time. Tommy took the band on a few low-paying ventures in order to tighten up the sound and then after a few months of woodshedding they made their debut at the Hotel Lincoln in New York.

There had been many personnel changes in the first few months of the band. Dorsey brought in drummer Davey Tough and tenor saxophonist Bud Freeman. He also stole trumpeter Joe Bauer, vocalist Jack Leonard and arranger Axel Stordahl from the Bert Block Band. The great trumpeter Bunny Berigan joined the band as did clarinetist Johnny Mince and guitarist Carmen Mastren.

Although the turnover in the band was always high—especially during its formative years—no other position suffered more changes then the vocalist's spot. Buddy Gately was the first singer but Cliff Weston soon replaced him. Later Jack Leonard took over. Leonard helped popularize the band while singing on such classics as "For Sentimental Reasons," "Dedicated to You," "If It's the Last Thing I Do," "Little White Lies," "You Taught Me to Love Again," "Once in a While," and the most famous "Marie." The flip side of "Marie" was "Song of India," another huge hit.

The Tommy Dorsey Orchestra was one of the most successful big bands from 1937 through 1944. In that period a veritable who's who of jazz greats of the period passed through. Tenor saxophonist Bud Freeman, drummers Louis Bellson, Gene Krupa, Buddy Rich, Dave Tough, trumpeters Charlie Shavers, Max Kaminsky, Bunny Berigan, Pee Wee Erwin, Yank Lawson, clarinetist Buddy De Franco, multi-instrumentalist Ziggy Elman, and pianist-trumpeter Joe Bushkin were Tommy Dorsey alumni. While many moved on to better situations others were driven away by Dorsey's short temper.

A number of important singers also had their start with the Tommy Dorsey Orchestra including Jack Leonard, Jo Stafford and Lucy Ann Polk. When Jack Leonard left, Allan DeWitt was hired but didn't last long. It was then that Tommy hired a skinny, young singer named Frank Sinatra. Although Sinatra (who began singing with Dorsey in 1940) would later achieve legendary status, the fact that Dorsey was willing to give the young unknown his first real break is a clear example of the bandleader's eye for talent.

The arrangers also played an important part in the Tommy Dorsey band during its reign at the top. Paul Weston and Axel Stordahl handled the commercial side of Dorsey's musical personality. In 1937, Dorsey was able to lure away Sy Oliver from Jimmie Lunceford's Orchestra, which was a major step in ensuring that there was some jazz content in his music. Dean Kincaide provided more serious pieces for the band.

In 1942, Dorsey shocked jazz purists when he added a string section.

The experiment was short-lived and Dorsey returned to the usual lineup. During the period with strings the group was augmented to a 31-piece ensemble. Although he remained popular Dorsey would periodically reorganize the band mainly because of the large turnover. But he persisted and kept his group at the top of the jazz world.

In 1942, he was forced to cut down on personnel and many other changes took place. Sinatra left and Ziggy Elman was drafted. Jo Stafford left the band and Buddy Rich went into the Marines. Teddy Walters, Betty Brewer, The Sentimentalists (a singing group), Gene Krupa, and arranger Bill Finegan joined the group.

The band was making frequent recordings and appearing throughout the country. Although they never played Europe, Dorsey would eventually accompany Mezz Mezzrow and Bill Coleman across the Atlantic during a break from touring with his own group. The time he spent in France with Mezzrow and Coleman was rewarding. Dorsey also occasionally moonlighted as a member of the Metronome Esquire All-Stars.

Aside from radio, live recordings, and studio recordings, Dorsey increased the band's popular appeal by appearing in numerous films. A partial list includes *Las Vegas Nights, Girl Crazy, Dubarry Was a Lady, Presenting Lily Mars, Ship Ahoy, Broadway Rhythm, I Dood It, A Song Is Born,* and *Reveille with Beverley.* This outlet allowed them to reach an even greater audience and to sell more records. Perhaps, from a personal perspective, the most important of his films was *The Fabulous Dorseys,* which began an armistice with older brother Jimmy. But it wasn't until 1953 that the two played in the same band as Jimmy had disbanded his outfit and joined Tommy's orchestra. The partnership lasted three years.

In December 1946, eight of the best big bands called it quits including Woody Herman, Benny Goodman, Harry James, Les Brown, Jack Teagarden, Benny Carter, Ina Ray Hutton and Tommy Dorsey. But the irresistible urge to create swing music was too much, and two years later Dorsey reformed his band. It included Charlie Shavers and Chuck Peterson on trumpets, Boomie Richman on tenor sax, Paul Smith on piano, Louis Bellson on drums and Lucy Ann Polk on vocals. The outfit also included Jimmy Dorsey. It was this group that was featured on the Jackie Gleason show. During his time on the show Dorsey introduced two unknown singers Elvis Presley and Connie Francis to the world.

On November 26, 1956, in Greenwich, Connecticut, Tommy Dorsey choked to death. He was fifty-one.

Tommy Dorsey was a key player in the big band and swing era as a bandleader and a musician. He was a notable talent scout, and provided music that became the soundtrack of a generation. His name was as well known as Glenn Miller's, Jimmy Dorsey's, Duke Ellington's, Count Basie's, and Benny Goodman's among big band leaders. His jazz-based dance group entertained millions via hundreds of concerts and numerous recordings.

Although he had fine touch on the clarinet, it was as a trombonist that he made his strongest musical contributions. His carefully crafted solos serve as an audio-bible for all aspiring novice players. His specialty was the smooth, perfectly controlled execution on ballads supporting the best singers including Frank Sinatra. He was a surprising improviser who could wrap his warm sound around a melody and turn it into magic.

Dorsey was featured on records he made as a bandleader as well as on those he participated in during the 1920s with such jazz personalities as Benny Goodman. He was excellent on recordings made with Joe Venuti and Eddie Lang, including *The Golden Days of Jazz* and *Stringing the Blues*. He blew hot on the record *The Bix Beiderbecke Legend*. Further example of Dorsey's excellent musicianship is on the *Jazz of the Thirties* recording with Adrian Rollini. He was also a standout on *Paul Whiteman & His Orchestra* and on various other recordings including Metronome All-Stars/Esquire All-Stars records.

Along with his brother Jimmy, Tommy was instrumental in transforming the Chicago Jazz style of the 1920s into the big band sound of the 1930s and 1940s. Both were leaders in emphasizing a more swinging style that could be played with a larger number of musicians. In each era they made significant contributions.

Tommy gave the world a number of classic songs. A partial list includes "On Treasure Island," "The Music Goes Round and Round," "Alone," "You," "Satan Takes a Holiday," "The Big Apple," "Once in a While," "Dipsey Doodle," "Music, Maestro, Please," "Our Love," "Marie," "Indian Summer," "All the Things You Are," "I'll Never Smile Again," "Dolores," "Things Are Such Things," "In the Blue of the Evening," "Boogie Woogie," "I'll Be Seeing You," "How Are Things in Glocca Morra?," "Until," and "The Hucklebuck." The Tommy Dorsey Orchestra's popularity is linked to its wide range appeal. It could swing with the best of them. Tommy Dorsey's band could do more things better than any other all-round dance band. They excelled at playing ballads. They were masterful in creating moods that were danceable and enjoyable to listen to.

Dorsey also had a life outside music. He was a proud family man and a baseball enthusiast; he adored toy trains, and became a successful businessman. He formed Tommy Dorsey, Inc., to deal with bookings. He also wisely invested in the career of Frank Sinatra after the latter left to pursue a solo path. Although he could be short-tempered, his furious outbursts were quickly over and he would laugh at himself.

But it was always about the music. His popularity continued long after his death, as his band kept recording and performing. He is a deserved member of the Jazz Hall of Fame. It is artists like Tommy Dorsey who gave jazz respect as a continuing musical form, and the "Sentimental Gentleman of Swing" always knew how to show the way.

Tommy Dorsey Orchestra 1938

SAXOPHONES

1st Sax	*2nd Sax*	*3rd Sax*
Hymie Shertzer	Babe Russin	Dean Kincaide

CLARINET

Johnny Mince

BRASS

1st Trumpet	*2nd Trumpet*	*3rd Trumpet*
Charles Spivak	Yank Lausen	Lee Castaldo

1st Trombone	*2nd Trombone*
Moe Zudicoff	Len Jenkins

RHYTHM

Piano	*Guitar*	*Bass*	*Drums*
Howard Smith	Carmen Mastren	Gene Traxler	Maurice Putrill

SINGERS

Edythe Wright and Jack Leonard

Discography

Trumpets and Trombones, Vol. 1, Broadway Intermission BR-112.
Trumpets and Trombones, Vol. 2, Broadway Intermission BR-113.
Big Bands, Time-Life 4TL-0002-R959-0.
Having a Wonderful Time, RCA 51643.
Music goes Round and Round, Bluebird/RCA 3140.
This Is Tommy Dorsey, Volume 2, RCA VPM-6064.
Radio Days, Vol. 1, Star Line SG-405.
Yes, Indeed! Bluebird/RCA 9987.
Saturday Afternoon at the Meadowbrook: 1940 [live], Jazz Band 2156.
Sentimental Gentleman, RCA PM-6003.

1942 War Bond Broadcasts [live], Jazz Hour 1013.
The Great Tommy Dorsey and His Orchestra, Pickwick SPC-3168.
I'm Gettin' Sentimental Over You, Pickwick CXS-1907.
The Post-War Era, Bluebird 66156.
In a Sentimental Mood, Decca D-5448.
Tommy Dorsey Orchestra, Vol. 1, Echo Jazz 1.
Tommy Dorsey Orchestra, Vol. 2, Echo Jazz 9.
Seventeen Number Ones, RCA 9973-2-R.
The Complete Tommy Dorsey, Vol. 1 (1935), Bluebird 5521.
The Complete Tommy Dorsey, Vol. 2 (1936), RCA 5549.
The Complete Tommy Dorsey, Vol. 3 (1936–1937), Bluebird 5560.
The Complete Tommy Dorsey, Vol. 4 (1937), RCA 5564.
The Complete Tommy Dorsey, Vol. 5 (1937), Bluebird 5573.
The Complete Tommy Dorsey, Vol. 6 (1937-1938), Bluebird 5578.
The Complete Tommy Dorsey, Vol. 7 (1938), Bluebird 5582.
The Complete Tommy Dorsey, Vol. 8 (1938-1939), Bluebird 5586.
The Dorsey/Sinatra Sessions, Vol. 1, Bluebird 4334.
The Dorsey/Sinatra Sessions, Vol. 2, Bluebird 4335.
The Dorsey/Sinatra Sessions, Vol. 3, Bluebird 4336.
Tommy Dorsey Plays Sweet and Hot, Tax 3075-2.
Sheik of Swing, Drive Archive 41081.
Panic Is On, Viper's Nest Gold 150.
Well Git It, Vintage Jazz 14.
Live in Hi-Fi at Casino Gardens, Jazz Hour 1018.
Tea for Two Cha-Chas, Decca 8842.
The Best of Tommy Dorsey and his Orchestra, Curb 77396.

BENNY GOODMAN (1909–1986)

Swing's the Thing

The swing era produced a bevy of jazz entertainers who gained immortality for their musical efforts. The big band sound captured the imagination of a nation mired in the depths of the depression and lifted its spirits. One of the major artists who was a prime driving force behind the popularity of the music always knew that swing was the thing. His name was Benny Goodman.

Benny Goodman was born Benjamin David Goodman on May 30, 1909, in Chicago, Illinois. He began to study music at the age of ten at the local synagogue and took up the clarinet when he was twelve. Two important teachers during his early development were Johnny Sylvester and the classical player Franz Schwepp. Goodman honed his skills quickly and by the time he was thirteen was already in the musicians union playing gigs on a regular basis. In 1921, he entered a talent contest in Chicago where he imitated Ted Lewis, the famous bandleader from Ohio.

Goodman was consumed by music and listened closely to the sounds of Bix Beiderbecke, King Oliver, Earl Hines and Jimmie Noone. In the early 1920s, a full decade before the advent of swing, Goodman was part of the Austin High Gang, a group of local Chicago teenagers who grooved on the music that they heard by sneaking into the clubs around town. Among the members of the Austin High Gang who would carve out successful jazz careers were Pee Wee Russell, trombonist Jack Teagarden, and drummers Dave Tough, Gene Krupa, Bud Freeman and Eddie Condon. Goodman would call upon the friendship of Krupa in later years.

In 1923, Goodman met one of his idols, Bix Beiderbecke, while working on a Great Lakes steamboat. To a young aspiring musician like Goodman (he was fourteen), Beiderbecke was a genuine hero. Bix encouraged Goodman to pursue his musical dreams because it was evident even in his tender teens that young Benjamin was something special on the clarinet.

After playing in a handful of local bands, Goodman landed a job with the Ben Pollack group, one of the more popular outfits at the time. He would play on and off with Pollack, leaving the band and returning only to depart once again. Although Pollack was a top bandleader the music they played was not how Goodman envisioned jazz. He wanted to swing, but that style was still in its infancy and it would be a few years before he would get a chance to make the people dance.

In the early 1930s, with the Great Depression crippling the entertainment industry, Goodman found employment as a freelancer in Broadway shows, on the radio and playing regular recording dates with Ted Lewis (his boyhood idol), Red Nichols, and Ben Pollack. Although he found work under the tutelage of various bandleaders, Goodman was determined to form his own group to play swing.

In 1932, during the depths of the Depression, he did just that. Although work was somewhat scarce he managed to somehow keep it all together. One of his first gigs was a residency at Billy Rose's Music Hall in New York City. Although the money was only adequate, the fact that they were featured on the National Biscuit Company's *Let's Dance* radio show, broadcast coast-to-coast, helped propel the band to greater prominence.

The *Let's Dance* program featured three bands: Goodman's, Xavier Cugat's Latin music, and Kel Murray's vanilla sound. The program lasted six months and then Goodman was booked into the Grill Room of the Roosevelt Hotel in New York in the spring of 1935. It was a less than stellar debut as two weeks later they were fired. Goodman turned to one-night performances and some record dates in order to pay the bills. The band cut some solid sides including "Blue Skies," "Sometimes I'm Happy," and "King Porter Stomp," all of which were Fletcher Henderson arrangements. Horace Henderson, Edgar Sampson and Jimmy Mundy also arranged for the group. Before leaving on a cross country tour Goodman and drummer Krupa cut four sides that included "After You've Gone," "Body and Soul," "Who," and "Someday Sweetheart" with a then little known pianist named Teddy Wilson. Wilson would eventually join the Goodman band.

But for the tour Jess Stacy was the piano player. Bunny Berigan was also in the band. In Denver, the Goodman band suffered a humiliating experience, but it was a much different scene in Oakland, California. It was now magic time. The quartet consisting of Goodman, Berigan, Stacy, and Krupa could suddenly do no wrong. A few nights later the group played at the Palomar in Los Angeles and decided to play the more risky numbers such as "King Porter Stomp." They were a huge hit. This important attention was the confidence builder that the band needed and from this point on they never looked back.

The press fueled Goodman's triumph in Los Angeles and he was dubbed the "King of Swing." The band continued their tour with one-night performances and eventually landed in Chicago where a three-week engagement at the Congress Hotel turned into an eight-month stay. They continued to record and it was during this period that they added "Stompin' at the Savoy," "Don't Be That Way," "Blue Lou," and with Helen Ward on vocals "Goody, Goody," "It's Been So Long," and "No Other One."

It was in Chicago that Teddy Wilson made his debut with the band. Because of his newfound popularity Goodman was able to create his interracial band without fear of being shunned. In an era where segregation was rigidly enforced, Goodman defied the social system. Upon the band's return to New York Murray McEachern added his trombone, alto sax and trumpet to the lineup. They also made their first movie, *The Big Broadcast of 1937*. It was this period—the summer of 1936—that tenor saxist Vido Musso joined the group as well as vibraphonist Lionel Hampton. They recorded "Dinah," "Moonglow," and "Vibraphone Blues." The song "Vibraphonist Blues" featured the extensive talents of Hampton.

In the fall of 1936, Goodman's band opened at the Madhattan Room in New York. The Big Apple crowd was able to witness firsthand what all the commotion was about and the king of swing did not disappoint. It was while in New York that trumpeters Harry James, Ziggy Elman and Chris Grifin joined the band. Although the musical personnel of the group were set, the vocalist position was another matter. Helen Ward left the band and Margaret McCrae replaced her. Francis Hunt replaced McCrae soon after. Peg LaCentra joined the band but left quickly and Betty Van was hired on. Finally, in the summer of 1937, Martha Tilton arrived and the vocalist problem was solved.

Perhaps the highlight of many great achievements for Goodman during the period between 1935 and 1938 was the concert at Carnegie Hall that featured Benny and his band as well as many famous guests. It was the crowning glory of his ride to the top, and from this point on, though he remained popular, he was soon to be eclipsed by bands led by Glenn Miller, Duke Ellington, Count Basie, and Jimmie Lunceford.

After the Carnegie Hall appearance Gene Krupa left the group to form his own big band. Davey Tough replaced Krupa. But Tough had personal problems and was replaced by Buddy Schutz. Schutz eventually gave way to Nick Fatool. Harry James left to form his own band. Lead Saxist Toots Mondello and guitarist George Rose joined the band. Louise Tobin (married at the time to Harry James) replaced singer Martha Tilton. Another important change was the switch from the Victor to the Columbia label. It was also around this time that Goodman added a young guitar protégé named Charlie Christian. In the span of two years Christian would reinvent the sound of jazz guitar.

But the greatest factor of all in the decline of the Goodman Band was the leader's health. Goodman, who was exhausted by the non-stop touring of the last four years, took a brief holiday in Europe and returned to form another band, but was forced to disband the group because of illness. Once he was treated for sciatica he reformed his sextet. The superb arrangements of Eddie Sauter, Mel Powell, Buster Harding and Jimmy Mundy enabled the group to remain at the top of the polls into the early 1940s.

The reformed band had several hits with "Benny Rides Again," "Clarinet a la King," "It Never Entered My Mind," "More Than You Know," "The Man I Love," and "Cornsilk." Charlie Christian, Artie Bernstein, trumpeters Jimmy Maxwell and Irving Goodman, as well as singer Helen Forrest (who had replaced Tilton), remained from the old band. Trombonist Lou McGarity, tenor saxist Georgie Auld, trumpeter Alec Fila, Bernie Leigton or Fletcher Henderson on piano, and Harry Jaeger on drums were added to the lineup. Tough returned and replaced Jaeger. It was this group that recorded the song "Scarecrow," one of Goodman's most swinging numbers ever. Later on when Artie Shaw disbanded his group Goodman grabbed pianist Johnny Guarnieri, trumpeter Billy Butterfield and lead saxophonist Les Robinson.

During this time Goodman appeared as a guest soloist with the New York Philharmonic Orchestra, and later he conducted the Philadelphia Orchestra to rave reviews. Of course, he continued with his band. Goodman included some featured performers in 1941, including singer Peggy Lee, who was featured on several songs the band cut including "My Old Flame," "Let's Do It," "I Got It Bad and That Ain't Good," "Somebody Else Is Taking My Place," " How Long Has This Been Going On?," "Blues in the Night," "All I Need Is You," and "Why Don't You Do Right?"

Because of the war the band underwent several personnel changes. Hymie Shertzer on lead sax, Miff Mole on trombone, Gene Krupa on drums, Allan Reuss on rhythm guitar, trumpeter Ralph Muzzilo, Lee Castaldo and trombonist Bill Harris worked with Goodman at one time or another. Shortly after Krupa, Castaldo and Muzzillo quit the band, Goodman disbanded the group and produced V-Discs for a while.

In 1945, he reformed the band that included Teddy Wilson, Red Norvo and Slam Stewart. Later Kai Winding and Stan Getz would join the group. The addition of Winding and Getz signaled a change for Goodman. With the advent of bebop, Goodman was forced to change his style to accommodate the new taste and briefly flirted with the new music. He organized an outfit that consisted of Stan Hasselgard and Wardell Gray, and even recorded with legendary bebop trumpeter Fats Navarro in 1949. But Goodman was not a bebopper at heart; his interests were in swing, and he returned to the big band format at the beginning of the 1950s.

Although for the remainder of his career he would never again experience the same mass popularity as he had in the late 1930s, Goodman continued to record and perform on a regular basis. He toured Europe in 1950, and Japan, Thailand, and Burma in 1956. In 1958, he appeared at the Brussels World's Fair. Although many of the stars who had propelled him to the title of "King of Swing" in the late 1930s were gone, he still featured some interesting sidemen such as Terry Gibbs, Buck Clayton, Ruby Braff, Paul Quinichette, Roland Hanna, Jack Sheldon, Bill Harris, Flip Phillips and Andre Previn. In 1957, *The Benny Goodman Story* was released to mixed reviews. Perhaps the fact that the movie was made and shown fifteen years too late accounted for its lukewarm reception.

Although he toured the USSR in 1962, Japan in 1964, and Belgium in 1966, Goodman began to slow down during this decade. He recorded less often and his performances (despite his globetrotting) were quite spread out. When he did record new material (often it was rehashed Henderson riffs), Goodman used alumni and even spotlighted up and coming names in jazz like keyboardist Herbie Hancock and guitarist George Benson.

During the early 1970s, he toured Europe. It seemed no matter how tired he was of playing the songs he had been performing for three decades, he could not resist playing them overseas. In the middle of the 1970s, he quit recording all together, but returned in 1978 to celebrate the highly anticipated 40th anniversary of the legendary Carnegie Hall concert. By this time, Goodman was mostly retired.

In the last few years of his life Goodman played few gigs but did make one memorable appearance on television in the early 1980s with his last big band. On June 13, 1986, in New York City, the man who turned the country on as the "King of Swing" died. He was 77 years old.

Benny Goodman is a jazz phenomenon. He played the music for almost fifty years; however, he will be remembered best for the four-year period (1935–1939) when he reached heights previously thought unattainable by jazz bands. Although he will be forever associated with the swing and big band era as the leader of one of its most successful groups, Goodman was also a first class clarinet player, perhaps the greatest ever. He made enormous contributions and was a definite pacesetter.

Although he moonlighted on different instrument such as the alto, baritone, and tenor saxes, he was definitely a licorice stick (clarinet) man. Goodman produced a smooth, exact sound that earned him accolades as one of the best swing musicians. Frank Teschemacher, Leon Rappolo and Jimmie Noone originally influenced Goodman. In turn, Goodman had a special effect on Kenny Davern, Buddy DeFranco, Johnny Mince, Phil Nimmons, and Benny Waters. But his excellent clarinet playing was only one of many contributions he made to jazz.

Goodman had an exceptional eye for talent that enabled him to recruit the most proficient players of the era. How can anyone argue with a band comprised of Teddy Wilson, Charlie Christian, Harry James, Lionel Hampton and Gene Krupa? More important was Goodman's color blindness. He had no problems bringing in African-American musicians such as Teddy Wilson, Charlie Christian, Lionel Hampton, and Fletcher Henderson into the fold. Goodman was instrumental in breaking down the racial barriers that existed in the music world at the time.

Goodman was also an excellent bandleader. He was a perfectionist and demanded a high level of performance from all those who were in his band. He ranks right among all the top bandleaders. That includes Duke Ellington, Count Basie, Tommy and Jimmy Dorsey, Artie Shaw, and Glenn Miller. He had a way of pulling magic from those in his big bands and small combos. The ability remained with him long after his halcyon days of the late 1930s.

Additionally, Goodman was wise enough to break his big band into small groups for recording purposes enabling the small combos to propel the popularity of the bigger band. Many people bought the records of the small combos and came to the performances to hear these songs played live. By separating his big band into smaller groups, Goodman was also giving the musicians confidence, credibility, and a chance to make extra money. Although he wasn't the first to do this, he did it probably more effectively than any other bandleader.

Goodman was immortalized more than any other bandleader with the possible exception of Duke Ellington. Although the movie made about his life was made when his popularity was waning, it was still a triumph since few movies were made of jazz musicians at that time. Goodman himself starred in a number of films including *The Big Broadcast of 1937*, *Hollywood Hotel*, *Stage Door Canteen*, *Sweet and Lowdown*, *The Powers Girl*, and *A Song Is Born*.

He delivered hundreds of performances, but his most memorable was at Carnegie Hall in 1938 because it had special significance. It marked the beginning of jazz being showcased in concert venues as opposed to being confined solely to dance halls and clubs. Jazz had to this point been considered the music of revelry, but after Goodman's debut at Carnegie Hall it was perceived as a more intellectually challenging genre. Goodman managed in one series of concerts what Duke Ellington had been striving to accomplish for years.

The Benny Goodman story is the tale of very good clarinetist who understood the mood of the nation during one of its most restless periods and was able to eliminate that frustration through music. He knew that swing was an elixir for the hardships of the Great Depression. Although he never regained the immense popularity once the big band era faded, Goodman was always aware that swing was the thing.

Benny Goodman Orchestra 1941

SAXOPHONES

1st Sax	2nd Sax	3rd Sax	4th Sax	5th Sax
Vido Musso	Clint Neagley	Julie Schwartz	George Berg	Chuck Gentry

CLARINET

Benny Goodman

BRASS

1st Trumpet	2nd Trumpet	3rd Trumpet
Jimmy Maxwell	Billy Butterfield	Al Davis

1st Trombone	2nd Trombone
Lou McGarity	Cutty Cutshall

RHYTHM

Piano	*Guitar*	*Bass*	*Drums*
Mel Powell	Tommy Morgan	Sid Weiss	Ralph Collier

SINGERS

Art London, Peggy Lee

Discography

The Early Years, Biograph 109.
Swing Sessions 1945–1946, HS 254.
Wrappin' It Up 1935–1939, AVD 608.
Runnin' Wild 1935–1938, AVD 609.
Blue Note, Chicago, CAN 1009.
Plays Henderson Vol. 2 1936–1941, HEP 1059.
1931–1935, CBC 1065.
The Radio Years 1940–1941, STC 2041.
V-Disc Recordings, CCM 3592.
When Buddha Smiles 1934–1939, ASL 5071.
The Small Groups, ASL 5144.
Sing, Sing, Sing 1935–1939, Bluebird 5630.
After You've Gone: The Original Benny Goodman Trio & Quartet Sessions 1935–1937, Bluebird 5631.
Benny Goodman Sextet 1950–1952, Sony 40379.
Small Groups 1941–1945, Sony 44437.
Best of the Big Bands, 1939–1945, Sony 45338.
Benny Goodman on the Air 1937–1938, Sony 48836.
Best of the Big Bands Featuring Helen Forrest, Sony 48902.
Featuring Peggy Lee, Sony 53422.
Swingsation, GRP 59954.
The Birth of Swing 1935–1936, Bluebird 61038.
Stompin' at the Savoy 1935–1938, Bluebird 61067.
Fabulous Benny Goodman, RCA 63555.
The Very Best of Benny Goodman, RCA 63730.
Live at Carnegie Hall—The Complete 1938 Concert, Sony 65143.
Greatest Hits, Victor 68489.
More Greatest Hits, Victor 68645.
The Complete Small Combinations Vol. 1 & 2, 1935–1937 Jazz 66542.

Masterpieces Vol. 5, EPM 158172.
Benny Goodman Big Band 1939–1946, EPM 158962.
Trio & Quartet 1935–1938, EPM 159132.
Benny Goodman & His Orchestra 1928–1931, Classic 693.
Benny Goodman & His Orchestra 1931–1933, Classic 719.
Benny Goodman & His Orchestra 1934–1935, Classic 744.
Benny Goodman & His Orchestra 1935, Classic 769.
Benny Goodman & His Orchestra 1935–1936, Classic 789.
Benny Goodman & His Orchestra 1936, Classic 817.
Benny Goodman & His Orchestra 1936 Vol. 2, Classic 836.
Benny Goodman & His Orchestra 1936–1937, Classic 858.
Benny Goodman & His Orchestra 1937, Classic 879.
Benny Goodman & His Orchestra 1937–1938, Classic 899.
Benny Goodman & His Orchestra 1938, Classic 925.
Benny Goodman & His Orchestra 1938 Vol. 2, Classic 961.
Benny Goodman & His Orchestra 1938–1939, Classic 990.
Benny Goodman & His Orchestra 1939, Classic 1025.
Benny Goodman & His Orchestra 1939 Vol. 2, Classic 1064.
Benny Goodman & His Orchestra 1939–1940, Classic 1098.
Benny Goodman & His Rhythm Makers: Good to Go, Bud 99624.
Benny Goodman Quartet Body and Soul 1937–1938, Pre 101.

CHICK WEBB (1909–1939)

I Got Rhythm

After Baby Dodds and Zutty Singleton opened the door of opportunity for drummers suddenly there was an abundance of stickmen all eager to show off their talents. In the 1930s, Buddy Rich, Gene Krupa, Jo Jones, and Louis Bellson all starred with various bands. There was also another timekeeper who was probably the most amazing of them all because of the many obstacles he faced to achieve his success. But he showed everyone that he had rhythm. His name was Chick Webb.

William Henry Webb was born on February 10, 1909, in Baltimore, Maryland. As a young boy he suffered from tuberculosis of the spine which left him physically challenged, but Webb would not be deterred from pursuing his musical dreams. In order to raise enough money to buy his first set of drums he delivered newspapers. At the age of eleven he was already honing the skills that would astonish crowds during the next decade.

He jammed with local groups, gaining valuable experience, and developed a close friendship with John Trueheart, who played the guitar and banjo. Together they spent summers working on pleasure boats entertaining the crowds. Already, by his teens, Webb was a dynamic force on the drums. Those who were lucky enough to listen and dance to the funky rhythms he produced knew he was going to be special.

Webb and Trueheart moved to New York to find work and joined Edgar Dowell's Orchestra for a short time. But Webb was a born leader despite his diminutive status and physical challenges. He formed his first five-piece band for a lengthy residence at the Black Bottom Club. A year later, he added three members to his group and enjoyed a long residency at the Paddocks Club. When he played the Rose Danceland, Webb added three more pieces and his big band swung hard, powered by the dynamics of Webb's impressive drumming skills.

He continued to work in New York in the late 1920s at the Rose, the Cotton Club and other venues throughout the city. He also toured in the Hot Chocolate Revue in 1930. In 1931, Webb's big band began a residency at the Savoy Ballroom and his name would become synonymous with that famous dance hall. He also found time at one point despite his busy schedule to tour with Louis Armstrong. Webb was a masterful musician who rarely had trouble finding work and was versatile enough to fit in in any situation.

Despite a talented line up that included Edgar Sampson on saxes, Taft Jordan and Bobby Stark on trumpet, Wayman Carver on flute and alto sax, Hilton Jefferson on alto sax, Louis Jordan on saxes, and Sandy Wilson on trombone, the Webb band didn't break through until the mid-1930s. But from around 1935 they became one of the most popular attractions. They were able to accomplish this feat because of their obvious musical skills, but even more so because they introduced an unknown, but incredible, seventeen-year-old singer by the name of Ella Fitzgerald to the jazz world.

Fitzgerald added an untold dimension to the Webb band that it had never possessed before. The recording of "A-Tisket A-Tasket" was the biggest hit the group ever enjoyed. With all the pieces of the puzzle in place, it soared to new heights and became one of the most popular big bands on the circuit. Although Jordan, Fitzgerald, and Sampson shared some of the acclaim, it was Webb's articulate and tasteful drumming that was the focus of the band. However, he was not an egomaniac bandleader;

he was a slick professional who allowed other members of the band to shine in the spotlight.

By 1938, the Chick Webb Band was truly at the top of their form. In one legendary cutting contest at the Savoy, they embarrassed the Benny Goodman Band, which had just returned from a triumphant West Coast tour that had garnered an immense amount of attention. Webb, like a field general, reveled in the ability to blow the most popular bands off the stage.

During this time Webb's group practically lived at the Savoy Ballroom as the house band. They enjoyed a solid period of economic stability when many other outfits were not so fortunate. Although their name was synonymous with the Savoy Ballroom, the group still toured all over the country on a regular basis. They were in constant demand because they possessed the musical magic that never failed to enchant audiences wherever they performed.

Unfortunately, plagued by health problems most of his life, Webb was hospitalized in 1938. After a major operation, however, he was behind the drum kit and back on tour with his group. But it was quite noticeable to everyone in the band that his health was failing and that his demise was inevitable. On June 16, 1939, in Baltimore, Maryland, William "Chick" Webb died from pleurisy. He was 30 years old.

Chick Webb was an important and influential drummer. He was also one of the best bandleaders and made maximum use of the musicians in his band. He was a generous man who insisted that every member of the group share the limelight. His premature death only enhanced his reputation as one of the major figures of the big band and swing era.

There were many faces to Webb's ability on drums. He was technically sound and able to create a swinging beat with his powerful arms and foot. He could groove with the rhythm section, riding the song for a long time, and then shift the patterns to a different level. He also tuned his drums to the other instruments in the band to attain more of a melodic tone, a practice that later drummers would eventually adopt.

He was one of the quickest drummers around. His power was astonishing; he was capable of unleashing a barrage of muscle that resembled a freight train rumbling down the tracks at breakneck speed. He made use of his entire drum kit better than anyone else of his generation. His speed and coordination often unnerved other musicians because of the physical challenges that he had to overcome. But he never allowed any barriers to come between him and his love of music.

He was an explosive drummer, dropping bombs in a furious attack of unmatched and uncanny skill. More than anything, he understood dynamics and his ability to create them with relative ease was his greatest asset as a stick man. He spurred on the other musicians in his band as well as his singer Fitzgerald. He was able to create a rhythm that everyone in his band could play off to create a swirling body of racing sounds.

He was also one of the first drummers to front a band. Later Gene Krupa, Kenny Clarke, Max Roach and Art Blakey would lead their own groups, taking a page from Webb's book. He was an exceptional leader and propelled his band to the top of the big band heap. During the group's moment in the sun, they were on equal terms with rivals Duke Ellington, Count Basie, The Dorsey Brothers, Benny Goodman, Artie Shaw, Jimmy Lunceford, Cab Calloway, Andy Kirk, Benny Carter, and Earl Hines.

He also had an eye for talent. It was Webb who introduced Ella Fitzgerald to jazz audiences. She was the brightest star in the group. Although Ted McRea, Hylton Jefferson, Taft Jordan, and Tommy Fulford never became household names, their contributions remain impressive. Therein lies the secret to the success of the group. Their intelligent leader was able to coax the best performances out of his lineup on a nightly basis, as well as select the right player to mesh perfectly with the other members. Instead of stacking his group with name musicians he picked personnel who fit better into a tight knit unit rather than for their solo abilities.

After his death Fitzgerald took over the group but without their leader for inspiration, the group folded a couple of years later. It would have been interesting if Webb had lived into the 1940s because he would have been able to carry the swing and big band banner on his diminutive, but strong, shoulders. He was one leader who cut a noteworthy figure during the era.

He influenced a whole group of drummers, including Louie Bellson, Jo Jones, Gene Krupa, Buddy Rich, Mario Bauza, Art Blakey, Kenny Clarke, Panama Francis, and J. C. Heard. It is interesting to note that many of his greatest rivals during his halcyon days, including Jones, Krupa, and Rich, admired Webb and incorporated some of his best elements into their own style.

Webb worked with Edgar Sampson, a brilliant arranger, and together they gave the world many classics. A partial lists includes: "Blue Lou," "Stompin' at the Savoy," "Don't Be That Way," "If Dreams Come True," "Stardust," "Liza," "Who Ya' Hunchin'," "Undecided," "Rock It for Me," "Holiday in Harlem," and "I Got Rhythm." The following songs included Ella Fitzgerald on vocals: "Sing Me A Swing Song," "Ella," "If You Can't Sing It (You'll Have to Swing It)," "Little White Lies," "Vote for Mr. Rhythm," and, of course, "A-Tisket A-Tasket."

Chick Webb is remembered for many things. He was the leader of one of the most successful big bands, he died too early, he helped Ella Fitzgerald break into the big time, and he was a great drummer admired by many of his closest rivals. Despite being physically challenged he could power a band harder and faster than others who did not suffer from his ill health. Time and time again, Webb proved that he had rhythm and that the rhythm was in him.

Chick Webb Band 1939

SAXOPHONES

1st Sax	2nd Sax	3rd Sax
Ted McRea	Hylton Jefferson	Wayman Canven

CLARINET
Chauncey Haughton

BRASS

1st Trumpet	2nd Trumpet	3rd Trumpet
Dick Vance	Bobby Stark	Taft Jordan

1st Trombone	2nd Trombone
Nat Storee	Sandy Williams

RHYTHM

Piano	Guitar	Bass	Drums
Tommy Fulford	Bobby Johnson	Beverley Peer	Chick Webb

SINGER
Ella Fitzgerald

Discography

Chick Webb, Strictly Jive 1935–1940, HEP 1063.
Chick Webb, Stomping at the Savoy with Ella Fitzgerald 1934–1949, EPM 159722.
Chick Webb & His Orchestra, 1929–1935, Classic 502.
Chick Webb & His Orchestra, 1935–1938, Classic 517.
Spinnin' the Webb, Decca Jazz 635.
Standing Tall, Drive Archive 42427.
Quintessence—New York 1929–39.
Rhythm Man 1934–35, HEP 1023.

Classic Tracks, BMG 318.
An Introduction to Chick Webb 1929–1939, Best of Jazz 4015.
King of the Savoy, Decca 9223.
The Immortal Chick Webb, Columbia CS-9439.
Chick Webb and His Savoy Ballroom Orchestra 1939, Tax 3706.
Original Sessions 1937–1939, Jazz Anthology 5113.
Chick Webb, Decca DL-79923.
Bronzeville Stomp, Jazz Archives 33.
Heritage: A Legend (1929–1936), MCAC-1303.
In the Groove, Affinity 1007.
Rhythm Man, Hep 1023.

ARTIE SHAW (1910–)

Blues in the Night

The big band era featured a group of individuals who propelled jazz from a particular musical style into the most popular music on the planet. Although many players made their mark during this era, it was the band-leader who like a field general displayed the ability to form the various personalities into a solid unit. One of these directors became known for the long list of star musicians who performed in his eponymous outfits as much as for his blues in the night. His name was Artie Shaw.

Artie Shaw was born Arthur Jacob Arshawsky on May 23, 1910, in New York City. At the age of seven he moved to New Haven, Connecticut, and three years later started his formal musical education. He played the ukulele at the age of ten, moved to the sax at the age of twelve, and later learned how to play the clarinet. In his teens he was a member of the New Haven High School band where he played several instruments. Although he was never allowed to conduct the school band Shaw was laying down the very foundation that would enable him to assume the leadership of a big band.

He matured quickly as a musician. He won a talent contest performing a duet with banjo player Gene Becker in the early 1920s. A few short months later he formed the Bellevue Ramblers who played gigs at some of the local clubs like the Liberty Pier. He left home when he was fifteen to work in Kentucky. Unfortunately, the big adventure turned sour and he was forced to make his way back home as part of a traveling band. Although the entire experience was not what Shaw had hoped for, it increased his traveling stamina and taught him valuable lessons about the entertainment world that would serve him well later on his career.

He eventually joined Don Cavallero's band in New Haven and traveled to Florida with him. He also played with Joe Cantor and Merle Jacobs in Cleveland. The young Shaw had seen much of the country before he was twenty years old. At seventeen he joined violinist Austin Wylie's band and stayed for two years. He moved on to Irving Aaronson's Commanders where he played tenor saxophone.

Shaw, an original New York native, moved back to the big city and played along side the legendary Willie "The Lion" Smith, one of the great stride pianists of the early 1920s and 1930s. But Shaw, who never seemed to be able to stay with one group very long, moved on to play with Paul Specht, Vincent Lopez, and Roger Wolfe Kahn. By this time his resume was a few pages long.

In 1931, Shaw, who was now a seasoned veteran at the age of twenty-one, played with Red Nichols, one of the great early cornetists of the 1920s. The group had a residency at the Park Central Hotel in New York. Shaw also did some studio work with Fred Rich, but despite having paid his dues for the past ten years his moment in the sun had not yet begun.

After another brief stint with Roger Wolf Kahn, Shaw did freelance radio and studio work before leaving the business for an entire year. One of the most outspoken critics of commercialism in music, he ran a farm in Pennsylvania. After his one-year sabbatical, he returned to New York and did some freelancing. As a studio musician he worked with Benny Goodman, The Dorsey Brothers, Bunny Berigan, Jack Teagarden and Claude Thornhill.

After performing at an all-star big band concert at the Imperial Theatre Shaw put together his first group. It consisted of clarinet, strings, and a Dixieland-type frontline with a vocalist. The group included trumpeter Lee Castle and tenor saxophonist Tony Pastor, among others. Joe Lipman wrote many of the arrangements. But Shaw was dissatisfied with this aggregation and broke it up. In between bands, Shaw found time to record with the great Billie Holiday, providing a moving blues solo behind the voice of jazz. Up to this point it was one of Shaw's finest moments as a musician.

Shaw reformed his group and enlarged the personnel in what became his second big band. Some of the individuals in the band included Leo Watson, John Best, Harry Rogers, Malcolm Crain, George Arus, Les Robinson, Tony Pastor, and Cliff Leeman. Shaw and his big band made their debut in Boston. They found success quickly with the song "Begin the Beguine." Life was never the same after that for the band. Suddenly, they became one of the most popular outfits on the concert circuit and more hits followed including "Indian Love Call," "Back Bay Shuffle," "Non-Stop Flight," "Yesterdays," and "Nightmare."

Despite their success there were personnel changes. The new version of the band featured Tony Pastor, Helen Forrest, Georgie Auld, George Wettling, Chuck Peterson, John Best, Leo Watson, Cliff Leeman, and Russell Brown. They were much in demand especially when drummer Buddy Rich joined replacing Wettling. But the pressure of success was more than Shaw could handle and he disbanded the group in 1939, living in Mexico for a few months in search of peace.

But the music bug was too strong to resist and Shaw jammed with local musicians in Mexico. He eventually returned to Hollywood organized a thirty-two piece band that included singer Pauline Byrne. His first recording session produced another major hit with the song "Frenesi." The band also scored big with "Gloomy Sunday," "Don't Fall Asleep," "Adios," and "Mariquita Linda."

Shaw could not escape success. He had the uncanny ability to give audiences the type of music they demanded and enjoyed. Soon after, Shaw formed his third orchestra. It featured a string section and star soloists in Billy Butterfield on trumpet and Johnny Guarnieri on piano. The group became known for the definitive version of "Stardust," as well as for the superb "Concerto for Clarinet." Even side projects produced hit singles. For example, the Gramercy Five, a small group drawn from the larger Shaw band, played the wildly popular "Summit Ridge Drive." On these sessions Guarnieri played the harpsichord. The group also enjoyed success with "Keepin' Myself for You" and "Cross Your Heart." It was this group that featured nine strings plus vocalist Anita Boyer.

Shaw broke up this band and studied music for a while with Hans Burns, who had conducted the Berlin Opera. Shaw recorded with saxophonist Benny Carter, trumpeter Henry "Red" Allen and trombonist J. C. Higginbotham. But the urge to lead his own big band would not let his spirit alone and it was only a matter of time before he took the plunge again.

In the fall of 1941, Shaw organized a larger version of his big band. It included "Hot Lips" Page, Auld and Guarnieri, as well as drummer Davey Tough, saxophonist Les Robinson, trumpeters Lee Castle and Maxie Kaminsky. This group recorded "Take Your Shoes Off, Baby (And Start Runnin' Through My Mind)." This version featured three great vocalists Bonnie Lake, Paula Kelly and Fedda Gibson. The group was called Artie Shaw and His Symphonic Swing.

Shaw disbanded the group when he joined the U.S. Navy for the war effort in 1942. While in the Pacific he fronted a naval outfit that entertained hundreds of thousands of soldiers stationed there. It consisted of trumpeters Conrad Gozzo, Frank Beach, Johnny Best, and Kaminsky. Sam Donahoe was an outstanding saxman. Davey Tough played drums and Claude Thornhill played piano and wrote arrangements. Unfortunately, that particular group never recorded any of their material.

Upon his discharge in 1944, Shaw returned to America and re-formed a big band that included Little Jazz, Roy Eldridge, as well as trombonist Ray Conniff, pianist Dodo Marmarosa, Herbie Steward and Barney Kessel, the talented guitarist. The style they played was a modern jazz with bebop strains. Shaw dissolved the group in 1946.

In 1949, he formed his last big band that included Zoot Sims, Al Cohn, and Don Fagerquist. It had stronger strains of bop but it seemed that he had lost his magic touch. No one seemed interested in the music he was making so he disbanded the group after only a few disappointing months. Despite the many successes that he had enjoyed, Shaw was disillusioned with the music industry so he retired a bitter man. He would return again to make several recordings with a version of the Grammercy Five that included Tal Farlow or Joe Puma on guitar, as well as pianist Hank Jones.

A talented individual, he became a writer and his book *The Trouble with Cinderella* raised a few eyebrows. Although he had retired, Shaw periodically formed small groups to play at various locations. A dedicated big band and swing enthusiast, he also flirted with bop arrangements during this time. His groups during this period were updated versions of his Gramercy Five, with which he had enjoyed so much success in the past.

He eventually retired for good in the mid–1950s to run a dairy farm. Later on, he went to live in Spain for five years before returning to the United States. He never appeared on the music scene again except for a brief time in 1983 when he co-fronted a band with Dick Johnson. He played the clarinet and his solos were engaging for someone who was past his seventies. Unfortunately, once Shaw was out of the music business completely, he received more publicity for his eight marriages that included brides Lana Turner, Ava Gardner, and Evelyn Keyes than for his past musical accomplishments.

Artie Shaw was the Midas of jazz in the 1930s and 1940s. Although his musical career did not stretch out as long as other bandleaders' such as Duke Ellington's, Benny Goodman's, and the Dorsey Brothers', Shaw did make his mark on the world of jazz with his many big and small outfits. He was always ahead of his time and his fine clarinet playing produced many memorable moments.

While he never reached the emotional depths of Sidney Bechet, Johnny Dodds, Jimmie Noone or Barney Bigard, there was a catchy side to Shaw's playing. He understood the appeal of a commercial song and this was often reflected in his style. He had a very melodic approach and demonstrated a knowledge for the subtle dynamics of swing as well as anyone else. He also played the tenor sax though he was never one of the outstanding practitioners of that instrument.

Like all great bandleaders, he had an eye for young talent. He enabled Buddy Rich, Roy Eldridge, Barney Kessel, Dodo Marmarosa, Herbie Steward, Billy Butterfield, and Johnny Guarnieri to gain some much needed exposure and broaden their budding careers. He was a selfless bandleader who made sure that the musicians in his band were given every chance to develop their skills.

Although he enjoyed working with his band he also backed some of the biggest musicians of the era. His musical skills can be heard in the recordings of Artie Bernstein, Billie Holiday, Sid Weiss, Hank Freeman, Helen Forrest, Chuck Peterson, Georgie Auld, George Wettling, Dick McDonough, Cozy Cole, and John Kirby. Shaw was always able to make some significant contribution to any project he participated in.

Another dimension of Shaw's contribution to jazz was the songs he wrote and performed. He gave the world a number of great ones including "Begin the Beguine," "I Can't Get Started with You," "Special Delivery Stomp," "Summit Ridge Drive," "My Blue Heaven," "The Grabtown Grapple," "Any Old Time," "Frenesi," "Stardust," and "Concerto for Clarinet." From 1937 through early 1941, it seemed that every song he recorded—no matter the lineup—was a hit.

The Artie Shaw story is a tale of a musically gifted player and composer who was a major force during the big band and swing era only to disappear from the scene later on by choice. It seems as if the world of jazz despite the numerous talented individuals it contained needed Shaw more than Shaw needed the world of jazz. Almost sixty years later, long after the period has faded into the history pages, his name remains vibrant as the man who gave the world his "Blues in the Night."

Artie Shaw Orchestra circa 1938

SAXOPHONES

1st Sax	2nd Sax	3rd Sax	4th Sax
Les Robinson	Tony Pastor	Hank Freeman	Ronny Perry

BRASS

1st Trumpet	*2nd Trumpet*	*3rd Trumpet*
John Best	Claude Bowen	Chuck Peterson

1st Trombone	*2nd Trombone*
Russell Brown	George Arus

RHYTHM

Piano	*Guitar*	*Bass*	*Drums*
Les Burness	Al Avola	Sid Weiss	Cliff Leeman

SINGER

Billie Holiday

Discography

Artie Shaw Vol. 1 1938, HS 139.
Artie Shaw Vol. 2 1938, HS 140.
Plays 22 Original Big Band 1938–1939, HS 401.
King of the Clarinet 1938–1939, HS 502.
Thou Swell 1936–1937, ASL 5056.
Begin the Beguine, ASL 5113.
Begin the Beguine 1938–1941, Bluebird 6274.
Artie Shaw V-Disc Recordings, CCM 6670.
Artie Shaw Vol. 2 1938–1941, Pearl 7038.
Artie Shaw: The Complete Gramercy Five Sessions 1940–1945, Bluebird 7637.
Artie Shaw and His Orchestra 1939–1940, Pearl 9779.
Frenesi Featuring Begin the Beguine, Bluebird 61064.
Personal Best 1938–1945, Bluebird 61099.
Greatest Hits 1938–1941, Victor 68494.
Artie Shaw Masterpieces Vol. 11, Original Historic Recordings 158272
Artie Shaw & His Orchestra 1936, Classic 855.
Artie Shaw & His Orchestra 1936–1937, Classic 886.
Artie Shaw & His Orchestra 1937, Classic 929.
Artie Shaw & His Orchestra 1938, Classic 965.
Artie Shaw & His Orchestra 1939, Classic 1007.
Artie Shaw & His Orchestra 1939 Vol. 2, Classic 1045.
Artie Shaw & His Orchestra 1940, Classic 1127.
Artie Shaw & His Orchestra: The Radio Years Vol. 1 1938, STC 2018.

Indian Love Call, JHR 73535.
The Chant, Hep 1046.
An Introduction to Artie Shaw, 1937–1942, Best of Jazz 4016.
Old Gold "Melody and Madness" Shows, 1938–39, Jazz Hour 1050.

PART FOUR

The Big Band and Swing Era: The Musicians

The big band and swing era was a romantic period. The music not only provided a soundtrack for a generation, it also marked the zenith of jazz as popular music. There was a fascination with the big bands and the legions of teenagers who followed the many groups religiously were true zealots. Many teenage boys dreamed of being the stylish, swinging drummer Gene Krupa in Benny Goodman's band. Jazz was no longer a musical style on the fringe of the entertainment industry; it *was* the entertainment industry. The era preceded the advent of television and provided the best option not only for the masses to have a good time, but for people's listening pleasure in their homes.

The music had matured since the Jazz Age. In the 1920s, the popularity of jazz demanded larger dance bands. Over the next decade the traditional New Orleans outfits would increase in size until they could be called big bands. Swing music differed from New Orleans Jazz and Dixieland in a variety of ways. The swing bands played simpler and more repetitious riff-filled music and the solos were more sophisticated.

The big band era presented something for everyone. For serious jazz fans there was the hard-driving swinging styles of Duke Ellington, Count Basie, Benny Goodman, Jimmie Lunceford, and Chick Webb. For those who wanted to dance there was the sound of the Dorsey Brothers, Artie Shaw, Harry James, Bob Crosby, and countless others. There were also the "sweet bands" like those of Lawrence Welk and Guy Lombardo, which played less driving swing music and had fewer impressive soloists.

The creation of the big bands meant more work for jazz artists since orchestras usually consisted of ten or more musicians and featured at least three trumpets, two or more trombonists, four or more saxophonists and a rhythm section that included a combination of piano, guitar, bass and drums. Thus, inevitably, there were hundreds of musicians able to make a good living during the big band era (1935–1945). It required a new breed of player who was able to sight-read and improvise at the same time. Although the 1920s produced some of the greatest soloists, it was in the 1930s that the jazz soloist really came to the forefront.

It was an exciting time to be a musician during the big band and swing era. For the top players there was a life of fame, glory and women. They were known throughout the country and in certain centers in Europe. They were given keys to cities and were the creators of history. There was a connection between the best-known musicians of the swing era and their fans that was pure magic. For the lesser players there were hardships. However, no matter the magnitude of the star the long hours of traveling, being away from home, stiff competition, and insecure employment were just some of the obstacles they faced.

Many of the biggest names of the swing era had their beginning in the 1920s including Louis Armstrong, Jack Teagarden, Benny Goodman, Coleman Hawkins, Ben Webster, and Benny Carter. Some of the most important musicians who are not featured in this section but should never be forgotten include trumpeters Bunny Berigan, Buck Clayton, Harry "Sweets" Edison, and Cootie Williams. Some of the important saxophonists include Chu Berry, Don Byas, Arnett Cobb, Hershal Evans, Johnny Mince, Bud Freeman, and Buddy Tate. Noted clarinetists include Kenny Davern, Bob Wilber, Woody Herman, and Pee Wee Russell. Important trombonists include Bobby Byrne, Lawrence Brown, Dickie Wells, Trummy Young, Vic Dickerson, and Benny Morton. Pianists such as Mary Lou Williams and Jess Stacey, as well as guitarists Freddie Green, Eddie Condon, Tiny Grimes, Les Paul, George Van Eps, and Chuck Wayne, also made a strong impact on the genre. The bassists Bill Taylor, Milt Hinton, Chubby Jackson, and Slam Stewart played a vital role. The famous drummers include Buddy Rich, Sonny Greer, Louis Bellson and Jimmy Crawford.

Those featured here were the best of a talented group that made the big band and swing era special.

Coleman Hawkins played complex solos that foreshadowed the path jazz would take in the next decade. He had a sound all of his own.

Benny Carter wore many hats, including first-rate multi-instrumentalist, talented arranger, and innovative composer. He was one of the biggest stars and continued to produce quality jazz long after the swing era was over.

Johnny Hodges was the finest example of Ellingtonia. Except for a brief period in the 1950s when he led his own band, Hodges spent his entire career with the Duke.

Ben Webster had a delicate touch on the tenor saxophone that made him one of the best for decades. He lent his talents to numerous bands over his career.

Lionel Hampton was the most noted vibraphonist throughout the history of jazz. An enthusiastic individual, as a bandleader he got his groups to swing hard and brilliantly.

Gene Krupa was one of the flashiest drummers in the history of jazz. He was a star and played in the Benny Goodman band. Perhaps more than any other jazz musician of the swing era, Krupa glamorized the lifestyle.

Lester Young, nicknamed "the Prez," was the most influential of all saxmen, and the legend that surrounds him helped shape the appeal of jazz over the last seventy years. He was a rebel who set his own standards with his highly unique approach to playing the saxophone.

Roy Eldridge was known as "Little Jazz." His unique trumpet sound was one of the most recognized in all of jazz, and is scattered throughout hundreds of recordings.

Jo Jones reinvented the art of drumming and set the table for the bop players Kenny Clarke and Max Roach. There is scarcely a drummer of the modern era who doesn't owe a debt to "Papa" Jones.

Teddy Wilson was a brilliant pianist who made his biggest splash in the Benny Goodman Band. He was known for his distinct style as well as helping to break the color barrier.

Jimmy Blanton was the first of the modern bassists and brought the instrument invaluable respect. He blazed the way for all others to follow.

Charlie Christian was one of the most important guitar players of the past sixty years. Like Django Reinhardt, his influence goes beyond the realms of jazz and spills into blues, rock, and soul.

COLEMAN HAWKINS (1904–1969)

The Boss of the Tenor Saxophone

The evolution of the saxophone from minor importance to prominence is tied to the life stories of the individuals who made it happen. At one time many musicians in jazz circles gave the saxophone little attention. It wasn't until the emergence of the "Boss of the Tenor Saxophone" that the instrument gained credibility in jazz. His name was Coleman Hawkins.

Coleman Randolph Hawkins was born November 21, 1904, in St. Joseph, Missouri. The music bug bit the man who would later be called the greatest saxophone player in history at a very early age. He started out on the piano, then switched to the cello, before settling on tenor sax when he was nine years old. He progressed quickly playing in school gigs when he was eleven. By the time he was sixteen he was a professional musician.

He caught his first big break when Mamie Smith spotted him. In 1920, she had scored an incredible hit with the song "Crazy Blues." It catapulted her to stardom even though it was relegated to the "race market." As part of her backing group, the Jazz Hounds, Hawkins made his recording debut in 1923. Although he was not yet the great soloist that he would later become, his days in Smith's band gave him more time to shape and control his style. He left the Jazz Hounds later the same year and freelanced for some time backing up singer Ginger Jones and blues queens Ma Rainey and Bessie Smith.

In 1924 Hawkins took a giant step forward in his cause to make the saxophone respectable when he joined Fletcher Henderson's orchestra, which was quickly becoming the best band of the era. Throughout the next decade Hawkins developed into the leading voice of the tenor sax and settled into the role of star in Fletcher's outfit. His reputation was based on his big-toned, rich and rhapsodic style featured on such numbers as "The Stampede," "Whiteman Stomp," "Hop Off," "Feeling Good," "Freeze an' Melt," "Blazin'," "Sweet & Hot," and "Hot and Anxious."

However, in 1934, fed up with the failings of Henderson's group, Hawkins left for Europe to work on his solo career. During his five-year stay overseas he recorded with a variety of acts including the Ramblers, the Berries, Jack Hylton, Jean Omer's Orchestra, Freddy Johnson, Michael Warlop, Benny Carter, sundry French musicians, Stephane

Grappelli, and the gypsy guitarist Django Reinhardt. He toured extensively throughout Britain, France, Holland, Switzerland, Belgium, Scandinavia, and many other countries spreading the gospel of jazz. He even appeared in the British film, *In Town To-night*. There was never a shortage of work for Hawkins in Europe.

But the impending threat of war forced Hawkins to return to New York in 1939. It was in the fall of that year that he entered the studio and recorded the definitive piece of his distinguished career. With the song "Body and Soul," Hawkins passed into jazz immortality long before his tenure was over.

In 1940, Hawkins formed his first big band, which played residencies at the Golden Gate Ballroom, the Savoy Ballroom, the Apollo Theatre, the Arcadia Ballroom and many others. However, Hawkins was forced to reduce the group to a smaller collection in 1941. Although it was not the most successful venture of his career, he still managed to keep his outfit working full-time.

Despite the difficult atmosphere of the war years that saw a ban on recording, Hawkins still spent more time in the studio than most. He was involved in making records sponsored by *Esquire* magazine as well as for the Signature and Keynote labels. It was during this phase that he worked with an impressive lineup of jazz contemporaries that included Buck Clayton, Charlie Shavers, Roy Eldridge, Tab Smith, Don Byas, Harry Carney, Teddy Wilson, Johnny Guarnieri, Cozy Cole and Big Sid Catlett.

One of the most important recording sessions that he participated in during the 1940s, and perhaps his entire career, occurred in 1944 with an eleven-piece band that featured Dizzy Gillespie. It is regarded as the first official bebop record date. While many of the elder statesman of jazz looked down upon bebop, Hawkins encouraged the young music revolutionists to follow their own path. Interestingly enough, Hawkins, who was so technically advanced on the tenor saxophone, fit right in with the young beboppers without having to drastically alter his style.

In 1945, Hawkins headed to the West Coast and brought with him Howard McGhee, Vic Dickenson, Allen Reuss and John Simmons. The bop-tinged band did well in the sunshine of California and even starred in a movie, *The Crimson Canary*. Upon his return from the West Coast Hawkins joined the Jazz at the Philharmonic tour that took him to Europe for the first time in almost a decade and thus began a yearly trek over the Atlantic where he satisfied and enlarged his fan base.

In the 1950s, Hawkins continued to build on his star status. He toured Europe several times as a solo act and as part of the Jazz at the Philharmonic package. He played solo dates at various small club venues and partnered with Roy Eldridge in a successful quintet. He also toured

American Armed Forces Bases in Europe with Illinois Jacquet. He played many of the major jazz festivals in the United States, and also did prolific freelance recordings.

By the 1960s, Hawkins was beginning his fifth decade in the spotlight as one of jazz's premier tenor saxophonists. He was able to reflect on many career highlights as the realm of his influence had spread throughout the world. He toured Europe on a frequent basis, recorded many strong records including one hot session with the upstart Sonny Rollins, and appeared as a solo act at various clubs in Greenwich Village in New York. He was a frequent act at the Village Vanguard, the Village Gate, The Metropole and other well-known jazz clubs in the Big Apple.

Despite the accolades, all was not well with Hawkins. Many jazz historians and some of his friends maintain that he was a frustrated, bitter man towards the end of his life.

Other accounts insist that after 1965 the sharp decline began that would lead to his demise by the end of the decade. Whichever facts correctly capture the real life of Coleman Hawkins in the end, not only the jazz world but also the entire international music community lost one of the greatest on May 19, 1969, in New York City. He died at the age of sixty-four from bronchial pneumonia shortly after appearing with Roy Eldridge on a Chicago television show.

Coleman Hawkins was the jazz poster boy for the tenor saxophone. Although he experimented with different instruments when he was a youngster, and even played the bass saxophone and occasionally soloed on the clarinet while a member of Henderson's big band, Hawkins will forever be identified with the tenor saxophone.

On the tenor sax Hawkins was a musical genius. He took the instrument down paths that had previously been thought impossible. He was so far advanced from other players that his talent was sometimes misunderstood and underappreciated. While jazz evolved from New Orleans to Chicago to big band to bebop to hard bop to avant-garde jazz during Hawkins' long, distinguished career, he never dramatically changed his style.

The Hawkins style, that distinctive rich, improvised big tone sound, still haunts tenor saxophonists to this day. He blew with an enthusiasm that went unmatched until Coltrane arrived on the scene in the late 1950s. More importantly, Hawkins was a man of rhythm and was second to none in his understanding of measured phrases. His solos were a series of bunched notes that followed rapidly in succession sounding like heavy raindrops falling hard. He was the first saxophonist to create moods with the instrument.

Hawkins was able to take apart the structure and melody of a song and reorganize it rhythmically. His round, beautiful notes, which contained a prettiness and sweetness, melted together and swept the listener away. There was an adventurous sound to his playing as he brought out the dynamics of the main rhythm to reveal the inner rhythm within the main beat. When he played there was much going on at many different levels. Because of his advanced musical prowess, Hawkins was a favorite to record with.

Throughout his forty-year recording career, he matched his uncanny skills and enthusiasm with fellow saxophonists Lester Young, Ben Webster, Benny Carter, Chu Berry, Don Byas, Johnny Hodges, Sonny Rollins and John Coltrane. But he also worked with a variety of piano players with different styles including Bud Powell, Oscar Peterson, Thelonious Monk, Billy Taylor, Red Garland, Tommy Flanagan, and Duke Ellington as they meshed their styles with his highly individualistic voice on horn. Guitarists Kenny Burrell, Django Reinhardt, Herb Ellis, Roy Eldridge, and bassist Oscar Pettiford also recorded with Hawkins drawing inspiration from his tireless solos and rhythmic magic. Hawkins also got together with noted vibraphonist Lionel Hampton; the combination proved to be interesting to all jazz fans.

There is hardly a jazz musician who has not been influenced by the brilliance of Coleman Hawkins. The breath and depth of the list is interesting. It includes such diverse talents as Hoagy Carmichael, George Adams, Pepper Adams, Arnett Cobb, Johnny Griffin, Buck Hill, Illinois Jacquet, Charles Lloyd, Billy Mitchell, Nick Nicholas, Flip Phillips, Sonny Rollins, Archie Shepp, Lew Tabackin, Buddy Tate, Cecil Taylor, Stanley Turrentine, Bennie Wallace, Tony Coe, and Noble "Thin Man" Watts. A complete list would fill a book.

While his career had an important effect on so many musicians, he also left jazz fans with a sparkling collection of songs that have endured the test of time. He gave the world "Body & Soul," "Old Black Joe's Blues," "The Stampede," "Whiteman Stomp," "Hop Off," "Feeling Good," "Freeze an' Melt," "My Ideal," "Woodyn You," "Bu-De-Dah," "What Is There to Say?," "I'm Thru with Love," "Lady Be Good," "It's the Talk of the Town," "The Man I Love," "How Deep Is the Ocean?," "Georgia on My Mind," "I Can't Believe That You're in Love with Me," "Chicago," and "Picasso."

But despite his obvious genius, wonderful collaborations, important influence, and the treasure trove of classic songs that make up his legacy, there was a dark side to Hawkins. He was reported to be a loner with very few close friends. He was a hard drinker who didn't always take good care of himself. He was a hard case, someone who was so far advanced musically that he grew impatient with those who could not keep up with him.

But whatever his personal shortcomings might have been, he remains an important figure in jazz history and is a member of the Hall of Fame. He paved the way for the modern jazz sound in the 1920s and 1930s long before anyone had heard of bop and hard bop. There was intensity, a stark feeling that enabled him to rearrange a song in his head and instantly translate it into his playing. There was no denying the claim that he was the "Boss of the Tenor Saxophone."

Discography

Rainbow Mist 1944, Delmark 459.
Body & Soul Revisited, 1951–1958, GRD 627.
In Holland: Dutch Treat, 1937–1939, AVD 638.
Hawk Talk 1963, TRD 1007.
Body & Soul, Pearl 1022.
In the Groove 1926–1939, Ind 2037.
The Hawk in Europe 1934–1937, ASL 5054.
The Body and Soul of the Saxophone, ASL 5378.
Cabu Collection, Masters of Jazz 8023.
April In Paris Featuring "Body And Soul" 1939–1956, Bluebird 61063.
Hollywood Stampede 1944–1945, Blue Note 92596.
Coleman Encounters Ben Webster, 1957, Verve Master Edition 521427.
The Genius of Coleman Hawkins, Verve Master Edition 539065.
The Complete Coleman Hawkins: The Keynote Recordings (1939–56),
    RCA Victor Jazz 68515–2.
Today and Now: Coleman Hawkins Quartet, Impulse IMPD 184.
Wrapped Tight, Impulse! GRD 109.
Duke Ellington Meets Coleman Hawkins: Duke Ellington & Coleman
    Hawkins, Impulse IMPD 162.
Desafinado, Impulse! IMPD 227.
The Hawk Relaxes, OJC 709.
At Ease With, OJC 181.
With Red Garland Trio, OJC 418.
Night Hawk, OJC 420.
In a Mellow Tone, OJC 6001.
Hawk Eyes, OJC 294.
Hawk Flies High, OJC 027.
Swingville: Coleman Hawkins All-Stars, OJC 225.
Sirius, OJC 861.
Very Saxy, OJC 458.
Bean and the Boys, Prestige PRCD 24124–2.
On Broadway, Prestige PRCD 24189–2.

Blues Wail: Coleman Hawkins Plays the Blues, Prestige PRCD 11006-2.
Jam Session in Swingville: Coleman Hawkins & Pee Wee Russell, Prestige PRCD 24051-2.
Bean Stalkin': Coleman Hawkins & Friends, Pablo PACD 2310933-2.
The Hawk Returns, Savoy Jazz SV 0182.
Coleman Hawkins Meets the Big Sax Section, Savoy Jazz SV 0248.
Ultimate Coleman Hawkins, Verve 557538-2.
Coleman Hawkins Encounters Ben Webster, Verve Master Edition 314 521427-2.
The Genius of Coleman Hawkins, Verve Master Edition 539065-2.
At the Opera House: Coleman Hawkins & Roy Eldridge, Verve 521641-2.
Compact Jazz: Coleman Hawkins & Ben Webster, Verve 833296-2.
Coleman Hawkins & Confreres, Verve 835255-2.
Hawkins! Eldridge ! Hodges! Alive! At the Village Gate, Verve 513755-2.
High and Mighty Hawk, Verve 820600-2.
Bean Bags: Milt Jackson & Coleman Hawkins, Koch Jazz KOC 8530.
1958-59: The Tenor for All Seasons, Jazz Classics 5017-2.
The Hawk in Europe 1934-1937, ASV Living Era 5054.
Jamestown N.Y. 1958, Uptown Jazz 2745.
Live from the London House Chicago, Jasmine 2521.
Passin' it Around, Jazz Hour JHR 73515.
Bean and Little Jazz: Coleman Hawkins & Roy Eldridge, Jazz Hour JHR 73574.

=====

JOHNNY HODGES (1906–1970)

The Earl of Ellingtonia

One of the most famous jazz bandleaders and personalities in the history of the genre was Duke Ellington. He was beyond category and for fifty years delighted millions of people in North America and around the world. The Duke Ellington Orchestra featured some of the most creative and best musicians in history. One of these individuals, because of his vast contributions to the Ellington sound for nearly half a century, earned the title "The Earl of Ellingtonia." His name was Johnny Hodges.

Johnny Hodges was born John Cornelius Hodges on July 25, 1906, in Cambridge, Massachusetts. Although his sisters were not musical they had a hand in boosting his career. One of Johnny's sisters married pianist-arranger Don Kirkpatrick, while another sister introduced him to the legendary Sidney Bechet. Hodges started on drums and moved to piano before settling on the alto saxophone by the age of fourteen. Through his sisters' connections Hodges received important lessons from Bechet, the New Orleans master who did much to shape his sound.

At eighteen, Hodges played in Willie "The Lion" Smith's quartet for a brief spell then shared the stage with his idol Bechet a year later. Although he remained in Boston during this period, he would travel to New York on the weekends to play at various gigs. It was during this period that Hodges was paying his dues as he spent time in a number of outfits including Lloyd Scott's, the Luckey Roberts Orchestra, and Chick Webb's. But the apprenticeships in these various groups were only preparation for a spot in Duke Ellington's Orchestra. In 1928, Hodges joined Ellington and remained there for almost all of the next forty-two years.

It was as a member of the Duke Ellington Orchestra that Hodges earned his reputation as a legendary alto saxophone player. The Ellington setting was the idyllic environment for someone of Hodges' ability. Duke loved to write for the musicians in his band and created many songs that emphasized Hodges' brilliance on the alto and for a while the baritone sax. There were doors opened for Hodges as part of Duke's band that would not have been available to him in another outfit.

That Hodges was able to join Ellington at the beginning of the bandleader's career enabled them to grow together. Although they had traveled different roads musically, once they met they were able to synthesize their various experiences into a formidable working partnership. As the Duke's fame spread so did that of his treasured alto sax player. That unmistakable whispery, warm tone became an integral part of the Ellington sound as much and probably more than the leader's piano. The name Johnny Hodges was immediately associated with the court of Ellingtonia.

By the mid-1930s he had established himself as the supreme voice of the alto saxophone. The musical voice of Johnny Hodges was one of the most recognizable sounds in all of jazz. His one serious rival, Benny Carter, was an excellent alto sax player, but was not fortunate enough to be part of Duke Ellington's Orchestra. While other bands struggled during the Depression era, Ellington and his men only increased their stranglehold on the jazz world.

As a member of the Duke Ellington Orchestra, Hodges contributed arrangements and also recorded in smaller contexts that included members of the band. As a result he was featured on hundreds of recordings over the years and produced an extensive catalog. He was also a highly in-demand session player and can be heard on the albums of countless jazz artists throughout the 1930s.

Hodges graced some of Billie Holiday's recordings with his match-less tone riding close with the rhythm section, challenging the horns, and providing a perfect foil to Lady Day's remarkable voice. He was one of the greatest soloists to ever back Holiday, and considering the list of musi-cians who played with the voice of jazz—that includes Lester Young, Teddy Wilson, Lionel Hampton, Benny Goodman, Roy Eldridge, Ben Webster, Benny Carter, Oscar Peterson—it is saying quite a lot.

Hodges would also lend his talents to the recordings of Teddy Wil-son, Earl Hines, Shelley Manne, and Gerry Mulligan, among others. Although his main loyalty was to Duke Ellington, Hodges would some-times lead his own group in session and on stage. In 1948, while Elling-ton was on a solo tour of England, Johnny gathered some of his fellow bandmates and played at the Apollo Club. He would also lead a session that involved Billy Strayhorn, Ellington's chief musical collaborator.

Perhaps one of the most interesting side projects in Hodges career was his teaming up with the immortal Charlie Parker and his rival Benny Carter. The three horns created pure magic as they traded solos and pushed each other to heights never achieved before. Parker, also an alto saxophonist, would eventually wrestle the crown from Hodges and Carter, but despite Parker's utter brilliance, Hodges proved that he could match Bird note for note on that session.

By the 1940s, Johnny "Rabbit" Hodges' name was synonymous with excellence in jazz circles. The creamy sound of his alto sax was such a part of the Ellington sound that it was inconceivable that the Duke could function without the premier soloist in his band. However, in 1951, Hodges stunned the jazz world when he temporarily left the Ellington fold.

Hodges formed his own group with trombonist Lawrence Brown and drummer Sonny Greer (who had also left the Ellington Orchestra), trumpeter Emmett Berry, and for a brief spell a young tenor saxophonist named John Coltrane. The group went through a few personnel changes, but managed to make some recordings. Hodges' septet also did TV stu-dio work on the *Ted Steele Show*. But despite his best efforts Hodges was not able to keep his outfit together and rejoined Ellington in the summer of 1955.

Although he returned to the Duke there seemed to be something that still bothered Hodges. He had wanted to go on his own and the fact that he was unsuccessful was a major disappointment. He had wanted to prove that he was more than just the star soloist in Ellington's orchestra. For many the coveted recognition of being a celebrated musician in one of the top groups in the world was enough. While he continued to make enormous contributions to the band upon his return, Hodges' best playing was in the 1930s and 1940s.

During his second stint, Hodges continued to record and appear in the various mediums that the band was involved in. Some of these venues included open-air concerts as well as television. He remained a good lieutenant for the next twenty-five years.

That Johnny Hodges was one of the great irreplaceables was proven during his hiatus from the Ellington Orchestra between 1951 and 1955. It was further proven on May 11, 1970, when Hodges, one of the seminal voices of the alto sax, died of a heart attack. It was a day of mourning for all jazz fans throughout the world.

Johnny "Rabbit" Hodges possessed one of the most identifiable tones in all of jazz history. He was—along with Coleman Hawkins and Benny Carter—the first great soloist of the saxophone. Despite the large number of incredible alto saxophonists in the history of jazz, Hodges must be evaluated as one of the top four sharing the exalted status with Charlie Parker, Benny Carter and Ornette Coleman. In some circles—particularly the Duke Ellington fan club—he is considered number one.

The Hodges style was one of complexity that created immense beauty. There was a subtlety in his overall tone that hinted at greater possibilities. This is not to say that he never tapped into his true potential, but it is a tribute to mastery of the instrument. He was able to deliver music on many levels that satisfied the casual and expert listener simultaneously.

Hodges had the ability to play a spattering of notes which were welded to the rhythm section, and, at the same time, challenged the other horns in the orchestra. His improvisational skills were impeccable. He was able to bolster a work's signature melody and chords with his own embellishments. He never wasted a note.

His solos were masterpieces that danced with pure delight. Hodges' dreamy, whispery solos could take a listener to some exotic location of tropical trees, sparkling oceans, pure white beaches and unlimited personal fantasies. However, his solos were by no means lightweight; they contained sureness and a subtle power that drove the song in interesting and unexplored directions.

Hodges' brilliance can be heard on hundreds of songs. A partial list includes "The Far East Suite," "His Mother Called Him Bill," "Loveless Love," "Weary Blues," "Wabash Blues," "Beale Street Blues," "Back to Back," "Good Gal Blues," "Jeep's Blues," "Magenta Haze," "Day Dream,"

"Empty Ballroom Blues," "Wanderlust," "Harmony in Harlem," and "Blue Goose." His diverse recording career allowed him to leave a massive catalog as leader of his own sessions, with Ellington, or on the albums of others.

The greatest influence on Hodges was Sidney Bechet. Bechet, one of the greatest soloists in the history of jazz, taught his young protégé well. Hodges' glissandos—smooth slides through a run of adjacent tones—were a trademark, and the technique that he passed on to a number of other saxophonists who followed the wide path he blazed. Charlie Barnet, Jan Garbarek, Woody Herman, Charlie Parker, Charlie Mariano, Oliver Nelson, Tab Smith, Barbara Thompson, Bennie Wallace, Ben Webster, Bob Wilber, Leo Wright, Captain John Handy, Chris Woods, Norris Turney, Leroy Harris, Cecil Scott and Eddie Metcalfe are just a few of the musicians who were touched by Hodges' magic.

Among the members of the Duke Ellington band, Hodges was the greatest soloist—a bold statement considering the wealth of talent that was part of the famous orchestra. Rex Stewart, Ray Nance, Joseph "Tricky Sam" Nanton, Lawrence Brown, Barney Bigard, Ben Webster, Harry Carney, Jimmie Blanton, Sonny Greer, and Cootie Williams all excelled in the ranks of Ellingtonia, but Hodges surpassed everyone of them. He was always a notch above the rest.

The legend of Johnny Hodges is one of the most heartwarming stories in jazz history. Within a genre that has produced such tragic figures as Billie Holiday, Charlie Parker, Bix Beiderbecke, Scott Joplin, Fats Navarro, and Lester Young, to name a few, Hodges was the exact opposite. He enjoyed a stable and remarkable career that earned him entry into the Jazz Hall of Fame. Undoubtedly, all must bow their heads in admiration for the man known as the "Earl of Ellingtonia."

Discography

Rarities & Private Recordings, Suisasa JZCD 361.
Hodge Podge, Epic 22001.
Ellingtonia!, Onyx 216.
The Rabbit in Paris, Inner City 7003.
Johnny Hodges Collates, Vol. 1, Mercury MGC-111.
Castle Rock, Norgran MGN-1048.
Memories of Ellington, Norgran MGN-1004.
More of Johnny Hodges, Norgran MGN-1009.
In a Tender Mood, Verve 8149.
The Blues, Norgran MGN-1061.

Perdido, Norgran MGN-1091.
Swing with Johnny Hodges, Clef MGC-151.
Johnny Hodges Collates, Vol. 2, Clef 128.
Alto Sax, RCA-Victor PT-3000.
Used to be Duke, Verve 849394–2.
Alto Blue, Verve 20.
A Man and His Music, Storyville 4073.
At a Dance, in a Studio, on Radio, Enigma 1052.
Dance Bash, Norgran MGN-1024.
Creamy, Norgran MGN-1045.
Ellingtonia, Norgran MGN-1055.
Duke's in Bed, Verve MGV-8203.
The Complete Johnny Hodges and His Orchestra, Le Jazz 8103.
The Complete Johnny Hodges Sessions, Mosaic 6126.
Johnny Hodges, Volume 1, Mercer P-1000.
Johnny Hodges, Volume 2, Mercer P-1006.

BENNY CARTER (1907–2003)

Ridin' in Rhythm

While some artists gained fame for their ability on a single instrument, others attained legendary status for their versatility and multiplicity. These multi-instrumentalists, arrangers, bandleaders, and singers were unique individuals who made an immeasurable impact on every era. The man who was always comfortable ridin' in rhythm wore many hats in the world of jazz. His name is Benny Carter.

Benny Carter was born Bennett Lester Carter on August 8, 1907, in New York City. Like many other jazz musicians he came from a musical family. His mother played organ and piano and two of his cousins, Theodore Cuban Bennet and Darnell Howard, would make their mark on the jazz world playing trumpet and guitar, respectively. As a child he was surrounded by music and absorbed all that he could like a sponge storing it for future use.

He began playing piano at an early age but gave it up for the trumpet. In order to save up for an instrument he did odd jobs as a milkman's assistant, laundry deliverer, and upholsterer. Despite his most honest attempts at mastering the trumpet, it proved too difficult and he traded it in for a C-melody saxophone. During this formative period he was attempting to constantly hone his skills on whatever instrument he picked up.

In 1924, at the tender age of seventeen, he joined June Clark's band where he switched from C-melody saxophone to alto sax. A short time later he left Clark's band and landed a coveted spot in Earl Hines' band. Despite the excitement and the wonderful opportunity of working with such a great talent as Hines, Carter left music for a brief spell in order to study theology at Wilberforce College. But jazz was in his blood and after a brief time at school, he joined Horace Henderson's Collegians, leaving the world of academia behind.

For the next couple of years Carter bounced around the band circuit. After leaving Horace's band he worked with Billy Fowler's group in Baltimore and New York. But soon he was adding his distinct alto saxophone sound to the outfits of James P. Johnson, Duke Ellington (briefly) and finally Fletcher Henderson. Unsatisfied with the working conditions in Henderson's band, Carter moved on to Charlie Johnson's group from 1927 to 1929, and later was part of Chick Webb's Orchestra.

In 1931 Carter joined McKinney's Cotton Pickers as the group's musical director and stayed for about a year. He was able to work with the great Don Redman and learned much about arrangement and writing. From this point on he doubled on trumpet. He also became the musical director of the Chocolate Dandies Band and stayed with them from 1930 until 1933. The fact that he was able to wear many hats at once only proved the depth of his versatility.

In 1932, Carter took the initiative to form his own swing band and assembled a group that played its first residency at the Arcadia Ballroom in New York. For the next couple of years he concentrated on running his own outfit but in the depths of the Great Depression he was forced to disband the group. He joined Fletcher Henderson again in the fall of 1934. Carter, a keen student of music, had been sharpening his abilities as an arranger and a composer throughout his career. He became so proficient that he supplied music to such well known bandleaders as Duke Ellington, Teddy Hill, McKinney's Cotton Pickers, Fletcher Henderson, and the soon to be crowned king of swing, Benny Goodman.

In 1935, Carter emigrated—temporarily—to Europe. His first job was with Willie Lewis's band in Paris. However, because of his remarkable multi-abilities Carter was highly in demand and was soon working as staff arranger for Henry Hall and His Orchestra in London. His first overseas recording was with Hall on the record *Swingin' at Malda Vale*, followed by a tour of Scandinavia and Holland. Upon his return to London he hooked up with Freddie Johnson and together they played in Copenhagen. In 1938, he was appointed to lead the International Band of Scheweningen in Holland. Despite his busy schedule, he found time to record two albums with the great Django Reinhardt.

Upon his return to America in 1939, Carter led his own big band for a couple of years. At various times his group was comprised of Tyree Glenn, Jonah Jones, Jimmy Archey, Sidney De Paris, Sonny White, Doc Cheatham, Benny Morton, Eddie Heywood, Joe Thomas, J. C. Heard and Coleman Hawkins. He recorded two classic albums, *Melancholy Benny* and *Benny Carter & His Orchestra*, at the turn of the decade. He also found time to sit on sessions with Coleman Hawkins and Billy Holiday. Later, when he cut his big band to a sextet it included Dizzy Gillespie and Jimmy Hamilton.

Carter, born with a traveling foot, moved to the West Coast in 1943 where he led his own band. It featured the emerging talents of drummer Max Roach, Henry Coker, Al Grey, trombonist J. J. Johnson, Joe Albany, Porter Kilbert, and Curley Russell. He played residencies at Billy Berg's and the Casa Mañana. During this period he devoted his time to writing film scores and his live performances were drastically reduced. He appeared in many films including *The Snows of Kilimanjaro*, *Stormy Weather*, *As Thousands Cheer* and *Clash By Night*.

In the 1950s, he had his own big band and played all over the Los Angeles area spending long residencies in the top clubs in town. With the advent of television, Carter found another lucrative market for his composing and arranging talents. He scored for several national television series including *"M" Squad*, *Alfred Hitchcock Presents*, and *Climax*. In 1955, he wrote the score for *The Benny Goodman Story* and *The Five Pennies*. He was also one of the many jazz luminaries to join Norman Ganz's Jazz at the Philharmonic series. He partook in numerous package tours of Europe, performing in France, England, Scandinavia, and Germany.

While many musicians begin to slow down as they advance in age, Carter was the exception to the rule. During the 1960s he continued to amaze many by playing as fiercely as he had when he had broken in forty years before. He performed all over the United States leading his own band as well as doing solo shows. He also toured much of the world giving a taste of his pleasant alto sax sound to everyone in jazz-starved countries.

Throughout the decade he was extremely busy and there seemed to be no limit to his versatility. He remained active on the scene, appearing in several JATP sessions in the United States as well as Europe. He also added Barney Bigard, Ben Webster, Milt Jackson, Joe Pass, Dizzy Gillespie, Tony Flanagan, Eddie "Lockjaw" Davis and Clark Terry to his already impressive list of recording mates. He toured Germany as a solo artist in 1961. Two of the many highlights he enjoyed during the decade occurred when he appeared with legends Count Basie and Duke Ellington.

In 1979, he celebrated his seventieth birthday, but Carter continued to defy all odds and stun all observers with his energy and creativity. He blew his alto sax with as much force, brilliance, and beauty as players half his age did. Perhaps the secret to his longevity was his constant work ethic.

As more jazz festivals began to take place around the country Carter was an important participant as a link between the new thing and the golden age of jazz of the pre-war years. In any outdoor facility, indoor club or arena, he could hold his own with anyone who dared take the stage with him. He also continued to score films for Hollywood and recorded at a steady pace. Long after many of his generation were out of the music business he continued to thrive on countless projects.

In the 1980s, during the jazz revival, young lions such as Wynton Marsalis, Marcus Roberts, Kenny Kirkland, Mark Whitfield, Kevin Eubanks, Robert Hurst III, Reginald Veal, Jeff "Tain" Watts, Herlin Riley, Robin Eubanks, Wallace Roney, Ryan Kisor, James Zollar and Roy Hargrove looked up to Carter. Although he was his seventies he graciously accepted his new role, but that isn't to say that he gave an inch to the new players. He continued to amaze all by holding his own against the new guard and reminding them that he might be the old man on the block but he had been around that block several times.

The 1990s did not see Carter slow down and his warm alto sax remained one of the most identifiable sounds in all of jazz. A master performer, his appearance at outdoor jazz festivals was a guaranteed event as new and old fans stood in awe of his energy and his sheer ability to still entertain a crowd.

Benny Carter passed away on July 12, 2003, following a brief illness. He had recorded and performed into his nineties, one of the last links to a bygone musical era.

Benny Carter was a jazz institution and encompassed everything that is the genre. He was one of the most accomplished musical personalities of any style. As a multi-instrumentalist, arranger, composer, and occasional singer, he made outstanding contributions to jazz. While the history of jazz is filled with many who died too young such as Charlie Parker, Jimmy Blanton, Charlie Christian, Bix Beiderbecke, and Fats Waller, to name a few, Carter defied the odds and enjoyed a long, prosperous career.

In any discussion of the greatest alto sax players in history four names are ranked together: Johnny Hodges, Charlie Parker, Ornette Coleman, and, of course, Carter. In the 1930s he was most definitely Hodges' peer and later was able to absorb the influence of Parker's unique vocabulary without losing his personal identity.

His elegant tone, with its sympathetic rhythm and uncluttered flow of melodic improvisation, is instantly recognizable. There is a consistent rousing emotion in his playing that contains a definite sophistication. He emotes a series of notes that literally fall together like perfect words in a classic poem. There is always an underlying subtlety to his clean, precise sound.

Carter also made recordings on tenor sax, clarinet, trombone, trumpet and piano during his extended career. One of his most remarkable traits as a musician is his versatility on such a wide assortment of instruments. There are only a handful of jazz musicians throughout its one hundred-plus-year history who can match his flexibility and ability.

His talents as an arranger and composer spilled over from the world of jazz and spread into movies and television. He wrote for the studios for fifty years and was one of the most prolific composers in music history. Carter opened the door of opportunity for modern artists.

He recorded with every legend in jazz. Ben Webster, John Kirby, Roy Eldridge, Teddy Wilson, Ray Brown, Billie Holiday, Johnny Hodges, Milt Hinton, Buster Bailey, Fletcher Henderson, Rex Stewart, Chu Berry, J.C. Higginbotham, Norman Granz, Cozy Cole, Lawrence Lucie, Russell Procope, Benny Morton, and Harry "Sweets" Edison are just a few of the names he worked with. A complete list would include just about anyone who ever appeared in jazz from 1920 and beyond.

Carter was also a long-time bandleader. Although the names of his bands would change over the years—Benny Carter & His Orchestra, Benny Carter & the American Jazz Orchestra, Benny Carter All-Star Sax Ensemble, Benny Carter Quartet, Benny Carter's Orchestra, Benny Carter & His Swing Quartet, and Benny Carter & The Rambles—the bands themselves always retained a strong quality. He maintained a talented and well-rounded outfit no matter how its name appeared on the bill.

Because of the many decades he spent in jazz, he had a profound influence on an incredibly large number of artists. A partial list includes Cannonball Adderley, Sonny Criss, Roy Eldridge, Al Grey, Art Pepper, Bud Shank, Ben Webster, Leo Wright, Alvin Alcorn, Eddie Barefield, Jimmy Hamilton, and Sahib Shihab. But in truth, he touched everyone whom he came in contact with over the years. Carter's music is an excellent starting point for anybody entering the world of jazz.

The life of Benny Carter was one of endurance, improvisation, creativity, change and individualism. In many ways his biography is the story of jazz itself. The one thread that was sewn throughout Carter's life and kept it together was the music that flowed from his endless imagination and ability. From the very beginning, without a doubt, Benny Carter was ridin' in rhythm.

Discography

California Ramblers Edison Laterals 1928–1929, DCP 301.
Benny Carter Vol. 1 1928–1931, Masters of Jazz 22.
Benny Carter Vol. 2 1931–1933, Masters of Jazz 23.
Benny Carter Vol. 3 1933–1934, Masters of Jazz 39.
Benny Carter Vol. 4 1934–1935, Masters of Jazz 59.
Benny Carter Vol. 5 1936, Masters of Jazz 73.
Benny Carter Vol. 6 1936, Masters of Jazz 81.
Benny Carter Vol. 7 1936–1937, Masters of Jazz 95.
Benny Carter Vol. 8 1937, Masters of Jazz 103.
Benny Carter Vol. 9 1938–1939, Masters of Jazz 124.
Masterpieces Vol. 17, EPM 158672.
Benny Carter—The Verve Years, Vol. 1, PLG 849395.
Benny Carter & His Orchestra 1929–1933, Classic 522.
Benny Carter & His Orchestra 1933–1936, Classic 530.
Benny Carter & His Orchestra 1936, Classic 541.
Benny Carter & His Orchestra 1937–1939, Classic 552.
Benny Carter & His Orchestra 1939–1940, Classic 579.
Benny Carter & His Orchestra 1940–1941, Classic 631.
Benny Carter & His Orchestra 1943–1946, Classic 974.
Benny Carter & His Orchestra 1946–1948, Classic 1043.
Benny Carter Songbook Vol. 2, Musicmasters 65155.
The Verve Small Group Sessions, Verve 849395.
A Gentleman and His Music, Concord Jazz 4285.
Advanced Swing, Drive Archive 42449.
Benny Carter and The Jazz Giants, Fantasy Records 60029.
Best of Benny Carter, Pablo Records 409.
Quintet Sessions 1946–1954, Blue Moon 3032.
Groovin' High in Los Angeles 1946, HEP 15.
Live and Well in Japan!, Original Jazz Classics 736.
The Best of Benny Carter, Musicmasters 65133.
The King, Original Jazz Classics 883.
Tickle Toe, Fresh Sound New Talent 24.
Benny Carter, Vol. 9 (1938–39), Masters Of Jazz 124.
Best of Benny Carter, Pablo Records 409.
Additions to Further Definitions, Impulse 19136.

Love Is Cynthia, BMG BVCJ-37172.
Swingin the Twenties (Limited Edition), JVC VICJ-60355.

BEN WEBSTER (1909–1973)

Cottontail Blues

Once the saxophone began to assume a more prominent role in jazz through the masterful playing of its pioneer practitioner Coleman Hawkins, it was inevitable that the new individuals who had taken up the instrument during the swing era would eventually receive proper recognition. Lester Young, Benny Carter, Sidney Bechet, and Johnny Hodges were those who followed in Hawkins' footsteps and elevated the status of the horn. There was another saxophonist who belongs to this distinguished group who charmed everyone with his "Cottontail" blues and became one of the best of all time. His name was Ben Webster.

Benjamin Francis Webster was born on March 27, 1909, in Kansas City, Missouri, a place that produced many famous jazz musicians including Count Basie, Charlie Parker, Walter Page, and Jimmy Rushing. Webster, primarily self-taught, first took up the violin then switched to the piano. He was passionate about music and continued to hone his skills. After attending Wilberforce College he found work playing the piano in a silent-movie house in Amarillo, Texas.

His first professional engagement was with Bretho Nelson's Band in Enid, Oklahoma. A few months later he joined Dutch Campbell's group for a brief stint. While a stream of talented piano players like Fats Waller, Jelly Roll Morton, and James P. Johnson dominated the world of jazz, there were few good saxmen. The saxophone had not yet made a major impact on the world of jazz as it would in the following decades.

When Webster discovered the possibilities of the instrument he switched to tenor saxophone and was encouraged by Budd Johnson. After a few months of hard practice, he became proficient enough to join his first group, W. H. Young's outfit (he was the father of Lester Young), as a tenor saxophone player. He started with the group in New Mexico and toured with the family show for a few months during which time he improved his skills tremendously.

Despite the tough economic circumstances brought on by the Great Depression, Webster enjoyed much success throughout most of the 1930s. Although he was able to find work almost on a consistent basis it was not exactly a decade of stability for Webster. For the entire decade he played in no less than twelve different bands including stints with Jap Allen, Blanche Calloway, Bennie Moten, Andy Kirk, Fletcher Henderson, Willie Bryant, Cab Calloway, Roy Eldridge and Teddy Wilson. However, it was during this period that his sound matured and he started to attract serious attention because of his abilities.

In 1940, Webster joined the Duke Ellington Orchestra and remained there for three years. Although the Ellington Orchestra was a top-notch outfit, Webster decided that after almost a decade and a half of being under one bandleader or another he desired to front his own group. In 1943, he formed his own aggregation, which he led for the next five years; the group played many of their gigs on 52nd Street in New York. However, on occasion, Webster would moonlight as a sideman with groups led by Raymond Scott, John Kirby, and Sid Catlett. In 1948, when given a second opportunity to play with Ellington, Webster took the leap and stayed with the Duke for a scant seven months. After leaving Ellington, Webster went back to working on 52nd Street, recording frequently as both a leader and a member of other groups.

It seemed that Webster could not sit still. For the next few years he played in Jay McShann's band and Bob Wilson's group, both Kansas City outfits. He also joined Jazz at the Philharmonic. He returned to New York City in the early 1950s to lead his own band, while freelancing and doing studio work. He moved to the West Coast in the mid–1950s, occasionally returning East to play at various venues including the Village Vanguard.

Webster remained active as he divided his time between the two coasts when not touring Europe. He found plenty of work as a session player (his skills had not diminished with age), leading his own group, and sitting in with various bands. Sometimes, Webster would have a pick-up band back him up for concert dates as he wove magic with his tenor saxophone. Without a doubt he was a free spirit who could not be tied down to any confining situation for a long period of time.

In 1964, he moved to Europe and made Holland his central base. He performed in England, France and many other countries. In 1966, he moved to Copenhagen and continued to build on his burgeoning international reputation. In 1967, a movie, filmed in Holland, documented the life and times of Ben Webster. It was a fine retrospective of the career of one of the most important jazz players of the past thirty years.

On September 20, 1973, Ben Webster, the kid from Missouri who had entertained millions with his brilliant ability on the tenor saxophone, died in Amsterdam of natural causes. He was sixty-three years old.

Ben Webster is one of the most important voices of the tenor saxophone to emerge from the swing period. In an era that also included the talented work of Lester Young, Benny Carter, Johnny Hodges, and Coleman Hawkins, the fact that Webster made such an impact is a tribute to his genius. He is one of the most memorable sax players for a variety of reasons.

The Webster style featured a dual personality that made for a distinct and unique sound. Webster could swing with the best and on fast and furious songs he played with an emotion that bordered on pure anger. He was fierce, coarse, dangerous—a genuine warrior on the tenor saxophone. On slower ballads he was earthy, tender, reserved, advancing the song along with a happy run of notes that melted like cream.

His schizophrenic playing can be traced to his range of personal feelings. Webster was an emotional man, more so than the average jazz player. He was capable of terrible torrents of anger that left many of his bandmates shocked and stunned. He could be sweet like a gentle bear, playful and funny. He was able to bring to the surface all of these feelings when playing, and that amplified his sound, bringing to it the full scope of human colors and tones.

Whether he is remembered as a hot head or a man capable of elegance and reserve, Webster was a major influence on a diverse number of future sax players. A partial list includes Archie Shepp, Lew Tabackin, Scott Hamilton, Bennie Wallace, Eddie Shaw, Dudu Pukwana, George Adams, Paul Gonsalves, Johnny Griffin, Buck Hill, Charles Lloyd, Nick Nicholas, Flip Phillips, Ike Quebec, Al Sears, Tony Coe, David Murray, Eddie "Lockjaw" Davis, and Willis "Gator" Jackson. It is in the records of these musicians and countless others that the full range of Webster's brilliance can be heard and truly appreciated.

Although he was not well known as a great jazz composer, Webster was a true studio ace, adding his emotionally filled split personality saxophone to the recorded efforts of many jazz greats. The songs "Danny Boy," "Love Is Here to Stay," "My Romance," "Cotton Tail," "All Too Soon," "Conga Brava," "Bojangles," "Sepia Panorama," "Just A-Settin' & A-Rockin'," "The Girl in My Dreams," "Chelsea Bridge," and "Blues Serge," all bear Ben Webster's distinct touch. He enhanced any session that he participated in whether he played lead or was just a member of the background group.

Some of the important concerts and sessions that feature Webster include the Carnegie Hall premiere of Duke Ellington's *Black, Brown and Beige* masterpiece. He also can be heard on Billie Holiday's *The Golden*

Years and *The Voice of Jazz*, on Jack Teagarden's *Jack Teagarden/Pee Wee Russell*, on *The Gillespie Jam Sessions* and with Red Norvo on *The Greatest of the Small Bands*. Webster was also prominently featured on Benny Carter's *Jazz Giant* and on *Gerry Mulligan Meets the Jazz Giants*. He recorded an album with Oscar Peterson called *Soulville* for the Verve label. He backed Jimmy Witherspoon up on a couple of his recordings. Aside from Gillespie, he also appeared with other bebop artists including Charlie Parker, Kenny Clarke, and Barney Kessel. There were hundreds of sessions that featured Webster's undisputed genius.

Webster has not been forgotten. He appeared in a few films during his career with Duke Ellington, and also appeared with Benny Carter's band in *Clash by Night* in 1952. Webster is included in all jazz compilations and many television series that celebrate the genre and its foremost players. There have been many books published on him; the most interesting two are *The Discography of Ben Webster, 1931–1973*, and *The Tenor Saxophone of Ben Webster, 1931–1943*.

In a career that lasted seven decades Ben Webster delighted all with his versatile tenor saxophone sound. A brooding man whose emotional outbursts were best heard through his music, he was an important stylist and remains one of the most recognizable voices of the swing era and thereafter with his "Cottontail" blues.

Discography

1944–1946, Classics 1017.
An Introduction to Ben Webster: His Best Recordings, Best of Jazz 4052.
At the Renaissance, Original Jazz Classics 390.
Ben Webster and Associates, Verve 543 302.
Ben Webster's Finest Hour, Verve 543 808.
Bounce Blues, Blue Moon 3042.
For the Guv'nor, Le Jazz 008.
Gone with the Wind, Music 9020.
In a Mellow Tone, Jazz House 601.
Jazz Round Midnight, Verve 517775.
King of the Tenors, Verve 519 806.
Live in Paris, 1972, Esoldun 2131.
Meets Oscar Peterson, Verve 521 448.
No Fool, No Fun: The Rehearsal, Storyville 8304.
Plays Ballads, Storyville—(import) 4118.
Plays Duke Ellington, Storyville 4133.
Quiet Now: Until Tonight, Verve 543 249.
See You at the Fair, Impulse! 121.

Soulville, Verve 833 551.
Stormy Weather, Intuition Music 9010.
Story 1934–1944, EPM 158612.
The Best of Ben Webster (1931–1944), ASV 5152.
The Frog, Giants of Jazz Recordings 53307.
The Soul of Ben Webster, Verve 527 475.
The Warm Moods, Reprise Archives 2001.
There Is No Greater Love, Music 9002.
Ultimate Ben Webster, Verve 557 537.
Verve Jazz Masters, Verve 525 431.
At the Renaissance, Original Jazz Classics 390.
Soul Mates, JVC VICJ-60514.
Stormy Weather, BCD JTM8100.
Victory Stride/Swing Sessions, EMI TOCJ-66014.

LIONEL HAMPTON (1909–2002)

The Jazz Ambassador

The history of jazz is filled with musicians who enjoyed long and distinguished careers that spanned every era of the genre. These individuals spread the magic of jazz throughout the entire world with their ability and sheer passion for the music. One of the most brilliant innovators earned the title "The Jazz Ambassador" for his accomplishments on a domestic and international front. His name was Lionel Hampton.

Lionel Hampton was born April 12, 1909, in Louisville, Kentucky. His father was an entertainer before World War I, and later on when his parents split up, Lionel and his mother moved to Birmingham, Alabama, then on to Chicago in hopes of a better life. It was in the Windy City that young Lionel first caught the music bug. From the beginning his interest in music was on the percussionist side.

As a youngster he liked to make noise by hammering on things. He worked at various odd jobs in order to buy his first drum kit. But Hampton's interest in creating rhythm went beyond the ordinary drums set-up. He realized that there were entire dimensions of sounds that were just waiting to be discovered and that was the path he decided to follow. He not only wanted to unearth these sounds but he desired to mesh them together and create something new.

During his development into one of the top rhythm creators in jazz history, Hampton learned from a variety of teachers. Jimmy Bertrand was his original hero; he played the xylophone—not one of the most dominant instruments in jazz at the time. Drummer Snags Jones also tutored Hampton. Once he had become proficient enough as a drummer he joined Major Smith's famous Chicago Defender Newsboy's Band.

After his stint in the Major's band, Hampton played with a number of Chicago area outfits, gaining valuable experience that would serve him well later in his career. At the age of eighteen he decided to move to the West Coast after having spent most of his time in the Midwest. On the left coast he found work with the Spike Brothers and Paul Howard's Quality Serenaders, with whom he made his recording debut in 1929.

His next engagement was with Les Hite's orchestra where he was able to participate in various film projects. He was also given the opportunity to play behind the great Louis Armstrong. He continued to record with Hite's Band and was quickly making a name for himself on the vibraphone. During a recording session with Armstrong, Hampton added vibraphone sounds and decided to dedicate his time to further studying the possibilities of the minor instrument.

During the depths of the Great Depression, 1932–35, Hampton was leading a busy life. He played in the Hite Orchestra and also attended the University of Southern California to add some musical theory to his practical experiences. He also moonlighted in the Armstrong movie *Pennies from Heaven*, where he donned a mask while playing the drums.

Soon after he began to lead his own band that appeared around the Los Angeles area picking up gigs at regular intervals. An enterprising young man, Hampton was learning the strings of becoming a good bandleader when one night he met another young man who was fronting his own group. His name was Benny Goodman, and he recognized Hampton's potential and invited him to be part of what would become the hottest band in America. Hampton, an adventurous young man, jumped at the chance.

For the next four years Hampton was part of Goodman's swing band. During this period, 1936–1940, the vibraphonist learned many important lessons that would enable him to further forge his own path in the jazz world. He made numerous recordings with smaller groups of Goodman's orchestra. It was one of the most prolific recording periods of his long, illustrious career. Together, Goodman and Hampton broke down the rigid color barrier that existed in music. In this sense he was a pioneer along with Teddy Wilson.

In August 1940, armed with renewed confidence and four years of tutelage under Goodman, Hampton re-formed his big band and they made their debut in Los Angeles that same year. From this point on Hampton led his own outfits and created a permanent name as one of the best bandleaders of the middle century. He surrounded himself with exceptional talent and over the years such names as Charles Mingus, Quincy Jones, Illinois Jacquet, Lucky Thompson, Joe Newman, Ernie Royal, Cat Anderson, Kenny Dorham, Art Farmer, and singers Dinah Washington and Joe Williams spent time in his group.

Although he became known as a leader of a wild, swinging band that roared with the power of a hurricane, Hampton was always organizing jam sessions with the elite of the jazz world. A classic example is the lineup assembled in 1937 for sessions on Victor Records. The band boasted a horn section of Coleman Hawkins, Ben Webster, Chu Berry, Benny Carter, Dizzy Gillespie, and a rhythm section comprised of Charlie Christian, Milt Hinton, Clyde Hart, Cozy Cole, Gene Krupa and Hampton. His super groups also included Harry James, Jonah Jones, and Nat King Cole, among others.

But amassing a talented lineup was only part of Hampton's longevity secret as a leader. He was an intelligent man who managed to survive the constant changes that occurred in jazz after the war. Although his roots were firmly planted in the big band and swing era, he was also able to incorporate certain elements of bebop and many other styles that became the rage in the 1960s and 1970s. His remarkable ability to accept change while not changing his style was the key to his enduring success.

Over the years his groups were legendary and his name became synonymous with mainstream jazz. While other bands started up only to fall apart a short time later, Hampton remained in the forefront of the music scene without breaking stride. He was a jazz giant who survived the fickleness of public taste, the ravages of old age, and the many strokes that robbed him of some of his exuberance, creativity and mobility.

On August 31, 2002, Lionel Hampton, the beloved vibes player who had thrilled millions with his enthusiastic percussionist skills, died. He was 94 years old.

Hampton was the greatest living ambassador for jazz. His career spanned back into the twenties and he could freely speak of the magic of the big band and swing era with confidence since he had a major hand in creating it. He was a walking encyclopedia of jazz history and continued to perform and record on an occasional basis until the very end. Many of his records were reissued in CD format.

He was a survivor who thrived on playing the music that he felt delighted audiences. A shrewd musician, arranger and bandleader, he always had an uncanny sense of what the people wanted to hear and then promptly wrote music to fit their needs. He long ago understood the adage of supply and demand: his audiences demanded dynamic jazz with flair, and Hampton supplied just that with sheer enthusiasm.

Hampton was the prime vibraphonist in jazz history. Although Red Norvo (born 1908) was of the same generation as Hampton, he began to experiment with the instrument a decade after Lionel had already established his expertise. Another contemporary of Hampton's, Milt "Bags" Jackson, also propelled the instrument in new directions. Although a masterful vibraphone player, he was most famous as a member of the Modern Jazz Quartet with pianist John Lewis. Jackson was more of an ensemble player than a prime soloist like Hampton.

While the vibraphone was Hampton's prime instrument he was also an acknowledged master of the drum kit. During the thousands of concerts he performed, many times he jumped on the drums and pounded out expert rhythms much to the crowd's delight. Undoubtedly, he was the king of the rhythm instruments.

Although not an accomplished piano player, Hampton had firm control of the instrument and was able to elate an audience with his primitive, but very effective two finger technique. While not in the same league as an Art Tatum, Oscar Peterson, or Fats Waller, Hampton, with his creative spark and unbound excitement, usually pulled off his piano exercises with splendid results. It was another dimension of his musical abilities.

In a career that spanned eight decades, he worked with many of the major names as well as with some lesser-known musicians. The musicians he played with included Benny Goodman, Gene Krupa, Jess Stacy, Ziggy Elman, Charlie Christian, Allan Reuss, Harry James, Milt Hinton, Ben Webster, Cootie Williams, Cozy Cole, Johnny Hodges, Vido Musso, Benny Carter, John Kirby, Coleman Hawkins, Jo Jones, Billy Mackel, and Harry Goodman.

Like all good bandleaders he displayed a remarkable eye for talent. It was Hampton who discovered the dynamic singer Dinah Washington. Washington, whose real name was Ruth Jones, was born in Tuscaloosa, Alabama, in 1924. Her first musical experience was singing gospel in church, but she moved beyond gospel in a hurry and won a talent contest in Chicago when she was fifteen. Four years later she made her debut with Hampton and cut many classics. From the beginning she proved to be a special talent who could handle any material. Her life came to a tragic end as a result of a drug overdose; it was a great loss for all music fans.

Throughout the years Quincy Jones, Wes Montgomery, Clifford Brown, Art Farmer, Jimmy Cleveland, Alan Dawson, Milt Buckner,

Dexter Gordon, Illinois Jacquet, Arnett Cobb, Chico Hamilton, Shadow Wilson, Cat Anderson, Gigi Gryce, Al Grey, Earl Bostic, and Johnny Griffin were just some of those who spent time in Hampton's band. An engaging leader, he was always able to spark his bandmates to reach greater heights. Many of those who served an apprentice in Hampton's group went on to front their own successful outfits.

Aside from providing a training school for future innovators and contributors to jazz, Hampton also gave the music world an incredible number of classic songs. "Stompin' at the Savoy," "Dizzy Spells," "Avalon," "The Man I Love," "Stardust," "Hamp's Boogie Woogie," "Midnight Sun," "Gin for Christmas," "Till Tom Special," and his most famous song, "Flying Home," are just a few of Hampton's gifts to the world. His complete catalog was immense because of the longevity of his career and his constant participation in various projects.

With the deaths of many greats in the 1990s including Dizzy Gillespie, Tito Fuente, Dexter Gordon, Stan Getz, Miles Davis, Billy Eckstine, Ella Fitzgerald, and Sarah Vaughan, Hampton became one of jazz's great spokesmen with roots that stretched back to the days of Louis Armstrong. His historical links to the past made him a true historian and he was a guiding light for the new generation of jazz musicians.

The scope of Hampton's accomplishments was truly remarkable and after nine decades as a musician, bandleader, arranger, and occasional vocalist, there was little that he hadn't seen or done. But without a doubt his greatest legacy has always been his enthusiasm for jazz and how he transmitted that spiritual impulse to audiences throughout the world, his bandmates, and anyone else who came in contact with him. He carried the torch despite numerous obstacles to remain the jazz ambassador.

Discography

Lionel Hampton Vol. 1, 1929–1936, Masters of Jazz 17.
Lionel Hampton Vol. 2, 1936–1937, Masters of Jazz 83.
Lionel Hampton Vol. 3, 1937, Masters of Jazz 133.
All Star Sessions Vol. 1—Open House, AVD 611.
All Star Sessions Vol. 2—Hot Mallets, AVD 612.
Midnight Sun 1946–1947, GRD 625.
Jazz in California, CBC 1934.
I'm in the Mood for Swing, 1937–1939, ASL 5090.
Cabu Collection, Masters of Jazz 8017.
Swingsation, GRP 59922.
Greatest Hits 1939–1956, Victor 68496.
Classics 1937–1939, EPM 157372.

Original Historic Recordings—Masterpieces Vol. 10, EPM 158252.
Just One of Those Things 1953–1954, Verve 547437.
The Complete Quartets & Quintets Featuring Oscar Peterson 1953–1954, Verve 559797.
Lionel Hampton & His Orchestra 1937–1938, Classic 524.
Lionel Hampton & His Orchestra 1938–1939, Classic 534.
Lionel Hampton & His Orchestra 1939–1940, Classic 562.
Lionel Hampton & His Orchestra 1940–1941, Classic 624.
Lionel Hampton & His Orchestra 1942–1944, Classic 803.
Lionel Hampton & His Orchestra 1945–1946, Classic 922.
Lionel Hampton & His Orchestra 1946, Classic 946.
Lionel Hampton & His Orchestra 1947, Classic 994.
Lionel Hampton Big Band: The Torrid Stuff 1944–1946, EPM 158902.
50th Anniversary Concert, Half Note Records 4201.
And His French New Sound Vol. 1, POLY 5494052.
And His French New Sound Vol. 2, POLY 5494062.
Golden Vibes/Silver Vibes, Collectables 6676.
'77 Vintage. Black and Blue 870.
1942–1944, Classics 803.
All-Star Sessions Vol. 1, Jazzterdays 102 407.
Basin Street Blues, Chrisly Records 15011.
Classics 1937–1939, EPM 157372.
Dark Eyes, Early Bird 1003.
Flyin' Home and Other Showstopping Favorites, EMI-Capitol Special Markets 57587.
Flying Home, The Empress Recording Company 858.
For the Love of Music, Mo Jazz 530 554.
Glad Hamp, Jazz Time Records 8156.
Greatest Hits, RCA Victor 68496.
Hamp in Harlem, Timeless 133.
Hamp's Blues, Laserlight 17090.
Hamp's Boogie, Laserlight 17091.
Hamp: The Legendary Decca Recordings, GRP Records 652.
Jazz After Dark: Great Songs, Public Music 8008.
Jazz Archives, PMF Music Collection 506.
Jivin' the Vibes, Jazz Hour 73537.
Jivin' the Vibes, Le Jazz 001.
Lionel Hampton and His All-Stars 1956, Musidisc 550152.
Lionel Hampton's Paris All-Stars, RCA Victor 51150.
Live in Cannes, Jazz Hour 73584.
Live in Paris: Concert Olympia 1961, Accord 401052.
Old-Fashioned Swing, Jazz Hour 73587.

Open House: All-Star Session Vol. 1, Avid 611.
Plays the Groove, Musidisc 500682.
Priceless Jazz Collection, GRP Records 9945.
Slide Hamp Slide, Drive Archive 41082.
Sound Of Jazz Volume 8: In Concert, Galaxy Sound of Jazz 388608.
Stardust, Jazz Time Records 8154.
Stompin' at the Savoy, Magnum 17.
Swingsation, GRP Records 9922.
The Best of Lionel Hampton, Giants of Jazz Recordings 53347.
The Big Band, West Wind Jazz 2404.
The Torrid Stuff 1944–1946, EPM 158902.
Vintage Hampton, Telarc 83321.
You Better Know It! Impulse! 140.
Hamp: The Legendary Decca Recordings, GRP Records 652.
The Complete Quartets & Quintets, Verve 559 797.
50th Anniversary Concert, UNIDI AGEK2–2008.
90th Anniversary, SOUND SSCD-8105.
Airmail Special, POLY—POCJ-2609.
All Star Big Band, SOMET TOCJ-8015.
Complete Vol. 1 & 2, RCA 21155252.
Complete Vol. 3 & 4, RCA 74321226142.
Complete Vol. 5 & 6, ARIOL 21355552.
Dizzy Spells, BCD JTM8116.
Essential Masters of Jazz, PROPE EMCD07.
Gold Collection, RETRO R2CD40–87.
Hamp's Big Band, BMG 74321218212.
Jazz Flamenco, RCA 21364002.
Jazzmaster, UNIDI UBK-4105.
Le Jazz De A-Z, BMG 74321247602.
Moods, UNIDI UBK-4107.
New Best One, MCA MVCR-2205.
New Look, UNIDI UBK-4106.
On the Sunny Side of the Street, BMG BVCJ-37176.
Paris All Stars, BMG 74321511502.
Planet Jazz, BMG 74321520592.
Please Sunrise/Stop I Don't Need No Symphony, Demon DIAB8014.
Story of Jazz, EMI P 5760682.

GENE KRUPA (1909–1973)

Drum Boogie

Often it is not the most talented performers who gain the greatest accolades. Ability is blended with charisma and the careful balance between the two is the foundation that many legends are based on. During the swing era, one drummer possessed an abundance of skill and personality that enabled him to storm onto the jazz scene with his drum boogie style. His name was Gene Krupa.

Gene Krupa was born on January 15, 1909, in Chicago, Illinois. His interest in jazz was fueled by the hotbed of music that existed in his hometown when he was in his teens. King Oliver, Freddie Keppard, Louis Armstrong, Sidney Bechet, Baby Dodds, Johnny Dodds, and Jelly Roll Morton were just some of the transplanted New Orleans jazzmen who had made Chicago the jazz center in the 1920s. Although the star of those early bands was usually the trumpet player, Krupa was attracted to the role of the drummer. His idol was Chick Webb.

Krupa started to play drums in his teens. He dreamed of stardom with pretty women lined up outside the hottest jazz clubs in every town in the country screaming his name. He studied with various percussion teachers, slowly honing his skills to a level that would allow him to play in one of the major bands that ruled the Chicago jazz scene. While in high school he jammed with the Austin High Gang that also included a shy clarinetist named Benny Goodman. Later, after both had paid their dues, Goodman would call upon Krupa's friendship.

In the middle of the 1920s, Krupa played for the Al Gayle Band, Joe Kayser, Leo Shukin, Thelma Terry, Mezz Mezzrow, the Benson Orchestra, and Eddie Neibauer's Seattle Harmony Kings. He eventually was given a chance to record with the McKenzie & Condon's Chicagoans. That enabled him to move close to his boyhood dream. Although Chicago offered many opportunities for a hungry, young musician like Krupa, he decided a change of scenery was needed and moved to the Big Apple.

In 1929, Krupa arrived in New York and landed a job working for Red Nichols. Nichols, originally from Utah, was one of the early cornet players. A much-traveled personality, he was a well-seasoned bandleader and musician when Krupa came under his direction. He was the exact type of leader the young drummer needed to shape his final development. He remained with Nichols for two years and absorbed all he could from the old master.

After leaving Nichols, Krupa worked for a variety of bands including Irving Aaronson, Russ Colombo, Mal Hallet, and Buddy Rogers. In 1934, his old friend from his high school days, Benny Goodman, came calling and asked him to join his band. Krupa jumped at the opportunity. At the time, neither one knew that they would be involved in one of the most glamorous periods of jazz.

Although the first few months were rough as the new band paid its dues, they eventually began to catch on. Krupa fit in the band handsomely. He had matinee idol good looks and a strong personality. He was quickly turning the role of the drummer that had been one of a background post into one of pure showmanship. He was an integral part in the meteoric rise of the Benny Goodman Band. He also swung as hard as any drummer did and soloed with as much enthusiasm and more flash than any other timekeeper at the time.

When the Goodman band became the most popular group in the country and gained international fame, Krupa shared the spotlight with the bandleader. He became the idol of hundreds of young drummers who were all very keen on being just like their hero Gene Krupa. He was young, good looking, played drums in the biggest group in the universe, and had dozens of women swooning over him. He had achieved his boyhood dream.

The Goodman-Krupa partnership lasted through the Carnegie Hall concert that featured the star drummer playing "Sing, Sing, Sing." His drum solo held the crowd breathless and he claimed a lion's share of the applause. The friction between Goodman and Krupa was generated by the latter's stealing much of the attention. The clashing of egos ended with Krupa leaving Goodman in 1938 after a concert at the Earle Theatre of Philadelphia.

It didn't take long for Krupa to organize his own big band. It included Vido Musso, Milt Raskin, Floyd O'Brien, Sam Donahue, Shorty Sherock and the very talented Irene Daye, who was featured on "Sweetheart, Honey, Darling, Dear" and the band's most famous tune, "Drum Boogie." The song "Drum Boogie" featured Krupa's best drum solo, an accumulation of twenty years of studying the intricacies of rhythmic textures.

Personnel changes were frequent. Roy Eldridge and singer Anita O'Day (upon Daye's departure) would join the orchestra giving the ensemble an energetic boost. But no matter the lineup the band was built around the leader's drumming and showmanship.

Krupa left Victor (where he had made some recordings) and signed with the Brunswick label. With the new company he struck gold with the instrumentals "Blue Rhythm Fantasy," "Wire Brush Stomp," and "Apurk-sody," whose title was a combination of Krupa spelled backwards and part of the word rhapsody. Helen Ward was on that first recording session. The band also boasted a writing team of Chapie Willett, Elton Hill and Fred Norman. Later vocalists Jerry Kruger and Leo Watson joined the group.

The outfit also recorded cover songs such as "I'll Never Smile Again," a Tommy Dorsey tune, "Yes, My Darling Daughter," originally sung by Dinah Shore, "Moonlight Serenade," from the creative pen of Glenn Miller, and "Tuxedo Junction," also by Miller in collaboration with Erskine Hawkins.

During Roy Eldridge's tenure the group enjoyed its most successful period. The band had further hits with "Georgia on My Mind," "Green Eyes," "Thanks for the Boogie Ride," "Murder, He Says," and "That's What You Think." The combination of O'Day and Eldridge came together beautifully on "Let Me Off Uptown," "Knock Me a Kiss," "After You've Gone," and "Rockin' Chair." Eventually the team was broken up when a rift erupted between O'Day and Eldridge. She left the band and Ray Eberle replaced her. Johnny Desmond eventually came in to replace Eberle.

The group remained together until 1943 when the leader was forced to disband the outfit because of a drug charge. The incident cost Krupa his band, tarnished his wholesome image, and shook his confidence. But he was a fighter and returned to the scene in 1944 with another big band that featured a string section, a short-lived experiment since it didn't suit the tastes of his fans. Eventually Krupa returned to his swinging style and scored a hit with "Leave Us Leap." But, once again, he was forced to disband his orchestra.

He rejoined his old friend Goodman for a brief stint then played with Tommy Dorsey and remained in that orchestra for a year. But Krupa wanted to front his own group again so he left Dorsey and began to assemble a large ensemble that contained some thirty members before settling down to a more workable number. Despite his best efforts, his group never really achieved any amount of success.

He then formed a trio with tenor saxist Charlie Ventura and pianist Teddy Napoleon. The trio had hits with "Dark Eyes" and "Body and Soul." O'Day joined the small group to make it a quartet and they recorded "Opus One" and "Boogie Blues." But the winds of change in jazz meant Krupa had to adjust and he did just that. He started to incorporate bop into his drumming style and added clarinetist Buddy DeFranco to his group that included Red Rodney and Ventura. Gerry Mulligan also wrote arrangements for the band including "Disc Jockey Jump."

From 1944 to 1951, he led this big band playing residencies in New York, Chicago, Detroit, Los Angeles, and the rest of the country. There were personnel changes and at various times the group included Don Fagerquist, altoist Charlie Kennedy, tenorman Buddy Wise and the return of Roy Eldridge near the end of the group's reign. Many of the musicians in this ensemble were boppers, but Krupa worked with the new kids. Although it was a successful adventure, the big band folded in 1951.

Krupa joined Jazz at the Philharmonic and toured under the name with his own trio. Sometimes he was pitted against Buddy Rich, another name drummer from the swing era. The battle between the two stick men was a genuine crowd pleaser and did nothing to hurt either of their reputations. The cutting contests that had existed between pianists and horn players didn't lose any velocity when they occurred between two drummers.

In 1954, Krupa opened a drum school with Cozy Cole in New York City. Although his popularity was not as great as it had been during the late 1930s, he was still a favorite among those who had grown up listening to him during the big band era. When not teaching aspiring drummers, he toured with his group all over the country and overseas. In 1959, *The Gene Krupa Story* (also known as *Drum Crazy* in some countries) premiered to enthusiastic audiences. Krupa supplied a drum track for the film. However, like *The Benny Goodman Story* of a few years before, the Hollywood angle of the biography never told the entire story.

Although he slowed down in the 1960s due to heart problems, Krupa continued to tour and record on an almost regular basis. Even though his best work was long behind him he still carried some weight in the jazz world since he was of the old guard and a link to one of the most glorious eras in jazz history.

On October 16, 1973, in Yonkers, New York, Gene Krupa, the man who had helped propel the Benny Goodman Band to its immense popularity, died of leukemia. He was 64 years old.

Gene Krupa was the archetypal showman-drummer. He raised the status of the rhythm men. They went from being nearly obscure to become cherished idols. He had the magnetism, the wit, and the charm to exude a mystique that young teenage musicians were drawn to like moths to the flame. He was one of the most important drummers in the history of jazz and modern music.

While he was an exciting percussionist, he was not the best timekeeper to ever occupy the drum stool. During Krupa's career, Jo Jones, Big Sid Catlett, Chick Webb, Buddy Rich, and David Tough were considered better technical drummers than Krupa. Rich even equaled Krupa in showmanship, as did Jo Jones and Chick Webb. But Krupa used all of his assets to forge his own star appeal. He was able to balance all of the weapons in his arsenal in order to create a complete attack.

He was a swing drummer without the speed of Buddy Rich or the finesse of Jo Jones and Chick Webb. But he could propel a band and its soloists to greater heights with his genuine enthusiasm. He used every trick in a drummer's vocabulary to create the excitement. He was able to accent the beat in a way that brought him the attention of fans and fellow musicians.

His biggest claim to fame was his determination to bring the drummer to front-line recognition. He reasoned that the drummer was an integral part of the band so therefore should receive as much respect and attention as the horn players, the pianists, and everyone else in the string section. He did just that and he became the first drum hero. In fact, he inspired generations of drummers to step forward and challenge the other instruments in the band for supremacy.

He made the drum solo part of a band's repertoire and influenced a number of future drummers including Peter Criss, Joe Morello, Cozy Cole, Danny Davis, Ginger Baker, Carl Palmer, Dennis Wilson, Keith Moon, and Ringo Starr. Krupa paved the way for drummers like Ringo Starr, who enjoyed an incredible amount of popularity as a member of the Beatles, by stepping out front and propelling the band to rock hard. He also influenced Phil Collins and Don Henley by proving that a drummer didn't have to stay barricaded behind his kit and could become a leader.

Kruppa made playing the drums look like fun. His constant smile and his uncanny ability to create excitement generated a tremendous amount of interest. He was able to transmit this power into the songs he made famous. "Drummin' Man," "Let Me Off Uptown," "Rockin' Chair," "After You've Gone," "Thanks for the Boogie Ride," "Disc Jockey Moon," "How High the Moon," "Drum Boogie," "Lemon Drop," "Stardust," and "Sing, Sing, Sing" were all part of his repertoire.

Gene Krupa will be remembered as the driving force behind the Benny Goodman band and as the first star drummer. While he was never considered the greatest stick man in the history of jazz, he was one of the most exciting. It was this enthusiasm that enabled him to create his own niche in jazz history where he will forever be known for his drum boogie.

Discography

Drummer Man 1956, HS 262.
The Gene Krupa Story, PPER 1001.

The Drummer 1935–1941, Pearl 7008.
Recordings from 1935–1945, SPVR 31032.
Drum Boogie 1941–1942, Sony 53425.
Original Historic Recordings—Masterpieces Vol. 13, EPM 158302.
That's Drummer's Band, 1938–1945 EPM 158592.
Drummer Man 1956, PLG 827843.
Gene Krupa & His Orchestra, 1935–1938, Classic 754.
Gene Krupa & His Orchestra, 1938, Classic 767.
Gene Krupa & His Orchestra, 1939, Classic 799.
Gene Krupa & His Orchestra, 1939–1940, Classic 834.
Gene Krupa & His Orchestra, 1940, Classic 859.
Gene Krupa & His Orchestra, 1940 Vol. 2, Classic 883.
Gene Krupa & His Orchestra, 1940 Vol.3, Classic 917.
Gene Krupa & His Orchestra, 1941, Classic 960.
Gene Krupa & His Orchestra, 1941 Vol. 2, Classic 1006.
Gene Krupa & His Orchestra, 1941–1942, Classic 1056.
Gene Krupa & His Orchestra, 1942–1945, Classic 1096.
Gene Krupa & His Orchestra: The Radio Years 1940, STC 2021.
The Instrumental Mr. Krupa, Jazz Masters 2572.
Gene Krupa/Buddy Rich, 1955, Verve 521643.

====

LESTER YOUNG (1909–1959)

The Prez

Throughout the history of jazz nicknames have been commonplace. Sometimes the monikers were self-imposed; sometimes they reflected the respect and admiration a player earned from his peers for his sheer ability on a given instrument or for his zany character. Gillespie earned his nickname "Dizzy" for his constant clowning around. Joe Oliver became known as "King" because he was the supreme cornet player during his prime. In the 1930s and 1940s, because of his superb solos on the tenor saxophone, one individual was dubbed "The Prez." His name was Lester Young.

Lester Willis Young was born August 27, 1909, in Woodville, Mississippi, into a musical family. His early days were spent roaming the countryside and he eventually settled in New Orleans where he spent much of his childhood. But by 1919, at the tender age of ten, he was living in Minneapolis after his parents split up. In order to deal with his disrupted family life, Young immersed himself in music.

William Young, Lester's father, had studied music at Tuskegee Institute and was a multi-instrumentalist who played the violin, saxophone, trombone, trumpet and drums. He also taught choirs and when he wasn't teaching was traveling with his carnival. Lester studied the violin, trumpet, and drums before settling on the alto sax at the age of thirteen.

Lester and his sister and brother traveled with their father's carnival. As part of the family band, Young acquired important musical lessons in showmanship, responsibility, and in playing his instrument. By the age of fifteen Lester had become adept at the tenor saxophone. Although his father was a wonderful teacher Lester was also influenced by two of the biggest names in jazz of the 1920s, Bix Beiderbecke and Frankie Trumbauer. Young incorporated Beiderbecke's cool trumpet sound and Trum's light-toned sax into his own style.

The elder Young chided his son for improvising rather than reading the music. Lester eventually learned how to read music to satisfy the demands of his father but was a much more effective musician when he played what he felt and not what was dictated to him. His style at the time only hinted at the beautiful maturity that he would eventually arrive at. But like all other serious jazz artists he had to pay his dues.

When Young balked at the thought of traveling through the racist South, it cost him a spot in the family band. But he quickly found a place in Art Bronson's Bostonians where he was relegated to the alto sax. Later, he would switch to the tenor sax. Since the pressures of playing in his father's group were lifted from his shoulders, Young was happy in Bronson's band.

But he eventually left the Bostonians and joined King Oliver's group. By this time Oliver had played his best jazz but was still instrumental in shaping the musical character and attitude of the impressionable Lester. The group, which consisted of three brass, three reeds and four rhythm players, toured mostly through Kansas and Missouri.

After much wandering, trying to find some consistency in his life, Young returned to Minneapolis to play in his father's traveling carnival band in 1929 but stayed only a few months. His restless spirit drove him away again. He drifted for a few years and became a hired gun. He spent time in Walter Page's Blue Devils and Eddie Barefield's band in 1931. He returned to the Blue Devils for a year before leaving again to lend his immense musical talents to Bennie Moten's and King Oliver's groups.

It was the Depression era and one gig didn't seem more secure than another one. As a Blue Devil he had lived as a hobo. But while he was seemingly wasting his life away, Young was honing his distinct sound that would make him a legend. He eventually made it to Kansas City where he was able to find work and stayed for a while. But later, he returned to Minnesota.

In 1934, Young joined the legendary Count Basie for the first of several stints. He left a few months later to take Coleman Hawkins' spot in Fletcher Henderson's band. That turned out to be a disastrous decision. Young was counted on to sound like the departed Hawkins, but the two tenor saxophonists had completely different styles. Hawkins had a forceful, robust sound, while Young's had a lighter, more lyrical tone that carried latent nuances. As a result, the Prez had a short stint in Henderson's group.

Young played in Andy Kirk's outfit for a brief spell before returning to Count Basie in 1936. It was during this second tenure that Lester established his legend. He appeared on numerous recording sessions with the Basie orchestra, as well as in small group settings with the classic Billy Holiday and Teddy Wilson. It was Young's laid back original sound that captivated audiences. Although he enthralled all with his wailings on alto sax, he also made recordings as a clarinetist with Basie and the Kansas City Six.

Young enjoyed the most stable period of his career between 1936 and 1940. Basie had signed a two-year recording contract with Decca and began touring the bigger cities instead of being relegated to the territories, taking trumpeter Carl Smith, drummer Jo Jones, bass player Walter Page, singer Jimmy Rushing and Young with him to New York. The subsequent bootleg album the group recorded ushered in Young's mellow style, especially on the song "Lady Be Good." It would be talked about for the rest of the century.

In New York, the band was enlarged to fifteen musicians and despite the number of players the group blended together and turned out hard, biting blues and pop with a solid kick. Although the Basie band would cut forty-seven sides for Decca during their contracted period, none would have the carnival bounce and sting of their live recordings. Once his Decca contract ran out Basie was immediately signed to Columbia. Young can be heard on roughly half of the more than one hundred songs the band cut thereafter.

On a musical level Young attracted serious recognition for his imaginative, happy solos, which greatly expanded the boundaries of the instrument's capabilities. On a personal level, it was around this time that he began to court Billie Holiday, the finest jazz singer of the era. They recorded together and their two plaintive voices blended as one, creating moments of pure jazz magic. The happiness would, however, not last forever.

After four years with Basie, Young left the Count and drifted around, uninterested in furthering a career that had built up much momentum. He formed his own combo and had a residency in New York. He also played in a band with his brother Lee Young in Los Angeles. In 1943, after three years of what many considered wasting his talent, Young, who had never recovered from the broken home of his youth, returned to the Basie band, his symbolic musical home. He recorded a memorable session with Slam Stewart and even starred in a film called *Jammin' the Blues*.

But this brief time of happiness was destroyed when he was drafted into the army in 1943. The experiences of blatant racism that were part of his short army career affected his mental state, and he never recovered from them. It was during this period that he was incarcerated on trumped-up charges of drug possession and sent to a detention barracks in Georgia for five years. Although he was released a year later the traumatic army experience left a permanent scar on his soul.

Upon his release, Young immediately went to the West Coast where he formed a six-piece combo that included trombonist Vic Dickenson and pianist Dodo Marmarosa, a member of the new bebop movement. The group cut four sides for Aladdin Records. On this session Young sarcastically recalled his brief stint in the army with the song "D. B. Drag." The initials D. B. stood for detention barracks. Young had gotten his revenge for his rough treatment at the hands of Uncle Sam's outfit.

He toured with Jazz at the Philharmonic through the 1940s and 1950s, adding thousands of followers to his already impressive fan base. With the JATP, many of the songs he performed live or in the studio were recorded by Norman Granz. In the thirteen years that Young was associated with JATP—1945 to 1958—over a hundred and fifty sides featured his extraordinary tenor saxophone. Although some of the cuts lacked polish, many captured the old magic and enhanced his reputation to a new generation of jazz fans and players. Most importantly, throughout this period, Young was never out of work and enjoyed a period of domestic bliss with his second wife. The marriage included a daughter and a son.

Despite the fact that his career was burning brightly the walls were slowly closing in on him. His health was erratic as his mental state noticeably deteriorated. He drank excessively to ward off the darkness that enveloped him and he took poor care of himself. He also increased his drug use. He entered Bellevue for the first time in 1955 for medical and psychological help.

Young continued to fight the demons that troubled him. He rejoined Basie's band in 1957 for a concert date at the Newport Jazz Festival but it was obvious that he was just a shell of the man who had changed the course of modern music more than a decade before. His best days were behind him.

Young slipped back into the dark shadows, but made one last stab at righting himself in 1958 with a few concert dates and a tour in Paris. But the demons that haunted him would not release him. He died on March 15, 1959, in New York City. He was fifty years old.

Lester Young is one of the jazz giants of the past hundred years. He remains a seminal figure more than forty years after his death and is revered by all saxophone players. But his legend goes much deeper than just the respect of his peers; everyone in jazz holds the Prez in awe because of his deep talent and totally unique sound.

Young was a non-conformist of the highest order. Although the saxophone was regarded as a novelty instrument when he first started out, Young used the unpopularity of the tenor sax to create a name for himself. He cared little that the style of the day happened to be Coleman Hawkins' with its fierce attack; Young was more interested in creating his own universe with his rhythmic subtlety. He did just that.

There is no natural image of the world or human emotion that Young could not produce with his horn. His calculated choice of the exact notes fit together like the perfect words to a classic story. There was a semblance and uniformity to his playing. Young never wasted a note. He never juxtaposed notes against each other to create chaos, but was interested in painting landscapes of lush meadows wet with morning dew, the calmness after a fresh rainstorm, the inner peace of a beautiful sunset, the tranquility of being the only person on a deserted, wind-swept beach. His solos were poetic masterpieces of sound.

He was a major influence on two of the greatest jazz artists in history. Charlie Parker listened intently to the Young style and learned every solo note for note. Young's detached style that ran against the accepted norm would greatly inspire Parker to seek his own voice even if he was derided by others.

Miles Davis, though a trumpet player, would take the Lester Young approach and maximize its elements to head the new style of jazz. With his indirect way of approaching emotion Young laid down the foundation of the Cool School of Jazz that would flourish in the 1950s. Others would follow Davis' lead.

When Cool Jazz gave way to Free Jazz, the leader was a tenor saxophonist by the name of John Coltrane. As Young had done thirty years before him, Coltrane sought his personal musical voice and didn't care if he went against conventional sounds. Eventually, Coltrane's spiritual quest led him to create free jazz, whose basic elements could be traced back to Young's breakthrough style.

If Lester Young had a soul mate in jazz it would have to have been Billie Holiday. Together they elevated the collaboration between voice and instrument to new heights that have never been reached again. They were both rebels of the period, individuals, two against the world and their loneliness, idealism, and romanticism drew them together. To listen to Young and Holiday together is to hear one single voice, a perfect blend of carefully chosen notes and liquid phrases.

Along with only a handful of other jazz figures, Young had his own small coterie of disciples including Stan Getz, Brew Moore, Al Cohn, Allen Eager, Zoot Sims, and Lee Konitz. He also had a deep impact on Alan Broadbent, Booker Ervin, Eddie Jefferson, Charles Lloyd, Warne Marsh, Bob Mintzer, King Pleasure, Sonny Stitt, Bob Wilber, Vincent York, Ted Brown, George Kelly, Chris Woods, Willis "Gator" Jackson, and Paul Quinichette. Young made the deepest impressions on every musician as well as on many singers. There are scarcely any modern artists who have escaped the shadow of the Prez.

Despite a large collection of followers and admirers, Young was often a dispirited man. For a time, many of the white tenor saxophonists who imitated their idol were making more money than he did. It was an infuriating point for the Prez. The adage that genius and melancholy go hand in hand speaks volumes about Young's career.

Young left the world many classics to enjoy, including "Shoe Shine Boy," "Evenin'," "Boogie Woogie," "Panassie Stomp," "Jumpin' at the Woodside," "Taxi War Dance," "Clap Hands," "Here Comes Charlie," "Ham 'n' Eggs," "Pound Cake," "Broadway," "Lester Leaps In," "D. B. Blues," "Blue Lester," and "Jump Lester Jump." This list does not cover the many classics he recorded with his favorite jazz queen Billie Holiday.

Perhaps Lester Young's greatest contribution was the widening of the narrow boundaries of jazz inventiveness. The standard way to improvise had been to create variations on an existing melody. But Young discarded this method by building his fresh solos on the standard series of chords. Young injected the sound of surprise into his solo improvisations and it was the path that everyone would follow for rest of the century.

As well as being one of the greatest musicians in the world Young was also one of the most genuine characters. He spoke in a vocabulary all his own that stunned other musicians. He was a loner, a man who could never leave the experiences of his life behind, whether his disastrous time in Fletcher Henderson's band, his short stint in the army, or his early alienation from his father.

There have been many jazz artists who have touched the world with their special gift. Billie Holiday, Duke Ellington, Louis Armstrong, Dizzy Gillespie, Art Tatum, Charlie Parker, Miles Davis, and John Coltrane are just a few names that immediately come to mind. Among those names is Lester Young, the man they called "The Prez."

Discography

Lester Young Vol. 1 1937–1939, Masters of Jazz 46.
Lester Young Vol. 2 1939–1942, Masters of Jazz 47.
Lester Young Vol. 3 1943, Masters of Jazz 64.
Lester Young Vol. 4 1944, Masters of Jazz 77.
Lester Young Vol. 5 1944, Masters of Jazz 89.
Lester Young Vol. 6, 1944, Masters of Jazz 99.
Lester Young Vol. 7 1945–1946, Masters of Jazz 118.
Lester Young Vol. 8 1946, Masters of Jazz 136.
Lester Young The Kansas City Sessions 1938, CMD 402.
Lester Young 1943–1946, Classic 932.
Lester Young 1946–1947, Classic 987.
Lester Young The Lester Young Story, PPER 1008.
Easy Does It 1936–1940, Indigo 2036.
Lester Young His Best Recordings 1936–1945, Best of Jazz 4042.
Lester Young Prez in Europe 1956, HIN 7054.
Lester Leaps In—His Greatest Recordings 1936–1944, ASL 5176.
Complete Aladdin Sessions 1942–1948, Blue Note 32787.
Lester Young with the Oscar Peterson Trio 1952, PLG 521451.
Lester Young Trio 1946, PLG 521650.
Lester Young The Complete Lester Young Studio Sessions 1946–1959, Verve 547087.
Lester Swings 1945, Verve 547772.
Jazz Giants 1956, PLG 825672.
Lester Young & Teddy Wilson Pres & Teddy 1956, PLG 831270.
1941–1944, EPM 158352.
Best of Lester Young, Pablo Records 2405–420.
Blue Lester (20-Bit), Savoy 78817.
Exercise in Swing, Giants of Jazz Recordings 53319.
In Washington D.C. 1956, Vol. 1, Original Jazz Classics 782.
In Washington D.C. 1956, Vol. 2, Original Jazz Classics 881.
In Washington D.C. 1956, Vol. 3, Original Jazz Classics 901.
In Washington D.C. 1956, Vol. 4, Original Jazz Classics 963.
In Washington D.C. 1956, Vol. 5, Original Jazz Classics 993.
Jammin' the Blues, Definitive 11117.
Lester Dreams, Definitive 11116.
Lester Leaps In, Jazz Hour 73571.
Lester Leaps In: His Greatest Recordings 1936–1944, Living Era 5176.

Lester Swings, Verve 547 772.
Lester Young Story, EPM 157342.
Live at Birdland, Vol. 1, Band Stand 1525.
Live at Birdland, Volume 2, Band Stand 1526.
Master's Touch, Savoy 18056.
Masters of Jazz Vol. 7 (1951–1956), Storyville 4107.
Pres, Collectables 5791.
Pres in Europe, Highnote Records, Inc. 7054.
The Be-Bop Days: The Famous Royal Roost Live, Definitive 11119.
The Complete Aladdin Recordings of Lester Young, Blue Note Records 32787.
The Complete Lester Young Studio, Verve 547 087.
The Kansas City Sessions, Commodore Records 402.
The Quintessence: New York-Los Angeles...Vol. 2, Fremeaux 233.
The Super Sessions, Le Jazz 36.
Ultimate Lester Young, Verve 539 772.
Verve Jazz Masters 30, Verve 521 859.
Les Incontournables, WEA 630154192.

ROY ELDRIDGE (1911–1989)

Little Jazz

A careful examination of jazz history reveals an interesting fact in that there has been a succession of great practitioners on each instrument. Take, for instance, the trumpet. Buddy Bolden hailed the birth of jazz with his classic New Orleans cornet. Freddie Keppard followed him. He was then succeeded by Joe "King" Oliver. Later on, the great Louis "Satchmo" Armstrong arrived on the scene and became one of the greatest trumpet soloists in the history of jazz. Twenty years later Dizzy Gillespie would usher in the bebop era. In between these two seminal figures there were many important trumpeters including the magnificent player known as "Little Jazz." His name was Roy Eldridge.

David Roy Eldridge was born on January 30, 1911, in Pittsburgh, Pennsylvania, into a musical family; his brother Joe was a professional trumpeter. His cousin Reunald Jones became an important trumpet player and played in the bands of Jimmie Lunceford, Teddy Hill, and Claude Hopkins. Roy took up the drums at age six and then received special tuition from his brother on trumpet. Eventually he decided to become a trumpeter and left his drum kit to gather dust.

Once he was proficient enough he played in local bands in his hometown and graduated to his own juvenile group that toured Pennsylvania and other nearby states. But after playing local venues Eldridge was determined to travel and see the world. He joined a carnival show and toured the south, then returned home to form his second band. It played in different venues around the Pittsburgh area. By the time he joined Horace Henderson in 1928 at the age of seventeen, Eldridge was a well-seasoned performer.

He stayed in Henderson's outfit, the Dixie Stompers, for eight months then returned to Pittsburgh. He then played with a number of bands including Speed Webb's, Zack Whyte's, and Johnny Neal's Midnite Ramblers, performing all over the Midwest. He moved to New York City where he padded his resume with stints in Teddy Hill's, Charlie Johnson's, Cecil Scott's and Elmer Snowden's bands. Eldridge grew tired of the Big Apple scene and returned home where he joined forces with his brother Joe to form a local group in 1933.

After a brief stint in the famous McKinney's Cotton Pickers, Eldridge rejoined Teddy Hill in New York. After much journeyman work, Eldridge joined Fletcher Henderson's Big Band in 1935, but left a few months later to lead his own outfit. They played a long residency at the Three Deuces in Chicago, as well as the Savoy Ballroom in the Big Apple. For the rest of the 1930s, Eldridge led his own ensemble through tours all over the United States. By this time he had acquired a major reputation as one of the most combative trumpeters in the business.

In 1941, he joined Gene Krupa's big band and starred there for a couple of years until the group broke up. Eldridge once again formed his own band and toured the major venues in Chicago and New York. Although he was a good leader he never made a lot of money with his own groups. In 1944, Eldridge took the plunge once again and joined Artie Shaw's Big Band. He left a few months later since he seemed to prefer running his own show.

He was able to find plenty of work fronting his own group and they toured all over the country. A restless figure who could not remain in one group or with one project for very long, he rejoined Krupa in 1949 and stayed for approximately eight months. Upon his departure, he joined the Jazz at the Philharmonic tour and added his powerful trumpet to the mix.

In 1950, he toured Europe with Benny Goodman, and remained behind after the latter had returned to America. Eldridge played a few solo dates while across the Atlantic and enjoyed his stay there. Upon his return to the United States he led his own group in New York City. For the rest of the decade he toured with his own outfit (it included Coleman Hawkins). The band was part of numerous package tours with JATP, and appeared at many jazz festivals, a growing phenomenon in the United States.

He was also recording at a furious pace, and some of his studio mates included Dizzy Gillespie, Ben Webster, Stan Getz, Lester Young, Buddy Tate, Gene Krupa, Buddy Rich, Oscar Peterson, Sonny Stitt, Johnny Hodges, and Bud Freeman. It was in the late 1950s that Eldridge began his association with clarinetist Sol Yaged. The pair recorded and toured together into the 1960s to enthusiastic audiences. The collaboration with Yaged was another musical adventure for Eldridge to add to his long list of credits.

In the 1960s, Eldridge formed a small combo and it appeared at the Village Vanguard, one of the premiere jazz venues during the decade. He backed up Ella Fitzgerald for a couple of years (1963 to 1965), and then returned to his small group. He joined Count Basie, one of the few jazz giants he did not record with during his varied career. Eldridge also became the favorite at outdoor concerts all over the Untied States and was also involved in many package tours that performed in Europe.

Eldridge never seemed happy as part of a group. He had spent little time in so many of them, and was only generally content to be leading his own small combo. For the rest of his career he did just that and his group became somewhat of a permanent house band at Jimmy Ryan's in New York. He continued to record and add to an impressive catalog of work.

In 1980, Eldridge suffered a stroke that ended his career. He spent the rest of the decade reliving the many memories that he had created during his long, illustrious time in the spotlight. On February 26, 1989, "Little Jazz," the beloved trumpet player who had left his mark on six decades of jazz, died in Valley Stream, New York. He was 78 years old.

Roy Eldridge played a vital role in jazz history. His contributions as a trumpeter, multi-instrumentalist, and composer are of seminal importance. He was part of a number of big bands, and recorded with a wealth of jazz figures covering many different eras and styles. Jazz artists are for the most part musicians with a traveling foot, jumping from one situation to another, and Eldridge made the rambling art his badge of courage. In his six decades in music he blazed his own path.

Although he made his greatest impact as a trumpeter, Eldridge was proficient enough on a number of instruments including the piano, flugel-horn, and the drums to play them on records. His multi-talent is scattered across the jazz recordings of Billie Holiday, Teddy Wilson, Oscar Peterson, Ben Webster, Ray Brown, Lester Young, Jo Jones, Gene Krupa, Chu Berry, John Kirby, Herb Ellis, Freddie Green, Buster Bailey, Johnny Hodges, Sidney "Big Sid" Catlett, Ella Fitzgerald, Cozy Cole, and Charlie Shavers.

But it was as a trumpet player that he is best remembered. He played with a fire and emotion that was rarely matched. He was a superb technician who was capable of hitting the notes with incredible accuracy and power. He played with incredible speed and his solos were triumphs of measured sweetness. He swung as hard as anyone else who came before or after him.

He was a survivor, a man who during the long span of his career saw a number of jazz trumpeters come and go. In the 1920s and 1930s, he had to out-duel Louis Armstrong, Henry "Red" Allen, Bunny Berigan, Buck Clayton, Harry "Sweets" Edison, Tommy Ladnier, Red Nichols, "Hot Lips" Page and Cootie Williams to gain attention. In the 1940s, he continued to swing, while Dizzy Gillespie, Fats Navarro and Clifford Brown were experimenting with bop. He was challenged by the cool one, Miles Davis, who paved the way for a whole new school of trumpeters that included Chet Baker, Lester Bowie, Tom Harrell, Freddie Hubbard, Lee Morgan, Woody Shaw, and Clark Terry. In the 1980s, the young lion, Wynton Marsalis was ready to challenge Little Jazz.

Eldridge's sound heavily influenced many of the trumpeters who challenged him for the instrument's crown. A short list includes Miles Davis, Dizzy Gillespie, Fats Navarro, Ernie Royal, Willie Mitchell, Howard McGhee, Wynton Marsalis, Dusko Goykovich, and Snooky Young. Not only was he a prime figure in the big band era, but Eldridge with his quick bursts of pure emotion paved the way for the bop revolution. However, until the end, Eldridge was a swing enthusiast.

He gave the world a number of classics including "Christopher Columbus," "Stealin' Apples," "Blue Lou," "Arcadia Shuffle," "Let Me Off Uptown," "Little Jazz," "Rockin' Chair," "After You've Gone," and "Nobody in Mind."

During his career, Eldridge guested on numerous sessions and there is scarcely an important jazz artist who starred between 1920 to 1970 he did not record or perform with. A short list includes Billie Holiday, Teddy Wilson, Oscar Peterson, Ben Webster, Ray Brown, Lester Young, Jo Jones, Gene Krupa, Chu Berry, John Kirby, Herb Ellis, Freddie Green, Buster Bailey, Johnny Hodges, Sidney "Big Sid" Catlett, Ella Fitzgerald, Cozy Cole, and Charlie Shavers.

Another part of history that Eldridge is associated with is the progression of venues. Eldridge played his hard swinging style in a number of different places. He began his career in the little clubs, moved on to the ballrooms, then to the large packed houses, and finally the outdoor festivals. But no matter the arena, Eldridge was always on top of the note and played as if it was his last concert or recording date. The sound of urgency in his playing gave it a sharp edge.

Eldridge remains a jazz icon. In any conversation about top trumpeters in jazz history the name Eldridge always pops up. Although he made his biggest impact during the swing and big band era, his presence could be felt in every decade he performed. With a career that stretched through the terms of twelve presidents, one could say that Little Jazz certainly made his mark on history.

Discography

Roy Eldridge, 1935–1940, Classic 725.
Roy Eldridge, 1943–1944, Classic 920.
Roy Eldridge, 1945–1947, Classic 983.
Roy Eldridge, Live 1957, JZBA 2107.
Uptown—Gene Krupa/Anita O'Day 1941–1942, Columbia CK-45448.
Roy Eldridge, Little Jazz 1935–1944, EPM 158362
The Amazing Trumpet of Little Jazz, 1936–1946, EPM 159612.
1957 Live, Jazz Band, 2107.
After You've Gone, GRP Records 605.
Fiesta in Jazz, Le Jazz 46.
Happy Time, Original Jazz Classics 628.
Heckler's Hop 1936–39, HEP 1030.
Live at the 3 Deuces Club, Jazz Archives 24.
Quintessence/Chicago—New York (1935–1945), Fremeaux 231.
Roy Eldridge & His Orchestra, Vol. 1, RCA Victor 51141.
Roy Eldridge 1935–1946, Best of Jazz 4051.
The Amazing Trumpet of Little Jazz 1936/1946, EPM 159612.
The Nifty Cat, New World Records 80349.
What It's All About, Original Jazz Classics 853.
Roy Eldridge and His Little Jazz, Vol. 1, BMG 74321511412.
Roy Eldridge and His Little Jazz, Vol. 2, BMG 74321559522.
Man I Love, BMG BVCJ-37179.
Planet Jazz, RCA 74321599752.
Montreux 1977, Pablo/OJC OJCCD-373-2.
Arcadia Shuffle, Jazz Archives 14.
At Jerry Newman's, Xanadu 186.
Jazz Heritage: All the Cats Join In, MCA 1385.
Little Jazz: Big Band, Sounds of Swing 108.

Roy Eldridge in Paris, Vogue 68209.
Little Jazz, Inner City 7002.
I Remember Harlem, Inner City 7012,
Roy Eldridge in Sweden, Prestige PRP-114.
Roy's Got Rhythms, EmArcy MG-36084.
Rockin' Chair, Clef MGC-704.
Dale's Wail, Verve MGC-705.
The Roy Eldridge Quartet, Clef MGC-150.
Roy Eldridge Collates, Mercury MGC-113.
Battle of Jazz, Vol. 7, Brunswick 58045.
The Strolling Mr. Eldridge, Clef MGC-162.
Tour de Force, MGV 8212.
Little Jazz Live In 1957, Jazz Band 408.
Swingin' on the Town, Verve MGV-8389.

JO JONES (1911–1985)

The Rhythm Maker

In the early jazz bands the drummers had limited roles. But as the music grew and matured so did the function of the drummer within a group. Drummers began to explore different rhythms and to challenge the mighty horn section for the solo spotlight. The swing timekeepers were the focus of the band as they propelled the music forward and laid down solid paths for the horn players to take off from. One of the greatest swing stick men was "The Rhythm Maker." His name was Jo Jones.

Jo Jones was born Jonathan Jones on October 7, 1911, in Chicago, Illinois. Jones went to school in Alabama, and his favorite subject from the age of ten was music. He played the trumpet, the piano and a variety of saxophones, before settling on the drums. He left home in his teens, finding work in touring carnival shows as a singer and tap-dancer.

Jones played in a number of groups including Ted Adam's Band, and he even served a spell as one of Walter Page's Blue Devils in Oklahoma. Later, in 1931, he moved to Lincoln, Nebraska, and worked in Harold Jones' Brownskin Syncopators. He jumped bands often, playing with Grant Moore, Jap Allen, Bennie Moten, and eventually Lloyd Hunter's

Serenaders stationed in Nebraska. While he was serving his apprentice-ship with all of these bands, Jones was growing as a drummer.

He had mastered the art of swing drumming. Although drummers were discouraged to solo in the early 1930s (a situation that would even-tually change), they were expected to keep a steady beat and propel all the other musicians with an endless wave of energy. He was capable of keeping precise time but he was also an innovator because he was slowly changing the way drummers were utilizing their kits.

The dues he paid playing in the various groups paved the way for him to earn the top spot with Count Basie, who led one of the most famous and exciting swing bands of the 1930s. Although he didn't stick with the Count the first time, in his second stint, in 1936, he accepted the drummer's chair full-time. He would remain with Basie for the next thir-teen years.

He was the perfect drummer for the Basie Band. Along with the Count on the piano, Freddie Green on rhythm guitar, and Walter Page on bass, the effervescent Jones was part of one of most dynamic rhythm sections in jazz. Although he would occasionally step up and override the others with his incredible talent and imagination, he perfected the role of the ultimate team player. He would lock in a groove with the rhythm section and allow the soloists in the band, including the great Lester Young, Lucky Thompson, Herschel Evans, and Harry "Sweets" Edison, to shine.

While many swing drummers made the base and snare the heart-beat of their sound, Jones used the high-hat, and the flexibility enabled him to out swing all of his peers. Unbeknownst to Jones, he was laying down the foundation for Kenny Clarke and Max Roach the future bebop drummers. A capable solo drummer, Jones could also steal the spotlight showcasing his impeccable timing and rhythmic genius.

He recorded often with the Count Basie band and his talents are scat-tered throughout such classic albums as *Best of Basie*, *The Count at the Chatterbox*, *Count Basie & His Orchestra*, *William & The Famous Door*, and *Basie Live!/Count Basie Live*. Jones was the pulse on the group's most famous song, "One O'clock Jump." All of the Basie classics from this era (1936–1949) feature Jones' unique style of drumming.

The Basie Band played a driving blues, riff-filled Kansas City style of jazz. Jones played an integral part in popularizing that style of swing that was in many ways a cousin to rhythm and blues and paved the way for the advent of rock and roll in the 1950s. Jones was a link between the music of the pre-war years and the later musical explosion of the post-war era.

In 1944, the army came calling and Jones lost two years of his musical career. He returned in 1946 and once again occupied the drum chair for the Count Basie Band until his departure a year later. He toured with Jazz at the Philharmonic for a brief spell, and then joined Illinois Jacquet for a couple of years.

In 1948, he led his own trio, but the responsibilities of running a band were too much for him and he joined his old bandmate Lester Young's outfit. Although the reunion lasted only one year it was a productive venture. There was something about the pairing of Jones and Young that inspired first-class jazz. Some of the best music the two played in their respective careers happened when they were in the same unit. After leaving Young's band, Jones then toured with JATP for a year before joining Joe Bushkin's Quartet.

Throughout most of the 1950s Jones did freelance work including recording sessions with Billie Holiday, Teddy Wilson, Duke Ellington, Johnny Hodges, Harry James, Benny Goodman, and Lionel Hampton. Because of his extraordinary abilities, Jones was never out of a job. He was also able to front a band on occasion and in 1960 took his all-star group to Puerto Rico on a successful tour.

Most of the 1960s he spent touring with Jazz at the Philharmonic making several sojourns into Europe. He also spent several months overseas with Milt Buckner in 1969. Sometimes he would put together a group to tour with throughout the United States or some far away land. He also played in many recording sessions. By this time Jones had been in jazz for thirty years and he commanded a tremendous amount of respect. Every project he participated in—whether it was with his band or some other group—was usually successful.

For the rest of his career Jones would become one of the most outspoken voices in jazz as one of its elder statesman. An opinionated individual, he never cared much about winning any popularity contests and some of his remarks were very critical, especially of other drummers. Although he appeared to be mean-spirited Jones had specific ideas of exactly how the instrument should be played, and when drummers didn't perform up to his expectations he felt slighted. He had spent his entire career elevating the status of the drummer and expected each successive stickman to only widen that circle of respect.

On September 3, 1985, in New York City, "Papa" Jo Jones, as he was affectionately known, died. He was 73 years old.

Jo Jones was one of the greatest jazz drummers in history. With his relentless drive, vast imagination, undeniable skills, and superior sense of timing, he opened the way for drummers and freed them from the boring chore of simple timekeeping. Never afraid to experiment, he continued to improve his ability on drums long after he had attained fame and enjoyed a storied career.

He was an amazing timekeeper who never missed a beat. Jones had an inner clock that allowed him to work more than one rhythm at once to create a series of overlapping and distinct grooves. He was always the glue that held the band together, working with the rhythm section and the soloists at the same time. He flailed away tirelessly, creating different subtexts and layers of tension. He did more with one crash of his cymbals than most drummers could do with a flurry of strikes.

His extensive use of the high-hat freed drummers from the mechanical monotony of the bass and snare drum. He didn't restrict himself to his drumsticks to create rhythm; Jones used his feet as well as his hands to explore the polyrhythms of his creative imagination. He was a serious student of the African beat and marveled at the language of rhythm and its infinite secrets. To Jones the entire drum kit was one large alphabet machine that challenged him to put different words together in a rhythmic way. He rarely failed to meet that challenge.

Jones was the drummer who came after pioneers Dodds, Singleton, Webb, and Krupa and before Kenny Clarke, Max Roach, Elvin Jones, and Art Blakey. In this sense he was the bridge between the older, New Orleans, swing style and the new thing. He blazed the trail for new drummers who would create different kinds of rhythm to keep up with the free jazz, jazz-fusion, and avant-garde sounds that the horns and string sections created in the latter half of the century.

He was a major influence on all of the drummers who came after him. The list includes Frank Butler, Michael Carvin, Max Roach, Kenny Clarke, Chico Hamilton, Mel Lewis, Ronald Shannon Jackson, Alphonse Mouzon, Tony Williams, Jack DeJohnette, Roy Haynes, Shelley Manne, Jeff "Taine" Watts, Billy Higgins, Jimmy Cobb, Danny Richmond, Cozy Cole, Philip Joe Jones, Billy Cobham, and J. C. Heard. Arguably he also had an indirect influence on some of the greatest rock drummers including John Bonham, Ginger Baker, Mitch Mitchell, Charlie Watts, Cozy Powell, John Densmore, Carl Palmer, and Keith Moon.

His name appears on the credits of hundreds of other albums by many of jazz's greatest stars. His influential timekeeping can be heard on the records of Billie Holiday, Earle Warren, Roy Eldridge, Jack Washington, Coleman Hawkins, Ben Webster, Ed Lewis, Jimmy Rushing, Benny Morton, Buddy Tate, Johnny Hodges, Dan Minor, Herschel Evans, Milt Hinton, and Benny Goodman.

Jo Jones' understanding of rhythm textures is second to none and it eventually earned him a spot in the Jazz Hall of Fame. He was a doorway for the later exploration of technique and rhythmic possibilities. Because he lived long enough to see many changes occur in jazz drumming, the rhythmic maker could be proud that he was the genesis of it all.

Discography

The Essential Jo Jones, Vol. 1, Vanguard 101.
The Essential Jo Jones, Vol. 2, Vanguard 102.
Percussion & Bass, Everest SDBR 1110.
The Main Man, Original Jazz Classics, Everest 869.
Jo Jones Trio, Fresh Sound FSR 40.
Our Man Papa Jones, Denon 81757–7047–2.
Jo Jones Special, Vanguard VRS 8503.
Jo Jones Plus Two, Vanguard VSDS 5575.
Jo Jones Trio, Everest SDBR 1023.
The Drums, Jazz Odyssey 8.
Vamp Till Ready, Everest SDBR 1099.
Jo Jones Sextet, Fresh Sound FSR 144.

TEDDY WILSON (1912–1986)

Limehouse Blues

There are a plethora of piano players who have made a purposeful splash in jazz. The piano runs throughout the entire history of the genre, even predating the music first recognized as jazz. The ragtime masters Scott Joplin, James Scott, Eubie Blake and Joseph Lamb and the best of the stride school—James P. Johnson, Willie "The Lion" Smith, and Fats Waller—were all pianists. Other jazz greats Jelly Roll Morton, Duke Ellington, Count Basie, Earl Hines, Oscar Peterson and Art Tatum were all important piano players. During the swing era a new voice was heard on the instrument and everyone took immediate notice of the man known for his "Limehouse Blues." His name was Teddy Wilson.

Theodore Shaw Wilson was born on November 24, 1912, in Austin, Texas. Although he became the most famous musician in the family, his brother Gus Wilson was a trombonist and arranger. When he was a boy Wilson's family moved to Tuskegee, Alabama, where his parents taught school. It was in Tuskegee that Wilson began his musical career studying piano, violin, E-flat clarinet and oboe. Later, he would major in music at Tuskegee College. By this time he had honed his piano skills to the point that they were sufficient enough to play in a group.

Wilson joined Speed Webb's band in 1929, at the tender age of seventeen, but already his style was quite remarkable. Influenced by Earl Hines, Art Tatum, and Fats Waller, Wilson took the best elements all three had to offer and molded them with his own personal vision. He had an unflashy, yet sophisticated style with a delicate but firm touch. Although he could play the music of the day as well as anyone and better than most, he had his own personal sound. It was apparent from the very beginning that he had no intention of taking a backseat to anyone.

After he left Webb's band, he worked with Milton Senior in Ohio before making his way to Chicago. His first gig was with Erskine Tate, but he played with a number of other outfits including Eddie Mallory's Band, Louis Armstrong, Jimmie Noone, Benny Carter's Orchestra, and Willie Bryant's group for a few months. During this time he also worked with Billie Holiday and ensured that Lady Day was surrounded with first class musicians, including Lester Young. Wilson played an important role in Holiday's early popularity in the mid-1930s. It was also around this time that he guested with Benny Goodman, an unknown clarinetist who was trying to make his way in the music world.

In 1936, he officially joined the Benny Goodman Trio that consisted of the noted bandleader and the charismatic drummer Gene Krupa. Later, Lionel Hampton joined to make it a quartet. Wilson thrived in Goodman's outfit despite the fact that he was African-American during a period when the color barrier was strictly enforced. His economic yet swinging piano style fit perfectly within the band's context.

When Goodman began his meteoric rise Wilson went along for the ride. It was a wonderful adventure because seemingly overnight they became the most popular band in the land. Wilson suddenly found himself in the best known group and relished the situation. With Goodman he cut many important jazz classics that all featured his distinct touch on the piano. Although his time in Goodman's band was an incredible shot to his career, Wilson needed a change of pace.

He left Goodman in 1939 to form his own big band. His new group debuted at the Famous Door in New York and a year later disbanded after their last residency at the Golden Gate Ballroom. Despite the enormous talent in Wilson's group that included the legendary Ben Webster, Doc Cheatham, J. C. Heard, and Harold "Shorty" Baker, they were unable to continue as a unit. There exists some recorded material of this extremely talented ensemble, but sadly there is not enough of it. Their mature sound was never realized before they disbanded.

For the next four years Wilson led his own successful small combos that included Hot Lips Page and Benny Morton. Later he formed another outfit, an exciting six-piece group that included Charlie Shavers and

Red Norvo. It also enjoyed much success. In 1945, Wilson rejoined Goodman and though they didn't create the same mass hysteria that they had just a few years before, it was a triumphant reunion.

In 1946, Wilson began a long association with CBS radio. He also taught at the famous Juilliard School as well as the Metropolitan Music School. He also did studio work for WNEW in the late 1940s and early 1950s. As if all of these projects weren't enough to keep him busy, he toured Scandinavia in 1952, and a year later visited Britain. He was able to spread the gospel of jazz with his particular brand of swinging piano music.

Since he had been an integral part of the rise to fame of Benny Goodman, it was only fitting that he should have a role in the movie *The Benny Goodman Story*. This brought together Hampton, Krupa, and Wilson to record as a trio and the result was the album *Krupa-Wilson-Hampton/Kings of Swing, Volume 1*. Although they came together occasionally to record and perform the trio never caught lightning in a bottle a second time.

While not reminiscing with his old bandmates, Wilson was leading his own trio, playing at concerts all over the country and internationally. In the summer of 1958, he appeared with his group at the Brussels World Fair. By this time he was recognized as one of the greatest pianists and with the death of Art Tatum in 1956, assumed the piano throne of jazz though he had a serious rival in Oscar Peterson.

Wilson also continued to record with some of the greatest names in jazz including Lester Young and the aforementioned Oscar Peterson. He was much in demand and divided his time between his own projects and that of others. Interestingly, despite the advent of bop and bebop, he did not change his style to suit the new tastes although he had recorded with Dizzy Gillespie and Charlie Parker a few years before.

During the 1960s, Wilson continued to expand on his earlier career achievements. Although not every one of his recording dates was a moment of pure magic, he did manage to return to his old form on occasion, most notably on the two excellent solo efforts *Striding After Fats*, and *With Billie in Mind*. There was also the occasional invitation to play with Goodman, Hampton, and Krupa. He toured constantly with his own band, playing dates all over the country and overseas in France and Great Britain. One of his more notable concerts was with Goodman in Russia in 1962.

By the 1970s, Wilson had lost some of the golden touch that had made him so famous during his salad days. But he still could dazzle on occasion, including during his appearance at the 1973 Montreux Jazz Festival where he was accompanied by a group of British musicians. Despite this highlight, his steady decline had begun. By the time of his death on

July 31, 1986, in New Britain, Connecticut, his best days were long behind him. He was 73 years old.

Teddy Wilson was one of the premier stars of the swing era. A piano player with his own unique sound and someone who never wavered from the narrow path that had proven successful for him, he remains one of the greatest pianists. Although his fame was sealed as a member of the Benny Goodman band, Wilson made many other significant contributions to jazz.

The Teddy Wilson sound, the sparkle, the drive, the economy of playing are certainly attractive elements. But there was more to his legacy that has continued to dazzle listeners. He swung with great rhythm, never flashy, but steady and reliable. There was a smoothness that appealed to listeners because he was so accessible. Those who heard him playing felt that his style was the one they could best copy. Although the Wilson method seemed easy to play, it was quite complex. In a world of imitators, he was an original.

With his confined yet imaginative playing he was an ace entrepreneur for a bevy of great lady jazz singers. He was instrumental in launching the Billie Holiday rocket by organizing and supervising her earliest recorded efforts. He also backed Mildred Bailey during many of her classic recordings of the 1930s. Bailey never sounded better than when Wilson was at the keyboards guiding her through one great song after another.

In addition, Wilson supervised and arranged one of the earliest recording sessions for the then unknown singer Ella Fitzgerald. The album *Ella, Billie, Lena, Sarah: 4 Grandes Dames du Jazz* was a record of seminal importance. Of the other two ladies on the record Lena Horne was never considered a pure jazz singer. She might have been if Wilson had been her constant accompanist. The last grande dame, Sarah Vaughan, benefited greatly by the session, and a decade later, when she was a big star, could point to the album as a turning point in her career. This ability to play behind the great female singers provided another side of Wilson's many facets as a pianist.

Often Wilson organized all-star bands, a common practice among jazz musicians. The talent he was able to draw at these super sessions included Roy Eldridge, Buster Bailey, Johnny Hodges, Harry James, Pee Wee Russell, Gene Krupa, and Harry Carney. The quality of these recordings often overshadowed the studio efforts that Wilson put together with his own proper bands. The fact that so many musicians were willing to take time out of their busy schedules to participate in these all-star jam sessions indicates the amount of respect that Wilson drew from others in the jazz community.

Although his style wasn't the greatest display of virtuoso, Wilson nevertheless managed to influence a great number of future keyboard players as well as other jazz musicians. This list includes Toshiko Akiyoshi, Dave Brubeck, Ray Bryant, John Bunch, Lionel Hampton, Eddie Heywood, Duke Jordan, Eiji Kitamura, Dave McKenna, Bud Powell, Hazel Scott, George Shearing, Joe Bushkin, Claude Williamson, Skitch Henderson, Nat King Cole, Thelonious Monk, George Winston, and Luqman Hamza. While he often comes up short in comparisons to Art Tatum, Oscar Peterson, and Earl Hines, Wilson still remains a prime force in jazz piano.

He also gave the world a large number of classics, including "Dizzy Spells," "Moonglow," "Body & Soul," "Time On My Hands," "China Boy," "Running Wild," "Have You Met Miss Jones?" "I'm A Ding Dong Daddy," "Smiles," "Limehouse Blues," and an interesting reworking of "Tea For Two" to name a few. Many of these songs were recorded as a member of the Benny Goodman trio and quartet. Wilson had the ability to give an old tune a fresh appeal and his cover versions often sounded better than the original cuts.

While he has been criticized for his quiet style from certain corners of jazz, Wilson remains one of the best pianists and undoubtedly the greatest swing pianist of all-time. He provided the jazz world with many memorable moments and performances as a soloist, ensemble player, and accompanist. His instantly recognizable style ensures that the man who thrilled the world with his "Limehouse Blues" left behind a unique legacy.

Discography

And Then They Wrote.../Mr. Wilson, Collectables 6680.
Alone, Storyville 8211.
Central Avenue Blues, Vintage Jazz Classics 1013.
Cole Porter Classics, 1201 Music 9024.
Interaction, Drive Archive 41094.
Jumpin' for Joy, Hep 1064.
Keystone Transcriptions 1939–1940, Storyville 8258.
Limehouse Blues, Jazz Time Records 8150.
Moments Like This, Hep 1043.
Nice Work If You Can Get It, Laserlight 17118.
Teddy & the Girls, Vol. 1, Masters of Jazz 106.
Teddy Wilson 1946, Melodie 997.
The Legendary Small Groups Vol. 1: 1935–37, Masters of Jazz 150.
Three Little Words, Black and Blue 869.
Too Hot for Words 1935, Hep 1012.
Warmin' Up 1935–36, Hep 1014.

Of Thee I Swing, Hep 1020.
Fine and Dandy 1937, Hep 1029.
Blue Mood, Hep 1035.
With Billie in Mind, Chiaroscuro 111.
For Quiet Lovers, Polygram POCJ-2587.
I Got Rhythm, Polygram POCJ-2586.
Impeccable Mr Wilson Verve POCJ-2747.
Piano Artistry of Teddy Wilson, JC JC98016.
Teddy Wilson & His Orchestra, The Best of Teddy Wilson & His
    Orchestra, CCM 126.
The Legendary Small Groups Vol.1 1935–1937, Masters of Jazz 150.
Jumpin' for Joy, HEP 1064.
His Piano & His Orchestra 1938–1939, STC 2068.
Teddy Wilson & His Orchestra 1934–1935, Classic 508.
Teddy Wilson & His Orchestra, 1935–1936, Classic 511.
Teddy Wilson & His Orchestra 1936–1937, Classic 521.
Teddy Wilson & His Orchestra 1937, Classic 531.
Teddy Wilson & His Orchestra 1937–1938, Classic 548.
Teddy Wilson & His Orchestra 1938, Classic 556.
Teddy Wilson & His Orchestra 1939, Classic 571.
Teddy Wilson & His Orchestra 1939–1941, Classic 620.
Teddy Wilson & His Orchestra 1942–1945, Classic 908.
Teddy Wilson & His Orchestra 1946, Classic 997.
His Piano & Orchestra with Billie Holiday 1934–1937, ASL 5053.

JIMMY BLANTON (1918–1942)

Mr. J.B.'s Blues

In jazz, every instrument has its innovator, one musician who takes the ideas and visions of what could be accomplished a step further. For many years the bass was delegated to being strictly a background voice as part of the rhythm section. However, during the swing era, one bassist stepped forward and set the jazz world on its ear by demonstrating the many layered textures of sound that the instrument could produce. He did it by playing "Mr. J. B Blues." His name was Jimmy Blanton.

Jimmy Blanton was born on October 5, 1918, in Chattanooga, Tennessee, the hometown of blues great Bessie Smith. Blanton had strong family musical roots. His mother was a successful musician, a pianist who led her own band around Tennessee. His uncle was a violinist who taught Blanton the basics of music theory. It was while attending Tennessee State College that Blanton discovered the bass and adopted it as his instrument of choice.

He cut his musical teeth playing with bands while in school. Blanton, not content with being buried in the rhythm section and doomed to keeping a steady beat, developed his virtuoso talents in order to upgrade his position within the band context. After school he moved to St. Louis and caught his first break working with Fate Marable during summers on a riverboat. It was good practical experience for the young musician and allowed him to put some of the theory his uncle had taught him to use.

He joined the Jeter-Pillars Orchestra in late 1937, playing a three string bass, and remained there until one night when Duke Ellington discovered him. The Duke, who had a keen ear for talent, recognized Blanton's latent genius and lured him away from the Jeter-Pillars Orchestra. Overnight, Blanton went from a third rate outfit to one of the most exciting and well-known big bands in the country. It was a giant step forward in his career.

Blanton joined Ellington's Orchestra in September of 1939 and made an immediate impact. Prior to the arrival of Blanton, the bass players in Ellington's musical outfits had been solid rhythm man with very little of an adventurous spirit. Billy Taylor, the other bass player in the band, remained for three months and then left because he was well aware that Blanton could play enough bass for both of them. Taylor was not happy to be playing second fiddle to the young Blanton.

Ellington, a genius songwriter, reveled in writing pieces built around the talents of the men in his band. With such a diamond as Blanton, the Duke was inspired to create vehicles that showcased his young bass player's best abilities. Since Blanton was intent on expanding the role of the bass in jazz he could not have found himself in a better situation.

A month after he joined Ellington, he was swept into the recording studio and cut "Mr J. B. Blues" which astonished listeners. Blanton's fluid, big tone sound sent Ellington's febrile imagination spiraling into higher levels of creativity, causing him to produce masterpieces of his eloquent jazz sound. The greater the virtuoso, the greater depth of Ellington's writing. The song "Mr. J. B. Blues" signaled a new era in jazz as far as bass players were concerned.

Although he was much younger than many of the seasoned musicians in the Ellington Orchestra (he was twenty when he joined) he carried himself like a veteran amongst the elitist company. While other musicians might have felt out of place, Blanton fit right in and proved that he belonged with some of the greatest names in jazz.

Blanton's energy and drive sparked the rest of the band and the kid who was constantly practicing his bass amazed everyone. A serious student of the instrument, he was never satisfied with the status quo and sought to improve his playing and expand his musical vocabulary whether it was through a teacher or a late night jam session.

In 1940, Blanton and Ellington recorded the duet "Pitter Panther Patter," and the world of bass playing would never be the same again. Blanton transformed the sluggish bass drone of the past into a powerful solo instrument of melody and virtuoso. He had no peers at the time. From this point on the bass would be used as a lone voice in an orchestra much the same way that the saxophone, trumpet, drums, piano and guitar had been used for so long.

Life in Duke Ellington's band was good since they traveled used first class and performed in many of the finest concert halls of the era. As a member of the orchestra he reached heights that would have otherwise taken him years to achieve in a less publicized ensemble. He was well paid for his services and within a short time had served notice that he was the resident bass genius in all of jazz.

However, during the musical *Jump for Joy*, it was clearly evident that Blanton was not well. He was later diagnosed with tuberculosis and had to quit the band. He moved to a sanitarium in Los Angeles where seven months later, on July 30, 1942, one of the greatest single bass voices in jazz was silenced forever. Blanton was only 23 years old.

Jimmie Blanton was the pioneer of the modern bass sound. He advanced the instrument from one of strict rhythm to heights of virtuosity that had never been heard before. What is so remarkable about Blanton's breakthrough is the short amount of time that he did it in. His too brief time in the spotlight makes his accomplishments that much more amazing.

He had a different approach to the bass from most who played the instrument at the time. He thought of the bass as a horn capable of playing melody, harmonies and rhythm simultaneously. He had an outstanding vocabulary with excellent articulation and a deep rich tone. His incessant drive was reminiscent of the bebop sound that he paved the wave for but never heard. He plucked and used a bow on the strings to create his magic.

He was the complete bass player, able to carry the melody of a song or to ride along with the rhythm that he and the rest of the group created, and he was content to lay down a fat, bass line. He could swing with the best of them, keeping a rock steady beat that made people want to groove to the music. But his undeniable talent for instant improvisation is what set him apart from the other bassists at the time.

Before the arrival of Jimmie Blanton, the outstanding bass players in jazz had been Wellman Braud, Pops Foster, John Kirby and Walter Page. Although all were capable players they were simple timekeepers, not allowed to step out with the front line instruments like the trumpet and clarinet. But Blanton changed all that. He pushed his way to the forefront and put the bass on par with the other lead instruments in jazz.

He had an adventurous streak and explored the extreme possibilities of the bass. He stretched the limitations of the instrument imposed by the unwritten "rules" of jazz and in doing so broke new territory for all bass players to follow. After Blanton's exploits, the bass would never be viewed the same way it had been before his meteoric career.

Blanton was a major influence on Charles Mingus, Ray Brown and Oscar Pettiford, the three great modern jazz bassists who would follow him. Other bass players who owe a debt to Blanton include Curtis Counce, Sam Jones, Jimmy Woode, Monty Budwig, Red Callender, Paul Chambers, Stanley Clarke, Milt Hinton, Buell Neidlinger, Chubby Jackson, Slam Stewart, Cecil McBee, Red Mitchell, Charlie Haden, Niels-Henning Orsted Pederson, Gary Peacock, Ron Carter, Charles Fambrough, and Christian McBride. Undoubtedly, it was Charles Mingus who most benefited from Blanton's breakthrough. Although the jazz of the pre-bop era featured incredible soloists, the bebop area era was when total attention was focused on the soloist. Blanton was one of the godfathers of bebop and inspired Mingus to pursue his own thing. Blanton pointed Mingus down the path and the student dutifully and eagerly followed.

But Blanton's influence extends beyond the boundaries of jazz and spills into the blues and rock circles. Willie Dixon, the blues bass great, fully understood what Blanton was trying to accomplish. There is an affinity between the bass playing of Dixon and Blanton. They both were able to make their instruments talk with a unique voice. Because of their virtuoso and expertise each became the champion of the bass in their chosen genre.

Blanton also had a huge influence on the rock and roll bass players who would appear in the latter part of the century. Celebrated rock bassists like John Paul Jones, Roger Glover, and Jack Bruce certainly borrowed a page or two from Blanton. When Jack Bruce starred with Cream, astonishing all with his improvisation and lead voice, he was only echoing the efforts of Blanton twenty-five years before. John Paul Jones adopted the quiet anonymity of the bassist in the hard rock band Led Zeppelin, but he occasionally burst out of his unmarked territory to challenge Jimmy Page's mighty lead guitar, Robert Plant's wild blues shriek, and John Bonham's swinging stone meters.

Although he was part of the Ellington Orchestra, Blanton often recorded in the band within the band that featured Johnny Hodges, Barney Bigard, Rex Stewart, and Cootie Williams. His amazing talent can be heard on "Jack the Bear," "Ko-Ko," "Bojangles," "Conga Brava," "Harlem Airshaft," "John Hardy's Wife," "Take the 'A' Train" and "Jumpin' Pumpkins." If he had lived there is no doubt that his discography would match that of other jazz artists who enjoyed longer careers.

Jimmie Blanton's time in the sun was brief, but he made the most of it. Even today, modern bass players attempting to find a handle on the instrument can simply listen to Blanton's recordings. While other bass players in jazz have taken the instrument down different paths and have built on Blanton's foundation, the pioneer of the bass will never be replaced, or forgotten for giving the world his "Mr. J. B. Blues."

Discography*

Solos, Duets and Trios, RCA 2178.
In Boston, 1939–1940, Jazz Unlimited 2022.
Through the Roof, Drive Archive 42416.
In a Mellotone, RCA 51364.
Fargo 1940, Vintage Jazz Classics 1019.
Sophisticated Lady, RCA 61071.
Reminiscing in Tempo, Sony 48684.
Stereo Reflections in Ellington, Natasha Imports 4016
Beyond Category, Musical Genius, RCA 49000.
Blanton-Webster Band, RCA 5659.

CHARLIE CHRISTIAN (1916–1942)

Solo Flights

The longevity of jazz careers varies greatly. Duke Ellington, Count Basie, Louis Armstrong, Oscar Peterson, and Eubie Blake, among others,

*Blanton recorded as part of the Duke Ellington Band or one of the smaller groups within the larger orchestra.

have enjoyed long and distinguished tenures as prominent artists in their field. Other practitioners have lived much shorter days in the sun, but still managed to make an important impact on the music. One of the figures who falls into the latter category had a serious influence on all modern guitarists, as he was known for his impressive solo flights. His name was Charlie Christian.

Charlie Christian was born July 29, 1916, in Dallas, Texas, into a musical family. His parents had been professional musicians in Dallas providing the music for a silent movie theatre. His mother played the piano while his father played the trumpet. Both of his brothers could play several musical instruments. In 1921, when Charlie was five, the family moved to Oklahoma City. It was here that Christian joined his father and two brothers in a group that played blues and popular songs of the day.

Music was a part of Christian's daily life. It was a simple fact and he received a tremendous musical education that would be the envy of his professional bandmates. He chose the trumpet as his first instrument before settling on guitar when he was about twelve. A multi-instrumentalist, he also played the string bass and piano in the early 1930s.

Since Oklahoma was a crossroads of every musical idea in the country, young Charlie was exposed to a variety of styles including blues, country, jazz, popular songs, Mexican, gospel, and classical. It was also a meeting place for itinerant musicians to gather and jam. One night, during a club date, he met the incomparable Lester Young, the president of the tenor saxophone. The fateful meeting was a turning point in the blossoming guitarist's career that left a deep and lasting effect on the young Texan. When he heard the Prez play his sax Christian was inspired to play his guitar like a horn, an unheard of method in jazz at the time.

For much of the early 1930s Christian led the life of a vagabond musician and often worked outside of the business. While he wasn't playing with his brothers in their band Lully Jugglers, he was earning his living as a tap-dancer, singer, baseball pitcher, and even as a prizefighter. But in 1935, he received his first big break when he was asked to join the Alphonso Trent band. Although he had to switch to bass guitar to join the group it enabled him to break out of the territory to gain further musical experiences.

Christian would eventually join Anna Mae Winburn's group as well as the newly formed Jeter-Pillars Orchestra, run by two individuals who had broken away from Trent. In each band he impressed everyone with his dexterity. Although he was a talented individual who played the guitar like a horn there was something else to his sound that enthralled all those who were fortunate enough to hear him play; Christian had gone electric.

Although he wasn't the first guitar player to plug in, he made the most use of the dimensions of volume. For years, many people had been experimenting with a way to produce a greater sound out of acoustic guitars. Several companies, Rickenbacker, Gibson, and an inventor by the name of Les Paul, had all fiddled with primitive equipment hoping to pull out latent sounds from the guitar. In 1937, when the first Gibson electric guitar rolled off the assembly line—the famous ES 150—the role of the six-string instrument in jazz had changed forever.

Now the guitar could take its rightful place with the loud horns, the saxophones and the trumpets. The guitar could be used as a solo instrument, a lead voice, rather than being delegated to rhythmic duty as it had been since the birth of jazz. But in order for the electric guitar to become a dominant instrument it needed a hero; that hero was Charlie Christian.

He started to lead his own outfit around 1936, playing amplified guitar and phrasing his chords and single line solos like a horn gone electric. When his group disbanded he found work with James Simpson in Oklahoma City and also toured with Alphonso Trent again, this time as a guitarist. By 1939, he was playing with his brother at the Ritz Café in Oklahoma City. Christian might have toiled in obscurity for the rest of his career if it hadn't been for piano player Mary Lou Williams urging John Hammond to come down and hear this extraordinary guitarist. Hammond, the legendary producer for Columbia Records, eventually gave in and flew down to see Christian play. He was floored and immediately traveled to the West Coast where he persuaded Benny Goodman to take the young guitarist in his band. Christian was now on a sure path to create his own legend.

He made his debut with the Goodman Big Band in September of 1939 in New York City. From the very beginning he brought a totally new dimension to the swing sound of Goodman's outfit and drove the crowd wild. Although they were an interracial band in segregated America, their immense appeal did not waver. Many in the audience saw beyond color lines. In the next four months Christian would record numerous sides in a small combo situation with members of the band, as well as with others in the jazz world including Mary Lou Williams.

For the next two and a half years, Charlie Christian did much to change the sound of jazz. His brilliant improvised solos of single note runs never failed to leave listeners stunned. He was also leading a double life. When he finished work with Goodman, he would run to Minton's where bebop was being invented. He jammed with Dizzy Gillespie, Kenny Clarke, Thelonious Monk, and Charles Mingus. Although he excelled in the established patterns of jazz, his pure creativity could never be denied and he constantly searched for new outlets to explore.

Although he was a genuine spark in the studio Christian was at his best in a small combo setting and many of his masterpieces were recorded in such an environment. The energy that flowed from his magical fingers inspired others to push themselves harder than they would on a normal session. It was these recordings that accelerated his legend as much as the live concerts.

While all seemed right in Christian's world, it unfortunately wasn't. He had been diagnosed with tuberculosis as far back as 1939 and had been told to slow down. But the guitar genius would not heed the warnings of the doctors and continued to push himself beyond his limits. His stamina was questionable and, unfortunately, like another young trailblazer, Jimmie Blanton, Christian's time in the spotlight was too brief.

In the spring of 1941 he was hospitalized in a sanitarium and never fully recovered. Despite a stream of well wishers that came to visit him, including John Hammond and Count Basie, he remained sickly. On March 2, 1942, Charlie Christian, the imaginative guitar player who had made enormous contributions to jazz, died at the Seaview Sanitarium on Staten Island. He was 23 years old.

Charlie Christian was a genuine pioneer of jazz. His stylings on the electric guitar influenced every jazz guitarist for the next sixty years. No one had heard such utter genius on the instrument until Christian came along and no one has quite matched his display of dazzling talent. In less than three years he had laid down the parameters of the electric guitar in jazz.

To better understand Christian's style one must understand its roots. Christian was from Texas, which boasted a hot blues and jazz scene as well as country, folk and lively Mexican music. One of Christian's early idols was Blind Lemon Jefferson, the "Father of Texas Blues." Jefferson influenced all Texas guitar players. Another firm disciple of Jefferson was Aaron "T-Bone" Walker.

Walker and Christian became fast friends and traded licks and ideas while learning how to play their guitars like horns. They both plugged in at around the same time and began to explore the myriad of sounds that the electric guitar could produce. While Christian made a huge impact on jazz, Walker made a huge impact on the blues. Interestingly, Walker was never a pure blues guitarist since many of his songs featured a strong jazz presence. Similarly, Christian's jazz playing contained a large dose of the blues.

Another noted blues guitar pioneer who was an important influence on Christian was Lonnie Johnson, who laid down some of the first guitar solos in the 1920s. Johnson would enjoy two more surges of popularity after his initial breakthrough during the Jazz Age, but it is his early blues-jazz stylings that had the largest impact on Christian. Johnson's partner Eddie Lang was yet another influence on Christian's style.

Arguably the greatest influence on Christian was not a guitar player. It was tenor saxophone player Lester Young. The Prez, with his long, inspired runs of notes that produced a breathtaking body of sound, drove Christian mad in his attempt to imitate Young's style on guitar. A comparison between Young's saxophone solos and Christian's guitar runs is a clear indication of the profound and lasting effect that the horn master had on the young electric guitar wizard.

Christian was able to unleash a bluesy cascade of notes that fell like raindrops. He was also able to incorporate meaty and complex chord patterns. His dexterity, speed, and imagination where unparalleled. There was a definite blues-drenched feeling to his intense playing. It was a reflection of his earliest roots. His pattern of riff, run and riff would confine jazz guitarists for the next generation.

Although he was without a doubt the most important swing guitarist, Christian did have his peers. Eddie Condon was a swing bandleader who made his mark in Chicago in the 1920s and 1930s. Freddie Green spent most of his productive years in Count Basie's band. Tiny Grimes, who had one foot in swing and the other in bop, enjoyed a lengthy career playing with Art Tatum and Coleman Hawkins among others. Les Paul was an excellent guitarist and an inventor whose love for the instrument has been well documented. George Van Eps, who enjoyed his best years with the swing bands of the Dorsey Brothers, had a career that spanned twice that of Christian's.

But not only was Christian the king of swing guitar, he was also a pioneer of bebop. He influenced Barney Kessel, Kenny Burrell, Bill DeArango, and Herb Ellis, as well as later jazz guitarists Wes Montgomery and George Benson. But Christian's impact spilled over the borders of jazz. He had a hand in shaping the styles of Pee Wee Crayton, blues great B. B. King, rocker Chuck Berry, as well as modern axe slinger Jimi Hendrix. Christian also had a profound impact on a slew of Texas guitarists including Stevie Ray Vaughan, Jimmie Vaughan, Johnny Winter, Albert Collins, Freddie King, Johnny "Guitar" Watson, Billy Gibbons, Chris Duarte, and Anson Funderburgh.

Although his recorded output was limited he did leave a handful of classics including "Swing to Bop," "A Smo-o-o-oth One," "Seven Come Eleven," and "Solo Flight," perhaps his best known piece. Ironically enough, although his body of work is not immense his playing reverberated throughout jazz for the next three decades. There was a definite touch. In each of the songs he created a guitarist's feeling for the perfect placing of notes and chords in precise and imaginative patterns.

Charlie Christian is a perfect example (along with Jimmie Blanton) of the young genius dying too soon. There is no telling what heights he would have scaled if he had lived. Despite the fact that he was tragically cut down in the prime of his life, Christian remains one of the most important jazz innovators. There is no denying his very special place in the history of jazz with his solo flights.

Discography

Celestial Express, Definitive 11122.
Charlie Christian 1939–1941, Best of Jazz 4032.
Immortal Charlie Christian, Legacy Records 373.
Solo Flight, Jazz Classics 5005.
Solo Flight, Topaz Jazz Records 1017.
The Genius of the Electric Guitar, Legacy Records 40846.
The Immortal Charlie Christian, Vol. 2, 1939, Laserlight 17032.
Vol. 3 (1939–39), Masters of Jazz 40.
Vol. 6 (1940–41), Masters of Jazz 68.
Volume 1: 1939, Masters of Jazz 024.
Volume 4: 1940, Masters of Jazz 44.
Volume 5: 1940, Masters of Jazz 67.
Volume 7, 1941, Masters of Jazz 74.
Volume 8, 1941, Masters of Jazz 75.
Masters of Jazz, RETRO RCD8004.
Swing 2 Bop, MASTE 503542.

PART FIVE

Other Major Figures

During the first fifty years of jazz history (1895–1945) there were hundreds of individuals who made enormous contributions to the history of the genre. Many of these artists became innovators, stars, and cult heroes.

The artists featured in this section have some of the most exotic stories in the annals of jazz. Included are ragtime performers, arrangers, singers, and the most famous jazz artist born outside the United States in over a hundred years of music. Although the seven personalities represented here made a large impact on the genre, they are just a few of the important names in the first fifty years of America's classical music.

Before the advent of the New Orleans Tradition there was ragtime. Although ragtime has been derided as a poor second cousin to jazz, the syncopated rhythms had a large influence on the stride pianists James P. Johnson, Willie "The Lion" Smith, and Fats Waller. Joseph Lamb and James Scott were important ragtime pianists.

One of the key elements that separated jazz from all other styles was the arrangements. Throughout the history of jazz the arranger has played a vital role in the popularity of the music as well as its consideration as a classical form. Some of the most important arrangers of the first fifty years include Sy Oliver, Billy Strayhorn, Van Alexander, Archie Bleyer, Sonny Burke, Ralph Flanagan, Joe Haymes, Carl Hoff, Quincy Jones, Bobby Sherwood and Billy May.

Although jazz has always been considered music of instruments, the hundreds of singers throughout its history are greatly responsible for the music's popularity. During the Jazz Age a number of blues singers, including Bessie Smith, Ma Rainey, Ida Cox, Sippie Wallace, Trixie Smith, and Alberta Hunter, performed songs with a jazz tinge.

During the Depression a number of singers emerged on the scene and became very popular. Connie Boswell, one of three sisters, was a major influence on a number of singers. Annette Hanshaw was one of Boswell's main competitors. But not all singers were female. One of the most noted jazz vocalists of the 1920s was the great Bing Crosby, who debuted with the Paul Whiteman band.

During the big band era there were dozens of singers who made their mark. A partial list includes Helen O'Connell, Peggy Lee, Bea Wain, Edythe Wright, Martha Tilton, Kay Starr, Helen Forrest, Mildred Bailey, Marion Hutton, Jo Stafford, Rosemary Clooney, Dale Evans, Amy Arnell, Helen Ward, Ginny Powell, Louise Tobin, Anita O'Day, Connie Hanes, June Christy, Dinah Washington, Nan Wynn and Bonnie Baker.

When jazz spread over to Europe many enthusiasts caught the bug. Soon the Europeans were playing in jazz clubs and the music spread like wild fire. Stephane Grappelli, Oscar Aleman, Philip Catherine, Birell Lagrene, and Rene Thomas are just a few of the early stars of European jazz.

The following seven jazz people are those who made enormous contributions to jazz as arrangers, singers, and pianists. They are those individuals who are difficult to categorize and therefore deserve their own section. Hence, the title "Other Major Figures."

Scott Joplin was the prime player of the ragtime tradition. He opened the door for all who would follow. Many of his songs became classics which were covered by dozens of jazz artists. In the early 1970s, more than fifty years after his death, Joplin would enjoy a renaissance.

Eubie Blake is the marathon man of the jazz world. While countless jazz musicians died young, Blake lived to be a hundred and never lost his taste for ragtime. He was a living historian.

Don Redman is the best "tailor" in the jazz business. In a music that celebrates the musicians and bandleaders, it was Redman as arranger who propelled Fletcher Henderson to stardom.

Art Tatum is considered the greatest piano player in the history of jazz as well as modern music. Nearly completely blind, he never allowed this obstacle to stop him form pursuing his true ambitions. Although sometimes classified as a swing artist, he possessed a much wider range.

Django Reinhardt's is one of the most exotic stories, and his influence spilled over the borders of jazz to include blues, country, and rock to inspire guitarists of every style as well as every era.

Billie Holiday was a tragic figure who became known as the voice of jazz. There is hardly a female singer—of any style—in the past fifty years who has not stolen a page or two from the Holiday vocal book.

Ella Fitzerald is synonymous with jazz. Her career was one of the longest and most brilliant in the annals of the genre. Her popularity could be matched against any other jazz figure's.

SCOTT JOPLIN (1868–1917)

Maple Leaf Rag

One of the early musical styles that had a strong impact on the development of jazz was ragtime. Although ragtime lacked blues and improvisation, which later characterized jazz, the elements of the primarily piano-driven, syncopated, good-time dance music could be heard in the early pioneers like Buddy Bolden, King Oliver, and Kid Ory. While there were many fine ragtime practitioners, including Tom Turpin, James Scott, Joseph Lamb, and Louis Chauvin, it was the man with his "Maple Leaf Rag" whose name became synonymous with the genre. His name was Scott Joplin.

Although Joplin's birthday is celebrated as November 24, 1868, there is some doubt as to his real birth date and the actual place of his birth. Some historians believe he was born earlier in 1868 somewhere in the northeast part of Texas. Whatever his true date and place of birth may be, Joplin was well acquainted with poverty. He was the son of former slaves and as a young boy the family left the farm to move to Texarkana on the Texas-Arkansas border.

Life in Texas was a desperate struggle so he turned to music for solace. If historical sources are correct Joplin began his musical education on the piano. His mother worked for a white family who possessed one. Years later, in his opera *Treemonisha*, Joplin made reference to the difficulties that his mother went through to ensure that he received an opportunity to pursue his musical ambitions. The piano became an important part of his life and he dreamed of someday creating an African-American art form that would be viewed with dignity and authority. Although he would eventually create a distinct musical style, he never fully realized his complete vision.

Joplin's musical ambitions did not go unnoticed, as a music teacher, Julius Weiss, took special interest in the young, studious boy and instructed him on the finer points of European music, including opera. This special tutoring created the foundation of Joplin's musical education and enabled him to understand the nuances of serious composition. The element of classical music had a strong identity in Joplin's sound, a trait he passed on to mainstream jazz.

Joplin made his first trip to Sedalia in the 1880s when he was a high school student. Since Sedalia was close to St. Louis, Joplin, an enterprising young man, would have found an excuse and a way to discover the thriving metropolitan city. St. Louis was a prime center for ragtime and would play a large part in Joplin's future musical direction.

Joplin returned to his native Texas in the late 1880s already having decided to pursue a career in music. Historical reports indicate that he was working with a minstrel troupe in the early 1890s. It was at this point that the twenty-year-old Joplin was paying his dues. He remained in Texas for the next couple of years and his next documented move was to Chicago where he fronted a band (he played cornet in the group) outside the gates of the World Fair.

After the Fair, Joplin made the decision to live in Sedalia and established a permanent residence there. He played first cornet in the Queen City Cornet Band. Although it was a good experience for the still developing young musician, Joplin only remained a year with the band and then moved on to form his own group.

He called his band the Texas Medley Quartette and they performed in Sedalia, carving a solid name for themselves. But Joplin had a traveling bone and took his small group all over the East Coast. It was on one of these tours that he was spotted in Syracuse, New York, by local businessmen, which resulted in his first two songs, "Please Say You Will" and "A Picture of Her Face," being published. The enthusiastic reception he received while on tour and the excitement of having his first two piano rolls published encouraged him to continue towards achieving his goal of creating a distinct African-American musical form.

When Joplin didn't have his band on the road he remained active in Sedalia playing at various clubs and events. One of these venues was called the Maple Leaf, a popular social club for black men. Joplin also found time to tutor local young musicians including Scott Hayden and Arthur Marshall. Later on, he and Marshall would collaborate on a number of rags.

Joplin continued his double life as musician on the road and quiet composer at home in Sedalia. He would publish two marches and a waltz in the late 1890s, but neither made him any real money. In 1898, he published "Original Rags," and learned a very important lesson about the music business in the process. Joplin had to share "credit" with a local staff arranger. On his next composition, "Maple Leaf Rag," Joplin, through the help of a local lawyer, made sure that the song credits belonged solely to him. It was this song, "Maple Leaf Rag," that would become his most famous composition and earn him a slight income for the rest of his life. Although he would publish a stage work, *The Ragtime Dance*, that would eventually be performed three years later, and one more rag, "Swipesy," in Sedalia, Joplin left the quietness of the small town for the hustle and bustle of St. Louis.

In 1901, Joplin moved to St. Louis with his new wife, Belle. In the big city he quickly made a name for himself not through live performances, but as a teacher and composer. Joplin's publisher, John Stark, had also traveled to St. Louis with his daughter Eleanor, who was instrumental in ensuring through her many contacts that her favorite ragtime pianist would not starve. It was with the help of Eleanor that he was able to form a friendship with Alfred Ernst, the conductor of the St. Louis Choral Symphony Society, a most vital contact for an aspiring musician like Joplin.

Joplin was very prolific in St. Louis as he had many songs published including "Sunflower Slow Drag," "Peacherine Rag," "The Easy Winners," "Cleopha," "The Strenuous Life," "A Breeze from Alabama," "Elite Syncopation," "The Entertainer," and the "Ragtime Dance," all in 1902. To say that Joplin flourished in the Arch City would be an understatement.

In 1903, he became even more ambitious as he had the opera *A Guest of Honor* copyrighted. In order to stage the work, Joplin formed an opera company, rehearsed the work in a local St. Louis theatre and then toured towns in the bordering states of Illinois, Iowa, Kansas, and Nebraska. A potential successful run was ruined when the box office receipts were stolen. A couple of weeks later the opera folded leaving him bitter.

Joplin needed a change of scenery after the opera debacle and moved to Chicago for some time before pushing on to Arkansas. It was in Arkansas that he met Freddie Alexander, a delicate flower to whom he dedicated the song "The Chrysanthemum." Upon his return to Sedalia he had the song copyrighted. He would later appear at the World's Fair in St. Louis where he would preview his song "Cascades," written specifically for the grand event. He would also publish "The Sycamore" and "The Favorite" in 1904.

After the break up of his marriage to Belle, Joplin returned to Arkansas and married the much younger Freddie Alexander. Joplin brought his bride back to Sedalia to live with him. However, ten months after their marriage, Alexander contracted pneumonia and died.

The memory of Alexander convinced Joplin that he needed another change of scenery and left Sedalia. He eventually drifted to St. Louis and earned a poor living although he continued to compose great works. In 1905, he published, "Bethena," a ragtime waltz, as well as the songs "Sarah Dear," "Leola" and "The Rose-Bud March." A year later he published his march "Antoinette," "Ragtime Dance," and "Eugenia."

By 1907, Joplin was living in Chicago where he met Louis Chauvin; together they composed "Heliotrope Bouquet," a very engaging rag. Joplin endured more tragedy in his life when his young protege died a few months later. His passing not only marked the loss of a musician with extraordinary skills, but also the potential of a very profitable partnership.

Joplin spent the last ten years of his life in New York where he enjoyed some success but also knew failure. In New York he renewed his business partnership with Stark who would publish many of Joplin's last compositions, including "Nonpareil," "Fig Leaf Rag," and "Heliotrope Bouquet." During this period—1907–1910—Joplin managed to publish "Searchlight Rag," "Gladiolus Rag," "Rose Leaf Rag," "Sugar Cane Rag," "Pine Apple Rag," "Wall Street Rag," "Solace," "Pleasant Moments," "Country Club," "Euphonic Sounds," "Paragon Rag," and "Stoptime Rag."

But his efforts to have his grand work *Treemonisha* published met with one failure after another. The opera was eventually published privately in 1911 though it never enjoyed a complete run in Joplin's life. He would also publish "Felicity Rag," "Kismet Rag," and "New Rag" later that year. In 1913, Joplin established his own publishing company with the help of his new wife Lottie. "Magnetic Rag" was the first song to be published under the name of his own company.

In the last two years of his life Joplin wrote several pieces of music including rags, a musical, a symphony, and a piano concerto, but none were ever published. Joplin, who had contracted syphilis, was an ill man by the early 1910s. He was eventually committed to a mental institution in New York City, and died there on April 11, 1917.

Scott Joplin was the most famous ragtime pianist-composer in the history of the genre. His contributions as a predecessor to jazz are immense. Ragtime was a necessary part of the evolution of jazz, and he had a leading role as a link in the chain. Without the efforts of Joplin, the earliest form of jazz would have sounded very different and affected later development of the genre.

How good a pianist was Joplin? There is practically no way of measuring his true skill, but his influence on others is one way of determining his abilities. It was Joplin who had a direct effect on Jelly Roll Morton and the Harlem stride piano school that includes James P. Johnson, Fats Waller, and Willie "The Lion" Smith among others.

More importantly Joplin was the first of the piano tradition that includes such famous names as Art Tatum, Oscar Peterson, Count Basie, Earl Hines, Duke Ellington, Mary Lou Williams, Jimmie Yancey, Erroll Garner, Teddy Wilson, Bud Powell, Fletcher Henderson, and Bennie Moten. He was also copied by some of the great blues pianists including Cow Cow Davenport, Pete Johnson, Albert Ammons, Meade "Lux"

Lewis, Sunnyland Slim, Roosevelt Sykes, Big Joe Turner, Otis Spann, Leroy Carr, and Professor Longhair.

Joplin was also a grand composer whose approach to creating music influenced every other jazz arranger to come after him. He gave the world an incredible body of music that includes "Elite Syncopations," "Weeping Willow," "Palm Leaf Rag," "The Chrysanthemum," "The Cascade," "The Sycamore," "Nonpareil," "Gladiolus," "Rose Leaf Rag," and "The Entertainer."

"The Entertainer" was used in the hit movie *The Sting*, which starred Paul Newman and Robert Redford. Suddenly, fifty-seven years after his death, the grand popularity that had eluded him during his lifetime was granted to Joplin. The song raced up the charts and became one of the biggest hits of the year. The influence of Joplin and ragtime were undeniable.

The spell he cast over his audience nearly one hundred years ago continues to this day among modern music fans. It is not only jazz buffs who have bought his compositions, but a cross-section of music fans. A spate of books has been published about Joplin. They only embellish the legend of the man rated as the greatest of the ragtime artists.

Although Joplin spent only a few years in Sedalia, Missouri, it became one of the centers that has kept his name alive years after his death. The annual Scott Joplin Festival is held in Sedalia and attracts ragtime enthusiasts from all over the world proving that the public never gets tired of a good thing. There are few jazz artists who can boast of an annual festival held in their honor.

Today, Scott Joplin is probably more popular than he was at the height of his career. Although ragtime has never been given major recognition because it lacked the blue notes and improvisations that characterized jazz, Joplin did his part to increase its popularity. With his "Maple Leaf Rag" there is no denying his place as an important pioneer in the evolution of jazz. The power of Joplin continues to reign.

Discography

Ragtime, Vol. 3 (Early 1900s), Biograph BLP 10100.
Piano Rags by Scott Joplin, Nonesuch 71248.
The Easy Winners, Angel 47170.
Digital Ragtime/Wall Street Rag, Angel 47199.
Piano Works, RCA 7993.
Original Rags, Jazz Classics 157262.
The Entertainer, Drive 3531.
Ragtime Guitar, Easydisc 7026.

Scott Joplin's Rag Time, Greener Pastures 1.
Magnetic Rag, Angel 36078.
Palm Leaf Rag, Angel 36074.
Piano Rags: Rifkin, Vol. 2, Nonesuch 1264.
Piano Rags, Rifkin, Vol. 3. Nonesuch 1305.
Ragtime, Vol. 2, Jazz Anthology 5137.
Ragtime, Vol. 1, Jazz Anthology 5134.
Ragtime, Vol. 2 (1900–1910) [live], Biograph BLP-1108.
1916 (Classic Solos from Piano Rolls), Biograph BLP-1006.

EUBIE BLAKE (1883–1983)

The Historian

The history of jazz is filled with those who left us too early—Bix
Beiderbecke, Charlie Parker, Billie Holiday, Chick Webb, Eddie Lang,
Bennie Moten, Buddy Bolden, Fats Waller, Charlie Christian, Jimmie
Blanton and John Coltrane, to name a few. However, there are some jazz
artists who enjoyed a long, prosperous life, including the man known as
"The Historian." His name was Eubie Blake.

James Eubie Blake was born on February 7, 1883, in Baltimore,
Maryland. One of the few early jazz pioneers unable to claim an authen-
tic New Orleans birth certificate, he nevertheless developed a love for the
root music of jazz. The son of former slaves, he received encouragement
from his parents and at six was already playing the organ. From the start
Blake showed a definite touch on the keyboards.

His biggest influence during his most impressionable years was Jesse
Pickett, a piano man who traveled throughout the East entertaining audiences with his unique brand of showmanship and musical ability.
Although he had an important impact on the young Blake, his young fan
would eventually surpass him in fame and capability. However, Pickett
was one of the many unsung heroes of early jazz who never received the
credit that he deserved mostly because he never had a chance to record.

At the age of sixteen Blake composed the "Charleston Rag," a considerable achievement for someone so young. He was also at this time playing in local sporting houses and at rent parties. Already an advanced

player, he was one of the prime ragtime pianists along with Scott Joplin, James Scott and Joseph Lamb. Eventually, Blake moved out of the sporting houses and joined a medicine show, a popular form of entertainment at the turn of the century.

As part of the Dr. Frazier Medicine Show, Blake played melodeon and delighted audiences as a dancer. But the rigors of the traveling show were too much for him and he moved to New York where he backed Madison Reed. Blake would return to Baltimore and remain there until 1915. However, he would on occasion play dates in nearby centers such as Atlantic City and other East Coast locales.

He was a mainstay at the Goldfield Hotel in Baltimore throughout much of the early 1910s. Blake also returned to playing other venues like sporting houses and rent parties. In the early days, the ragtime-influenced jazz that he was such a proud practitioner of was deemed unfit music. "Jass," as it was known at the turn of the century, was crude music intended for frequenters of bordellos. But, eventually jazz would be hailed as American's classical music and performed in the best venues in the country.

Blake gained a solid reputation as one of the best ragtime pianists and even earned an encouraging word from stride piano legend James P. Johnson. It would require the brilliance of Johnson to transform the best elements of ragtime into jazz. As jazz developed into a more sophisticated music and left ragtime behind, Blake remained dedicated and unwilling to change with the times.

Despite the shift from ragtime to a more bluesy sound, Blake made a good living as a piano player in the Baltimore area and played Atlantic City in the summertime. In 1914, he caught a break when the first of his compositions, "Chevy Chase," was published. Interestingly, it was not a ragtime piece but more of a musical comedy. It was a stage piece and writing music for the stage would be the path that he would follow for the next several years.

In 1915, Blake joined Joe Porter's Serenaders, a six-piece outfit. It was in Porter's band that he met composer, bandleader, and vocalist Nobel Sissle. Since Sissle was such an important part of the Eubie Blake story it is necessary to include him in Blake's biography.

Sissle was born August 10, 1899, in Indianapolis, Indiana. He was more of a singer than a musician. After honing his skills he formed his first group in 1914 in his hometown of Indianapolis, but the band folded in a few short months. Later, he found work in Baltimore with Porter's Serenaders. Sissle assembled his second group in 1915 called the Marcato Band. It was an eight-piece outfit that included Blake on piano, two trumpets, trombone, clarinet, string bass, banjo and drums. Although they played a few dates they never found enough work to keep them going and they disbanded by the beginning of the summer. An outstanding lyricist, Sissle was the perfect partner for Blake. One of the first songs they wrote together was "Its All Your Fault," and singer Sophie Tucker turned it into a hit. The partnership would last through the many changes that occurred in jazz.

Once they had tasted success Blake and Sissle left Baltimore and moved to New York where they joined James Reese Europe's Society Orchestra. Europe was a pioneer who composed for large ensembles which contained over fifty members. He had a major influence on the big bands of the 1930s. Europe incorporated ragtime into his own style and was swinging hard long before anyone heard of Goodman, Basie, Ellington, Henderson, or any of the other big bands. When Europe was stabbed to death in 1919, Blake and Sissle moved on.

They found work on the vaudeville circuit and continued to write songs together. They eventually graduated to Broadway and played in *Shuffle Along*, a show that drew praise and made money. Although successful, the duo of Blake and Sissle would break up and Eubie would team up with Andy Razaf who wrote lyrics for Fats Waller. But like many musicians, Blake's career was decimated by the Depression. His wife died at this time and Blake was at the lowest ebb of his personal and professional life.

It wasn't until after the attack on Pearl Harbor that Blake's career turned around and headed in a positive direction. He played in hundreds of USO shows criss-crossing the country. He also remarried during this period of time. After the war, Blake found work in a variety of venues including teaching and later on in the 1950s in the new medium of television.

In the 1950s, amidst the creation of free jazz, hard bop, and avant-garde, there was a ragtime revival. At the center of the renaissance was Eubie Blake, who was a living master. He played many of the ragtime festivals throughout the United States and Canada. Despite the increase in concert dates the recording side of Blake's career was severely neglected. This wrong was righted with the Columbia product *The 86 Years of Eubie Blake*.

It was this album, released in the heavy flower power and psychedelic days of 1969, that truly re-energized Blake's recording career. Sudden interest in the early blues and ragtime made Blake a cult hero among interested fans. Not only could he still play with the power and agility of a younger man, but he was also a living link to the bygone era of ragtime. With the release of the movie *The Sting*, ragtime enjoyed an even greater revival and Blake soaked up his newly found fame.

His 1969 appearance at the Newport Jazz Festival, where he

delighted crowds with his still superior technique, opened other concert venues. He played the Montreux Jazz Festival in 1973 at the age of 91. He would continue to appear in concerts and Broadway shows until he was 98. He also owned his own label, Eubie Blake Music, for a time.

On February 12, 1983, one hundred years and five days after his birth, Eubie Blake, the brilliant ragtime pianist who survived many peaks and valleys in his long, illustrious career, died.

Eubie Blake is a genuine legend of jazz. For eighty years he entertained audiences in various venues including bordellos, rent house parties, vaudeville, Broadway, medicine shows, open-air concerts, festivals, and USO shows. Although he experienced first hand the entire history of jazz, Blake never wavered in his dedication to his ragtime roots. There is something to say for this dedication.

He was a two-handed piano player with incredibly long, dexterous fingers capable of dancing along the keys to produce the intricate syncopation of ragtime and basic blues. He was also quite able to play show tunes (many of them he wrote himself) with a particular twinkle that added dimensions to each song. Arguably not the greatest piano player in the history of jazz, he was one of the most interesting and versatile. He could have easily participated in any of the later schools that mushroomed before and after the Second World War, but remained rooted in ragtime.

Blake, along with Lucky Roberts, Willie Gant, James P. Johnson, Willie "The Lion" Smith, and Stephen Henderson influenced the next generation of piano players which included Fats Waller, Donald Lambert, Bill Basie, and Earl Hines. But Blake was also an influence on any musician who decided to take up the piano. There was fluidity to his music, a personal touch that separated him from other ivory ticklers.

He was also a historian. He witnessed the creation of jazz, lived through the New Orleans Tradition, the jazz age, the big band and swing era, bebop, hard bop, free jazz, avant-garde, jazz fusion, acid jazz, third stream, universal, the new traditionalist and other offshoots of the genre. He is the only jazz artist to live to be a hundred years old. In a field where so many have died young he was an anomaly. Almost as remarkable was his musical facility into his 90s. Blake not only could still play powerfully, he could also sing with a warm, rich voice.

He gave the world an incredible amount of music throughout his long career. A partial lists includes "Charleston Rag," "Dicties on Seventh Avenue," "Black Keys on Parade," "Troublesome Ivories," "Chevy Chase," "The Dream," "Memories of You," "I'm Just Wild About Harry," "You're Lucky to Me," "Old Fashioned Love," "If I Could Be with You One Hour Tonight," "Love Will Find a Way," "Bandanna Days," "Gypsy Blues," "If

You've Never Been Vamped by a Brownskin (You've Never Been Vamped at All)," "In Honeysuckle Time," and an interesting version of "Maple Leaf Rag."

In his long career, he worked with an impressive list of artists. Alberta Hunter, George Brashear, Ernest Elliott, Elmer Chambers, Fletcher Henderson, Charlie Dixon, Don Redman, Bob Darch, Chink Johnson, Frank Signorelli, Johnny Mercer, Jimmy Lytell, Joe Jordan, B.G. DeSylva, Eddie Daniels, Andy Razaf, Joe Augustine, Phil Napoleon, Buster Bailey, Bernard Addison, Ethel Waters, and of course Noble Sissle were just some of his partners throughout the years. There is scarcely a jazz musician whom Blake did not share the stage with at one time or another.

Although other jazz artists have gained more fame than Blake and are better remembered, he remains a legend. There is not one single individual who can boast the same walk through jazz history that Blake enjoyed. He was a unique performer and because of the wide musical path he cut, the Eubie Blake story is one of the most heartwarming tales in jazz.

Discography

The Wizard of the Ragtime Piano, 20th Century 3003.
The Marches I Played on the Old Ragtime Piano, RCA 610.
Golden Reunion in Ragtime, Stereoddities 1900.
The 86 Years of Eubie Blake, Columbia 2223.
Live Concert, Eubie Blake EBM 5.
Eubie Blake Introducing Jim Hession, Eubie Blake EBM 6.
Eubie Blake and His Friends, Eubie Blake EBM 3.
Eubie Blake & His Protégés, Eubie Blake EBM 8.
Wild About Eubie, Columbia 34504.
Eubie Blake Song Hits, Eubie Blake 9.
Tricky Fingers, Quicksilver 9003.
Memories of You, Biograph 112.
Blues and Rags (1917–1921), Biograph 1011.
Blues & Spirituals (1921), Biograph 1012.
Rags to Classics, Stash 128.
That's Ragtime! ARI 2116.
More Ragtime! ARI 2124.
Jazz Piano Masters, Chiaroscuro 170.
An American Classic: Eubie Blake, Music Masters 20013.

DON REDMAN (1900–1964)

The Arranger

Throughout the history of jazz many individuals have made enormous impacts because of their dedication, skill, and love for the music. Different personalities are remembered for what they gave to the genre. Louis Armstrong was a fountainhead, a first-rate trumpeter. Charlie Parker was hailed as the messiah of the modern jazz movement. Jo Jones holds a special place among drummers for his revolutionary approach to playing the instrument. But there are others who were important in their own right for the contributions they made including the man known as "The Arranger." His name was Don Redman.

Donald Mathew Redman was born on July 29, 1900, in Piedmont, West Virginia. He came from a musical family. His father was a music teacher and his brother Lewis led a band in Maryland and on the East Coast for many years. Redman was a child prodigy and began playing the trumpet at the age of three. By his twelfth year he was proficient on all the wind instruments including oboe. It was this ability as a multi-instrumentalist that would enable him to achieve immortal status as an arranger. His familiarity with the range and color of sound that each instrument could produce allowed him to compose his intricate masterpieces.

Perhaps the most important musical training he obtained was as a student at the conservatories in Boston and Chicago, as well as at Storer's College and Harper's Ferry. At these schools he learned theory and structure. But while he was absorbing the rudiments of music on paper and studying all the great composers, he was also digging deeply into the practical musical scene where a new blues-oriented music called jazz was beginning to take shape.

In 1922, he joined Billie Page's Broadway Syncopators and traveled to New York with the group. It was in the Big Apple that he met Fletcher Henderson who was leading his own big band. Although a skilled musician, Redman joined Henderson's outfit as the arranger and began to experiment with the current state of jazz. From his starting date in 1923 Redman began to lay the groundwork for the big band era that would last until the middle of the 1940s.

Redman blended his taste for New Orleans bluesy and elastic but precise ensemble playing with a desire to swing with improvisation. His task was facilitated with the arrival of Louis Armstrong into the Henderson ranks in 1924. It was Armstrong's ability to play brilliant solos that inspired Redman to pit the horns against each other in the call-and-response mode of the early blues hollers of the field workers. Redman also wrote arrangements that called for the saxophonists to play in harmony thus creating one wall of sound. With the great Armstrong capable of playing fiery solos he used this great weapon like a lyrical serpent to wrap around the sound of the other horns.

Redman also introduced the use of advanced harmonies that were much more sophisticated than those that emerged from New Orleans. He also brought in sudden changes in rhythm as the song took on different and interesting twists and turns. All of the elements added up to the most creative, swinging songs in jazz at the time and propelled the Henderson Band to the forefront. Although Coleman Hawkins, Louis Armstrong, Charlie Green, Fletcher Henderson, Buster Bailey, and Tommy Ladnier gained most of the fame, it was Redman's arrangements that were the true source of the group's popularity.

For four years Redman wrote innovative arrangements for Fletcher Henderson's big band. But Redman was a restless soul and shocked the jazz world in 1927 when he left Henderson to become musical director of Detroit's McKinney's Cotton Pickers. Although it was a novelty band, Redman wasted no time in transforming the Cotton Pickers into a full-fledged big band, mostly by stealing some of Henderson's best soloists, including Joe Smith, Benny Carter and Coleman Hawkins.

Within a year he had rearranged the saxophone section and had written a number of first-rate arrangements that were perfectly executed by his revamped and more talented lineup. The Cotton Pickers enjoyed great commercial success and replaced the Henderson orchestra as the top band in the land. In the four years that Redman was the musical director of the Cotton Pickers they enjoyed unprecedented fame.

After he left McKinney's and before he formed his own group, Redman was reunited with Louis Armstrong. He recorded and arranged for Satchmo during this brief time. The combination of the greatest trumpeter and the greatest arranger of all-time created an interesting brand of music. However, their collaboration together was too short-lived.

In the fall of 1931 Redman formed his first band, made up of a number of ex–McKinney players and members of Horace Henderson's outfit. Throughout the 1930s Redman would mold his band into one of the most exciting groups of the era. Although there were many personnel changes at one time or another, the brass section boasted trombonists Benny Morton, Fred Robinson, Claude Jones, and trumpeters Sidney De Paris, Shirley Clay, and Leonard Davis. The sax section included Edward Inge,

Robert Carroll, and Rupert Cole. The rhythm unit was comprised of drummer Manzie Johnson, pianist Horace Henderson, guitarist Talcott Reeves and bassist Robert Ysaguirre. On occasion, Redman played alto sax. The group would remain together as a unit and toured regularly until 1940. They played many important radio shows and in films, and recorded a number of songs, mostly Redman compositions. However the group never could crack the upper echelon of the jazz scene.

Although he was extremely busy with his own aggregation Redman found time to write for Paul Whiteman, Ben Pollack, Isham Jones, Nat Shilkret and a host of others. He also created special arrangements for crooner Bing Crosby and composed two of the most famous songs in jazz at this juncture of his career—"Deep Purple" for Jimmy Dorsey and "Three O'clock Whistle" for Count Basie. He would also contribute to the songbooks of Harry James, Jimmy Lunceford, Charlie Barnet, Ella Fitzgerald and Pearl Bailey. After a brief time as a freelancer, Redman reorganized another band. However the group didn't last long.

Although he would re-form bands for special residencies during the Second World War, Redman was primarily an arranger for a number of big bands. In 1946, with travel to Europe once again a possibility, he formed a big band and went overseas and remained in Europe until the summer of 1947. In 1949, he had his own television series. It was a short-lived project and by 1951 he was the musical director for Pearl Bailey.

In the last years of his life Redman made few public appearances, but when he did they were special treats. He played piano at the Georgia Minstrels concert in 1962. At the Sissle-Blake Grass Roots concert in 1964, Redman backed the legendary duo on soprano saxophone. He continued to write arrangements for various bands. On November 30, 1964, Don Redman, the brilliant arranger who left his musical fingerprints on four decades of jazz, died in New York City.

Don Redman was an innovator of the highest order. His brilliant compositions pointed to the future and the big band sound. He was constantly ahead of his peers and although his musical abilities were sharp, it was his skill in writing that created his legend. Without Don Redman, the history of jazz would be different in inexplicable ways.

He enjoyed creating walls of sound that swung against each other as well as complimented one another. He was the first to group sections together so that they were as overpowering as a single voice. His understanding of rhythms, melodies, harmonies, and the proper blend of all three is second to none. He saw the multi-dimensional aspects of the structure of music in layers. His musical imagination was equal to that of any of the great composers.

It is Redman who is responsible for providing jazz with the respect and class it earned as a serious music played boisterously by excellent musicians. In the early days jazz was considered decadent and declasse; Redman turned it into an art form. He was always blessed with extremely talented musicians who were able to breathe life into his compositions.

Redman gave the world a number of classics. A partial list includes "Sugar Foot Stomp," "Words," "Copenhagen," "Albany Bound," "Henderson Stomp," "Whiteman Stomp," "If I Could Be with You One Hour," "Rocky Road," "Gee Baby, Ain't I Good to You?," "Shakin,'" "The African," "Chant of the Weed," "Got the Jitters," "Sophisticated Lady," "Exactly Like You," "Sunny Side of the Street," "Sweet Sue," "Deep Purple," and "Three O'clock Whistle." Hundreds of his arrangements were recorded. With the exception of Duke Ellington, he is arguably the most prolific jazz songwriter of all time.

At the end of his life he wrote a number of extended compositions that were never published. These works, if they were ever brought forth, would shed some light on a side of him that the public is unaware of. It would, of course, only enhance his reputation as the most brilliant arranger of the twentieth century.

Although he will be remembered as the most imaginative and important arranger in the history of jazz, he was also a capable musician and singer. It was Redman who inadvertently recorded the first improvised scat solo on the song "My Papa Doesn't Two Time." Arguably, as a musician, he never received the credit he was due.

Don Redman helped build the career of Fletcher Henderson, and without his arranger it is doubtful that Henderson would have achieved the recognition he did. Even more than that, he taught Henderson how to write and arrange big band numbers. Redman was more than just a right hand man with any project he was involved with; he was the brain. He proved his genius when he took over McKinney's Cotton Pickers and turned them around, creating a big band that rivaled the best including Henderson's own outfit. There is hardly a big band of the 1920s and 1930s that didn't benefit from Redman's incredible imagination.

As a session man, musician, bandleader, singer, and especially as an arranger, Redman made enormous contributions to the world of jazz. While many of the most famous names in jazz will be remembered for their outstanding musical abilities, and others are known for their position as bandleaders, Redman will always live in the pages of jazz history with his own special place as "The Arranger."

Discography

Shakin' the African, HEP 1001.

Doin' the New Lowdown, HEP 1004.
For Europeans Only (Live) Steeplechase 36020.
Don Redman's Park Avenue Patter, Golden Crest CR 3017.
Dixieland in High Society, Roulette 25070.
Master of the Big Band, RCA PV-520.
Star Dreams, Drive Archive 41211.
1931–1933, Classics 543.
1933–1936, Classics 553.
1936–1939, Classics 574.
Doin' What I Please, ASV/Living Era 5110-2.
Chant of the Weed, Pearl 1043.
Swiss Radio Days, Vol. 11: Live from Geneva, TCB 2112.

ART TATUM (1909–1956)

King of Jazz Piano

The world of jazz has been blessed with some of the most talented piano players to ever sit down at the instrument. Not only did these individuals contribute widely to the creation and progress of jazz, but they also added to the wealth of world music. While many practitioners have been cited for their wonderful achievements, one particular artist was revered for his unsurpassed technical skills and earned the title "King of Jazz Piano." His name was Art Tatum.

Arthur Tatum, Jr., was born on October 13, 1909, in Toledo, Ohio. A spirited young boy who was born nearly blind, he did not let his physical limitations get in the way of his musical ambitions. While he did pick up some formal instruction at the school for the blind in Toledo, he was primarily self-taught. Perhaps the fact that his parents were amateur musicians—his father played the guitar and his mother played the piano—had something to do with his gift for music. Although he would make his mark in the world of jazz as a pianist, he also studied guitar, violin, and accordion.

Like every other piano player discovering the limits of the instrument, he was steered towards a classical style. However, Tatum was more enthralled with the big three stride and ragtime pianists: James P. Johnson,

Willie "The Lion" Smith, and Fats Waller. Although Johnson and Smith had a solid influence on Tatum, it was Waller who would make the greatest impact. Interestingly, although Tatum worshiped Waller, it was the latter who was in awe of the former. In interviews Fats was constantly praising Tatum, a major ego boost for Art.

By the time he was sixteen he was ready to seek his fame and fortune. He formed his own band and toured through the Toledo area and other parts of Ohio. Although he had not reached his musical maturity there was no doubt that Tatum was the focus of the group. Although still in his teens, he was drawing praise from critics, fans and fellow musicians for his remarkable style.

Tatum disbanded his group and found work in Speed Webb's band where he continued to astonish everyone who heard him play with his superior piano skills. Although he never recorded with Webb, the experience proved to be a positive one for Tatum. He learned important show business practices that would serve him well for his entire career.

Tatum also began to carve out his outstanding reputation because of his ability to win every cutting contest he entered. In jazz, it was a matter of great pride to emerge from the vicious cutthroat piano battles as the victor. Tatum rarely lost. When other piano players heard his range, sophistication and sheer dominance of the instrument, they knew they would have to change their style. Already as a young man Tatum was influencing much older and more experienced pianists.

After a short stint in Speed Webb's band, Tatum became a disc jockey spinning the platters that mattered for station WSPD in Toledo. He also continued to gig in local nightclubs like the Tabernella and Chateau La France. While employment at the radio station provided a steady income, Tatum possessed a traveling foot. His itch was satisfied when Adelaide Hall asked him to join her on tour. He came highly recommended from a variety of jazz sources. Hall, at the strong urging of blues shouter Big Joe Turner, realized that Tatum would make an invaluable addition to her band.

Tatum arrived in the Big Apple in order to join Hall. Although he remained with her for barely over a year, he made his recording debut with her band. One of two piano players on the session, the true genius of Art Tatum was not realized on these recordings. It wasn't until a year later that he began to assert himself as one of the more dominant jazz pianists when he cut a number of classics including "Get Happy," "Indiana," "Gone With The Wind," and the definitive version of "Tiger Rag." Nearly every jazz personality for the next sixty years would record the latter song in one form or another. From this point on, he would be acknowledged as one of the masters of the piano.

He spent much of the 1930s in concert as a solo performer playing residencies in Cleveland, Chicago, New York, and Los Angeles. In 1938, he went to England and was well received across the Atlantic, creating a second fan base. He returned to the United States and worked on the West Coast for a while before playing a residency at Café Society and Kelley's.

After years of working as a soloist, Tatum formed a trio with guitarist Tiny Grimes and bass player Slam Stewart. For the next nine years he worked the concert tours and regular club circuit within the trio format. Although they developed a strong feel for one another's talents, Tatum was the featured star and expanded his burgeoning reputation during this period. If he wasn't acknowledged as the greatest piano player at the time he was at least considered one of the top three in all of jazz. Tiny Grimes would leave after a year. Stewart would also leave but would return to serve in two separate stints.

In the 1950s, Tatum recorded for Norman Granz and also continued to tour throughout the United States and Canada. On August 15, 1956, he gave his last big concert at the Hollywood Bowl. Tatum, who had been ill with kidney problems for the past eighteen months, died on November 5, 1956. He was 47 years old.

Art Tatum is considered by many to be the greatest piano player in the history of jazz. Fellow musicians, critics, and diehard jazz fans all speak of him with breathless wonder. His complex technique elevated jazz into the realm of classical music. In a world plentiful of good musicians, Tatum was great.

His dexterity was truly astonishing. He was capable of playing long runs of notes that sounded like a train rushing through a wall. He also laid down killer chord combinations that bridged his improvised solos of perfect craftsmanship. While he was technically superb, he played with a definite emotion that gave his music a dangerous edge.

He had an impeccable sense of timing, rhythm, harmony and melody. The sounds that he transferred from his creative mind to his nimble hands flowed like the surge of uninterrupted electricity. There was nothing he could not do on the piano. He was a complete player and recorded innumerable classics that captured the attention of the entire jazz world. However, despite the many accolades heaped on Tatum, many felt that he never really tapped into his immense talent.

He was a rare blend of tremendous technique and emotional nuance. He played with frightening speed and a comprehensive understanding of the piano that had never been seen before or since. The sheer velocity of his attack helped him pave the way for bebop pianists Thelonious Monk and Bud Powell. Many of the great keyboard virtuosos who would surface in the next forty years, including Keith Jarrett, Chick Corea, and Herbie Hancock, owe a debt to Tatum.

Tatum's sound was so complex because his right hand could work independently of his left hand. Often, on many of his recordings and during his live performances, he made it sound as if there were two piano players instead of just one. He advanced the basic elements of stride into the twenty first century although he died forty-five years before the start of the new millennium. He began where James P. Johnson, Fats Waller, and Willie "The Lion" Smith left off.

Although he was classified as a swing artist and there were swing elements in his playing, Tatum was more than that. He was far ahead of his time and foretold the direction that the piano would take in years to come. He sounded as if he belonged in the past, the present and the future simultaneously. There was such a complex element in his playing that it was beyond category.

He shares a special place in jazz piano history with Oscar Peterson and Erroll Garner. Both Peterson and Garner, although categorized as swing artists, were capable of doing much more. These three pianists ushered in the modern age of jazz piano while maintaining the best elements of the old guard. With every note they played they were assimilating different periods in jazz history.

Tatum left a lasting impression on a number of jazz figures including Ray Bryant, Russ Freeman, Buddy Greco, Charles Mingus, Bob Moses, Oscar Peterson, Michel Petrucciani, Hazel Scott, Lennie Tristano, Joe Bushkin, John Coates, Jr., Mickey Tucker, Ramsey Lewis, Sammy Price, Joe Zawinul, Jon Hendricks, and Junior Mance. Countless musicians have plundered his extensive recorded catalog over the years and every time someone records another of his songs it is a tribute to Tatum.

He gave the world a large number of classics. A partial lists includes "Get Happy," "Indiana," "Gone with the Wind," "I've Got My Love to Keep Me Warm," "I Know That You Know," "Aunt Hagar's Blues," "The Man I Love," "Jitterbug Waltz," "Too Marvelous for Words," "It's the Talk of the Town," "Stompin' at the Savoy," "Caravan," "You're Driving Me Crazy," "This Can't Be Love," "Fine and Dandy," "Ain't Misbehavin'," "How High the Moon," and "Perdido." More importantly, many of his songs were the starting points for the compositions of others.

His contributions extend beyond the abundance of classics he created; he also played on numerous sessions for a number of important jazz artists. His distinctive piano skills can be heard on records made by Louis Armstrong, Coleman Hawkins, Roy Eldridge, Adelaide Hall, Billie Holiday, Big Joe Turner and Benny Carter, among others. By appearing on the recordings of others Tatum was simply supplementing his already impressive credentials.

The story of Art Tatum is one of inspiration, courage, and understanding. He was an individual who overcame many obstacles to achieve his widespread fame. He lived and died for his art. He loved the music that he created with his unlimited genius and never wanted to stop playing. Although he left us almost fifty years ago no one has forgotten the genius hailed as the "King of Jazz Piano."

Discography

Art Tatum, Classic Piano Solos 1934–1937, GRD 607.
I Got Rhythm Vol. 3, 1935–1944, GRD 630.
1932–1934, Classic 507.
1934–1940, Classic 560.
1940–1944, Classic 800.
1944, Classic 825.
1945–1947, Classic 982.
1949, Classic 1104.
On the Sunny Side, 1944–1945, Pearl 1066.
The Art of Tatum, ASL 5164.
Cabu Collection, Masters of Jazz 8020.
The Complete Jazz Chronicle: Solo Sessions, STC 8253.
The Standard Transcriptions—Piano Solos, 1935–1945, STC 8260.
The V-Discs, Great Jazz Masters 9008.
Standards—From Standard Transcriptions, Great Jazz Masters 9022.
Piano Starts Here, 1933–1949, Sony 64690.
Masterpieces Vol. 16—Original Historic Recordings, EPM 158632.
20th Century Piano Genius 1955, PLG 531763.
Ultimate Art Tatum, Verve 559877.
The Art Tatum Solo Masterpieces, Vol. 1, Pablo PACD-2405-432-2.
The Art Tatum Solo Masterpieces, Vol. 2, Pablo PACD-2405-433-2.
The Art Tatum Solo Masterpieces, Vol. 3, Pablo PACD-2405-434-2.
The Art Tatum Solo Masterpieces, Vol. 4, Pablo PACD-2405-435-2.
The Art Tatum Solo Masterpieces, Vol. 5, Pablo PACD-2405-436-2.
The Art Tatum Solo Masterpieces, Vol. 6, Pablo PACD-2405-437-2.
The Art Tatum Solo Masterpieces, Vol. 7, Pablo PACD-2405-438-2.
The Art Tatum Solo Masterpieces, Vol. 8, Pablo PACD-2405-439-2.
The Complete Pablo Group Masterpieces, Pablo 6PACD-4401-2.
The Complete Pablo Solo Masterpieces, Pablo 7PACD-4404-2.
Art the Best of Art Tatum, Pablo PACD-2405–418-2.
The Tatum Group Masterpieces, Vol. 1, Pablo PACD-2405-424-2.

The Tatum Group Masterpieces, vol. 2, Pablo PACD-2405-425-2.
The Tatum Group Masterpieces, vol. 3, Pablo PACD-2405-426-2.
The Tatum Group Masterpieces, vol. 4, Pablo PACD-2405-427-2.
The Tatum Group Masterpieces, vol. 5, Pablo PACD-2405-428-2.
The Tatum Group Masterpieces, vol. 6, Pablo PACD-2405-429-2.
The Tatum Group Masterpieces, vol. 7, Pablo PACD-2405-430-2.
The Tatum Group Masterpieces, vol. 8, Pablo PACD-2405-431-2.
Tatum, Piano Starts Here, Columbia 64690.
Art Tatum, Art of Tatum, Decca DL-8715.
Art Tatum Masterpieces, MCA MCAC2-4019.
Art Tatum, God Is in the House, High Note 7030.
Art Tatum, At the Piano, Vol. 1, GNP-9025.
Art Tatum, At the Piano, Vol. 2, GNP-9026.
Art Tatum, Vol. 1, Verve MGV-8101-5.
Art Tatum, Vol. 2, Verve MGV-8102-5.
Genius of Art Tatum, Vol. 1, Verve 8036.
Genius of Art Tatum, Vol. 2, Verve 8037.
Genius of Art Tatum, Vol. 3, Verve 8038.
Genius of Art Tatum, Vol. 4, Verve 8039.
Genius of Art Tatum, Vol. 5, Verve 8040.
Genius of Art Tatum, Vol. 6, Verve 8055.
Genius of Art Tatum, Vol. 7, Verve 8056.
Genius of Art Tatum, Vol. 8, Verve 8057.
Genius of Art Tatum, Vol. 9, Verve 8058.

DJANGO REINHARDT (1910–1953)

The Gypsy Soul

There is a vast assortment of heartwarming and fascinating biographies of jazz personalities in the genre's one hundred plus year history. The one underlining characteristic of each story is how the music managed to capture a player's imagination. While the United States is the foremost land of jazz, the rich textured music spread throughout the globe. One of the most exotic tales in jazz is that of "The Gypsy Soul." His name was Django Reinhardt.

Jean Baptiste Reinhardt was born on January 23, 1910, in Liverchies, Belgium. A gypsy, Reinhardt grew up enthralled by the hypnotic strains of gypsy music. Like all budding musicians he was obsessed with imitating the captivating sounds that he heard. He first picked up the violin before switching to the guitar later on in life. When he was eighteen, he had made sufficient progress, but a disaster almost put an end to his musical ambitions. Reinhardt burned his fingers in a caravan fire that severely limited his dexterity.

However, it is a tribute to Reinhardt's musical genius and his human spirit that he was able to fashion an intricate guitar style that allowed him the maximum use of the three fingers available to him. It was around this time that he discovered the treasure trove that was American jazz—notably Louis Armstrong—which pointed him down a direct path. Although he yearned to be a successful jazz musician, he needed to team up with someone to work with, a partner and a kindred spirit. He found one in Stephane Grappelli.

Stephane Grappelli was born in 1908 in Paris, and by the age of twelve he had acquired his first violin. His first professional gigs were with theatre bands and then he discovered jazz. Although the violin was not an important instrument in jazz, Grappelli had definite ambitions to make it one. One night, in a club, Philippe Brun introduced Grappelli to Reinhardt. Together they decided to form an all string group, an anomaly in jazz at the time, but the two European rebels were determined to make it work.

Reinhardt and Grappelli were a formidable duo. They called their group the Quintet of the Hot Club of France. The outfit was comprised of two rhythm guitars and a string bass plus Reinhardt and Grappelli who improvised hot solos over the solid, swinging beat of the rhythm section. The chemistry between Reinhardt and Grappelli was the focus of the band. Grappelli was a perfect foil to the fire and intensity of Reinhardt's single run notes of pure ecstasy.

The recordings the duo made with their unique group were of seminal importance. The two became the first true jazz stars to emerge from countries other than the United States. It was a period of good times, good friends, and good music. Unfortunately, the shadow of the impending war broke them up. Grappelli remained in Great Britain while Reinhardt returned to France.

During the occupation of France, Reinhardt would not be subdued and continued to make music. He formed a quintet with clarinetist Hubert Rostaing and although the latter was a fine musician, he was unable to inspire Reinhardt like his old bandmate Grappelli. The group consisted of Reinhardt, Rostaing, a bass player, a drummer and a second guitarist.

Reinhardt, always defiant, was fortunate not to have been dragged to a concentration camp because of his gypsy roots. He emerged at the end of the war unscathed.

The last few years of his career were marked with inconsistency as he enjoyed limited success jamming with American jazz artists who were passing through Europe. He even traveled to America and played in a series of solo concerts including an appearance with Duke Ellington. However, he was poorly received. Also in 1947, Reinhardt switched to electric guitar and as a result his style changed. He played fewer chords and the magic of his earlier flourishes was diminished.

Perhaps the best times that Reinhardt enjoyed during the last few years of his life were the sporadic meetings with his old friend Grappelli. Although they didn't swing as hard as they had done during their golden years together, they were still able to conjure up some of the old magic. Unfortunately, Reinhardt was retreating into his own universe and near the end of his life he recorded and played infrequently.

On May 16, 1953, in Fontainebleau, France, Django Reinhardt, the majestic gypsy soul with the rapid-fire licks and jazz sensibility that would influence generations of guitarists, died of a stroke. He was only 43 years old.

Django Reinhardt is one of the unique characters in jazz history. His exotic background, his physical disability, his distinct technique, his passion for the music, his flair, his individualism are all part of the package that made him such a legend. While there have been better musicians who have attained greater heights, none ever possessed the uniqueness of Reinhardt. He wrote an important chapter in jazz that has been admired by fans throughout the world.

There was his captivating style. He combined the rich, folksy European music of his youth with the dynamics of swing. His understanding of exotic rhythms was second to none. He possessed an inherent and uncanny feel and passion for improvisation as well as a vision of the blues, the two foundations of jazz. His inborn musical genius, honed to a fine skill, was like an irresistible flame was drawn to everyone.

He was first and foremost a lead guitarist who played like a lead guitarist. He rode over and under the rhythm that his band created, weaving long, intricate passages of beauty. His solos were beautifully crafted works that revealed a true artist. His quick run of notes and octave passages were like a wave that carried the listener away to another dimension of life. There was a depth to his solos, a wizard-like edge that never failed to stun his listeners and those who tried to imitate him.

To better understand the genius of Reinhardt one must understand the role of jazz guitarists of the time. Jefferson Mumford is credited as the first jazz guitarist and he played in Buddy Bolden's band. But Mumford and Johnny St. Cyr, who later backed Louis Armstrong, Jelly Roll Morton, Kid Ory, Freddie Keppard, and King Oliver, among others, were accompanists, strumming chords behind the soloists. It wasn't until Lonnie Johnson and Eddie Lang showed up on the scene in the 1920s that the guitar took on more of an individual voice in jazz bands. Although Lang and Johnson did much to expand the role of the guitar, none played with the same delicacy, drive, or passion as Reinhardt.

In many ways, Reinhardt was the Robert Johnson of jazz guitar. During the 1930s, while bluesman Robert Johnson was recording his best licks, which would influence blues guitar playing for the next sixty years, Reinhardt was doing his own thing with six strings that would inspire the best jazz guitarists for the rest of the century. Although they led much different lives, both remain outstanding starting points for aspiring blues and jazz guitarists. The study of Reinhardt's technique is an essential learning process for any musician serious about becoming a jazz guitarist.

Reinhardt was a guitar hero long before the term was coined. Although he never received the credit he was due during his lifetime, he has been awarded his proper accolades since then. After his death a small coterie of guitarists intended to maintain the Reinhardt legacy. The Argentinean Oscar Aleman, in an effort to duplicate Django's sound, played the same type of oval-shaped guitar as his hero. Philip Catherine was so inspired by Reinhardt that he became a guitar player. Birell Legren, a Belgian, churned out hard bop that captured the same emotions as his idol. Rene Thomas, another Belgian, also drew his main inspiration from Django. But Reinhardt's influence goes much deeper.

A partial list of those in the jazz and blues world whom he influenced includes B. B. King, Jethro Burns, Tiny Moore, Bola Sete, Cal Collins, Dave Holland, John McLaughlin, Wes Montgomery, Babik Reinhardt, Gabor Szabo, Bill Harris, Attila Zoller, Maria Muldaur, George Benson, and Sam T. Brown. Without a doubt, Reinhardt also had an indirect influence on rock guitarists such as Eric Clapton, Jimmy Page, Jimi Hendrix, Jeff Beck, Eric Johnson, and Duane Allman.

Reinhardt received much respect from jazz artists who passed through his area. He played and recorded with Rex Stewart, Dicky Wells, Coleman Hawkins, Benny Carter, Barney Bigard, Eddie South, and Bill Coleman. Without a doubt, among his peers, and many of those who followed after him, Reinhardt had an everlasting effect.

Because of his undeniable talent and creativity it is not surprising that he gave the world a body of classics that have stood the test of time. A partial list includes *"Vendredi 13,"* "Lover," "Apple Honey," "Crazy Rhythm," *"Nuages et Crepuscule,"* "Limehouse Blues," "China Boy," "It

Don't Mean a Thing," "Them There Eyes," "Three Little Words" and "Swing '39." Each song contained a part of him, a touch of magic from the master.

But there is more to the Django Reinhardt story than his music. There was the man himself who was obsessed with the game of billiards, cared little for schedules and was unable to read music. He was a restless spirit, spent lavishly on whatever turned his fancy, and burned with an intensity that is reserved for geniuses. He was never interested in following the crowd; he had his own agenda to attend to and set out to meet it.

In a very short time Reinhardt wrote his own page in jazz history that is parallel with anything else anyone has ever done. He was so different that he could not be copied, just admired for his spark of imagination, and his ability to mold sounds into masterpieces. He clearly demonstrated that a person didn't have to be American to be an exceptional jazz artist. There is no denying the greatness of the man with the gypsy soul and his own special place in jazz history.

Discography

Django Reinhardt: The Early Years, 1928–1934, EMI Jazz Time 7989 75-2.
The Art of Django/Django the Unforgettable, BGO 198.
Django Reinhardt and His American Friends Vol. 1 & 2, BGO 249.
Djangology, RCAL 307.
Chronological Vol. 3, Paris, JSP 343.
Art of Jazz Guitar, Leg 411.
Django Reinhardt 1934–1935, Classic 703.
Django Reinhardt 1935, Classic 727.
Django Reinhardt 1935–1936, Classic 739.
Django Reinhardt 1937, Classic 748.
Django Reinhardt 1937 Vol. 2, Classic 762.
Django Reinhardt 1937–1938, Classic 777.
Django Reinhardt 1938–1939, Classic 793.
Django Reinhardt 1939–1940, Classic 813.
Django Reinhardt 1940, Classic 831.
Django Reinhardt 1940–1941, Classic 852.
Django Reinhardt 1941–1942, Classic 877.
Django Reinhardt 1942–1943, Classic 905.
Django Reinhardt 1944–1946, Classic 945.
Django Reinhardt 1947, Classic 1001.
Django Reinhardt 1947 Vol. 2, Classic 1046.
Django Reinhardt Plays the Great Standards, EPR 808.

Django Reinhardt The Classic Early Recordings in Chronological Order, JSP 901.
Django Reinhardt His Best Recordings 1934–1942, Best of Jazz 4036.
Django Reinhardt Cabu Collection, Masters of Jazz 8018.
Django Reinhardt & Friends, Pearl 9792.
Djangology 1949, Bluebird 9988.
Best of Django Reinhardt, Bluebird 37138.
The Indispensable Django Reinhardt 1949–1950, Jazz 66468.
Django Reinhardt *Nuages* Vol. 2, 1938–1940, EPM 157222.
Le Quintette du Hot Club, EPM 157522.
Django Reinhardt Vol. 5 The Solo Sessions 1937–1943, EPM 158202.
Django Reinhardt Verve Jazz Masters 38, PLG 516931.
Django Reinhardt Souvenirs w/Stephane Grappelli, PLG 820591.
Django Reinhardt & Hubert Rostaing Vol. 4, *En Belgique* 1942, EPM 157972.
Django Reinhardt & Stephane Grappelli Parisian Swing AVD 648.
Django Reinhardt & Stephane Grappelli Swing from Paris 1935–1939, ASL 5070.
Django Reinhardt–Stephane Grappelli *Nuages*, ASL 5138.
Django Reinhardt & Stephane Grappelli: The Quintessential *Le Quintette du Hot Club de France*, ASL 5267.
Django Reinhardt & Stephane Grappelli: Original Recordings, Pearl 9738.

BILLIE HOLIDAY (1915–1959)

The Voice of Jazz

There are a number of jazz giants who have made a large impact on the music in the course of the past one hundred years. There are even those who have crossed over to enjoy success beyond the traditional borders of jazz. There are also a handful who have gained immortality for their contributions to music in the twentieth century. One such performer was dubbed the voice of jazz. Her name was Billie Holiday.

Billie Holiday was born Eleanora Fagan Gough on April 7, 1915, in Baltimore, Maryland. Holiday's life was troubled and difficult from the start. She was the daughter of Clarence Holiday, a jazz guitarist, and Sadie Fagan. The two were teenagers when Billie was born and never married. Her father would eventually occupy the guitar seat in the Fletcher Henderson Orchestra. Their paths would cross later on when Billie was a big star, but there was never any reconciliation between them.

Her teenage mother was unprepared for the rigors of single parenthood and Holiday was shuffled off from one relative to another. When she was still a young girl she witnessed the death of her great-grandmother. Young Eleanora was no stranger to hard work and was scrubbing steps and bathrooms to keep body and soul together before her teenage years. Her mother returned from New York and took Eleanora from her grandparent's place. Her mother bought a house and rented it out to roomers. She also remarried and for the first time in years Eleanora was enjoying a family life. But the death of her stepfather Bill Gough left a huge hole in her heart.

By the age of thirteen she was a working child of the ghetto, but had the mature body of a woman. She was a radiant beauty who had managed to overcome the many tragedies of her poverty-stricken life. But most importantly she had discovered music. Her favorites were Louis Armstrong and Bessie Smith. While she was scrubbing the steps of the large white houses in Baltimore and then New York, Eleanora sang, making the hard work tolerable. It was also at this time that she began to call herself Billie.

When she was thirteen Billie was raped by one of the roomers who rented from her mother. The rapist received five years in prison; Billie was sentenced to eleven years in a Catholic institution. It took her mother several months to obtain Billie's release. The scar would last the rest of her life. Billie and her mother moved to New Jersey, then to Brooklyn, New York. In order to make ends meet, the two worked as housekeepers, but underage Holiday often moonlighted as a prostitute in order to earn more money.

Although her chaotic life could have turned out to be a definite tale of tragedy, Holiday possessed a unique gift. She could sing the blues with the passion and skill of her idol, Bessie Smith. She had her own sound and needed to develop her voice, but there was no money or time for proper lessons. Billie's mother fell ill and Billie needed a regular job in order to keep them from being evicted. She walked from one Harlem club to another until she entered Pod's and Jerry's. She tried to audition as a dancer, but her gift was singing, not dancing. Finally, in a desperate attempt to secure a job, she sang. The crowd was stunned with the painful brilliance that emoted from the beautiful girl who looked much older than her fifteen years.

Billie gained a gig at the Log Cabin in Harlem. It was a good place to woodshed as it afforded her the time to get her act together. It was while at the Log Cabin that she began to gain a reputation as a special singer and met influential people. The most important contact she made was legendary Columbia producer John Hammond, who was just beginning his own personal musical journey. The man, who would record Holiday, Bruce Springsteen and Stevie Ray Vaughan, knew talent when he heard it. He realized that Holiday had a natural jazz voice and that with the right material and back up band she could be a big star. He hooked up Billie with Joe Glaser, a savvy music agent who boasted Louis Armstrong among his stable of clients.

Her first recording date was with members of Benny Goodman's band in November of 1933 when she was eighteen. The group included Charlie and Jack Teagarden and drummer Gene Krupa. She cut two songs, "Your Mother's Son-in-Law" and "Riffin' the Scotch." It was not overnight success for Holiday despite the clear fact that she possessed a magical voice. But it was only a matter of time before everyone realized that she was something special.

Since the songs didn't go over that well Holiday had no chance but to return to the Harlem dives and await her next big break. Hammond had not forgotten her and set up a recording session that included Teddy Wilson, Goodman, Roy Eldridge, Ben Webster, and Cozy Cole. During these sessions she cut "What a Little Moonlight Can Do," one of her masterpieces; it proved she was indeed something unique.

Her next recording date occurred in 1934 when she appeared in *Symphony in Black*, a one-reel film starring the Duke Ellington Orchestra. Her memorable rendition of "Big City Blues" was another positive step forward, but did not catapult her into a star role. However, the next time she would record would prove to be much different.

By 1935, Holiday had worked her way up the thriving and competitive New York bar scene and astonished the crowd at the Apollo. The entire Harlem club scene was open to her as she was able to appear anywhere she wanted to when just a couple of years before she had been banned from those same venues. Although the performance side of her career was marching ahead, it was the recording part that she struggled to establish. After several failures, it was magic time.

In 1936, she recorded with a Teddy Wilson group that included Johnny Hodges and Harry Carney from the Duke Ellington Orchestra. The next sessions she would record—under her own name—included Bunny Berigan, Artie Shaw, and Joe Bushkin. It was at this date that Billie cut "Summertime" and "Billie's Blues." Both enhanced her name in jazz circles. Over the next two years she would participate in eighteen separate recording sessions, cutting many of her famous classics, often with a Teddy Wilson band. From this point on she enjoyed the luxury of working with the elite jazzmen of the era, including Freddie Green, Jo Jones, Walter Page, Buck Clayton, and Lester Young.

Lester Young arrived in New York City with the Count Basie Band in 1937 and the special chemistry between Young and Holiday that produced pure moments of jazz magic that have never been equaled was present from the very beginning. There was a shared melancholy between the blues singer who had seen too much life and the sad saxophonist who fought personal demons. His sublime and superb tenor saxophone lines complimented her coarse, blues-tinged voice perfectly to the point that voice and instrument were seamless. They also shared a love that neither could believe and allowed to slip away.

Although she would work with big bands including Count Basie, Artie Shaw, Benny Goodman, and Duke Ellington, Holiday was better suited to small combos. In 1937, Billie traveled with Artie Shaw's Big Band, an unusual event in those days since black singers were supposed to be backed by black bands, not white ones. Shaw and Holiday were breaking down barriers. But eventually the pressures were too much and Holiday returned to Harlem, to her black world.

Although she was a popular singer, she hadn't yet attained her legendary status. It took her residency as a solo act at the Café Society to bring her the fame that she had been seeking ever since that fateful day when, as a frightened fifteen year old, she had stunned the crowd. The Frankie Newton Orchestra was the house band and the combination of Holiday and Newton's Orchestra was a dream come true. It was with Newton's band that she cut the classics "Strange Fruit," "Fine and Mellow," and "Yesterdays," and reached the apex of her recording career. Holiday stayed at the Café Society for two years and when she left she was a superstar.

Her recording sessions were events, her concerts legendary and she was a household name. Everyone was hypnotized by her stellar ability to render a song in such a way that it got into the psyche of each listener. She had a distinguished, firm, bluesy-edged voice. She had broken the color barrier, and whites enjoyed her as much as her African-American fans did.

In 1941, Holiday, who had looked for love all her life but had never found it, married Jimmy Monroe. Her mother had died and she needed someone to fill the empty void in her heart. But the marriage was not a joyous one since he was not the great comfort that she sought. Instead of security he gave her something very dangerous: a heroin habit.

While the latter part of the 1930s had been good, the next decade proved to be her most glorious and also her most frustrating. Those who were unaware of Billie Holiday at the beginning of 1940 would recognize the name by the end of the decade as much for her tragic life as for her distinguished singing abilities. She continued to record one masterpiece after another and her live performances were great happenings. But the heroin habit was sucking the life out of her. She attempted to kick the habit but was unable to do so.

She criss-crossed the country playing residencies in Los Angeles, Chicago, Detroit, St. Louis and New York. But it seems as if Holiday was doomed from the very start. In 1947, she served a one-year prison sentence for narcotics offense at the Federal Reformatory in Alderson, West Virginia. There has been much controversy about the arrest and whether the drugs found in her possession were planted. It seemed, like other black entertainers before her—Bessie Smith, Louis Armstrong—and others after her—Charlie Parker, Chuck Berry and Jimi Hendrix—that she was something of a *bête noire* in the eyes of the law establishment. She was black and successful. She would later clear similar narcotic possession charges in 1948. Her singing, which reached a height in the middle of the decade, began to deteriorate by the early 1950s.

Throughout the 1950s, Holiday worked as a solo attraction in many of the clubs, theatres and concert halls throughout the country. While she appeared at theatres in San Francisco, Boston, Chicago, Detroit, Los Angeles, and many other cities, law prohibited her from working the club scene in New York. Her cabaret card was revoked, preventing her from earning a living there.

Holiday would make two separate trips to Europe, the first in 1954 as part of a package tour and again in 1958 where she appeared on television in Great Britain. Although the European tours were a triumph she continued to be a marked person by the law in the United States. She faced numerous charges, sometimes winning acquittal, sometimes being convicted. She slid down the slippery rope and by the middle of the decade she looked tired and used.

Her last few years were marked with serious inconsistency. There were periods when she was able to produce the old magic. In 1957 she appeared on the television show called *The Sound of Jazz* and she wowed the audience with that inimitable Holiday sound. On May 25, 1959, after hundreds of concerts, Holiday appeared for the last time at the Phoenix Theatre in New York. Her dominant voice that had moved listeners for almost thirty years was by now ravaged and a shell of its once tremendous beauty.

On July 17, 1959, at the Metropolitan Hospital in New York City, "Lady Day," the irrepressible singer with the definitive jazz voice, died of heroin withdrawal and heart disease. It was a day of international mourn-ing. Until the bitter end, Holiday was persecuted as the police waited outside her hospital room in order to charge her with possession of illicit drugs. Interestingly, her greatest jazz mate, Lester Young, died a scant two months before her.

Billie Holiday is the queen of all jazz singers. Despite a life that was riddled with frustration, tragedy, despair and pain, she produced some of the greatest music in history. Along with Louis Armstrong, she owns the most distinctive voice among hundreds of vocalists spanning over a cen-tury.

Billy Holiday was an original. Although Bessie Smith and Louis Armstrong were her biggest influences she possessed her own unique sound that defies description. Although never classified as a blues singer, many of her greatest songs contained a blues tinge. Her voice often sounded like the brightest and loudest, but loneliest horn in the entire band.

She gave the world more treasures than it deserved for the way she was treated throughout her lifetime. A partial list includes "This Year's Kisses," "Why Was I Born?," "I Must Have That Man," "Mean to Me," "Fooling Myself," "Easy Living," "Me, Myself, and I," "A Sailboat in the Moonlight," "He's Funny That Way," "Lover Man," "Strange Fruit," "If Dreams Come True," "When a Woman Loves a Man," "Body & Soul," "God Bless the Child," and "Gloomy Sunday." She had the ability to wrap her voice around a song and bring it to life like no one at the time and no one since.

She influenced legions of singers. Nina Simone, Frank Sinatra, Aretha Franklin, Mildred Bailey, Betty Carter, Urszula Dudziak, Dinah Wash-ington, Jean Carne, Anita O'Day, Yusef Lateef, Abbey Lincoln, Carmen McRae, Fiona Apple, and Shirley Witherspoon are just a few who were hypnotized by the Holiday power. Every singer in the past half decade has been touched by the Holiday magic in some way despite the myriad of musical styles. A complete list would fill volumes.

The legend of Billie Holiday continues to this day over fifty years after her death. She published her own memoir, *Lady Sings the Blues*, in 1956, and the hard cold facts were sometimes blurred by a foggy mem-ory. Later, in 1973, Diana Ross starred in *Lady Sings the Blues*, a movie based on Billie's life. Despite a fine performance by Ross, the film was severely panned by critics.

Holiday's powerful legacy lies in the fact that the emotion she was able to inject in her songs came from practical experience. A lonely girl whose marriage to trumpeter Joe Guy ended in the late 1940s, she was unable to overcome a heroin addiction that eventually spelled the end for her. She didn't just sing the blues—she lived the life.

Although her life can be seen as a tragedy, it must also be examined in a positive light. Holiday is one of the certified giants of jazz who changed the course of the genre forever. Often the vast contributions of troubled artists like Janis Joplin, Jimi Hendrix, Jim Morrison, Charlie Parker, and Marylin Monroe override the sordid details of their life. Although some detractors might judge Holiday for her questionable lifestyle, there is no silencing the voice of jazz.

Discography

Billie Holiday: Vol. 1, 1933–1936, Masters of Jazz 10.
Billie Holiday: Vol. 2, 1936–1937, Masters of Jazz 11.
Billie Holiday: Vol. 3, 1934–1937, Masters of Jazz 12.
Billie Holiday: Vol. 4, 1937, Masters of Jazz 36.
Billie Holiday: Vol. 5, 1937–1938, Masters of Jazz 37.
Billie Holiday: Vol. 6, 1938, Masters of Jazz 61.
Billie Holiday: Vol. 7, 1938–1939, Masters of Jazz 62.
Billie Holiday: Vol. 8, 1939, Masters of Jazz 70.
Billie Holiday: Vol. 9, February—September 1940, Masters of Jazz 82.
Billie Holiday: Vol. 10, 1940–1941, Masters of Jazz 90.
Billie Holiday: Vol. 11, 1941–1942, Masters of Jazz 102.
Billie Holiday: Vol. 12, 1942–1944, Masters of Jazz 114.
Billie Holiday: Vol. 14, 1944–1945, Masters of Jazz 141.
Billie Holiday: Vol. 16, 1946–1948, Masters of Jazz 184.
Billie Holiday: No Regrets, RCAL 281.
The Complete Commodore Recordings: 1939–1944, CMD 401.
Billie's Blues 1935–1939, AVD 572.
Billie Holiday's Greatest Hits 1945–1950, GRD 653.
Billie's Love Songs: 1935–1949, Nim 2000.
Control Booth Series: Vol. 1, 1940–1941, STC 2014.
Control Booth Series: Vol. 2, 1941–1942, STC 2015.
The Complete Decca Recordings 1940's, GRD 2601.
Billie Holiday: 1949–1952 Radio & TV Broadcasts, Cai 3002.
Billie Holiday: 1953–1956 Radio & TV Broadcasts, Cai 3003.
Billie Holiday: Her Best Recordings 1935–1942, Best of Jazz 4003.
Billie Holiday: V-Disc Recordings, CCM 4502.
Lady Day's 25 Greatest 1933–1944, ASL 5181.
Wishing on the Moon: 1935–1936, ASL 5277.
Lady Sings the Blues, Columbia 6133.
At Storyville: Early 1950's, GJM 9001.
Billie Holiday: The Early Classics, Pearl 9756.
Billie Holiday: Priceless Jazz, GRD 9871.

God Bless the Child, Sony 30782.
The Original Recordings, Sony 32060.
Billie's Blues, Sony 32080.
The Quintessential Billie Holiday: Vol. 1, 1933–1935, Sony 40646.
The Quintessential Billie Holiday: Vol. 2, 1936, Sony 40790.
The Quintessential Billie Holiday: Vol. 3, 1936–1937, Sony 44048.
The Quintessential Billie Holiday: Vol. 4, 1937, Sony 44252.
The Quintessential Billie Holiday: Vol. 5, 1937–1938, Sony 44423.
The Quintessential Billie Holiday: Vol. 6, 1938, Sony 45449.
The Quintessential Billie Holiday: Vol. 7, 1937–1938, Sony 46180.
The Quintessential Billie Holiday: Vol. 8, 1939–1940, Sony 47030.
The Quintessential Billie Holiday: Vol. 9, 1940–1942, Sony 47031.
I Like Jazz: The Essence of Billie Holiday, Sony 47917.
Billie's Blues 1942–1954, Blue Note 48786.
16 Most Requested Songs, Sony 53776.
This Is Jazz #15, Sony 64622.
Love Songs, Sony 64853.
Lady in Satin, Sony 65144.
Essential Billie Holiday: Songs of Lost Love, PLG 517172.
Jazz at the Philharmonic: Billie Holiday Story Vol. 1, PLG 521642.
Solitude—Billie Holiday Story Vol. 2, PLG 519810.
Verve Jazz Masters 12, PLG 519825.
Lady Sings the Blues 1954–1956, PLG 521429.
Billie Holiday: Jazz 'Round Midnight-Ballads, PLG 521653.
Recital by Billie Holiday, PLG 521868.
Sings the Great American Songbook, PLG 523003.
Music for Touching, PLG 527455.
Verve Jazz Masters 47 1945–1959, PLG 527650.
At Carnegie Hall 1956, Verve 527777.
All or Nothing at All: 1955–1956, PLG 529226.
Ultimate Billie Holiday, PLG 539051.
Songs for Distingue Lovers—Verve Master Edition 1956, PLG 539056.
The Billie Holiday Songbook 1952–1958, PLG 823246.
Silver Collection 1940's—1950's, PLG 823449.
Compact Jazz Live! PLG 841434.
Lady in Autumn: Best of the Verve Years, PLG 849434.

ELLA FITZGERALD (1917–1996)

Scat 'n' Things

The female contribution to jazz has been deep and very important. Ethel Waters, Mildred Bailey, Billie Holiday, Dinah Washington, Mary Lou Williams, and Sarah Vaughan are just some of the classic female singers who were integral in the development and spread of the popularity of the music they cherished so much. Each singer possessed her own unique voice, charisma and talent that separated her from others in the field. One voice that is essential to the above list is the singer who gave us her scat 'n' things. Her name was Ella Fitzgerald.

Ella Fitzgerald was born April 25, 1917, in Newport News, Virginia. Sadly, she never knew her father, who died shortly after the end of World War I. The tragedy left Ella and her mother in dire straits and they joined the great migration north. They settled in Yonkers across the Hudson River from the Bronx.

Music became important to her from a very young age. She grew up listening to the records of Louis Armstrong, Fletcher Henderson, Jimmy Lunceford, Jack Teagarden, the Dorsey Brothers, and the blues of Mamie Smith, Trixie Smith, Ma Rainey, Ida Cox, and the greatest of them all, Bessie Smith. She also enjoyed the radio broadcasts of Duke Ellington and his Orchestra from the Cotton Club. Another source of musical inspiration was the moving gospel sounds she heard in the church.

As a teenager, she took the first steps to establishing her career when she entered the amateur contest held at the Harlem Opera House. It was an unruly affair. The hardened crowds were famous for the immediate dissatisfaction they showed anyone who couldn't cut it on stage. Although she had promised to dance, her nerves were so sharp that she opted to sing instead. She selected "The Object of My Affection," a Connie Boswell number.

Boswell, a white singer from New Orleans, was Fitzgerald's idol at the time. Boswell sang with her two sisters Martha and Helvetia in a close harmony style that predated all of the female acts that would sing with the big bands in the swing era. After Fitzgerald finished the song the audience demanded more and Ella sang "Judy," another Boswell selection. Fitzgerald won the contest. Her first-place finish at the Harlem Opera House convinced her to enter other amateur contests. Although she didn't win all of them and was booed off the stage on occasion, she possessed great determination and continued to try and ignite her singing career.

She won first prize at another amateur contest at the Harlem Opera House, which was a week's work with bandleader Tiny Bradshaw. During her one-week stint she impressed the audience and some important jazz people including Benny Carter. Carter told his friend John Hammond, who had dedicated his life to recording the best names that jazz and blues had to offer. Just as she was poised to join Arthur Tracy, Ella's mother died, making her an orphan without a legal guardian. Fitzgerald was sent to the Riverdale Orphanage in Yonkers.

Although her dream of a career as a famous singer was temporarily put on hold, Ella would not be deterred. She continued to enter amateur contests and overwhelmed the no mercy crowd at the Apollo. First prize was fifty dollars and a week's work at the famous theatre. It was at the Apollo that Bardu Ali, the master of ceremonies for Chick Webb's Big Band, first saw Ella Fitzgerald. He told his boss and after a tryout, Ella became a part of the Chick Webb Big Band.

Chick Webb's band was nearly a permanent fixture at the Savoy Ballroom. Gradually Webb began to realize her immense potential, but refused to rush her along. One of Webb's most significant moves was to adopt Ella, thus enabling her to leave the orphanage. For the first time in a long time Ella had a family again.

In 1935, Ella made her first recordings with Chick Webb's band with the song "Love and Kisses," but it didn't make her an instant star. Fitzgerald, painfully shy, began to hit her stride, getting better and better every night at the Savoy and other engagements. She felt comfortable surrounded by the members of Webb's band, which included Taft Jordan, Edgar Sampson, Sandy Williams and Louis Jordan along with their drummer and leader Webb. It was also that year that Ella made her radio debut with the band. Her voice was broadcast throughout the nation as well as in Great Britain.

During her stay in Webb's group Ella grew as a singer and a songwriter. She began to pen songs such as "In a Mellotone" and "Oh, But I Do." She also recorded outside the Webb band. One of these sessions was with the Mills Brothers and together they cut "Boy Big Blue," which didn't break any sales record. She also recorded sides with Teddy Wilson and other members of the Benny Goodman band. In 1938, while on tour, Ella sang the number "A-Tisket, A-Tasket," which guaranteed her an instant place among the best jazz vocalists of the time.

The song "A-Tisket, A-Tasket," was the type of hit that every aspiring singer dreams about. Many spend a career in vain trying to record a song that catapults them to the top of the charts and into every home in the country. Fitzgerald recorded that song very early in her career and sealed her fate with the classic that would lead her to international fame.

She became a star with the Webb band. She toured throughout the country and cut many records that sold hundreds of thousands of copies. She helped the group attain a higher level of popularity and was an anticipated part of the show that helped filled seats at every venue that they played. She also placed first in popularity polls over other famous singers, including Billie Holiday.

When Webb died, in 1939, Fitzgerald took over leadership of the band at the tender age of twenty-one. Because of the veteran musicians in it, the band didn't need a strong leader. Fitzgerald scored another major hit with "Stairway to the Stars." Although work became harder to find with the decline of swing in the 1940s, the group struggled on and remained on the road for most of the war years despite the loss of key members to the draft. In 1943, a young trumpet player from North Carolina joined the band. His name was Dizzy Gillespie. Despite the musicians' ban on recording, Fitzgerald would score with the Duke Ellington composition "I'm Beginning to See the Light" in 1945. In 1946, Fitzgerald disbanded the group.

She continued to widen her appeal with the Decca recordings she made during this period despite the lack of a permanent band. The Ink Spots, Louis Jordan, and the Delta Rhythm Boys were some of the performers who backed her up in the studio. Many groups wanted to record with Fitzgerald because of her star appeal and because her records were commercial successes.

Another outlet for her was movies. In 1941, Fitzgerald had a large role in *Ride 'Em Cowboy* with Abbott and Costello. She played a maid (a typical stereotype role for blacks in that period), and sang her monster hit "A-Tisket, A-Tasket," as well as "Rockin' and Reelin.'" It was a rewarding experience that exposed her to an even larger crowd.

In 1947, Ella joined Dizzy Gillespie's big band that featured a young bass player named Ray Brown. She would eventually marry Brown and together they would adopt a son. Although the marriage would last only three years, Fitzgerald raised her son on her own. Gillespie's band played bebop and in her attempt to keep up with the frantic pace of the music she began to scat sing. Although not the first jazz singer to use this method, it became one of her vocal trademarks.

In 1948, she joined Jazz at the Philharmonic, the brainchild of Norman Granz. She became a favorite of JATP and with the decline of Billie Holiday, Fitzgerald assumed the top spot among jazz vocalists (though fans of Sarah Vaughan would strongly disagree). Ella was a perennial

Down Beat Poll winner. She also toured England in 1948 to enthusiastic reviews.

While married to bass player Ray Brown, Fitzgerald appeared with his trio. She also recorded a number of duets with pianist Ellis Larkins, and they interpreted George Gershwin songs. She was by this time capable of taking any song and making it a hit with her vast talent.

Although she had been under Norman Granz's management since 1953, it wasn't until 1955 that she was able to record on his Verve label. Under his directorship, Fitzgerald began her "songbook" period when most of her recorded material was derived from the work of Cole Porter, the Gershwins, Rodgers and Hart, Duke Ellington, Harold Arlen, Jerome Kern and Johnny Mercer. The life she pumped into these songs made them instantly recognizable and they received major radio airplay that only enlarged her fan base.

While she was criticized for straying away from her jazz roots since many of the "songbook" recordings were more pop oriented than pure jazz, they were big sellers. In many ways she never betrayed her jazz roots, but widened the parameters to include a different element. She also recorded with some of Granz's stable of stars including Oscar Peterson. Teamed with such a talented pianist, she never sounded better.

In 1960, Fitzgerald was at the very peak of her career and recorded and performed all over the country and throughout Europe. She was a household name to people who didn't even listen to jazz or pop music. It seemed that practically every song she recorded, no matter how many versions of it existed, was a hit. Her popularity reached such wide proportions that she appeared in crossword puzzles in the daily newspapers.

By the end of the decade she was recording more popular material such as "I Heard It Through the Grapevine." Although she could handle any material with relative ease, she was better suited to jazz backed by a small combo. Granz, an intelligent, driven man, was determined not to let his star fall into obscurity and decided to record her once again as a jazz singer.

The return to a more jazz-oriented sound enabled her to recapture some of the audience she had lost and introduced her to a whole new generation. She teamed with such jazz legends as Count Basie, Oscar Peterson, and Joe Pass. During the 1970s when many of the great names in jazz such as Louis Armstrong, Duke Ellington, Kid Ory, Ethel Waters, Bennie Carter, Ben Webster, Johnny Hodges, Gene Krupa and others passed away, Fitzgerald became a leading ambassador of the genre. While she sang with conviction and power, the 1970s were the last good decade she enjoyed. From this point on her decline in health was quite noticeable.

Throughout the 1980s she made infrequent recordings and appearances, but her performances were genuine events. She could still draw in a large crowd and could boast of fans from a career that had spanned six decades. Those who were fortunate enough to see her live in the 1980s were witnessing history in the making.

In 1994, after a career that had lasted fifty-seven years, she retired permanently. Two years later, on June 15, 1996, Ella Fitzgerald, the great vocalist who had dozens of awards and honors bestowed upon her, died in Beverly Hills, California. She was 79 years old.

Ella Fitzgerald was a jazz fixture for over fifty years. She had been called the greatest singer of all, though fans of both Billie Holiday and Sarah Vaughan would strongly deny that claim. Whether or not she is considered the best, there is no denying her place among the elite of jazz vocalists.

Perhaps one of the most interesting aspects of the Ella Fitzgerald story is her metamorphosis as a singer. At the start of her career, her voice possessed a sweet quality that eventually gave way to a more mature sound. She began as an excellent interpreter and finished her career as a true virtuoso. She was constantly polishing her craft adding depth and dimensions long after she had become a star. Her tireless efforts to improve were one of the main reasons why she remained so popular throughout her career.

Her ability to improvise with anyone in the band gained her an amount of respect that was her true calling card. Her voice sounded more like a distinct instrument than a human song box. Although considered a star of the swing era, she also incorporated the frenetic energy of bebop into her style, which enabled her to challenge trumpeters, saxophonists, and clarinetists. When she pitted her powerful voice against a single instrument the ensuing battle was one of the most cherished moments in jazz.

Despite the fact that her name became synonymous with jazz, she was criticized for her lack of emotional depth when compared to the likes of Billie Holiday. However, to compare them is to diminish the efforts and contributions of both singers because they were both so individually unique. They approached a song from a very different perspective. If one is to compare Fitzgerald and Holiday then the strengths of each individual singer should be pointed out.

Since she was a jazz fixture for so many years it is understandable that she would have a large influence over a number of female and male singers. A short list includes Rosemary Clooney, Urszula Dudziak, Fionna Duncan, Billy Harper, Karin Krog, Gloria Lynne, Helen Merrill, Dakota Staton, Norma Winstone, Jackie Paris, Eileen Farrell, Flora Purim, Joe Lee Wilson, Alice Day, Jody Sandhaus, and Uvee Hayes. But her sphere of influence also affected singers from every style of music. Janis Joplin, the great blues-rock singer of the late 1960s, and soul artist Aretha Franklin are just two female singers who owe a debt to Fitzgerald. She broke new ground and broke through the barriers, an African-American woman making her way in a white male dominated world had to face.

She worked with just about every big name in jazz. A who's who list includes Ray Brown, Louis Armstrong, Oscar Peterson, Herb Ellis, Johnny Hodges, Duke Ellington, Louie Bellson, Benny Goodman, Teddy McRae, Paul Smith, Roy Eldridge, Harry Carney, Dizzy Gillespie, Charlie Parker, Max Roach, Count Basie, Joe Mondragon, Clark Terry, Taft Jordan, John Trueheart, and Jimmy Hamilton.

Ella Fitzgerald remains one of the jewels of modern jazz. She gave the world a number of classics which lifted the spirits because of the genuine sunny disposition that came through her singing so clearly. Everyone was touched by the Fitzgerald magic from colleagues to fans. Undoubtedly, when the "First Lady of Song" was on everyone was entertained by her scat 'n' things.

Discography

The Enchanting Ella Fitzgerald: Live at Birdland 1950–1952, BSM 309.
One Side of Me: 1935–1941, AVD 565.
75th Anniversary Collection: 1938–1955, GRD 619.
Ella—The Legendary Decca Recordings: 1938–1955, GRD 648.
Last Decca Years: 1949–1954, GRD 668.
Roseland Dance City, New York, Can 1007.
Ella Fitzgerald and Her Famous Orchestra: The Radio Years 1940, STC 2065.
The Early Years Part 1—With Chick Webb & His Orchestra, GRD 2618.
The Early Years Part 2—With Chick Webb & His Orchestra, GRD 2623.
Rhythm & Romance—25 Early Hits, ASL 5212.
In the Groove 1935–1941, Bud 99702.
Young Ella, EPM 157962.
Like Someone in Love 1957, PLG 511524.
Ella Swings Lightly 1958, PLG 517535.
Get Happy 1957, Verve 523321.
Something to Live For, 1930s–1960s, Verve 547800.
Rodgers & Hart Songbook Vol. 1, 1956, PLG 821579
Rodgers & Hart Songbook Vol. 2, 1956, PLG 821580.
Cole Porter Songbook Vol. 1, 1956, PLG 821989
Cole Porter Songbook Vol. 2, 1956, PLG 821990.
The Gershwin Songbook 1959, PLG 825024.

The Irving Berlin Songbook Vol. 1, 1958, PLG 829534.
The Irving Berlin Songbook Vol. 2, 1958, PLG 920535.
At the Opera House 1957, PLG 831269.
Compact Jazz, PLG 831367.
Ella in Rome—The Birthday Concert 1958, PLG 835454.
Ellington Songbook 1956–1957, PLG 837035.
Fitzgerald, Ella / Count Basie / Joe Williams: One O'Clock Jump 1956–1957, Verve 559806.
Ella & Louis 1956, Verve 543304.
Compact Jazz: Ella & Louis 1956–1957, Verve 835313.

Bibliography

Armstrong, Louis. *Louis Armstrong: My Life in New Orleans*. New York: Da Capo, 1990.

_____. *Satchmo*. New York: Signet/New American Library, 1955.

Balliett, Whitney. *American Singers*. London: Oxford University Press, 1982.

_____. *Jelly Roll, Jabbo, and Fats*. London: Oxford University Press, 1983.

Barnet, Charlie. *Those Swinging Years*. New York: Da Capo, 1992.

Basie, Count, and Albert Murray. *Good Morning Blues: The Autobiography of Count Basie*. New York: William Heinemann, 1985.

Belker, Loren. *Seems Like Old Times: The Big Bands of the Mid–West*. New York: J&L Lee, 1992.

Berton, Ralph. *Remembering Bix: A Memoir of the Jazz Age*. New York: Harper & Row, 1974.

Broadbent, Peter. *Charlie Christian*. New York: Hal Leonard, 1997.

Buchmann-Moller, Frank. *You Got to Be Original, Man! The Music of Lester Young*. Westport, Connecticut: Greenwood, 1989.

Burnett, James. *Bix Beiderbecke*. London: Cassell, 1959.

Carver, Reginald. *Jazz Profiles*. New York: Billboard, 1998.

Case, Brian. *Illustrated Encyclopedia of Jazz*. New York: Harmony Books, 1978.

Chilton, John. *Billie's Blues: A Survey of Billie Holiday's Career 1933–59*. London: Quartet, 1975.

_____. *Sidney Bechet: The Wizard of Jazz*. New York: Macmillan, 1987.

_____. *The Song of the Hawk*. London: Quartet, 1990.

_____. *Who's Who in Jazz*. New York: Da Capo, 1972.

Claghorn, Charles. *Biographical Dictionary of Jazz*. New York: Prentice Hall, 1982.

Cohn, Sid. *Ella: The Life and Times of Ella Fitzgerald*. London: Elm Tree Books, 1986.

Collier, James Lincoln. *Benny Goodman and the Swing Era*. London: Oxford University Press, 1990.

_____. *Louis Armstrong: An American Genius*. London: Oxford University Press, 1983.

_____. *Louis Armstrong: An American Success Story*. New York: Macmillan, 1985.

Connor, D. Russell, and Warren W. Hicks. *B. G. on the Record: A Bio-Discography of Benny Goodman*. New York: Arlington House, 1969.

Connor, Donald Russell. *B.G. Off the Record: A Bio-Discography of Benny Goodman*. Fairless Hills, Pennsylvania: Crown, 1958.

_____. *Benny Goodman: Listen to His Legacy*. Lanham, Maryland: Scarecrow, 1988.

Cook, Richard. *Penguin Guide to Jazz on CD 3rd Edition*. New York: Penguin, 1992.

Courlander, Harold. *The World of Earl Hines*. New York: Scribner's, 1977.

Crow, Bill. *Jazz Anecdotes*. London: Oxford, 1990.

Crowther, Bruce. *Benny Goodman*. New York: Apollo, 1988.

Dahl, Linda. *Morning Glory: Biography of Mary Lou Williams*. New York: Pantheon, 1999.

_____. *Stormy Weather: The Music and Lives of a Century of Jazz Women*. New York: Quartet, 1984.

Dance, Stanley. *Jazz Era: The Forties*. New York: Da Capo, 1961.

_____. *The World of Count Basie*. New York: Da Capo, 1984.

_____. *The World of Duke Ellington*. New York: Da Capo 1980.

_____. *The World of Earl Hines*. New York: Da Capo, 1977.

_____. *The World of Swing*. New York: Charles Scribner's Sons, 1974.

_____, and Mercer Ellington. *Duke Ellington in Person: A Memoir*. New York: Da Capo, 1979.

Deffaa, Chip. *Jazz Veterans: A Portrait Gallery*. Leawood, Kansas: Cypress House, 1996.

DeLong, Thomas. *Radio Stars*. Jefferson, North Carolina: McFarland, 1996.

Dodds, Warren Baby and Larry Gara. *The Baby Dodds Story*. Los Angeles: Contemporary, 1959.

Dupuis, Roger. *Bunny Berigan: Elusive Legend of Jazz*. Baton Rouge: Louisiana State University Press, 1993.

Ellington, Duke. *Music Is My Mistress*. New York: Da Capo 1973.

Fernett, Gene. *Swing Out: Great Negro Dance Bands*. New York: Da Capo, 1993.

Friedwald, Will. *Jazz Singing*. New York: Da Capo, 1996.

Gammond, Peter. *Scott Joplin and the Ragtime Era*. London: St. Martin's, 1975.

George, Don R. *Sweet Man: The Real Duke Ellington*. New York: Putnam, 1981.

Giddins, Gary. *Satchmo*. New York: Doubleday, 1988.

Goffin, Robert. *Jazz from the Congo to the Metropolitan*. New York: Doubleday, 1944.

_____. *Horn of Plenty: The Story of Louis Armstrong*. New York: Allen, Towne, and Heath, 1947.

Goodman, Benny. *Benny, King of Swing: A Pictorial Biography Based on Benny Goodman's Personal Archives.* London: Thames and Hudson, 1979.

_____, and Irving Kolodin. *The Kingdom of Swing.* New York: Stackpole, 1939.

Gottlieb, William P. *The Golden Age of Jazz.* New York: Simon and Schuster, 1979.

Gourse, Leslie. *The Ella Fitzerald Companion—Seven Decades of Commentary.* New York: Omnibus Press, 1998.

Green, Sharony Andrews, and Grant Green. *Rediscovering the Forgotten Genius of Jazz Guitar.* New York: Miller-Freeman, 1999.

Grudens, Richard. *Song Stars: The Ladies Who Sang with the Big Bands.* Stoney Brook, New York: Celebrity Profiles, 1997.

Hall, Fred. *Dialogues in Swing.* Oxnard: Pathfinder Publishing of California, 1989.

_____. *More Dialogues in Swing.* Oxnard: Pathfinder Publishing of California, 1991.

Hampton, Lionel. *Hamp.* New York: Warner, 1989.

Handy, D. Antonette. *Black Women in American Bands and Orchestras.* Lanham, Maryland: Scarecrow, 1998.

Haskins, James and Kathleen Benson. *Scott Joplin: The Man Who Made Ragtime.* New York: Doubleday, 1978.

Hippenmeyer, Jean-Roland. *Sidney Bechet, Ou, L'Extraordinaire Odyssée d'un Musicien de Jazz.* Geneva: Tribune, 1980.

Holiday, Billie, and William Duity. *Lady Sings the Blues.* New York: Doubleday, 1956.

Horricks, Raymond. *Count Basie and His Orchestra: Its Music and Its Musicians.* New York: Citadel, 1957.

Jasen, David. *Spreadin' Rhythm Around: Black Popular Songwriters (1880–1930).* New York: Schirmer, 1998.

_____. *Tin Pan Alley.* New York: Donald I. Fine, 1988.

Jones, Max, and John Louis Chilton. *The Louis Armstrong Story 1900–1971.* London: Studio Vista, 1971.

Joplin, Scott. *The Collected Works of Scott Joplin.* New York: New York Public Library, 1971.

Kinkle, Roger. *Complete Encyclopedia of Popular Music and Jazz 1900–1950.* 4 vols. New York: Arlington House, 1974.

Kirkeby, Ed, Duncan P. Schiedt, and Sinclair Traill. *Ain't Misbehavin': The Story of Fats Waller.* New York: Dodd, Mead, 1966.

Knopper, Steve. *Swing! The Essential Album Guide.* Canton, Michigan: Visible Ink, 1999.

Lambert, G. E. *Johnny Dodds.* New York: A. S. Barnes, 1961.

Lester, James. *Too Marvelous for Words: The Life and Genius of Art Tatum.* New York: Oxford University Press, 1994.

Lomax, Alan, and Mister Jelly Roll. *The Fortunes of Jelly Roll Morton: New*

Orleans Creole and "Inventor of Jazz." New York: Duell, Sloan & Pearce, 1950.

Luckey, Robert. *A Study of Lester Young and His Influence Upon His Contemporaries.* Ph.D. diss. University of Pittsburgh, 1981.

Marquis, Donald. *In Search of Buddy Bolden.* New York: Da Capo, 1978.

McCarthy, Albert. *The Dance Band Era: The Dancing Decades from Ragtime to Swing—1910–1950.* Philadelphia: Chilton, 1971.

Meryman, Richard. *Louis Armstrong: A Self-Portrait.* New York: Eakins, 1971.

Miller, Marc. *Louis Armstrong: A Cultural Legacy.* New York: Queens Museum Books, 1994.

Nicholson, Stuart. *Ella Fitzgerald.* New York: Scribner's, 1993.

Ostransky, Leroy. *Anatomy of Jazz.* Washington: University of Washington Press, 1978.

Panassie, Hughes. *Louis Armstrong.* New York: Scribner's, 1971.

Peretti, Burton. *Creation of Jazz.* Chicago: University of Illinois Press, 1992.

Perhonis, J. P. *The Bix Beiderbecke Story: The Jazz Musician in Legend, Fiction, and Fact.* Minneapolis: University of Minnesota Press, 1978.

Pinfold, Mike. *Louis Armstrong: His Life and Times.* New York: Universe, 1987.

Placksin, Sally. *American Women in Jazz: 1900 to the Present: Their Words, Their Lives, Their Music.* New York: Penguin, 1982.

Rose, Al. *The New Orleans Jazz Family Album.* Baton Rouge: Louisiana State University Press, 1967.

Russell, Ross. *Jazz Styles in Kansas City.* Berkeley: University of California Press, 1971.

Rust, Brian. *American Dance Band Discography: 1917–1942, Volume 1–2.* New York: Arlington House, 1975.

Schuller, Gunther. *The Swing Era.* London: Oxford University Press, 1989.

Sheridan, Chris. *Count Basie: A Bio-discography.* Westport, Connecticut: Greenwood, 1986.

Shipton, Alyn. *Fats Waller: His Life and Times.* New York: Universe, 1988.

Simon, George T. *Glenn Miller and His Orchestra.* New York: Da Capo, 1974.

Smith, Jay D, and Len Guttridge. *Jack Teagarden: The Story of a Jazz Maverick.* London: Classell, 1960.

Sudhalter, Richard M., and Philip Evans. *Bix: Man & Legend.* New York: Arlington House, 1974.

Vance, Joel. *Fats Waller: His Life and Times.* Chicago: Contemporary, 1977.

Walker, Leo. *The Big Band Almanac.* Pasadena, California: Ward Ritchie, 1978.

_____. *The Wonderful Era of the Great Dance Bands.* New York: Da Capo, 1964.

Waters, Ethel. *To Me It's Wonderful.* New York: Harper & Row, 1972.

Williams, Martin. *Jazz Changes.* London: Oxford University Press, 1992.

_____. *Jelly Roll Morton.* London: Cassell, 1962.

Wilson, John S. *The Collector's Jazz—Traditional and Swing.* Philadelphia: Lippincott Williams & Wilkins, 1958.

Index